ROUTLEDGE LIBRARY EDITIONS:
ACCOUNTING HISTORY

Volume 16

CONTRIBUTIONS OF LIMPERG AND SCHMIDT TO THE REPLACEMENT COST DEBATE IN THE 1920S

CONTRIBUTIONS OF LIMPERG AND SCHMIDT TO THE REPLACEMENT COST DEBATE IN THE 1920S

FRANK L. CLARKE AND GRAEME W. DEAN

Routledge
Taylor & Francis Group
LONDON AND NEW YORK

First published in 1990 by Garland Publishing, Inc.

This edition first published in 2021
by Routledge
2 Park Square, Milton Park, Abingdon, Oxon OX14 4RN

and by Routledge
52 Vanderbilt Avenue, New York, NY 10017

Routledge is an imprint of the Taylor & Francis Group, an informa business

British Library Cataloguing in Publication Data
A catalogue record for this book is available from the British Library

ISBN: 978-0-367-33564-9 (Set)
ISBN: 978-1-00-304636-3 (Set) (ebk)
ISBN: 978-0-367-50864-7 (Volume 16) (hbk)
ISBN: 978-1-00-305158-9 (Volume 16) (ebk)

Publisher's Note
The publisher has gone to great lengths to ensure the quality of this reprint but points out that some imperfections in the original copies may be apparent.

Disclaimer
The publisher has made every effort to trace copyright holders and would welcome correspondence from those they have been unable to trace.

Contributions of Limperg and Schmidt to the Replacement Cost Debate in the 1920s

Frank L. Clarke
Graeme W. Dean

GARLAND PUBLISHING, INC.
New York / London
1990

Library of Congress Cataloging-in-Publication Data

Clarke, Frank L.
Conributions of Limperg and Schmidt to the replacement cost debate in the 1920s / Frank L. Clarke, Graeme Dean.
p. cm. — (New works in accounting history)
Includes bibliographical references.
ISBN 0-8153-0007-7 (alk. paper)
1. Replacement of industrial equipment—Accounting. 2. Limperg, Theodore, 1879–1961—Contributions in accounting. 3. Schmidt, Fritz, 1882–1950—Contributions in accounting. I. Dean, G.W. II. Title. III. Series.
HF5681.R34C62 1990
647'.73—dc20 90-27264

Printed on acid-free, 250-year-life paper

Printed in the United States of America

Contributions of Limperg and Schmidt to the Replacement Cost Debate in the 1920s

Preface

References to Limpergian thought and to Limperg's founding of the *Dutch School* of asset valuation allude to Theodore Limperg's contribution in the development of the case for replacement price valuations. In contrast with Limperg, Fritz Schmidt's work on current value systems generally takes a back-seat in the chronicling of those 1920s developments in asset valuation. Schmidt being in the back-seat is curious. For, whereas he had published his ideas widely, Limperg is well known to have published little.

This volume, inquires into which of Limperg's and Schmidt's contributions was the most prominent and whether either was the genesis of an evolutionary development of replacement price valuations. The evidence possibly favours Schmidt on the former count and neither of them on the second. We conjecture that Schmidt's contribution to the German *Betriebswirtschaftslehre* during the 1920s has been misinterpreted in the Anglo-American literature. Attempts to explain the dissimilarity between his *organic* theory and the *Bedrijfseconomie* theory attributed to Limperg, have confounded rather than lessened confusion.

In the Anglo-American literature there is a dearth of primary source material of the works of both Schmidt and Limperg. This has limited accounting historians in their attempts to piece together the myriad of factors having an effect on the development of replacement cost accounting ideas. Specifically, to date little attention has been given to the influence of the theories of Mahlberg, Schmalenbach and Schmidt on Sweeney's *Stabilized Accounting*.

Our monograph partly fills this void. It provides previously untranslated material coupled to biographical data and our analysis of both Limperg's and Schmidt's ideas. We hope this exploratory work with our conjectures will allow subsequent researchers to further investigate the complex underpinnings of replacement cost accounting, as it developed in Europe and subsequently was transported to Anglo-American countries.

This analysis of Schmidt and Limperg is apposite. For history indicates we will experience further periods of inflation and accompanying debate on the serviceability of accounting proposals to incorporate the financial effects of price and price-level changes.

Frank L. Clarke
Graeme W. Dean

Acknowledgements

Translated extracts are taken from the original German material of Schmidt (1921), [1926], [1927], [1928], Geldmacher (1920), von Kast (1920), von Schlesinger (1920), Mahlberg (1921, 1923a, 1923b), Isaac (1950), Schwantag [1951], Voigtländer [1952], Seicht (1970 & 1982), and Schneider (1981). For these translations we are indebted to Walter Thanner, Thomas Junge, Warwick Rodden, Angelika Dean, Sonja Wienker, Marc and Kathrin Joye. In respect of the Dutch translations (Limperg, [1937] and Groeneveld *et al.*, (1964) and [1968]; and Schmidt [1923]), we are thankful for the assistance of Dorothy Simons and Ineke Bergsma. Any errors or omissions, and the use of English accounting terminology, remain our responsibility. Research on this project commenced whilst Graeme Dean was visiting Universität Hohenheim, Stuttgart in 1984. The help of the staff at Hohenheim, in particular Professor Klaus Macharzina, Jörg Neubling, Rolf Scholl and Joachim Wolff, is acknowledged. It continued with overseas visits to European universities by Graeme Dean in 1988 and 1990 and Frank Clarke in 1984 and 1990. For the support of the Universities of Sydney and Newcastle and the financial support from Price Waterhouse (Newcastle) and the Accounting and Finance Foundation of the University of Sydney, we are grateful.

Last to be noted, but primary in significance, is our debt to Emeritus Professor Raymond J. Chambers. Over the past twenty years we have been privileged to be able to share his insights into the development of ideas in accounting. RJC's enthusiasm for delving into the ideas of Limperg, Schmidt and their contemporaries rubbed-off onto us. We are grateful that it did. Unquestionably, the inspiration for this project was his!

Translator's Note

The texts included in the present anthology have been translated *dem Sinne nach*, that is, according to meaning rather than verbatim. Accordingly, we have worked with the translators on their drafts in an attempt to ensure that we capture the correct idiom and tenor of the works. Yet we believe that we have remained faithful to the originals. We have, for example, avoided interpreting ambiguous passages; such passages remain ambiguous in the English. In several instances lengthy German and Dutch sentences have been simplified either by creating two or more sentences or enclosing explanatory clauses in parentheses. Parentheses, accordingly, are both the authors' and ours, although the material enclosed is entirely the authors'. Footnotes, too, are in the main the authors', although we have changed their format slightly and used italics where they used underlining. Materials in square brackets are ours.

Material in this anthology draws and elaborates on the exploratory work in this area by Clarke and Dean (1986 and 1989); Dean and Clarke (1989); Graves, Dean and Clarke, (1989) and Graves (1985, 1987 and 1989). Original citations for the items included in this volume are in chronological order (the order of their inclusion), as follows:

1. R. Burgert, "Reservations about 'Replacement Value' Accounting in the Netherlands", *Abacus*, December 1972, pp.111-126.

2. G.I. Groeneveld *et al.*, *Bedrijfseconomie*, Vol II 1968, sections A.III "De theorie der vervangingswaarde" (Replacement Value Theory) and B.I "De kostprijs en zijn functie in de voortbrenging" (The Basic Principles of Costing), pp.49-140.

3. Th. Limperg, "De gevolgen van de depreciatie van de gulden voor de berekening van waarde en winst" (The Consequences of the Depreciation of the Guilder for the Calculation of Value and Profit), *Maanblad voor Accountancy en Bedrijfshuishoudkunde*, January 1937, pp.14-31.

4. Karl Schwantag, "F. Schmidts wissenschaftliches Werk" (The Academic Work of Fritz Schmidt), *Abacus*, September 1986, pp.90-99; translation of original which appeared in *Zeitschrift für Betriebswirtschaft*, January 1951, pp.1-14.

5. Dr. Voigtländer, "Bibliographie: Das wissenschaftliche Werk von F. Schmidt" (Bibliography: Fritz Schmidt's Academic Work), *Abacus*, September 1986, pp.99-102; translation of original which appeared in *Zeitschrift für Betriebswirtschaft*, January 1952, pp.182-5.

6. Fritz Schmidt, "De winst van de onderneming" (Enterprise Profit), *De naamlooze vennootschap roermond*, 15 February & 15 March 1923, pp.302-4 and 332-34.

7. Fritz Schmidt, "Gewinn und Bilanzwert" (Profit and Balance Sheet Value), *Proceedings, Het Internationaal Accountantscongres*, 1926, pp.381-419.

8. Fritz Schmidt, "Indexziffern" (Index Numbers), in H. Nicklisch, *Handwörterbuch der Betriebswirtschaftslehre*, 1927, pp.274-82.

9. Fritz Schmidt, "Ist Wertänderung am ruhenden Vermögen Gewinn oder Verlust?" (Do Holding Gains or Losses Represent Profit or Loss?), *Zeitschrift für Betriebswirtschaft*, 1928, pp.1-19.

CONTENTS

1. LIMPERG'S *BEDRIJFSECONOMIE* AND SCHMIDT'S *BETRIEBSWIRTSCHAFT*

In many Anglo-American countries during the 1970's Current Cost Accounting (CCA) proposals appeared likely to supplant, or at least supplement, the extant historical cost accounting system (Tweedie and Whittington, 1984). Modern prescriptions of accounting for changing prices and changing price levels have close parallels with the major European prescriptions arising from the 1921-23 hyperinflation crisis in Europe, specifically in Germany and Holland. To date such similarities have not been explored. Recent professional prescriptions suggest an ignorance, or at best unawareness, of the political, social and economic vicissitudes underpinning those earlier accounting proposals. An ignorance of non Anglo-American ideas generally, was recognised by Chambers in 1966, when, as the editor of an international accounting journal, *Abacus*, he lamented:

> The theoretical literature of accounting and business economics in the English language contains few conspicuous expositions of the views of those who have written principally in another language. (fn. p.3)

Two leading European business economists, Fritz Schmidt from the German *Betriebswirtschaftslehre* and Theodore Limperg from the Netherlands *Bedrijfseconomie* movement,[1] produced accounting reform proposals in the early part of the 1920s which have been accorded seminal status in the recent accounting literature (Graves, 1985, 1987) and Clarke & Dean 1986, 1989). They contained the basic ideas of modern day replacement cost accounting proposals. This monograph analyses the writings of early 20th Century European writers in general, and Schmidt and Limperg in particular, with the aim of tracing the development of ideas underlying modern day current cost accounting systems. Specifically it aims to place the ideas of Schmidt and Limperg in their proper historical perspective. It thus strives to bring order to the Anglo-American accounting literature on this subject. It is the culmination of a series of studies by the authors on this topic (Clarke and Dean, 1986; Dean and Clarke (1989), Clarke and Dean (1989), Graves, Clarke and Dean (1989). An added justification for this study is the increase in the rate of inflation in Western developed countries in the late 1980s and in 1990: Sweden (11%), Great Britain (10.6%), Australia (8%) and Germany (3.5%). In underdeveloped countries the rate is substantially higher with Brazil 1000% in 1988 and over 100% in some months in

---

1 *Betriebswirtschaftslehre* and *Bedrijfseconomie movement* are the German and Dutch respectively for the teaching of business economics or business economics movement.

1989; whilst Bolivia 40,000% inflation p.a in 1985.[2] Such rates of hyperinflation prompted an international accounting standard (IAS29) on the subject in 1988.

A collation of writings by Schmidt and Limperg, together with biographies and bibliographies previously unavailable in English, are drawn upon to enable inferences on many issues, including whether there:

- are any similarities in or differences between the ideas of Schmidt and Limperg;

- has been proper recognition of their relative influences on modern replacement cost accounting proposals;

- is any credence in the proposition that *value to the owner* and *gearing* adjustments are simply ad hoc mechanisms within modern replacement cost proposals;

- is universal suitability of replacement cost proposals to modern environments, (e.g. Peru, Argentina, Brazil, and Israel) given differences in the cultural, social, political and economic factors that existed in 1920s Europe which spawned these proposals;

- is any identifiable pattern in the myriad of factors underpinning Henry Sweeney's perceived pathbreaking stabilization proposals and his preference, only recently recognised, for a stabilized replacement cost system of accounting; and

- are any general features of the European administrative theories which would explain why those proposals stumbled in dealing with the problem of accounting *simultaneously* for the effects of changing prices and changes in the general level of prices?

Chapter two provides a brief overview of the major political, social and economic events in Europe post-World War 1 till 1924. Concomitantly major accounting techniques proposed to overcome the prices and price-level problems resulting from those events are detailed; in particular those of Schmidt and Limperg. Those only speaking English are confronted with considerable confusion regarding the precise nature of both authors' works. Fritz Schmidt's contribution to the German *Betriebswirtschaftslehre* during the 1920s has been misinterpreted, whilst the similarity between his organic theory and the *Bedrijfseconomie* theory attributed to Theodore Limperg has also been less than clear. Tweedie and Whittington (1984) note that "there is also some doubt as to the extent to which [Limperg] was influenced by Schmidt" (p.30); and later they suggest there are "probable doubts as to the

---

2 These rates were cited in *The Economist, Newsweek, Time, and The Wall Street Journal* during 1989 and 1990. They were the product of *actual* rates and *projected* annual rates based on actual monthly figures.

originalities of his system" (p.32). Such doubts which had surfaced earlier (MacDonald, 1977, p.246), were revived by Clarke and Dean (1986, p.65) and Clarke and Dean (1988). A possible cause for these uncertainties has been the reliance on secondary sources since little of the respective works has been translated from original German and Dutch sources and published in English. The next two *chapters* (*3* and *4*) attempt to redress the deficiency.

Chapters 3 and *4* consist, inter alia, of extracts from works by Limperg and Schmidt respectively, published (it is believed) for the first time in English. *Chapter 3* contains translations taken from two of the few *major* publications of Theodore Limperg. One, entitled *Bedrijfseconomie*, is an edited version (seven volumes) of Limperg's draft lecture notes, and published posthumously over the period 1964 to 1968. There is undeniably conjecture as to the extent to which Limperg published his ideas. For example, one commentator, Muis (1980), noted that "during his lifetime Limperg had failed to publish an overview of his main thinking, except for a series of ad hoc articles" (p.69). On the basis of analysis of original source material our assessment is similar to that of Muis. Also included in this *chapter* is an article by Burgert [1972],[3] a leading Dutch authority on Limperg. Finally the first full length publication of Limperg's replacement cost ideas [1937] is provided in translation. The combination of these translations and our accompanying commentary partially redresses the oft-made complaint that "Limperg never wrote", but rather "Limperg said" (e.g. Muis, 1980, p.69), and the lament that "by virtue of the sparsity of Limperg's publications, (modern day) support for replacement cost theories has been more an act of faith, than the product of reasoning" (Clarke and Dean, 1986, p.66).

Chapter 4 consisting of two parts, provides translations of four major works of Schmidt containing the essence of his *organic relativist* theory. These are coupled with translations of Schwantag's [1951] biography of Schmidt and Voigtländer's [1952] bibliography of Schmidt's publications. Bridging *chapters 3* and *4* is a translation of a 1923 article by Schmidt originally published in Dutch and containing the major elements of his theory. That Limperg was cognizant of Schmidt's ideas appears beyond doubt.

The aforementioned Schmidt [1923] article was written for the Dutch audience following lengthy periods of fluctuations in both prices and price levels in the Netherlands. The article, "De winst van de onderneming", appeared in the first two issues of a *Bedrijfseconomie* journal, *De naamlooze vennootschap roermond* (15 February & 15 March 1923). To our knowledge the first reference, in the Anglo-American literature to this 1923 Dutch publication occurred only recently (Clarke & Dean, 1986). Its subject matter, a thorough discussion of what constitutes business

3 References in [ ] brackets refer to items and page references reproduced in this monograph.

profit, essentially is a summary of Schmidt's organic theory, as initially developed and published in 1921 as *Die organische Bilanz im Rahmen der Wirtschaft*. This 1921/23 organic theme was expanded subsequently to form the basis of his 2nd International Accountants Congress paper, "Profit and Balance Sheet Value"[4] delivered in German. The International Congress was held in Holland in October 1926.

The significance of this [1926] paper is evident from its reproduction, virtually verbatim in Schmidt's 1929 3rd ed. (pp.54-90) of *Die organische Tageswertbilanz*, and also with the recognition that a relatively little known, and little referenced 1929 article by Schmidt appearing in *The Accountant* (1929b), also consisted primarily of a rearrangement of this 1926 paper. The existence of the 1923 Dutch publication, coupled to the consistency of Schmidt's ideas over time, lends added support for those arguing that Schmidt's theory was complete and accessible in Germany and Holland by as early as 1923. It is likely that MacDonald, an early speculator on this subject, was unaware of the existence of the 1923 paper as he drew his controversial inference about the primacy of Schmidt's work, with reference only to the 1926 international congress paper delivered in Amsterdam (1977, p.246). But the 1923 article, because of its temporal significance, its exposure of Schmidt's ideas in the Dutch language, and since those ideas were retained by Schmidt (see Schwantag [1951]), ought to be examined by everyone undertaking a thorough analysis of the development of CCA proposals. It forms the basis of many of our speculations in *chapter 5*.

Based on these expositions the main conclusion of *chapter 5* is that, in contrast to previous allusions in the literature, both by Dutch and Anglo-American authorities, (e.g. van Seventer, 1975) and (Goudeket, 1960 or 1952), evidence now suggests that Schmidt's formulation of his replacement cost system not only pre-dates Limperg's, but that its theoretical structure is in many respects similar. More importantly it is equally formidable. On the basis of available translations of both authors' works, it appears that there are more similarities than dissimilarities in the ideas of Schmidt and Limperg. Other myths debunked include the suggestion that Schmidt neither addressed changes in the general level of prices in his theory nor distinguished between price and price-level changes (see Zeff, 1976); and that Schmidt's account adjustment mechanisms were "incident-specific" (hyperinflation) and not an integral part of a theory of business economics (Groeneveld *et al.*, Vol. I 1964). We agree with the proposition of MacDonald (1977, p.246) that it is Schmidt's work that was

4 The 2nd International Congress was also the venue of Limperg's "now famous congress speech of 1926 about 'The meaning of the Accountant's Certificate in Connection with the Accountants' Responsibilities'" (*Bedrijfseconomie*, 1964). It is of interest that his major address at this congress did not discuss business economics issues but rather auditing issues. He did, however, comment on Schmidt's business profit paper and J.M. Clark's paper on Valuation.

probably the catalyst for the development of replacement cost accounting, as we know it today. MacDonald concludes that it was Schmidt's system of accounting (expatiated upon by Dutch academics), that was subsequently applied by Philips. This proposition gains further credence, when one considers the substance of Schmidt's 1923 paper, and the fact that prior to its publication Limperg had published nothing (substantial) in this area; a point recognised even by supporters of Limperg (e.g. van Seventer, 1975, p.68).

The penultimate *chapter* examines the transportation of European ideas on how to account for inflation into the Anglo-American accounting literature. The vehicle was Henry Sweeney's magnum opus, *Stabilized Accounting*. Based on Clarke & Dean (1989) and Dean & Clarke (1989) we provide a synthesis of the myriad of factors influencing the development of Sweeney's *Stabilized Accounting*. *Goldmarkbilanz* and *Tageswertbilanz* proposals of *Betriebswirtschaft* theorists are examined and speculation proffered that Schmidt's ideas on stabilization had the greatest impact on Sweeney's *Stabilized Accounting*. This is not to downgrade the impact of either Malhberg or Schmalenbach on Sweeney's work (see Graves, 1985, 1987, 1989 and 1990).

We conclude by providing speculations on the utility of modern day inflation accounting prescriptions. Based on ideas emanating from the economic circumstances or malaise of the 1920s hyperinflation in Europe, we posit that CPP and CCA prescriptions, except for limited circumstances, are inappropriate for the 1990s and beyond. However, the ideas forged from the vicissitudes of the 1921-23 hyperinflation do provide a basis for arriving at a solution to the ongoing problem of how the accounts of entities could be prepared so as to incorporate the financial effects of *both* price and price-level changes. The effects of the war and the hyperinflation aftermath highlighted the distinction between price and price-level changes and reinforced their differential impacts on businesses. Undoubtedly both types of price changes need to be incorporated in any accounting reform proposal if the resulting information is to be of use for *all* parties interested in an entity's affairs.

Appendices to the book contain (i) a comparison in tabular form of the fundamental characteristics underlying the 1921-26 French and German hyperinflation accounting proposals; (ii) annotated listings of the major works of other leading 1921-23 European business economists; and (iii) a comparison of the ideas in the three editions of Schmidt's *Die organische Tageswertbilanz* (1921, 1922 and 1929).

2. LIMPERG AND SCHMIDT: AN INTRODUCTION TO THEIR IDEAS AND THE PREVAILING ECONOMIC BACKGROUND

(i) Renewed Interest in Schmidt and Limperg

Utilising existing commentaries as well as analysing the products of more recent translations provides historiographical evidence regarding the ideas of two leading 1920's European business economists, the German Fritz Schmidt and Theodore Limperg from Holland. Many people in the Anglo-American literature and even the European literature have alluded to the significance of Limperg's ideas in the context of developing systematic current cost accounting proposals (e.g. Goudeket, 1952, and van Seventer, 1975, p.68 in the former and van der Schroeff, 1959, p.558 in the latter). However, Schmidt's influence has also been gaining recognition, especially in the Anglo-American literature, (Zeff, 1976; Mattessich, 1982; Tweedie and Whittington, 1984; Graves, 1985; Clarke and Dean, 1986 and 1989 and Dean and Clarke, 1989). Renewed interest in both authors' works however, has produced contradictory evidence regarding the primacy issue and whether their respective theories differed. Some now even suggest that Schmidt's work not only predates Limperg's but that its theoretical structure is equally formidable (MacDonald, 1977; Tweedie and Whittington, 1984 and Clarke and Dean, 1986). We suggest in this chapter that the recent evidence now supports an inference that there are more similarities than dissimilarities in the authors' works. In sifting through recent translations, many provided in this monograph, certain myths are exposed. Included are the suggestions that Schmidt did not address the general price-level problem in his theory and that his accounting adjustment mechanisms were incident specific (hyperinflation) and not an integral part of a theory of business economics. There is also support for the suggestion that the so-called developments associated with modern CCA prescriptions, the *value to the owner* and the *Hyde* gearing proposals, were in fact contained in the proposals of Limperg or Schmidt. Previous doubts as to the originality of Limperg's works are also explored. Finally evidence is provided supportive of the proposition that the development of Schmidt's ideas on current value accounting, especially in published form, predates Limperg, even in his own native Dutch.

(ii) From Chaos to Pattern

The idea of entropy, that everything tends to disorder, is not as universal as tradition would have us believe. Pattern and cohesion emerge in what, at first glance, appears unconnected. There is order or a peculiar grammar in most things (Campbell, 1984). *Bedrijfseconomie* and *Betriebswirtschaft* theories emerged and prospered, gained coherence, during periods of inflation, only differing in intensity from those which spawned the Anglo-American replacement cost proposals of the 1950s and the full-blown Sandilands variety CCA proposals of the 1970s.

Chaos and *Pattern* are words used to describe the development of modern inflation accounting proposals of the CCA variety with specific reference to the respective contributions of Limperg and Schmidt. They portray not only the uncertainties associated with the origin of those proposals but the inherent similarities in those proposals over time. A presumption of a definite *pattern* runs through many of the commentaries on the development of modern inflation accounting proposals (Mumford, 1979).

Notwithstanding any similarities in their ideas Limperg's strident criticism of Schmidt has contributed to the overriding impression that the fundamental ideas of the two were at odds with one another. Some evidence of the resulting confusion is appears in the works of van Seventer (1969 and 1975), MacDonald (1977) and (say) Tweedie and Whittington (1984). It has been exacerbated by a dearth of translated primary source material, particularly in respect of Limperg who published nothing in English and "little (of substance) in his native Dutch" (Clarke and Dean, 1986, p.65).

Recent translations of Limperg's *Bedrijfseconomie* suggest that in fact "nearly 100 publications flowed from (Limperg's) pen". In that seven volume collection, however, no bibliography is provided. The collection is stated to be a synthesis of his *unpublished* manuscripts, "in the form of detailed lecture notes". However, if the published articles had contained substantive and systematically developed ideas, then it is unlikely that the editors of the *Bedrijfseconomie* collected works would have had to state that prior to his death in December 1961, "a complete version of his system or theory has never been written", or that Limperg's "theories are far less widely known than at first sight would appear to be the case". This is supported by Van Seventer (1969, p.2) who notes "Limperg has never published a full presentation of his theory . . . and his writings are limited to a *number* of articles and essays" (*emphasis added*). Another interpretation of the content of these *100* articles is provided by Muis, (1980, p.69) "He was throughout his career, entirely sensitive to criticism, and tended to dismiss rather than counter his critics. Whether from a need for perfection or an unwillingness to commit himself to paper he never published an overview of his main thinking, except for a series of *ad hoc* articles" (*emphasis added*).

(iii) Controversies of Schmidt and Limperg

(a) Primacy of Ideas

Considerable impediment to forming an unequivocal impression of interconnections between the current state of replacement cost and current cost systems and the respective works of Limperg and Schmidt arises by virtue of the contradictory commentaries on each in the literature. Some of the confusion might be rooted in the trenchant criticism of Schmidt attributed to Limperg in *Bedrijfseconomie* (Groeneveld *et al.*, Vol. I and II). How widely that criticism was disseminated during the 1920s (and after) is unclear. But we might presume the prominence it has in *Bedrijfseconomie* is indicative of the intensity of Limperg's attacks on Schmidt in the course of his teaching and promotion of his own version of business economics. It seems that then, (at least as far as Limperg was concerned), as now, establishing a primacy for Limperg's or Schmidt's expositions in first presenting coherent seeds of the replacement cost or replacement value case, has diverted attention from the real substance of their proposals.

The possible sequence of events does, however, provide insight to the pattern referred to above. Van Seventer (1975, p.68), apparently relying on van der Schroeff (1959, p.558), has suggested that Limperg "conceptualized his ideas about replacement value as early as 1917-1918", thereby predating the first published works of Schmidt. In contrast MacDonald (1977, p.246) has promoted the ideas of Schmidt as the antecedents of modern versions of replacement value accounting. It is difficult to obtain evidence to either support or refute these propositions. In the Biographical Notes section in *Bedrijfseconomie* (Groeneveld *et al.*, Vol. I 1964) the editors refer to some obscure pre-1920 publications on the topic of commercial dealings, concluding that they did not achieve "the complete development of his business economics". They explain also that Limperg started to develop his full potential as an economist after appointment as professor of economics in 1922. His inaugural Professorial Address on 8 May 1922, was titled "Some Observations on *cost-price* and the *price-making* processes as problems in business economics". Nonetheless, the first published full-length explication of his theory of replacement value accounting appeared as recently as 1937 as "De gevolgen van de depreciatie van de gulden voor de berekening van waarde en winst in het bedrijf" (The consequences of the depreciation of the guilder for the calculation of value and profit for the enterprise [1937]). It was a reprint of a lecture given at Nederlandsch Instituut van Accountants, 7 November, 1936. In the Anglo-American literature Goudeket (1952) was probably the first to acknowledge this article, whilst van Seventer (1969 and 1975) and Burgert (1972) and Ashton (1981) subsequently refer to it.

(b) Integrated income and capital concepts

Many have maintained that their capital and income concepts differed. It has been suggested, for example, that Limperg's theory proposed an integrated set of concepts which nevertheless contrasted with that of Schmidt's. Van Seventer (1975, p.74-5) was adamant that Limperg's was "not a substantialistic" theory and that Limperg's continuity principle and Schmidt's "relative maintenance of value concept" (1969, p.8) differed. Ashton (1981, p.17) is not so sure, describing Limperg's theory as follows:

> The income flow of the business was dependent on output which in turn was dependent on the capacity of the enterprise . . . (leading him to assume) a permanent income source, the basis of which was a fund of unchanging capital assets. From this he derived that income measures (sic) the amount which can be distributed without encroaching on the income source (or fund of capital assets).

Our translation of Schmidt's 1923 article, and the similarity of ideas in it and, say Limperg's 1937 article, provides circumstantial evidence against the proposition that the income and capital concepts *substantially* differed. This point is further explored in chapters *3* and *5*.

(c) Replacement Cost (Price) or Replacement Value?

Dispute over the supposed differences between Schmidt's replacement prices and Limperg's replacement values also has added to the impression of a substantial theoretical rift between them. In *Bedrijfseconomie* (Groeneveld *et al.*, Vol. II 1968) there is reference to the point made subsequently by Mey (1966 pp. 14-15; Bloom and Debessay, 1984, p.138) that Limperg's replacement value and Schmidt's replacement cost concepts differ. The entrenched idea that the differences are significant comes through strongly, for example in the following extracts from Groeneveld *et al.*, [Vol. II 1968]:

> At page 62 . . . Replacement value is nothing but the quantitative representation of the significance of a good, seen from the point of view of the *Sacrifices* which have to be made for its replacement.
>
> At page 66 regarding sacrifices . . . it is not a matter of *replacement* but of *substitution* of the same capacity.
>
> At page 72 . . . It is fundamentally important that the significance of the difference (between replacement value and replacement cost) should be kept in mind: it being hidden in the varying conditions of the stock and of the market personnel for the price formation of the good which has already been produced and the good which still has to be produced.

It is unclear just what Mey perceives to be the differences between *replacement cost* and *replacement value*. His explanations at that point are less than satisfactory for distinguishing one from the other. This is especially disturbing, bearing in mind that he uses the allusion to those differences as a point of significance for distinguishing Limperg's theory of business economics from Schmidt's. Earlier in the same (1966) article Mey had contrasted *outlays (expenditures)*, with costs. The former, he explained, were "derived from cash based accounting," whereas the latter related to "sacrifices, technically required and economically unavoidable. . ." (p.4). Aggregating the current or replacement values of those factor inputs gave the *value of the product* (p.5). It seems, according to Mey, that Limperg's notion of replacement value was equivalent to the dollar value of the current factor inputs, including the imputed *value* of administration (pp.6, 9, 11 & 12). This *integral* unit cost ". . . measures the replacement value of a product to its producer", he explains (p.6).

Mey's contrasting of the respective theories of Limperg and Schmidt might be seen in the context of those passages as a distinction between a variety of imputed current factor cost (supposedly Limperg's replacement value) and the actual current cost of replacing the good sold (Schmidt's replacement price).

Such a distinction is worth making, if that is what Mey intended. For it does distinguish between the notions of current cost or current value that Limperg and Schmidt were *perceived* to have been using. But there are problems with that interpretation of the distinction as Mey describes it. Certainly, that interpretation of Limperg's theory of replacement value would give little comfort to those who have alluded to his theory to draw support for their own variety of replacement price accounting (current cost accounting). Imputing a factor cost corresponding to Mey's description, has not been part of the generic varieties of replacement price (or current cost) proposals which have alluded for theoretical support to what legend has it Limperg said. Mey's purpose was to illustrate how Limperg's value was objectively determined by recourse to current prices of those factor inputs as, usually, there are *available market quotations* (p.15). But imputation of factor costs is likely to involve allocation of common costs, which is almost certain to be highly subjective, no matter how sophisticated one might be in devising the basis (or cost-driver) therefor. At this point it is worth noting that as early as [1923] Schmidt in his Dutch article had suggested the need to include the current costs of all factor inputs, including depreciation of fixed assets.

A further essential of Mey's explanation was to illustrate how Schmidt's notion of replacement price entailed the *transfer of the confusion between outlays and values from the past, to the future,* on the grounds that Schmidt's replacement price was an estimate of the future price that would be paid when replacement occurred. That seems at odds with Schmidt's explanation that his organic income calculation would inject the current prices for the goods *sold* and property *consumed* in the production process prevailing at the date of sale, those existing during the *turnover cycle*. That stands in stark contrast with Mey's description and interpretation of *Schmidt's organic theory*. It also appears to accord more with the current cost accounting proposals of the 1970s and 1980s than Limperg's system, at least as Mey explains it.

This appearance of conflict between what Limperg and Schmidt are considered to have meant is indicative of the confusion which surrounds their contributions. No doubt some of this is due to the traditional perceptions that Limperg and Schmidt were miles apart in their thinking. Some of those perceptions must be rooted home to those who authored *Bedrijfseconomie* and reproduced their recollections of Limperg's criticism of Schmidt's work. But the fact remains that the thinness of Limperg's own written explanations of his theory has placed everyone who tries to reconstruct it at a distinct disadvantage.

No doubt some of the above was input to Limperg's case that Schmidt was on the wrong track. For in Limperg's strident criticisms of Schmidt, as documented in Groeneveld *et al.*, [Vol.II 1968], he was at pains to dispel any doubts that his *Bedrijfseconomie* ideas and the German *Betriebswirtschaft* ideas in general, and Schmidt's ideas in particular, were similar. His criticism of Schmidt, or at least that reported, was vehement (Groeneveld *et al.*, *Bedrijfseconomie*, Vol. I, pp.222-226 and Vol. II, pp.124-9). The editors of *Bedrijfseconomie* lament (i) that Limperg's *substitution value* has been equated with Schmidt's *substitutionwert*, referring to the latter as a "yield or profit value", as well as (ii) that Limperg has "pursued Schmidt's ideas". Specifically, they explained:

> This (similarity) school of thought could take root and grow, because of the lack of publication on our side, thereby failing to indicate when (Limperg's theory) was developed and how it was completely expanded. However, we are of the opinion and wish to make it clear that the resemblance is more external than internal . . . not everyone is adequately acquainted with Schmidt's theory. For a correct insight into the sense of Schmidt's theory you need to know the period from which it was formulated. Two aspects are especially important. The theory was developed when German business economists were under the misconception that ideas in their subdiscipline were unrelated to ideas about social or national economics. Also the theory was born during times of devaluation in the German currency following the Great War . . . (Schmidt's) *substitutionwert* value grew outside the (Social Economics) domain and the manner of the development of value theory in economics. Because of this, the fact that neither in Schmidt's theory nor in any related theories, can we discern any possible connection with value theory in Social Economics. . . . Schmidt's theory of value begins its existence without any connection with economic theory . . . it is forced upon him because of the circumstance of the time and the urgency of the state of business. . . . With this we have come to the second phenomenon

> influencing Schmidt's theory. The inflation, once released developed in a frighteningly rapid manner; it destroyed buying power of the consumer and also threatened business with total destruction. . . . Under these conditions a number of manufacturers seized the obvious means of preventing their demise . . . so replacement price made its appearance in the calculations of producers and it is this spontaneous change which resulted . . . in Schmidt basing his *substitutionwert* theory. . . . From the preceding it appears that Schmidt did not intend to create an economic theory of value. (Vol. I, pp.222-226).

As indicated in the extract below, this view continues in *Bedrijfseconomie*, Volume II:

> The most fundamental objection [to Schmidt's ideas] is that a new value concept is introduced incidentally, without it being based on a general value theory or without using it as a basis for a general value theory. Errors are found in business policy as well as illogical ideas on price policy in general and in that of companies; in particular a different price policy and a different business policy are suggested without a theoretical explanation. [Schmidt's replacement price/cost] theory of the "Weiderbeschaffungswert" is not a value theory. It is an artificial construction in order to arrive at a price policy and a finance policy and it provides a course of action for drawing up the balance sheet of the company. As such it has great merit, especially for the past, for the period of inflation, even though it was conceived too late. But it misses out on the illuminating moment which true theory needs. It shows up the mistakes caused by a different policy but it does not explain why the value of goods is determined by their replacement costs. It has no connection with, neither does it attack, the economic value theory in general; it leaves it undisturbed. [p.125]
>
> The second fundamental objection against Schmidt's theory is that it is essentially a theory for a time of price-increase and specifically for the period of inflation after the first World War. It is not a sound basis for a period of deflation. Here the incidental nature of the theory shows up very strongly. [p.125]
>
> Our third objection against the German views is that the value problem was considered too much - and dealt with too much - as a balance sheet problem. Schmidt is in this respect one of the least guilty. It is Schmalenbach and other theorists who were very much oriented in this direction. We remind readers of the dispute on the static, dynamic or organic balance sheets. This dispute is probably a result of the fact that business economists in Germany were oriented strongly to the techniques of accounting. [p.126]

To the contrary Schmidt's objective of relative capital maintenance on an economy-wide basis places his organic theory no less in the context of a general theory of business economics than Limperg's *Bedrijfseconomie*. Limperg's assessment of the *generality* of Schmidt's theory reemerged when van Seventer (1969 p.8) opened up those old wounds. Comparing Schmidt's and Limperg's expositions he concluded:

> The (Limpergian) theory does not conclude that there is a requirement that the firm be perpetuated in *permanent* existence, or that the flow of services and purchasing power must be maintained or safeguarded. Neither does the theory follow the teaching of Fritz Schmidt who required the *relative* function of the business unit in the organic structure of the social economy be maintained (see F. Schmidt, *Die organische Tageswertbilanz*, 3rd ed. G.A. Gloeckner, Verlagsbuchhandlung, 1929, pp.71, and 127). (van Seventer, 1969, p.8, *emphasis added*)

and again in 1975 (pp.73-74):

> Limperg's theory, placing the economic value theory in the centre of the theoretical framework, is not a substantialistic theory like the one developed by Geldmacher, Schmidt and Sommerfeld. The replacement value theory, taken as a whole, differs substantially from the German theorem of *Substanzerhaltung*. Neither Limperg nor any of his followers would subscribe to the premise that the fund of productive resources of the firm - in its size and composition - must be kept intact, irrespective of the purchasing power required therefor.

To appreciate fully, and properly place in order of events the ideas of Limperg and Schmidt the next subsection contains an indication of the possible external influences, the observed particulars, on the development of their ideas. Specifically the events prior to, and consequences of, the hyperinflation are detailed. This is followed by a description of the German *Betriebswirtschaftslehre* responses to the monetary crisis.

(iv) Prevailing Economic Circumstances in 1920's Europe

Schmidt was one of a number of German academics in the 1920s pursuing the theory of business economics. Schmalenbach, Walb, Prion, Kalveram and Mahlberg were also prominent members of that group advocating a move from the *static (balance sheet oriented)* to the *dynamic (income account oriented)* perspective.[1] Despite the prestige of the others, Schmidt appears to have been acknowledged as the intellectual leader of theorists advocating the organic perspective which incorporated and extended the static and dynamic conceptions. The *Betriebswirtschaftslehre* gained popularity following the dramatic economic decline in Germany after World War I and the concomitant inflation. Seicht (1982)[2] comprehensively analysed the

1 See Schneider (1981) and Seicht (1982). Both publications appear in German only. De Motte Greene (1937) provides an extensive description of these German accounting theories in English whilst a summary is contained in Schranz (1930).

2 This is a condensed version of his doctoral work (1970). Both appear in German only. Older summaries of these proposals abound, including Kalveram (1922), Mahlberg (1923, pp.206-246) and Schmidt (1924, pp.80-121). For a critique of Seicht's work see Schneider (1973). We thank Alfred Wagenhofer, Technische Universität Wien, for this reference.

accounting *alternatives* proposed to overcome the consequential distortion of the financial information accounting proposals that emerged. These were:

(1) Utilization of the *normal* or *base stock* method of inventory valuation; resulting in absolute maintenance of values;[3] that is, retention of capital in terms of a *base* quantity of stock on hand, so that capital is not run down by virtue of sales revenue being insufficient to finance the replacement of the same quantity of stock sold,

(2) Indexed paper mark accounts correction procedures (*Indexbuchführung*) that provided surrogates for replacement costs (for pricing decisions); a better data base for investment decisions and evaluation, or both. Restatements of accounts data were made *progressively forwards* to recast them in terms of the number of current paper marks having the equivalent general purchasing power of the paper mark at the time of the relevant transaction,

(3) Balance sheet stabilization procedures; e.g. *Goldmarkbilanz*, aimed at presenting balance sheet figures in comparable purchasing power terms. Restatements were made backwards to recast the data in terms of the number of 1914 gold marks having the equivalent general purchasing power of the paper marks at the time of the relevant transaction, and

(4) Relative maintenance of values via use of replacement cost as at the sales date (for items sold) and replacement costs as at the balance date (for unsold items). Restatements were made in terms of current replacement costs so that the *value* of the firm's capital was retained in the same proportion to the *value* of the total capital in the economy, as it bore at the date of the transaction giving rise to the original transaction data.

Inflation, unemployment and industrial dislocation in Germany immediately following World War I, encouraged pragmatism in accounting practice. Following a short period post World War I when replacement costs of factor inputs were proposed, systems of indexed based accounting (type 2 above) were put forward to rectify distortions in the accounts of German companies as inflation gathered momentum. They were implemented mainly by large companies (see Mahlberg 1923, p.189). Main academic support for these indexed methods came initially from Mahlberg (1921), Prion (1921), Schmalenbach (1921) and Kalveram (1922). (An extended list of these and other authors and their corresponding bibliographical details are contained in Clarke and Dean, 1986, *Appendix A*; an extended list appears as *Appendix II*).[4]

---

3 For discussion of the use of this method refer to Schmidt (1931, p.292) and Sweeney (1936, pp.169-70).

4 *Appendix II* highlights the amount of academic and practitioner interest in this subject. From the material listed it is apparent that inflation was perceived as a problem in several cognate disciplines; in accounting (the distortions of reported income and financial position), in economics (the trade cycle effect), in engineering (depreciation as an input cost), and in law (the assessment of taxable income or distribution of dividends / maintenance of capital). The inflation accounting debate was lengthy, mirroring the prolonged period of inflation following

The justification for the American, Henry Whitcomb Sweeney, to examine the *Goldmarkbilanz* category (3) above, was its extensive use by larger concerns in late 1922 and during 1923 and that "it was probably among the simplest . . . probably the best of balance-sheet equalization methods" (1928, p.107). He viewed it as representing the "most practical promise to accountants in the United States" (1928, p.105). Why it was *probably the best*, and had *the most practical promise* are unstated. But, it may be presumed that Sweeney was relying on some kind of rough extrapolation[5] of the German business setting into the extant American business environment. If so, it was completely unwarranted, for the German experience was unique. It was incident specific, as the following table and brief chronology of the commercial environment before and during the hyperinflation show.[6] And by the time Sweeney's first articles appeared in 1927-1928 the drive for some form of *Goldmarkbilanz* had stopped. Further discussion of the *Betriebswirtschaftslehre* influences on Sweeney's writings appear later in this subsection as well as in *chapter 6*.[7]

World War I and continuing throughout the 1920s. Germany's hyperinflation reached its zenith during October and November, 1923, however, the debate has lingered much longer.

5 Katano (1967, p.21) describes Sweeney's *Stabilized Accounting* as the product of "the theory of Gold Mark accounting . . . (being) *transplanted* to the United States (*emphasis added*)".

6 This chronology, by necessity is truncated; however, it details the major events as perceived recently by economic historians Holtfrerich (1980, 1985 and 1986), Feldman (1983), and Kindelberger (1982 and 1984). It also accords with earlier accounts of Bresciani-Turroni (1937) and Beusch (1928). Graves (1985, pp.13-23) provides a similar account of this period, basing it on the study by Stolper *et al.* (1967).

7 It is based on Clarke and Dean (1989).

Table 1

Comparative movements of the German wholesale price index and the dollar/mark exchange rate 1914-23 (1913 = 1) (E = exchange rate index; W = wholesale price index).

Month	1914		1915		1916		1917		1918	
	E	W	E	W	E	W	E	W	E	W
January	1.002	0.96	1.10	1.26	1.27	1.50	1.38	1.56	1.24	2.04
February	1.001	0.96	1.12	1.33	1.28	1.51	1.40	1.58	1.26	1.98
March	1.000	0.96	1.15	1.39	1.32	1.48	1.39	1.59	1.24	1.98
April	0.999	0.95	1.16	1.42	1.30	1.49	1.54	1.63	1.22	2.04
May	0.999	0.97	1.15	1.39	1.24	1.51	1.56	1.63	1.22	2.03
June	0.998	0.99	1.16	1.39	1.26	1.52	1.69	1.65	1.28	2.09
July	0.999	0.99	1.17	1.50	1.31	1.61	1.70	1.72	1.38	2.08
August	0.998	1.09	1.17	1.46	1.33	1.59	1.70	2.03	1.45	2.35
September	0.997	1.11	1.16	1.45	1.37	1.54	1.72	1.99	1.57	2.30
October	1.043	1.18	1.16	1.47	1.36	1.53	1.74	2.01	1.57	2.34
November	1.097	1.23	1.18	1.47	1.38	1.51	1.65	2.03	1.77	2.34
December	1.072	1.25	1.23	1.48	1.36	1.51	1.35	2.03	1.97	2.45
Annual Average	1.017	1.05	1.16	1.42	1.32	1.52	1.57	1.79	1.43	2.17

Month	1919		1920		1921		1922		1923	
	E	W	E	W	E	W	E	W	E	W
January	1.95	2.62	15.43	12.56	15.46	14.39	45.69	36.65	4281	2783
February	2.17	2.70	23.60	16.85	14.60	13.76	49.51	41.03	6650	5585
March	2.48	2.74	19.97	17.09	14.87	13.38	67.70	54.33	5048	4888
April	3.00	2.86	14.20	15.67	15.13	13.26	69.32	63.55	5826	5212
May	3.06	2.97	11.07	15.08	14.83	13.08	69.11	64.58	11355	8170
June	3.34	3.08	9.32	13.82	16.51	13.66	75.62	70.30	26202	19385
July	3.59	3.39	9.40	13.67	18.26	14.28	117.49	100.59	84186	74787
August	4.48	4.22	11.37	14.50	20.07	19.17	270.26	192.0	1100632	944041
									in mil.	in mil.
September	5.73	4.93	13.81	14.98	24.98	20.67	349.18	287.0	23.5	23.9
									in bn.	in bn.
October	6.39	5.62	16.23	14.66	35.76	24.60	757.73	566.0	6.0	7.1
November	9.12	6.78	18.39	15.09	62.64	34.16	1711.08	1154	522	725.7
December	11.14	8.03	17.38	14.40	45.72	34.87	1807.83	1475	1000	1261.6
Annual Average	4.70	4.15	15.01	14.86	24.91	19.11	449.21	341.82		

Source: *Statistisches Reichsamt: Zahlen zur Geldentwertung in Deutschland 1914 bis 1923* (Berlin, 1925), pp.6,16,17.

[**Table 1** is reproduced from Holtfrerich, *The German Inflation 1914-23*, 1986, p.17].

(v) Economic and Accounting Consequences of the 1921-23 German Hyperinflation

(a) *Phase 1*

Several significant matters emerge from the above data. Consistent with propositions in monetary theory relating to the quantity theory of money, the intensity of post World War 1 inflation was not uniform. It is best considered as comprising two phases. The first began in 1918 and culminated in a plateau of prices from April 1920 till May 1921. It forms the backdrop for the early articles on the price-level problem by the German *Betriebswirtschaftslehre*. Mahlberg (1923a, p.ix) noted that small essays discussing the price-level problem began to appear, mainly in newspapers or trade journals, as early as 1919 and 1920. Authors included Schmalenbach (1919), Klein (1920), Geldmacher (1920), Mahlberg (1920), Prion (1920), Kast (1920) and many others (see Clarke and Dean 1986, pp.83-84 for details; whilst Dean, Clarke and Graves, 1990 provide translations of some of these articles). According to Mahlberg (1923, p.ix) the most notable early contributor was the appropriately named, Geldmacher (1920), who commented on *accounting problems* created by periods of large fluctuations in the value of *money*:

> The weighty inheritance of the war, the constantly falling buying power of the Reich Mark is bearing down on our German trading enterprises like a mill-stone. . . . Annual profits are growing, as evidenced by many balance sheets! Mere tricks with figures! . . . Commercial profit and loss accounting is sabotaged and has gone wrong in this day and age. . . . Especially since November 1919 many business people have been complaining almost ceaselessly that the money they are getting their hands on through the sale of their goods and products is often far less than what they have to invest . . . in immediately replacing the goods sold. . . . (then, in the context of the 3,000 marks *reported* profits of a piano dealer, he decries) had the dealer not sold his ten pianos, he would not have made *any* profit, but he would now own ten pianos of the same quality (and valued at 100,000 marks), instead of only one (valued at 10,000 marks). (1920, p.364, *emphasis added*)

The circumstances spawned numerous books by, for example, Prion (1919 and 1921), Schmalenbach (1919 and 1921), Mahlberg (1921), Schmidt (1921), and many others (Clarke and Dean, 1986, pp.87-87). The stabilization proposals they presented were intended to incorporate the fluctuations in the value of money by means of the techniques described earlier.

It is possible to discern the overriding focus of German business economists during this first phase from the *titles* of articles published at this time: "False business cost estimation", "The influence of changes in the purchasing power of money on cost estimation" and "Proper and fictitious business profits" (Clarke and Dean, 1986, p.83

detailed the articles appearing in industrial and engineering newspapers, viz. *Plutus*, *Industrie- und Handelszeitung* and *Werkstattstechnik*, whilst Dean, Clarke and Graves, 1990, provide translations of these early works); and from the contents of Geldmacher (1920, see above). Mahlberg expressed it this way:

> Individual business is threatened insofar as it is forced by state price control to sell its products and output or services not on a profit markup based on replacement costs but on acquisition prime costs. . . . Although Professor Schmalenbach from the University of Cologne (*Basics of Dynamic Accounting*) has already explained this connection one year ago and a short time ago (1920) in another connection ("Replacement Cost Accounting"). . . . (1920, p.183)

> If one wishes to acknowledge the effect of the shifting of values on income accounting (or income determination). . . . We shall examine two extreme cases in order to recognise the effect of this price rise on the measure of success of a merchandise account and thus of an expense and performance account. . . . (1923b, p.2)

> To determine profit the calculation formula should not read "prime costs incurred plus profit" but "replacement costs plus profit". Long before the war (1908/9) Schmalenbach had suggested this calculation formula. . . . The economic calculation formula, replacement costs plus profit, does not only apply for materials, salaries and expenses, but also for the inclusion of allowance for depreciation. . . . (1923b, p.3)

Although arguably *data comparability* was the primary underlying objective of these writers during this phase, it was to be achieved by matching the current costs of resources consumed with current revenues, for costing, pricing and financial reporting purposes. Sweeney recognised this focus:

> The necessity of recomputing original book costs to allow for price changes became well recognised during the great inflation. . . . (1931, p.176, *emphasis added*)

In respect of financial reporting Schmidt's (1921) early writings on the price-level problem represented one of the earliest comprehensive forms of current value accounting.[8] In this work an appreciation of the intertwined problems created by changing money values and changing relative prices is evident.

Although a current cost (physical capital replacement) perspective is evident during this phase, concern with reporting the effect of inflation, thereby reflecting a homogeneity perspective, also surfaces. Mahlberg's first major essay (1920),

8 Initially published in 1921 as *Die organische Bilanz im Rahmen der Wirtschaft*, it was extended and republished under the same title in 1922 and then a substantially enlarged version appeared in 1921 under the title, *Die organische Tageswertbilanz*. For details of the specifics of his work see Clarke and Dean, 1986, especially Schwantag's 1951 translated biography, provided as Appendix B to that article and reproduced in *chapter 4*, section *B*.

"Economic Relativity", comprised two main parts - the first concerned the impact of inflation on the German economy of 1920, in order to compare it with its 1914 counterpart. In the second the impact of inflation on businesses was examined. Below is an extract from that second section:

> When we look at the fixed asset values in the balance sheets of companies for instance, land and buildings and plant, these represent on average, assets acquired in peace time and expressed in peace time prices. They surely therefore represent gold mark, resulting in an enormous undisclosed reserve according to today's prices. The shareholder is the owner of these physical goods, the bondholder a mere creditor, only an owner of assets in marks, the value of which has *melted away with inflation*. (p. 182, emphasis *added*)

Even in 1920 arithmetical homogeneity may be inferred as one of his concerns.[9] In the same article the section on private enterprise was the forerunner of his major 1921 publication in which he suggested a modified variety of *forward* adjusting stabilization (see *subsection iv b below*).

Publication of Mahlberg (1921) coincided with Prion's, *Financing and Balance Sheet Reporting of Economic Operations Under the Influence of Currency Depreciation*, certainly one of the earliest comprehensive German books describing the impact of inflation on business and accounting. Prion's (1921, p.11) merchant example illustrates his concern of matching current costs and revenues: "The more I earn as a businessman, the poorer I become and the more I take in, the less able I am to pay my debts". It reinforced the point made by Geldmacher (1920) regarding the piano dealer (see extract above). And it has been the basis of many modern day justifications for various forms of replacement cost accounting.

(b) *Phase 2*

The May 1921 London Ultimatum on Germany's final War Reparations obligations disrupted the price plateau. Unexpected demand for increased repayments in the Ultimatum sent the financial markets into panic. Undoubtedly it acted as the catalyst of the increase in the rate of inflation during the latter part of 1921 and, was in fact, the seed of the eventual hyperinflation, which is generally agreed by historians to have begun in June 1922 (for example, Feldman, 1982; Kindelberger, 1984; Holtfrerich, 1986). Hyperinflation fuelled the second surge of academic interest in

---

9 Similar concerns were expressed by Von Kast (1920, p.1): "Inflation after the war tossed out the principle that one can add apples to oranges" and von Schlesinger (1920, p. 507): "Thus, not only do we have a new standard of measure in use whose graduations are wider but remain constant; unfortunately, we also have a rubber standard of measure whose length expands and contracts daily."

the impact of the price-level problem on accounting and business. From our perspective its importance is the change in focus it precipitated.

Sweeney's stabilization proposals (discussed in detail in *chapter 6*) were drawn from an array of *Betriebswirtschaftslehre* restatement mechanisms having their origins during phase 2. Predominant, particularly during the hyperinflation period, was *Goldmarkbilanz* as *the* accounting solution to (hyperinflation) price-level distortions.

Again, Schmidt's (1922 and 1923) *organic* - *operating capacity* based - form of stabilization was the main exception. But the exception was to be expected. For, economic historians have shown, the price-level problem and accounting policy choice were very much *public* rather than *private* or purely business issues. In the main this seems to have been overlooked in the accounting literature, with the result that explanation for accounting methods has been sought only in accountants' writings.

Possibly relying on the ideas of Mahlberg (1923a and 1923b) that "forward adjusting" was inappropriate when the currency's purchasing power became too volatile Sweeney did not regard the switch from forwards adjusting *Indexbuchführung* to backwards adjusting *Goldmarkbilanz* as surprising (1928, p.108 and 1935, p.186). Tweedie and Whittington (1984, p.19) seem to have accepted this thesis. But, the economic and social history of the period strongly implies that the switch was as much the product of political compromise, as the product of a cold, clinical, assessment of the business circumstances. The odds are that it was not a well thought out, accounting solution, selected from the many forwards and backwards restatement proposals being offered by business economists at the time (see Mahlberg, 1923b, pp.206-46 and Schmidt 1924, pp.80-121 for an annotated listing and illustration of the major proposals). The maelstrom of debate and the variety of adjustment mechanisms at that time are indicative of the general state of disorder from which the German *Goldmarkbilanz* solution emerged. The respective works of Schmalenbach and Mahlberg played an important role in the socio-economic process of exposing an acceptable, pragmatic, business, accounting and societal solution. An understanding of how these accounting ideas were intertwined with political and social issues is yet to be fully understood.

(c) *Schmalenbach and Mahlberg: Stabilization via Indexation*

Clearly the majority of Mahlberg's early work (pre 1921) was consistent with the *paramount* concern of the German *Bertiebswirtschaftslehre* during 1920 and the early part of 1921 - determination of the most appropriate cost calculation for business decision making and its consequential effect on profit determination.[10] Even in some of his later writings there is further evidence in support of this proposition. For example, in the *Introduction* to a 1923 monograph he explains:

> The unstable value of money means an unstable disturbance to all those calculations where *amounts in marks from previous periods* are connected with each other, e.g. cost calculations, statements of revenue and expenditure, profit and loss accounting. . . . (1923b, p.32, *emphasis added*)

Also, as noted earlier, in 1908 Schmalenbach had suggested that *business pricing* policy should be based on a replacement cost rather than the historical cost formula. From Schmidt's works [1923 and 1926] it appears such a policy had been suggested initially in the economics literature by Ricardo (1817) and picked up by Carey (1837). If this managerial policy were to be extended to profit determination and financial reporting Schmalenbach could be viewed as a replacement cost advocate. However, on another tack Schmalenbach is regarded by German accounting historians as the "father of *Indexbuchführung*" (see for example, Seicht 1970, p.413). His 1921 article on indexed accounting (which followed the aforementioned 1919 and 1920 *Betriebswirtschaftslehre* proposals) is regarded in the German literature as seminal, since it changed the focus of the inflation accounting debate. But it has only recently been accorded its deserved recognition in the Anglo-American accounting literature (Clarke and Dean, 1989 and Graves, Dean and Clarke 1989). In his commentary, Graves (1985, p.121), although discussing Schmalenbach's 1921 article, claims that "Mahlberg evidently enjoys the distinction of having presented the first comprehensive model for accounting for inflation in the accounting literature", in particular for the model in the First edition of *Bilanztechnik und Bewertung bei schwankender Währung*. But, Mahlberg was adamant that Schmalenbach's October 1921 article was more *complete* than either of his own 1920 or 1921 suggestions. In the Foreword to the 1922 Second edition of *Bilanztechnik* Mahlberg explains that Schmalenbach "inspired this second revised edition. . . . He recognised the *account* distortions arising from balance sheet corrections due to *money value* changes . . . " (1923, p.viii, *emphasis added*).

Mahlberg's initial (1921) stabilization proposal was partial and exploratory. It involved restatement of data relating to only real, physical items (*Realwerte*), such as Plant, Buildings and Merchandise, from the opening balance sheet. However, monetary items (*Geldwerte*) and Capital were not restated. The restatement procedure was based on movements in the price of gold (*Goldagio*), whilst the closing

10 Translations of some of these theorists' works and analysis appears in Dean, Clarke and Graves (1990).

balance sheet was established using capitalized or programmed values (*etatsmässiger Wert*).[11] Mahlberg regarded all of the increase in paper mark wealth as profit.

In contrast Schmalenbach's 1921 stabilization method entailed restatement of the historical cost values of both real and monetary items. Although there is no preferred measuring unit advocated in his 1921 article, he does discuss numerous possibilities, including: retail or wholesale price indices, foreign currency exchange rates, the price of gold and numerous other indexes. His forwards indexing procedure produced the same profit result as the *Goldmarkbilanz* solution, subsequently used by larger concerns during the 1922-1923 hyperinflation, and ultimately recommended by both Mahlberg and Schmalenbach in 1922 following deliberation of the Indexation Committee. Under Schmalenbach's 1921 method:

- The opening balance sheet acquisition values (both real and monetary items were restated to their equivalent ending paper mark value. *General* index numbers were used.

- Any difference between the adjusted opening and closing capital amounts, was regarded as *Profit.*

- Significantly Schmalenbach regarded part of the value (wealth) change between the opening and closing balance sheets as a business profit, whereas Mahlberg saw it as only a *value adjustment* entry resulting from the *value fluctuation in capital.* Profit variations arising from Mahlberg's and Schmalenbach's methods were due to their different treatment of monetary items.

- Gains and losses on the opening balances of monetary items (Cash, Debtors and Creditors) were included in the Profit and Loss Account.

Nevertheless, Schmalenbach appears to have been wedded to historical cost valuation for accounting purposes. Recognition of the necessity for indexing historical costs is first evident in his 1919 monograph. And again in his 1921 article. But by 1922 Schmalenbach had changed tack, advocating stabilization on a *deflated* gold-mark basis. Graves (1985, pp.61-64) claims that the "progression" of Schmalenbach's ideas on indexation mirrored the degree of inflation experienced in Germany from 1919 to 1922, a view with which we concur. Again we accept Graves' description that Schmalenbach's inflation accounting theory was an extension of his "dynamic balance sheet theory dating back to 1908 (p.24) . . . the model is based on price level adjustments and seems to be put forward as a temporary measure . . . [the object of which was] a concern with achieving comparable periodic income figures (p.58) . . . [requiring] an all encompassing stabilization . . . [Schmalenbach chose] indexation for the measuring unit". The suggestion that Schmalenbach's aim was

11 Graves (1985), pp.141-55 and 1989) details Mahlberg's valuation theory.

income comparability accords with our analysis of the concerns of the pre 1922 *Betriebswirtschaftslehre*. But it differs from our posited *data homogeneity* rationale of post 1922 *Betriebswirtschaftslehre* theorists. And it was the latter, of course, that formed the basis of Sweeney's work both pre and post 1928 (see *chapter 6* below).

In accepting that Schmalenbach saw the "stabilization technique" as a temporary measure Graves (1985, p.60) agrees with the observation of Hanns-Martin Schoenfeld (1979): that Schmalenbach was unenthusiastic about *inflationary* adjustments and only turned to indexation when "his nominalistic approach did not yield usable (in terms of comparable data) results any longer".

Tweedie and Whittington (1984) point to an apparent similarity in the approaches of Mahlberg (1921) and Schmalenbach (1921):

> Mahlberg was a pupil of Schmalenbach, and both *preferred the stabilization of historical* costs as a method of dealing with inflation rather than the alternative of replacement cost, although Mahlberg preferred the gold-Mark as the constant unit of measurement, whereas Schmalenbach preferred a unit based upon a general price index, such as was later used in the CPP proposals of the early 1970's. (p.19, *emphasis added*)

But it is to be noted that Schmalenbach's "preferred historical cost stabilization" method apparently was Mahlberg's "second best" solution. In contrast to Schmalenbach, after the hyperinflation Mahlberg continued to advocate an alternative to the extant historical cost valuation. It was not an indexation solution, but rather one based on programmed or forecast valuations (1925 and 1927). This suggests a fundamental difference in their approaches and the ordering of their preferences to changing prices and the price-level problems. Recently Graves (1989) speculated that Mahlberg's preferred method of "valuation" had the greatest effect on Sweeney's preferred replacement cost based stabilization system. We promote a combined view in *chapter 6*. These differences are significant for assessing the relative influence of these authors on subsequent events.

Ordering the relative importance of Schmalenbach's and Mahlberg's contributions is more than a matter of cleaning up the detail. It gives insight to the source of pressure for the adoption of particular procedures, thereby allowing a more informed evaluation of their appropriateness for today's environment.

Schmalenbach's status in the inflation accounting debate is apparent from his appointment in November 1921 to chair the *Indexkommission*, a German private-industry-sponsored Balance Sheet Commission of the Society for Economic Development. This was a critical point of departure in the hyperinflation accounting saga. As Holtfrerich's Table 1 indicates, by then prices had begun to accelerate and the hyerinflation was near. According to Schmalenbach (1922, pp.1-3) the Index

Commission was called within the private sector after hearings on the matter by the Reich Economic Advisory Council had come to a standstill in late 1920 and it was directed to explore the following issues arising from the hyperinflation:

- Which of the known Index numbers series was most suited for balance sheet purposes? - reporters were Ernst Kahn and Professor Fritz Schmidt.[12]

- Which of the suggested methods of computation was to be selected for balance sheet conversion? - reporter was Professor Walter Mahlberg.

- What were the practical consequences of changes for accounting law and revenue law? - reporter was the lawyer, Richard Fischer.

Mahlberg (1923a, Foreword to Second Edition) notes that "the work of the Commission resulted in the recommendation that accounting be based on a fixed monetary value (in short, gold mark accounting)". Notwithstanding Schmalenbach's status, his pupil Mahlberg was undoubtedly influential in the adoption of this gold-mark stabilization method. Graves (1985, p.121), citing Schmalenbach (1922, pp.2-3 and 1925, p.210), claimed the committee of the Index Commission recommended the gold-mark method on the basis of Mahlberg's speech at their conference held in late 1921. Thus, whereas Schmalenbach has been described correctly as the "father of *Indexbuchführung*", and Mahlberg is placed properly as the "developer of *Goldmarkbilanz*" (Schmidt, 1924, pp.94-95; Schoenfeld, 1979, p.60 and Graves, 1985, p.121), the picture remains incomplete without identifying the background relationship between the two.

Indexbuchführung proposals were quickly replaced with *Goldmarkbilanz* methods. This change was not surprising, since "progressive (forward adjusting) indexing methods" were not appropriate with the onset of hyperinflation as the currency's purchasing power became too volatile (Sweeney, 1928, p.108, citing Mahlberg (1923)). Accounting theorists, adopting methods used by large companies, were in the vanguard of that change. Mahlberg by then preferred the *Goldmarkbilanz* solution (Schmidt, 1924, p.94) whilst Schmalenbach had taken up and adapted Mahlberg's approach especially after the Index Commission to examine the gold mark proposal in detail was established in 1922 (Schmidt, 1924, pp.94-5). *Goldmarkbilanz* eventually became the legally endorsed accounting practice for certain companies on 28 December 1923 (details of the legislation appear in Schmalenbach, 1922; Schmidt, 1924, pp.151-205; as well as in translation in Graves, Dean and Clarke, 1989). But

12 Schmidt's appointment for this task may well be indicative of the status accorded by the *Indexkommission* regarding his expertise with respect to the construction of price indexes and their use in the *stabilization* of accounts. Schmidt's [1927] article, "Index Numbers" is included herein on pp.247-54.

the new accounting rules were not an isolated event. *Goldmarkbilanz* methods were part of an economic package which included the issue of the *Rentenmark* and the restoration of the gold mark in the early part of 1924 (Kindelberger, 1984, pp.325-8).

(d) *Hyperinflation and the Goldmarkbilanz Proposals*

We speculate that *Goldmarkbilanz* proposals, appearing when hyperinflation was at its zenith in 1922 and 1923, signalled a switch in emphasis by *Betriebswirtschaftslehre* theorists - from profit measurement to asset and equity data homogeneity. Matching current costs with current revenues now had been fully supplanted by the focus on balance sheet comparability.[13] Mahlberg (1923b), hammered home the new emphasis:

> The obvious precondition of *the arithmetical idea* underlying the *balance sheet* is . . . that a uniform value of money must be used as a standard for the *measurement of balance sheet figures* (p.32, *emphasis added*).

Mahlberg (1922), and later Schmalenbach (1922), were two of the many who, at one time of another, embraced *Goldmarkbilanz*. As noted by Graves (1987, p.48 *emphasis added*) the Indexation Committee of the *Indexkommission* was pragmatic in its response, electing "to endorse Mahlberg's method of restating accounting values in terms of their pre-war gold-mark value albeit by the *more practicable* means of indexation". However, it is arguable that it was "the *more practicable*" for business dealings. It is to be noted that Mahlberg's *Goldmarkbilanz* involved a backwards adjustment of *all* balance sheet items to August 1914 gold mark values, thereby valuing all assets and liabilities and thus net worth, on the same real (not merely nominal) basis. The main *advantage* claimed for it was that adjustments could be made continuously - thereby facilitating *immediate* intertemporal comparison. Prior year balances did not require restating as was the case with the *Indexbuchführung* (and modern CPP-type) mechanisms. The method, however, produced a profit figure representing the same amount of general purchasing power, as in Schmalenbach's 1921 indexation proposal involving forward adjustments.

---

13 Again Schmidt is the exception. As noted his classic, *Die organische Bilanz . . .*, first appeared in 1921 and was revised in 1922. Notwithstanding the massive increase in the inflation rate during 1921 and 1922 the latter edition retained the suggestion for including current costs in accounts. (See Holtfrerich, 1986, Table 1 or Bresciani-Turroni, 1937, Tables 3-5). There was no suggestion of incorporating a general price-level adjustment of the type proposed by Mahlberg and Schmalenbach. This is not to suggest that Schmidt did not recognise the importance of inflation; necessitating the matching of monetary assets and liabilities (see Clarke and Dean, 1986, pp.76-77 for details of Schmidt's managerial policy, "his principle of identity of values", to negate the impact of general price-level changes on a company).

Another, and arguably more plausible explanation for the Indexation Committee's pragmatism is that it was politically expedient. This economic consequences explanation is now explored further, based on earlier work by Clarke (1982), Clarke and Dean (1989) and Graves, Clarke and Dean (1989).

It is reasonable to infer that, at least in Germany, some officially prescribed form of stabilized accounting was inevitable from as early as 1922 following the Index Commission's advocacy of *Goldmarkbilanz*. Although not required by legislation immediately, interest in stabilization procedures in business, political and academic quarters was evident in the latter part of 1921 and the beginning of 1922, intensifying after June 1922 with the onset of the hyperinflation. Holtfrerich (1985, p.125) is instructive:

> (Prior to August 1923) wage conventions were negotiated on the average about every two months in 1921, every month during most of 1922, biweekly at the beginning of 1923 and weekly as the hyperinflation spiralled. . . . About then the decision was taken in principle to stabilize the mark because as a government publication declared in 1924 - with indexed wages no one was left to carry the burden of inflation. . . . A sliding price scale for industrial goods had been generally adopted by the end of 1921 to avoid the consequences of the currency's depreciation between the time of sale and time of payment.

It was not uncommon in Germany for other commercial documents, such as bond agreements, to have valorization clauses and by November 1923 large quantities of value maintaining currencies (*Notgelde*) were in circulation.[14] Also indicative of this intensification was the number of accounting books and articles published in 1922/23 having *Goldmarkbilanz* in their title (Clarke and Dean, 1986, p.88 and *Appendix II* of this volume).

Although it was mainly the larger concerns that adopted *Goldmarkbilanz* (Mahlberg, 1923, p.189), it is apparent from economic historians (such as Feldman (1982), Kindelberger (1984) and Holtfrerich (1986)) that many of the commercial undertakings had accommodated the "ills of hyperinflation" in various ways in their commercial dealings without formally changing their system of record keeping. Several economic historians claim "de facto stabilization existed" prior to the end of 1923, preceding the "de jure stabilization" embodied in the *15 November 1923 Monetary Reform* (Holtfrerich, 1985, p.125). This begs the question of why formal accounting stabilization procedures had not been implemented universally.

Political and commercial discussions on the best method of *monetary* stabilization during 1921-23 were lengthy and controversial. Beusch (1928)

14 At about this time in the Anglo-American "economics" literature Irving Fisher was advocating the use of indexed adjustment clauses for bonds.

categorized the various stabilization proposals into three groups with (2) and (3) involving the introduction of a new currency alongside the old *Papiermark*:

(1) Plans to use taxation policy, a ban on credit and regulations regarding foreign currency holdings in order to stabilize the currency. Such plans seek to generalize the adoption of a value maintaining unit of account, and by introducing "index-linked" assessment of tax liability would seek to halt the collapse of the paper mark; they did not purpose [propose] to introduce a new currency in place of or alongside it . . . ,

(2) Plans by industry (say, Kramer) and politicians such as Schacht, Hilferding, Hirsch and Bernard for a return to the gold currency in order to provide an internationally acceptable means of payment.

(3) Plans to stabilize on the basis of a currency secured against the mortgage of land or commodities. The plans of Helfferich and Minoux, a long standing colleague of Hugo Stinnes, are the main members of this class (as reported in Holtfrerich, 1986, pp.314-15).

The eventual compromise *Rentenmark* stabilization proposal (a special form of *Goldmarkbilanz*) was part of a package of government measures known as the November 1923 Monetary Reform. Unequivocally it was a political compromise, aimed at *saving the Reich*. Accordingly, the accounting and taxation stabilization proposals embodied in this reform package could have been arrived at independently of any *Betriebswirtschaftslehre* arguments pertaining to the theoretical accounting superiority of *Goldmarkbilanz*. The "simplicity" argument posited by Mahlberg (1923) and accepted by Sweeney (1928, p.106) or the "volatility" argument suggested by Sweeney (1928, p.108), are just two of the possible political reasons leading to the Index Commission's selection of *Goldmarkbilanz* in early 1922, and ultimately the *Rentenmark* adopted by the Reich in November 1923.

Most importantly, it is likely that the quest for financial or accounting purity was a matter of little influence in the ultimate decision - possibly furthest from the minds of those deliberating. Political expediency was the foremost. Accepting this economic consequences explanation the change is viewed as more seductive, than subtle. Holtfrerich, for example, is adamant that the monetary reform measures (including the *Rentenmark* as the unit of account for business and tax purposes)[15] were the result of powerful political forces - the result of compromise. Holtfrerich viewed their implementation as a necessity for the survival of the German political system - economic factors, although relevant, were deemed to be of lesser import:

15 As Sweeney (1928, p.106) noted, "paper marks could not be eliminated from the bookkeeping system altogether in most cases because, first, being still legal tender, they could not be refused when offered in payment of debts, and because, second, each business was required by law to prepare a balance sheet at least once annually and to express it in terms of the imperial mark (the 'paper mark')".

> As the incidence of "inflation tax" became confined to an ever shrinking class of paper mark users - chiefly wage and salary earners paid in paper marks - its burden on them weighed more progressively, but by the same token its "yield" to the state diminished. Revolutionary potential built up that threatened domestic public order and the integrity of the Reich. Currency (and with it accounting) stabilization thus became a *necessity of the political system*, if the Reich were to survive; to a far lesser degree was it a necessity for the continued functioning of the economic system. (Holtfrerich, 1986, p.334, *emphasis added*)

The mechanics of the *Rentenmark* stabilization proposal exemplify this compromise:

> The government scheme (introduced by Luther with the aid of Hilferding) borrows from Helferrich's (*Roggenmark*) "rye currency" and from Hilferding's "registration of tangible assets".... (Mahlberg, 1923a, p.vi)

> [The reworking of Helferrich's plan eliminated] the dependence of the new currency on the value of the rye, and (brought) it into a fixed relationship with gold instead. They [Luther and Hilferding] chose to make the gold value of the new currency identical to that of the pre-war mark. Further modifications imposed a credit ceiling of 1.2 billion marks on the new bank's dealings with the private sector - not least in order not to make the Reichsbank wholly redundant - and reduced the ceiling on credit to the Reich to 1.2 billion marks likewise. The "Currency Bank" became the "Rentenbank" and the "rye mark" became the "rentenmark". (Holtfrerich, 1986, p.316)

Historians note that the adoption of the *Rentenmark* proved an immediate and outstanding success. Identification of why, has proven more difficult. Guttmann and Meehan (1975, p.222) suggest that:

> The public's confidence was created by the conviction that the *Rentenmark* was backed by land and industrial property, and this in the public's mind was accepted as a *Sachwert*, as stable value.

In contrast Beusch (1928, p.62) claimed the success was due to:

> [T]he return to the accounting basis of the peacetime [i.e. pre-war] gold currency. Since the new currency was identical with the former national gold currency as a unit of account, and the government took all manner of steps to ensure its value remained stable, the German people felt itself liberated from the oppressive burden of astronomical figures and with astonishing rapidity found its way back to reckoning in the old unit of account. The "miracle of the rentenmark" lay in appreciating the psychological importance of enabling this return to take place. With a "rye mark" this magic property would have been missed. (As cited in Holtfrerich, 1986, p.317)

Even so, it is questionable whether Beusch refers there to accounting in the technical sense - as practised by accountants - as much as to "accounting", the mechanism of calculating as applied in financial matters, for the "confidence" was a "public" rather than a "professional" phenomenon.

(vi) Summary

In brief, *Betriebswirtschaftslehre* responses to the post World War I price and price-level problems were of two generic types. Initially, given the obvious need to replace worn out or destroyed capital, economic pragmatism dictated that firms utilised replacement cost data for costing and pricing purposes. This need spilled over into the external reporting domain. Schmalenbach (1919) (possibly inadvertently), Mahlberg (1920 and primarily Schmidt (1921) were the main means of transporting this idea into financial accounting. This initial reform phase was displaced by forwards indexed CPP-type adjustments when the level of prices started to dramatically increase early in 1921 (see proposals by Schmalenbach, 1921 and Mahlberg, 1921). As this rate of increase changed to hyperinflation in 1922/23 the indexation proposals reversed to backwards (*Goldmarkbilanz*) techniques - best illustrated by Mahlberg (1922) and Schmalenbach (1922). The focus of this latter reform phase however, shifted from pricing/budgeting. *Fictitious profits* and *excessive tax* were now the primary focus. Balance Sheet indexation had two visible impacts. First, it promoted the importance of achieving arithmetical homogeneity in balance sheet data. Second it evoked increased interest in the balance sheet *per se*.

To appreciate fully and to properly place in the order of events the ideas of Limperg and Schmidt, the next two chapters provide a comparative analysis of the possible influences on their respective ideas as they appeared in published form. Each chapter is prefaced by a description of their early professional lives and a brief overview of their main ideas in the area of replacement cost accounting. It is followed by translation of each authors' main works coupled to biographical and bibliographical information.

3. DR THEODORE LIMPERG, JR

(A) Limperg and the Background to his Replacement Cost Accounting

(i) Early Professional Associations[1]

Little is known in the Anglo-American literature of Limperg's writing and even less of his professional activities and potential influences on the development of his ideas. What is evident is that Limperg was a critic of conventional wisdom. Mey (1966, p.3) observes that Limperg would only accept views "logically and empirically defensible". A summary of Limperg's professional life appeared in the Preface of *Bedrijfseconomie* (Groeneveld, *et al.*, Vol. I 1964).

> Limperg was born in Amsterdam on 21 December 1879 and died in the same city on 6 December 1961. In 1907 he matriculated from the famous school of Raamplein, Amsterdam and a year later acquired a diploma in accounting, which in those days was a qualification of practical value. From the beginning he displayed industry and showed concern for public matters. From 1908 he was a board member of the association of *Houw en Trouw* where he played a useful role in the development of economics training, the training of his younger days. As early as 1910 Limperg, as the representative of *Houw en Trouw* at the 9th International Congress for the Teaching of Commerce, pleaded for the desirability of teaching commerce at tertiary level.... In 1922 his striving for tertiary education met with success: at the Municipal University in Amsterdam the Faculty of Business Science was founded.... Limperg has the right to be looked upon as a great systematician, who broke with the "business management teaching approach" (*bedreijfsleiding Kunstleer*); and as the builder of a science of business economics. A somewhat similar development took place in the wider area of accountancy. Originally Limperg and a colleague, Volmer (J.G. Ch.) were united in their fight against the "old school", as it was called. To please Volmer, whom he sided with in a conflict with the then board of the Dutch Institute of Accountants, Limperg even had himself expelled as a member of the Institute. This was followed by the formation of the Dutch Accountants' Association, later to merge with the old Institute, but not before it had been established that the new ways of thinking, crystallized in (Limperg's) Dutch Accountants' Association, would prevail.

From Mey's (1966) account of Limperg's early life, we glean a concern for a wide ranging fields of interest - "a leading personality in the [Dutch] Institute's struggle for legislative regulation of the profession" as well as "a pioneer in the scientific management movement". He "contributed to the development of the study

---

1 This subsection draws heavily from the works of Burgert [1972] and more recently, van Sloten (1981) and Ashton (1981).

and practice of industrial economics, administrative organization, accounting and auditing". (p.4)

From this account and other analyses of his writings by Burgert [1972], van Seventer, 1969 and 1975; Vos, 1970; van Sloten, 1981 and Ashton, 1981, it is obvious that Limperg was a leader and outstanding thinker of his time. Muis (1980, p.70) notes that Limperg's work comprises a "total commitment to system, to methodology, to comprehensive in-depth analysis, to clarity of expression". Notwithstanding this, it would not be too harsh to describe Limperg as an enigma. Muis, for instance noted: "The expression is never Limperg wrote, but rather Limperg said, and consequently much of what is attributed to him by later generations may well be apocryphal" (1980, p.69), and Clarke and Dean (1986, p.66) suggested: "But, by virtue of the sparsity of Limperg's publications, support for replacement cost theories relying upon the presumed authority of his work has been more an act of faith, than the product of reasoning".

(ii) Limperg's Theory

Tweedie and Whittington (1984) refer to the *impact* of Limperg's work. In commenting on the *flexibility* accorded accountants in complying with standards enacted in Holland (The Act on Annual Accounts of Enterprises, 1971), they suggest this is due to the pioneering efforts of Limperg:

> The influence of the replacement cost ideas of Limperg has enabled certain leading companies, notably Philips, to adopt replacement cost methods in their financial reports. . . . (1984, p.226)

We noted earlier that van Seventer (1975, p.68), relying on van der Schroeff (1959, p.558) claimed that Limperg conceptualized his ideas about replacement value as early as 1917-18, but noted that it is difficult to obtain evidence to either support or refute such a proposition. Drawing on a number of analyses (e.g. Mey, 1966; van Seventer, 1969 and 1975; Vos, 1970; Burgert, 1972; Ashton, 1981 and Tweedie and Whittington, 1984), as well as translated extracts from Limperg's *Bedrijfseconomie*, the following characteristics of his theory pertaining to accounting are discernible:

(1) There is no profit without a sale; so that the realization principle is adhered to.

(2) Differences between replacement cost and historic cost are charged to a special capital adjustment account.

(3) *Basic Valuation Rule*: The value of any asset is determined by what has subsequently been described as the *value to the owner* method of valuation. Following this approach, and in keeping with the now popular interpretation of that line of thinking, the value of any asset is determined in *today's idiom* by the lower of:

a) RC and NRV, where NRV is greater than EPV, and

b) RC and EPV, where EPV is greater than NRV.

(see Limperg [1937, p.3 and extract in *chapter 5*).

(4) Value is determined mainly by supply side factors, in particular replacement cost.

(5) Limperg integrated income and value theory. Ashton (1981, p.17) describes it in the following way. "The income flow of the business was dependent on output which in turn was dependent on the capacity of the enterprise . . . (leading him to assume) a permanent income source, the basis of which was a fund of unchanging capital assets. From this he derived the notion that income measures [sic] the amount which can be distributed without encroaching on the income source (or fund of capital assets)." This line of reasoning leads to (6) and (7) below.

(6) Holding gains are not regarded as a component of distributable income. All holding gains are credited to a capital reserve account, *rekening voor prijsverschillen.*

(7) Holding losses are to be charged to the special reserve account until the balance thereof has been exhausted. With further holding losses then charged to profit and loss, to give expression to the *double minimum postulate.*

(8) Limperg's income notion relates only to the accounting for non-monetary assets. Effects of general price-level changes on monetary assets are not accounted for.

(9) Income and capital concepts are used systematically to "indicate efficiency, inefficiency or excess capacity in production, marketing, administration and other centres" (Mey, 1966, p.6). These concepts also are viewed as pertinent to the financing of business activities.

To summarise, we rely on Mey's (1966, p.8) assessment: "Limperg's ideas are clearly marked by an integral quality, a unity of conception, a deep understanding of the relationship between macro-economic phenomena and industrial economic theory and experience".

These and other issues are described in the following (*section B*) biographical material (Burgert) and the primary material relating to Limperg's theory. Comparisons of the respective theories of Limperg and Schmidt are made below in *chapters 5* and *6* (pp.277-301).

(B) Biographical Data and Other Translations of Limperg's Ideas

(1) R. Burgert, "Reservations about 'Replacement Value' Accounting in the Netherlands", *Abacus*, December 1972, pp.111-126.

(2) Th. Limperg, "De gevolgen van de depreciatie van de gulden voor de berekening van waarde en winst", (The Consequences of the Depreciation of the Guilder for the Calculation of Value and Profit), *Maanblad voor Accountancy en Bedrijfshuishoudkunde*, January 1937, pp.1-14.

(3) G.I. Groeneveld *et al.*, *Bedrijfseconomie*, Vol II 1968, sections A.III "Replacement Value Theory" and B.I "The Basic Principles of Costing", pp.49-140.

Reservations About "Replacement Value" Accounting in the Netherlands

Professor R. Burgert*

An extensive search is taking place by accountants for soundly conceived current values for financial statements. In this connection some attention has been paid over the years to replacement value accounting as advocated in theory and practised by some firms in the Netherlands.

Many accountants might have gained the impression from published articles[1] that the Dutch have "solved" the problem of current value accounting, and that there is a sound theory underlying these practices. In all fairness to objectivity, I feel the need to correct some misconceptions that exist about replacement value accounting in the Netherlands, and to evaluate some of its weaknesses.[2] Professional literature in Holland has criticised many aspects of the replacement value theory.

In this article I shall set forth briefly the theory of replacement value as devised by Professor Th. Limperg, the *auctor intellectualis* of the replacement value theory, his theory of income measurement and the main points of criticism mentioned above.

For readers who are interested in how uniformly replacement value accounting is adhered to in the Netherlands, an appendix states the result of a survey.

I. Limperg's Theory of Replacement Value

When Limperg started lecturing as a professor at Amsterdam University in the 1920s, the breakthrough of the marginal utility school in economic theory was complete. Limperg had such serious objections to this theory, however, that he deemed it

---

1 A list of such articles is given in Appendix II [to this article].

2 In writing this article I have drawn to a great extent from a paper I submitted to the Accountants' Day of the Netherlands Institute of Registered Accountants (N.I.V.R.A.) in 1967. This paper in Dutch reflected the views of writers in the Netherlands, either as defenders or challengers of the replacement value theory. "Defenders" have been: G. Diephuis. H.H.M. Foppe, A.B. Frielink, A. Goudeket, G.L. Groenveld, A. Th. de Lange, Th. Limperg, H.J. van der Schroeff, A.F. Tempelar: and "challengers", D. Bakker, J.C. Brezet, R. Burgert, M.J.H. Cobbenhagen. B. van Deventer, J.L. Mey, F.L. van Muiswinkel. B. Pruijt, H. van Ravestijn, H.C. van Straaten. All quotations from Dutch literature are translations for which I am responsible.

* [The author, R. Burgert is Professor of Accounting and Business Economics at the Netherlands School of Economics, Rotterdam.]

necessary to formulate a theory of value of his own. His objections can be summarized as follows:

- the concept of marginal utility is not as generally useful as the Austrians thought;

- the qualification of subjectivity as handled in the theory of marginal utility is deemed unfit for use;

- the concept of cost as the basis of value should be given the role it deserves.[3]

I shall not go into these objections in detail, but merely mention them to illustrate that Limperg, although he stressed the importance of the concept of value as a basis for economic decisions and consequently considered a theory of value indispensable, dissociated himself from the then prevailing theory. Limperg's own value theory is summarized below; it culminated in the following valuation-rule:

> The value of a commodity is its realizable value or its replacement value, but always the lower of the two. As to the realizable value, a distinction should be made with regard to factors of production between the direct and the indirect realizable value; of these two the higher is always relevant.

From the producer's point of view, the direct realizable value corresponds to the proceeds by immediate sale, whereas the indirect realizable value should be understood as the proceeds to be realized in the normal course of business. Although it is not clear whether Limperg thought of calculating the indirect realizable value as the present value of future proceeds less associated costs, other authors have indeed taken this view. The difficulty of the allocation of total proceeds and costs to individual means of production inherent in this concept is, after severe but in my opinion unsound criticism of the Austrian theory, eliminated by the thesis, that:

> usually, the indirect realizable value of the combined means of production, governed by the sales price of their products is higher than their combined replacement costs. Usually, that is to say for the profit-showing company, the combined replacement costs assess a specific contribution to the proceeds and to the income; from this it follows logically that the value of each means of production is assessed as its cost of replacement.[4]

---

3 Th. Limperg, *Bedrijfseconomie*, Verzameld Werk (Industrial Economy, Collected Works posthumously published in 1964), Part I, p.141.

4 Limperg, *Bedrijfseconomie*, p.209.

Because:

> in practice the matter is in most cases decided upon in favour of the replacement value, the concept of replacement value becomes extremely important for the problems of production, for which the judgment of value plays a role: it plays therein a role which greatly exceeds the role attributed to it by the theory of marginal utility; this is not just for practical reasons but on the foundation of a consistent elaboration of the concept of utility that is the basis for the theory of marginal utility as well.[5]

It follows that, for the profit-showing company, the entire rule of evaluation given above is reduced to the simple maxim that value is governed by replacement cost. Limperg thus achieved his aim - "to give the concept of cost as the basis for value the role it deserves".

To amplify the above information about Limperg's theory of value I refer to an article in English, published in 1966 by the late Abram Mey, who had always energetically disseminated the Limperg ideas.[6] Here the reader can find two arguments for the central evaluation rule, one taken from the marginal utility school and one based on the doctrine of continuity of production in society as a whole.

The first argument is, that the economists belonging to the marginal utility school "affirm, . . . that the value of a good, for which there is available in the market any substitute good, cannot exceed the market price at the time of valuation".[7] Though not in conformity with his need to fortify this affirmation as much as possible, he goes on to say that the marginal utility school gives this affirmation "without further explanation.[8] In doing so Mey implicitly claims that this explanation is offered by Limperg's theory. In Part III, I below, it will appear that this explanation is far from convincing.

The second argument states that to satisfy consumer wants in society continually, the supply of all input factors must be maintained or reproduced. This aim can be realized by using "integral unit cost" as a basis for pricing. Integral unit cost is to be understood as the sum total of a number of multiplications of economically unavoidable quantities of input factors by their current replacement values. This reasoning ends with the conclusion:

---

5 Limperg, *Bedrijfseconomie*, p.210.

6 Abram Mey, "Theodore Limperg and his Theory of Value and Costs", *Abacus*, Vol.2, No. 1, Sept. 1966.

7 Mey, "Theodore Limperg. . . . ", p.10.

8 Mey, "Theodore Limperg. . . . ", p.10.

> As long as goods or services are produced in a regular and systematic flow, no good or service can have a higher value to its owner than the cost of replacement, whether by production or by purchase in the market.[9]

This conclusion comes to the same as Limperg's saying, quoted above, that *usually* . . . the value of each means of production is assessed at its cost of replacement. As did Limperg himself, Mey considered realizable value only as an exception to the general rule:

> If the flow is interrupted, replacement value can no longer express the significance of the good for its owner's welfare. Then the producer can only value his marketable goods at the amount of money they will command in the market.[10]

The question may be asked: what valuation rule should be used for goods which are not so readily marketable?

So much for Limperg's theory of value. In Part III I shall give some critical remarks on it. Now I turn to his theory of income measurement which is based on the theory of value.

II. Limperg's Theory of Income Measurement

The theory of value contains the foundations of the theory of income measurement for, "there is, in principle, no . . . difference between the problem of valuation and the problem of income measurement at the moment of sale and in composing annual financial statements".[11] At both instants of time Limperg considers the theory of value of decisive importance. However, the annual financial statements give rise to an additional problem with regard to the meaning of the difference between replacement value and historic cost. In answering this problem the purpose of income calculation must be borne in mind; this purpose is formulated by Limperg in his concept of profit; the aim is the determination of consumable income for the suppliers of equity capital, that is, the increase in capital which can be consumed on the condition that the source of income is maintained intact.

The means to this end are quite simple in nature, although they require much work when put into practice in complex circumstances. Moreover, the proper ascertainment of replacement values is sometimes less easy than it looks at first sight. This is especially true with regard to fixed assets. The necessary accounting

9 Mey, "Theodore Limperg. . . . ", p.12.

10 Mey, "Theodore Limperg. . . . ", p.14.

11 Th. Limperg, *Bedrijfseconomie*, Part VI, p.291.

techniques for implementing this theory will not be discussed in detail here, because they have already been explained by Goudeket with respect to a large enterprise, although not entirely in harmony with the theory.[12] The rules given in Limperg's theory are the following:

- there can never be a profit without a sale, so that the realization principle is consistently adhered to;
- the favourable difference between replacement value and historic cost cannot be profit, either for goods sold or for goods not yet sold:
- the unfavourable difference between historic cost and replacement value is always a loss.

The most frequently used application is broadly the revaluation of fixed assets and stocks of goods in the accounts after every material price change; the difference in value is credited or debited to a "revaluation account" which belongs to the equity capital group. If the credit balance of this account becomes zero by debiting price falls, any further price fall leads to the entrance of corresponding losses in the income statement. In ideal circumstances the latter account would show only so-called "transaction" profits or losses, being the difference at the moment of sale between the sales price and cost on the basis of replacement value.[13] These ideal circumstances occur if a sale and a corresponding replenishing purchase always take place at the same moment. In such a case, "economic stock" would continuously amount to nothing. "Economic stock" is the quantity of goods for which the company runs the risk of changing prices; in other words, this stock equals the algebraic sum of goods on hand plus purchase transactions on which delivery still has to take place, minus sales transactions on which the company still has to make delivery.

In practice, this ideal situation of nil economic stock will not present itself except for those goods for which there is a future market. From the point of view of the original theory, this signifies postponement and/or anticipation of transactions sometimes condemned as "speculation", the philosophy being that a businessman ought to make profits only through the differences between prices at the same moment in different markets (sales market/buying market). In principle, profiting from differences between prices at different instants of time on the same market

12 A Goudeket, "An Application of Replacement Value Theory", *Journal of Accountancy*, July 1960. Since the present article was written, it has heen announced that, beginning with financial year 1971, the method used by the Philips company has been changed, in respect of the treatment of tax liabilities on the revaluation account and the treatment of price increases for stocks which for technological reasons fall short of the increase of prices in general.

13 We shall not enter here into the problem of accurate calculation of the total unit costs of all articles sold. This figure is indispensable for the concept of transaction profit.

should not be encouraged; this is viewed as a form of speculation as opposed to serving society by bringing products further on their way to the ultimate consumers.

In order to bridge the gap between the theoretically ideal situation and reality, the theory has been extended by recourse to the concept of "normal stock", that is, a stock of goods of such quantity that the company can be sure of being able to continue its production process without disturbance. Speculation occurs when real stock differs from normal stock. The rule about the importance of price variations is now changed in such a way that only alterations in the value of normal stock are credited or debited to the "revaluation account". Price changes on a surplus or shortage of stock give rise to profits or losses from speculation, which are entered directly in the income statement.

In this respect, fixed assets create a special problem because of their indivisibility and their usability for a whole series of production processes. It is implicitly assumed that the normal stock of a certain fixed asset, e.g., machinery, consists of a number of entirely new machines. As soon as a machine has been used for a certain period, e.g., a year, then there is a shortage of normal stock. Assuming that for depreciation purposes, the economic lifetime is considered to be ten years, this shortage will amount to one-tenth of a whole machine, and so on. In periods of rising prices, such a shortage of normal stock leads to consequences comparable with a "loss by speculation". This loss is taken as such in the income statement under "additional (make-up) depreciation". Another explanation is that in a period of constantly rising prices the depreciation on a replacement value basis of an asset in a certain year is always higher than in previous years; in such circumstances, the income statement for year 2, for instance, has to be charged with depreciation based on the replacement value at the end of that year and also for the "additional (make-up) depreciation" for year 1. The latter equals the difference between the depreciation originally calculated for year 1 and that which would have been calculated for year 1 if the replacement value at the end of year 2 had then been known. This process continues for the entire lifetime of the machine. The result is that at the end of the lifetime a total depreciation (original + additional) will have been calculated which equals the replacement value at the end of the lifetime. A new machine can then be bought without raising additional money from elsewhere.

This procedure is not adhered to by Goudeket in his article on the Philips application referred to above. In fact, it is argued by Goudeket that the Philips concern has approximately a so-called "ideal complex" of all durable production factors. Theoretically, this is a complex of units showing ideal diversity in their remaining lifetime, so that depreciation always equals the new purchases. An additional argument put forward by Goudeket is that if and insofar as the diversity is not entirely ideal, so that amounts of depreciation must be held as monetary assets, Philips allows for maintaining the purchasing power of net monetary assets.

By applying these rules, Limperg states that consumable income, under the condition of maintaining the source of income intact, can be calculated "unambiguously and with certitude".[14] Before discussing the criticisms of this theory, I wish to draw attention to the considerable correspondence between Limperg's concept of income - indubitably an ex-post concept - and the economic concept of income aiming at the maintenance of economic capital as presented by writers such as Lindahl, Hicks and Palle Hansen. The latter consider that maintaining economic capital intact is only theoretically feasible as an ex-ante calculation on the supposition of perfect foresight. Once this assumption has to be discarded, as when making actual ex-post calculations of income, great difficulties arise. The concept of income then becomes, as Hicks says, "rough approximation(s), used by the businessman to steer himself through the bewildering changes of situation which confront him".[15] The measurement of income is such a difficult task that it hardly seems possible that consumable income can be calculated "unambiguously and with certitude" by the techniques advocated by Limperg, with the source of income maintained intact.

III. The Criticisms of Limperg's Theory

In this section we shall review the criticisms brought forward in the Netherlands against Limperg's theory of value and income measurement based on replacement values.

1. *The Theory of Value*

> In this world therefore every plain and simple doctrine as to the relations between cost of production, demand and value is necessarily false: and the greater the appearance of lucidity which is given to it by skilful exposition, the more mischievous it is. (Alfred Marshall, *Principles of Economics*, (8th printing, Book V, Ch. V, p.306)

As we have stated previously, the theory of value is the foundation of the theory of income measurement: rejection of the former automatically implies rejection of the latter. In this respect, it is interesting that Limperg sees his theory as a "normative

---

14 Limperg, *Bedrijfseconomie*, Part VI, p.282.

15 J.R. Hicks, *Value and Capital*, 2nd printing 1946, p.171.

theory", that is to say, that the theory not only offers a causal explanation of events in reality, but also gives a rule of conduct.

In all fairness to the critics, it must be noted that not until after Limperg's death was an authorized presentation of his thoughts made available in 1964.

In 1967 I tried to demonstrate the fundamental weakness of Limperg's valuation rule, the central question being, why the value of a good is governed by its replacement value or its realizable value, but always the lower of the two. In my opinion this rule is an apriorism for which no explanation is offered. This becomes clear from the way in which Limperg explains the relation between the two concepts: replacement value and realizable value, on the one hand, and the concept of value in general, on the other hand.

So runs Limperg's argument,

> Immediately we can ascertain that it is impossible, that both quantitative presentations can express at the same time the value. If the figures of two measurements differ - and only for that case does the question have sense - then only one of them can express the importance of the object to be valued; it is logically impossible that the availability of an object for a person's wealth depends on two different amounts of money. Therefore the question remains, which of the two expresses that dependence. It is not difficult to find the answer to that question; *it is easy to see* that the value is governed by the lower of the two quantitative presentations.[16]

This apriorism is the ultimate theoretical basis of Limperg's rule of valuation.

In Part I above, I pointed out that Limperg rejected the then prevailing marginal utility theory of value; therefore he engaged himself in a hard fight with the Austrians. The reader cannot escape the impression that Limperg somehow was nostalgically longing for the times during which economists thought that value is governed by cost only, I have mentioned that he wanted to give the concept of cost, as the basis for value, the role it deserves. In my opinion, a value theory that does not thoroughly consider the possibility that there may be irreplaceable goods or that there may be goods which are more or less difficult to replace (e.g., because some time has to elapse before replacement is complete) and that those more or less irreplaceable goods can sometimes be used in different directions and may yield in each of them different (marginal) utilities, cannot be very helpful in making managerial decisions. Unless these decisions are no more difficult than making replacements all the time, in order to maintain continuity in the flow of goods and cost-factors in society as a whole. A striking point is the obviously great difficulty of reconciling the theory with the concept of opportunity cost, so important in managerial economics.

---

16 Limperg, *Bedrijfseconomie*, Part I, pp.179-80, *emphasis added.*

It would be incorrect to think that professional literature in the Netherlands always agreed with Limperg as to the value of production factors for a company. In 1924, Professor Polak of the Netherlands School of Economics offered a further elaboration of the ideas on production of Böhm-Bawerk and Marshall. His appreciation of replacement values is clear from the following. "That nobody would valuate any commodity higher than the cost for which he can acquire or replace this commodity" is a "seeming axiom that has already given rise to many misunderstandings in the theory of value."[17] Polak derives the value of a commodity for the producer from the expected future proceeds and the costs to be incurred. He explains the possible coincidence between this value and replacement value as follows for goods and services capable of serving only one process of production: "the value the company attaches to such goods in its possession can, *statically considered*, equal the replacement value". However, the value, "which such a commodity has for the company is derived from the future proceeds and the cost to be incurred in realizing them; only under certain rather rare conditions does this value equal the replacement value".[18] Under static conditions, the value of durable factors of production shows the same tendency to correspond to the replacement value. However, on the basis of Marshall's analysis, distinguishing between short and long periods and leading to the concept of "quasi-rents", Polak concludes that for "performances of durable factors of production the value to the company can differ considerably from the replacement value".[19]

This opinion seems to be more in harmony with contemporary economic theory than with Limperg's reasoning, and proves that not everyone in the Netherlands can be considered to advocate replacement value theory.

The criticism leaves the impression that there may be one theoretical situation in which it may be true that value or utility equals replacement cost. That is a situation of complete equilibrium in which no entrepreneur sees opportunities for innovation and new production processes and in which no consumer is induced to correct or change his scale of preferences, including his preference for saving or consumption. That would be the condition of a stationary economy.

I shall now attempt to evaluate Limperg's theory of income measurement on its own merits without further reference to the theory of value. Dealing with the whole structure in this manner can be considered permissible since, as a reaction to my 1967 paper, an authoritative advocate of the replacement value theory, Professor van der

---

17 N.J. Polak, "Waarderings - en balansproblemen" ("Problems of Valuation and Balancing") *Verspreide Geschriften*, 1924, p.206.

18 Polak "Waarderings...", pp.203 and 207 respectively.

19 H.J. van der Schroeff, *Kosten en kostprijs* (Cost and Cost Price), 7th printing 1970, p.xvi.

Schroeff, drew the conclusion that it is better not to tie the theory of income measurement explicitly to the theory of value.

2. *The Theory of Income Measurement*

In considering the criticisms of Limperg's theory, it is important to be well aware of its aim and the means advocated.

Aim: to calculate unambiguously and correctly the income that can be consumed under the condition of maintaining intact the source of income.

Means: rises in replacement value never constitute income; declines in replacement value always constitute a loss unless they can be debited to a revaluation account showing a credit balance.

a. Do rises in value of normal stocks never constitute income? This question must be answered in the negative. The disadvantage of the theory is that it does not consider what is going to happen on the sales market once the replacement value of one or more production factors has risen. The source of income would be maintained intact only if it could be taken for granted that the future total absolute margin of profit on total production would remain unchanged. In general economics, price theory explains without further ado that this situation will only occur by mere chance and that such a development of prices, costs and volume is most improbable. If the absolute margin of profit increases, the rise in value can be considered wholly or partly as income; in order to arrive at the same income as before it is not essential to have the same production capacity available. Full replacement of present assets is not strictly necessary. If the absolute margin of profit decreases, withholding the rise in value of assets will not suffice to maintain the source of income intact. In that case, a greater production capacity, requiring more assets, is essential in order to reach this aim. The conclusion must be drawn that the advocated treatment of rises in value in most cases either falls short of what is necessary or overshoots its mark.

To put it in another way, the theory works well only in the case of a purely monetary rise in the general price level. Purely monetary price changes should be such that the proportion between all prices remains the same. In our dynamic and complicated society, however, such equi-proportionate price changes, even when triggered off by a monetary cause, do not occur. The theory itself does not distinguish between monetary price changes and specific real price changes. Presumably the theory is intended for the latter, but after the devaluation of the Dutch guilder in 1936 Limperg wrote: "The circumstance whereby the guilder is the cause of the rise in replacement cost in itself does not change the reasoning".[20] The field of application of the theory seems to have been extended in 1937, with the remarkable consequence that the effectiveness of calculation techniques has a better chance of succeeding in the new field than in the old. If it is intended to keep the source of income intact, the theory on the economic concept of profit should be further explored, present quantities and prices being ineffective guides. It should be noted, however, that profit calculations would then become much more subjective. Withholding increases in value from income could be defended by an entirely different argument, viz., that increases in value have to be financed without the acquisition of new capital, either loan or equity capital. The theory should then refute the argument that financing by new capital is acceptable. It is difficult to see, however, that this argument is really unacceptable when it can be ascertained that the given allocation of production factors is still rational after the price rise. In such a case all costs, including the cost of the additional capital, will be recovered.

b. *Do decreases in value of normal stocks always constitute a loss?* To prove this thesis, the theory should explain that replenishment of capital equal to the decrease in value of assets is an inevitable condition for keeping the source of income intact. However, it does not do so. This thesis can only be accepted if the aim of the theory is extended to include maintaining nominal capital. It should then be realized that the theory does not lead to the actual nominal capital being kept intact but the amount of capital that has been historically invested in the company. This becomes clear from the fact that decreases in value are to be debited to the revaluation account as long as this shows a positive balance. If actual nominal capital is to be maintained, every decrease in value should be immediately entered in the income statement.

c. *Non-identical replacement.* In our dynamic society non-identical replacements occur so frequently, especially in regard to fixed assets, that it is unacceptable to think only of more or less automatic pure replacement purchases which are known beforehand. In actual fact, management is continually confronted with the problem of selecting capital investment projects. Sometimes management buys a copy of an existing asset; more often, the purchase of an identical production factor will not be among the available alternatives.

When calculating income, this means that it will often be impossible to assess objectively the replacement value of existing assets. The theory does not offer a solution to this problem, and goes no further than a description of the concept of non-

---

20 Limperg, "De gevolgen van de depreciatie van de gulden voor de berekening van waarde en winst", ("The Consequences of the Depreciation of the Guilder for the Calculation of Value and Profit"), *Maanblad voor Accountancy en Bedrijfshuishoudkunde*, January 1937.

identical replacement - which, in the terminology of the theory, is erroneously called "economic replacement" as opposed to "technical replacement" - as replacement by an asset that fulfils the same function. Strictly speaking, this should be: replacement by an asset that offers the same contribution to net income. In fact, the theory has thus far not succeeded in offering a solution to the problem of assessment of replacement values of assets which will not be identically replaced. This problem can only be solved by planning future activities, specifying in particular the assets indispensable to these activities, existing assets which are still useful, and the investments in additional production factors necessary to realize planned activities. Furthermore, it should be ascertained how much money would be needed and how much could be found in some acceptable transaction on the capital market. It may then prove that a balance remains which the company has to provide from its own means; this amount could be withheld from income according to a timetable set up for this purpose. Only then can it be said that the best possible means are used in order to maintain the source of income. However, it would no longer be possible to say that income is calculated "without ambiguity and with certitude".

This argument concerning the difficulties of non-identical replacement has been countered by the statement that the theory aims at an objective ex-post income calculation and that, as a consequence, it should be restricted to the valuation of production factors that are actually in the possession of the company. No attention should be given to production factors by which the former could or should be replaced. It is admitted that it then becomes very doubtful whether the aim of maintaining the source of income will be realized under dynamic circumstances.

According to this reasoning, any shortcomings should be allowed for in the income distribution phase. No solution, however, is offered to the problem of finding values for production factors which will no longer be replaced in kind.

The theory appears to be rather too optimistic about the replaceability of production factors; this can be traced back to the exposition of the replacement value theory, especially Limperg's remarks on the theory of Böhm-Bawerk.

d. The concept of normal stock. The role of this concept has been explained previously. As far as the qualitative aspect is concerned, its precise definition is linked with what has been stated under (c) above. We shall therefore now consider the quantitative aspect only. Assuming that we are certain that there will only be identical replacement: what should be the volume of normal stocks of goods?

It will be remembered that the volume of normal stock does not influence the amount of transaction profit. However, in cases of rising prices, this volume is decisive for the amount of speculation profit or loss and for the amount to be credited to the revaluation account, and consequently for the amount of total profit and for the amount of increase in value that is retained in order to maintain the source of income.

In the beginning there was little concern about the problem of the volume of normal stock. Later, it was realized that management was unable to control all factors influencing the volume of real stock effectively; this resulted in the appearance of a greater or lesser amount of speculative profit or loss on the income statement without genuine speculation on the part of management. To mitigate this, the notion was put forward by other writers of distinguishing a zone within which stocks fluctuate without their surplus or shortage on normal stock giving rise to a speculative position. This development was in recognition of the fact that the crucial problem is not to find an acceptable figure for the volume of normal stock, but to assess whether and to what extent a shortage must be provided for in order to maintain the source of income. In dynamic circumstances this question can only be answered with regard to the future, by a managerial decision comparable with that needed in the case of non-identical replacement. Again, the objectivity of the income calculation is greatly endangered.

Another problem is: what should happen to previously retained increases in value in the revaluation account when the volume of normal stock is reduced? Limperg's theory does not answer this question. An opinion frequently voiced is that amounts that have once been added to the revaluation account can never return to income except, of course, in the case of decrease in value.

Addition of past depreciation. The procedure concerning additional past depreciation or the revaluation of performances of durable production factors used in the past has been dealt with earlier. The essential element is that a rise in the replacement value of fixed assets leads at the same time to a non-consumable increase in capital and also to a loss by way of a correction of past depreciation.

"Go to the margin and find the truth" is a maxim well-known to economists. Assume that the value of a building increases considerably during its last year of service. The building has been financed to a great extent by a mortgage loan and the company is certain that such a loan will again be made for the acquisition of a new building. It is then difficult to understand why, in order to keep the source of income intact, we should be obliged to charge the income statement with an amount practically equal to the entire rise in replacement cost of the building. This procedure can only be defended by an aprioristic argument, viz., that the rise in value has to be financed with equity capital which in fact is acquired by retaining profit in the business. Whether financing by new capital or even by loan capital is feasible is not even considered.

f. *Lack of interest in assets other than durable production factors and stocks of goods.* It is not easy to understand how the source of income can be maintained by paying attention to non-monetary assets only. Rising prices, for instance, also affect monetary assets. It is quite logical, therefore, that the Philips concern has extended its application of replacement value by taking measures with respect to monetary items. The company calculates that part of equity capital that is invested in net monetary assets by comparing total monetary assets with total liabilities. If this comparison shows a debit balance, part of the equity capital is then considered to be invested in monetary assets. On the basis of an index number expressing the changes in the purchasing power of money, a charge in the income statement is made to make up for the corresponding loss of purchasing power. This is an interesting amplification of the theory. It should be noted that Philips does not strive to maintain the source of income. Its system may perhaps be best defined as aiming at maintaining the specific purchasing power of that part of equity capital that is invested in non-monetary assets and also the general purchasing power of that part of equity capital, if any, that is invested in monetary assets.

g. *Special problems in times of price falls and recession.* Taking for granted that the indirect realizable value of individual factors of production is unfit for practical objective calculation, an enormous new problem comes up. Then the evaluation rule is reduced practically to the rule that value equals the lower of replacement cost and direct realizable value, the latter being extremely low in many cases. The lower of the two being relevant, the number of cases in which the replacement value is decisive, will be reduced enormously.

The problem is acute in times of recession and price falls. Supposing that direct realizable values for durable means of production can be found in all cases, it continues to be possible to calculate income "unambiguously and with certitude"; but the income-figure is not expected to be very acceptable. In other words, the theory does not offer a solution for situations which are remedied in the United States by "quasi-reorganizations".

The theory is confronted with an unexpected new situation under conditions currently described as "stagflation", the combination of recession and inflation. In traditional recessions, replacement values showed a tendency to fall; but nowadays they continue to rise in a situation for many companies in which stocks increase, while turnover and contribution-margins decrease. Then the use of replacement values in income calculations puts a heavy burden on profit figures.

We thus have seven rather severe criticisms of Limperg's theory which, in our opinion, does not represent the last word on the problem of income measurement, even in the Netherlands.

IV. Summary and Conclusion

In this article, we have brought forward the more important critical observations made in the Netherlands against replacement value accounting according to Limperg's theory. The main points may be summarized as follows:

a. The theory shows inconsistency between ends and means. The valuation methods and accounting techniques together are unable to yield objectively the income that can be consumed without endangering the source of income.

b. It is an exaggeration to say that favourable increases in value can never constitute a profit, with the exception of "speculative" stock positions.

c. Similarly, to say that unfavourable changes in value always constitute a loss is going too far, unless a second aim is introduced, viz., maintenance of nominal capital.

d. The problem of the inevitable time lags between purchases and sales has been solved by introducing the concept of normal stocks, but it is extremely difficult to assess their volume "unambiguously and with certainty".

e. This argument is more important for fixed assets than for stocks of goods. For the former it raises the question of "additional depreciation", which is essentially a loss in times of rising prices on a shortage of normal stocks. Its necessity seems to be based on an aprioristic thesis in the field of finance.

f. The theory has never offered a solution to the problem of non-identical replacement. This, too, is more important for durable production factors than for stocks of goods. Moreover, in many situations, it is more difficult especially for the former to find replacement values than it seems at first sight.

g. There is serious doubt about the validity of Limperg's theory of value.

h. The theory wrongly disregards monetary assets; the Philips applications provides a solution to this problem.

i. From the appendix it appears that Dutch companies which really apply replacement values are in the minority.

It should be remembered, however, that the means advocated by the theory might in themselves be important if the aim of calculating the consumable income while keeping the source of income intact is done away with. In doing so, a bridge might be built between Limperg's ideas and those of recent American writers, such as

Edwards and Bell, and Sprouse and Moonitz. Perhaps it would be worthwhile to consider whether any similarity exists between, on the one hand, Limperg's saying that "normally, that is, for the profit showing company, values are governed by replacement costs" and his obvious preference for transaction profits and, on the other hand, Edwards and Bell's saying that "current operating profit . . . is essentially the long-run profit associated with the existing process of production carried on under existing conditions".[21]

I am inclined to seek a solution for the problem of income measurement by way of "different concepts of profit for different purposes".

APPENDIX I

Practical Adherence to Replacement Value Accounting in The Netherlands

There are several reasons for distinguishing between durable and non-durable production factors for the purpose of income calculation. The arguments in favour of replacement values for non-durable goods are theoretically stronger than for the other, and thanks to the L.I.F.0. and base-stock-methods, the application in the accounts is less complicated. The touchstone for the inquiry into the practical application of replacement values is to be found in the field of fixed assets. A recent research project carried out by the Economic Institute of the Free University, Amsterdam,[22] has provided quantitative information on the matter. In this research four methods of valuation of fixed assets were distinguished:

I. Valuation in the balance sheet on the basis of historic cost and depreciation on this basis;

II. Valuation in the balance sheet on the basis of historic cost, but with extra depreciation above historic cost, which is subtracted in the balance sheet from the historic cost of the assets;

III. Valuation of fixed depreciation in the balance sheet at historic cost, from which depreciation on that basis is subtracted; as a charge lo income, however, extra depreciation is calculated, and this sometimes has the effect of bringing original depreciation to the level of depreciation on the basis of replacement value. The extra depreciation is credited to an account belonging to equity capital;

IV. Valuation of fixed assets at replacement value and depreciation on that basis according to the theory.

The inquiry covered all industrial and trading companies which have their shares quoted on the Amsterdam Stock Exchange (259). These were divided into four groups according to the amount of total net fixed assets. The following tables illustrate the results achieved, the first in absolute figures, the second in percentages.

	Evaluation Method					
Net fixed assets in million gld.	I	II	III	IV	Total Comp.	Total in %
0-10	100	27	21	8	156	60.2
10-25	16	10	9	8	43	16.6
25-75	12	7	7	11	37	14.3
> 75	3	3	5	12	23	8.9
Total	131	47	42	39	259	100.0

The same table in which all figures are expressed in percentages of the number of companies gives the following picture:

	Evaluation Method				
Net fixed assets in million gld.	I	II	III	IV	Total
0-10	64.1	17.3	13.5	5.1	100
10-25	37.2	23.3	20.9	18.6	100
25-75	32.4	18.9	15.9	29.8	100
> 75	13.0	13.0	21.7	52.2	100
Total	50.6	18.1	16.2	15.0	100

From this it appears that the traditional method (I) based on historic cost, is by far the most frequently used (50.6% or 131 companies). Method IV, valuing fixed assets at replacement cost and depreciation on that basis, is the least used (15% or 39 companies). Large companies apply the latter method more frequently than fairly small companies, so that the method is used by 52.2% of the large companies or 12 of the 23 forming this group.

These research results make it clear that replacement value accounting is not in general use in the Netherlands. This country can be considered an interesting source of experience only insofar as a number of larger companies, in particular Philips, apply replacement values. The most important thing to be learned from these companies may be their method of assessing replacement values. As far as Philips is concerned, this information has already been made public by Goudeket in his article mentioned above.

No doubt there is a limiting factor to this research: it covers only a period (1 April 1967 to 31 March 1968) in which there were rather regular price increases and no deep recession, so that, on the whole, satisfactory profits could be made.

As far as tax purposes are concerned, lifo and base-stock are permitted for the valuation of stocks of goods and for fixed assets only method I is permitted.

APPENDIX II

Selected Articles on Replacement Value Accounting in the Netherlands (Chronological Order)

A. Goudeket, "How inflation is being recognized in financial statements in the Netherlands", *Journal of Accountancy*, Vol. 94 (October 1952). (Paper read before the Sixth International Congress of Accountants, London 1952.)

I. Kleerekoper "Some aspects of accounting and auditing in the Netherlands", Seventh Summer School (St Andrews University: The Institute of Chartered Accountants of Scotland, 12-17 June 1959).

A. Goudeket, "An application of replacement value theory", *Journal of Accountancy*, Vol. 1 10, No. J (July 1960).

Gerhard G. Mueller, *Accounting Practices in the Netherlands*, International Business Series, Studies in Accounting, University of Washington, Seattle, 1962.

J. Kleerekoper, "Economic approach to accounting", *Journal of Accountancy*, March 1963.

Abram Mey and Kenneth S. Most, "Replacement value accounting", *The Accountant*, Vol. CXLIX, No. 4629, 7 September 1963.

J.H.M. van Vlerken, "Financial reporting in Holland", *Canadian Chartered Accountant*, November 1965.

Abram Mey, "Theodore Limperg and his theory of values and costs", *Abacus*, Vol. 2, No. 1, September 1966.

L.S. Rosen, "Replacement value accounting", *The Accounting Review*, January 1967.

A. van Seventer, "The continuity postulate in the Dutch theory of income", *International Journal of Accounting Education and Research*, Vol. 4, No. 2, Spring 1969.

George M. Scott, "A business economics foundation for accounting: the Dutch experience", *International Journal of Accounting Education and Research*, Vol. 5, No. 2, Spring 1970.

J. Vos, "Replacement value accounting", *Abacus*, Vol. 6, No. 2, December 1970.

Abram Mey, "On the application of business economics and replacement value accounting in the Netherlands", publication of International Accounting Studies, Institute and the Graduate School of Business Administration, University of Washington, Seattle, 1970.

Consequences of Depreciation of the Guilder for Enterprise Value and Profit Determination of the Enterprise[1]

Theodore Limperg, Jr

Introduction

On 7th November 1936 the Netherlands Institute of Accountants held a workshop at which I gave a talk about the above topic. As was customary for Institute workshops, the meetings were not public and the reports were not disclosed to non-members. In the mean time I gathered that there was an outside interest in what I said at those meetings. Moreover, the editors of this journal [*Maanblad voor Accountancy en Bedrijfshuishoudkunde*] were interested in having this topic discussed in one of their issues. Hence I am presenting the readers with this article, which is based on my notes for the talk. Apart from a few additions here and there, the article follows the talk closely.

The issues discussed below are of considerable theoretical and practical interest to accountants which is sufficient reason to reflect on them for a moment or two.

It is quite clear that in practice accountants are confronted with these issues, and it will be a problem shortly when it is time to draw up the annual balance;[2]. The accountant must have solved the problem if he wants to be able to give his opinion about the balance sheet. But first of all a question arises which has occupied the minds and hearts of economists right from the start: the question of cost price and profit at the point of exchange. Perhaps as far as this question is concerned, some people might object that it is not a matter of cost price or profit determination but one of price policy and as such outside the accountant's area; after all we are only talking here about whether prices should or may be put up or not. Indeed, this is a matter of price policy. But it is undoubtedly based on value determination and one can only implement a rational price policy if this problem has been solved. The issue of value determination for the balance sheet is also linked with business policy; and yet nobody would deny that that particular process is within the scope of the work of an accountant. Anyway, there is no doubt in my mind that everywhere accountants will be approached for advice about these matters, also in connection with business policy.

1 Theodore Limperg, "De gevolgen van de depreciatie van de gulden voor de berekening van waarde en winst," *Maanblad voor Accountancy en Bedrijfshuishoudkunde*, January, 1937.

2 Annual balance is synonymous with balance sheet or annual accounts.

Anyone avoiding this because of unwarranted fear of dealings with management, would harm business life and also underrate the value of accountancy. Nobody is in a better position to educate in this area than the accountant. So it is his duty to provide this education, especially so, because in the course of time this issue will be intensified and grow into a major fiscal problem. It is the accountant who, on both sides of the fiscal arena, will be the best qualified adviser or rather for both parties the best qualified referee.

In this article I do not want to try and answer the many question which are sure to arise in the near future or have in fact already arisen. What I want to do first and foremost is to lay some general and practical foundations. In other words, I want to put the issue on a theoretical footing; without theory we will not be able to reach a satisfactory solution. Not even for a practical application. Because also in practice we will need a well argued solution; a categorical or dogmatic answer will not be good enough. And we had better bear in mind that businessmen and accountants will have to come well prepared if they want to have any chance of success in discussions with the Government Taxation Department.

Some general theoretical principles about value and profit in business enterprises.

From a theoretical point of view the above problem occupies a very special position in value and profit theory. So it is necessary to have a look at the foundation principles of that theory because the solution to value and profit problems will be based on them. Before everything else, then, we have to establish what we mean by these words - especially in connection with the value and profit problem. We need some concrete definitions.

What, for instance, do we mean by *profit?*

As always, we could attach different meanings to the word. Obviously we are here concerned with profit in the economic sense and not so much the bookkeeping sense. It is generally useful if in business accounting one sticks to the economic sense of the word; this will be useful when bookkeeping is used as an economic yard-stick and it will prevent misunderstandings. But even if one does not want to follow this line of thinking, the meaning of the concept we have to employ within this framework stays the same: it remains an economic concept. Economically speaking, then, the concept "profit" only makes sense as basis for the rational satisfaction of wants of those people, whose size of income depends on the net result of the production process. If these people want to organize their consumption in a rational manner they will definitely want to know how much of their income is available for consumption. That is absolutely vital knowledge. In other words, it is an economic requirement that one knows how much of one's capital accrued though the production process is *income*.

Income, in an economic sense, is that part of one's capital which is available for consumption. When discussing our topic I usually employ the term *disposable income*, which is really a pleonasm but nevertheless useful, because people are not in the habit of using the word "income" in the real economic sense; the concept "income" is not sufficiently covered by just the bare word "income".

After all, "income" is also used for gross income or fictitious income. Within the framework of our present discussion, then, profit is the *(disposable) income*, which a business yields to those people who link up the size of their income with their business proceeds. They have to know the size of that income to be aware of how much they can consume without eating into their business capital - the production apparatus with which the income is brought about in the first place.

Value is another word which covers many different concepts. Economic theory shows us that it even covers widely divergent *economic* concepts. Fortunately I do not have to worry here about the endless number of controversies about the concept of value which have arisen and partly continue to exist. I will limit myself to voicing my personal opinion because I am presently only concerned about general theoretical principles upon which I want to base the analysis of the particular problem in this paper (i.e. value and profit determination). My definition of the economic value of a good is: *the quantitative representation of the significance of a good for the satisfaction of the owner's or prospective buyer's wants*. In this article we are particularly concerned with the quantitative representation of the significance of goods for the owner of the business to which our observations refer.

With this concept we have also inextricably linked the two aspects of our problem: value determination and profit determination. Value determines the size of the profit and so value determination is made subservient to the profit question; a tricky problem which we are seeking to solve to ensure a rational consumption and consequently a rational satisfaction of wants.

This problem comes mainly to the fore at two stages in the business enterprise, namely at the point of the exchange and at the moment of drawing up the annual balance. The problem is present in any exchange. The business manager needs to know what the value of his product is, so that he can know what he sacrifices in the exchange and what he acquires in disposable income.

Without this knowledge rational production is impossible. It is usually worded as follows: without knowledge of the *cost price* the producer is unable to know whether the exchange and thus the production is rational; one can put it either way, though, because cost price and value, though different concepts, represent identical amounts. My definition of cost price is: *the quantitative representation of the sacrifices in the exchange*; and apparently the sacrifice made by the producer in the exchange of his product amounts to exactly the value this product has for him. It is a different matter - because there is also a quantitative difference - if by cost price is meant the sacrifice brought earlier to acquire the production means and the product; that is the *historic* cost price or *purchase price*, the meaning of which will be discussed below.

We must surely all be agreed on the question of how significant is the difference between the *value* of the exchanged product and the proceeds. Apparently a positive difference is disposable income, because the business receives proceeds that exceed the amount indicating the *value* of the exchanged product, i.e. above the amount that is significant for the satisfaction of the owner's wants. And a negative difference is apparently a loss, i.e. a decrease in income that would otherwise have been obtained.

Meanwhile we still have time to find an answer to the question: what is the value of the good at the moment of exchange? How is this value determined? The answer to that question is: *usually the value equals the replacement value, i.e. the value measured in terms of replacement costs of the good.* It is impossible to present the reader here with an exhaustive explanation - that would require a lecture on replacement theory. I will have to limit myself to mentioning the fact that my analysis of the problem under discussion is based on this theory and I assume the readers of this journal are familiar with it. One does not have to agree with it in order to follow the course of my analysis.

One should be aware, though, of the fact that I am talking here about the replacement theory as I developed it and not about the one adhered to in Germany which now goes by the name of *Wiederbeschaffungswert* but was originally known as *organic* value theory or the theory of *reproduction value.* The two theories have a totally different starting-point and only share a small amount of theoretical argument. The theory I developed is based on the phenomenon that every good has a sales value and a replacement value and that the *value* of a good is determined by whichever is the lowest of the two, in business usually the replacement value. But even the advocates of the German theory will be able to agree with the discussion below, because in most cases - and especially in our test case - both theories arrive at the same quantitative outcome.

Whatever one thinks of replacement theory, I assume that in the circle of experts there will not be anyone who continues to think that the value of the exchanged good is determined by the price which was paid in the past for the good or its means of production. Whatever is represented by the historic cost price or the purchase price, it is definitely not the *value* of the good at the moment of exchange. And thus the difference between the sales price and the purchase price can not be the profit or the loss that comes about through the exchange either. The income from the exchange is determined by the positive difference between the value, i.e. the replacement value, of the product and the sales price. There remains the question of what is the significance of the difference between the purchase price and the replacement value of the exchanged goods. Before we proceed I will answer this question briefly.

For the problem under discussion only a positive difference is apparently important. While working out the principle of replacement value, theory teaches us that this positive difference does not represent disposable income. The increase in *purchase price* to a higher replacement value is really nothing but an increase in replacement value from the moment of purchase right down to the moment of exchange of the product. This increase does not create income. The difference in value is tied up in the good and in the business. There is no yield.

From this reasoning it follows that also after drawing up the annual balance any positive difference between the purchase price and the replacement value of the unsold goods is not income either. In practice it had often been intuitively worked out that way; admittedly arguments were clumsy and incorrect - they talked about "non-realized profit" - but people understood even without theory that, when drawing up the annual balance, the resulting increases in value *per se* could not be counted as income. That means, that an increase in value of stocks (of goods) and of fixed assets - which can also be looked upon as stocks, stocks of labour units - does not of itself create disposable income or profit.

And with this we have laid the foundation for solving the general problem of what the increase in prices and values means in relation to the annual balance. We have to bear in mind that the economic function of the annual balance is to identify the disposable income of a business; an absolutely indispensable piece of information for society in order to achieve rational satisfaction of wants. We now know that only those capital increases that result from positive differences of replacement value and proceeds of sold goods are disposable income; none of the others, neither positive differences between the purchase price and replacement value of the sold goods nor the positive difference between those of unsold goods and fixed assets are disposable income or profit.

General Principles During Currency Depreciation

If we are going to tackle the central issue from this general point of view we can establish first of all that depreciation of the guilder leads to price increases and that this consequence of depreciation in particular has given rise to the issue. Any further consequences which eventually will come out of the price increases we will leave out of the picture, especially the possibility of more price increases, future wage increases, etc. We will limit ourselves to the immediate consequences. We will see, then, that businessmen, dealers as well as wholesalers and retailers after the depreciation of the guilder will have to buy any goods they sell without processing, for a higher price, that is to say, if they are imported goods. And there is no doubt that later on they in their turn will have to sell the goods they had to spend more money on, at a higher price to their customers. But now there is a problem with increasing the price of the goods they still have in stock. I shall just leave price politics as such for a minute; first I want to look at this question in relation to value and profit, because objections to this price increase are based on specific ideas about it.

One is familiar with this line of thought. The shopkeeper, the dealer has still got old stock which cost him less than new stock will. If he now sells old stock at old sales prices, he earns just as much as he did before, he still gets the same profit he received earlier; so, increasing the price for these goods would be unreasonable. Anybody who has understood anything about replacement price valuation realizes this kind of reasoning is totally wrong; there is no need, then, for me to explain in detail that dealers, who sell at old prices, do so at the cost of their own disposable income, their profit. Nor do I need to spend a lot of time on clarifying that the value of the goods in stock and therefore the cost of the exchange - and thus the cost price - has gone up at the same rate as the replacement cost of the exchanged goods, a replacement that has been necessitated by this exchange. The goods released by the dealer will have to be replaced by him at a much higher price and if this difference in price is not covered in some way he will have to eat into his capital to the amount of that difference. And if he does increase his sales prices at the same rate as the increase in prime cost, not so much because he realizes that the value of his goods and hence his sacrifice in the exchange has increased, but rather because he wants to make the most of the situation. I mean, when he later on calculates his own "profit" on the old stock in the same way at too high a rate, he will miscalculate his disposable income and will be eating into that part of the proceeds which he will need for replenishing his stock.

Obviously the same principal applies to the manufacturer. The production process is more complicated, cost calculations are more complex, but the principle remains the same. Nevertheless there is one aspect here that could give rise to controversy and misunderstanding. Hence it deserves a brief mention.

What I said just now about the dealer's goods can without too many problems be applied to the raw and auxiliary materials of the manufacturer. The question is, does this kind of reasoning apply in the same measure to machinery and other fixed assets?

Experience has taught us that this is not nearly as easy and that the analogy escapes a lot of people. And I am not thinking here of those people who reject replacement theory - it's understandable that they resist the theory also in respect of - and perhaps even more so - fixed assets - but I have in mind those people who in general accept the theory. Among them there are some who stick to the purchase price as a base for profit determination for fixed assets, more than for liquid assets. Looked at superficially there is a reason for that, because replacement theory also works with purchase price as the basis for determining depreciation; so it looks as if purchase price does play a crucial role. Any one, however, who has gained insight into the theory, knows that it indeed only looks that way. The replacement value of the still existing production capacity of the machinery, currently being used, of the still available labour units, suddenly increases as a result of the depreciation of the guilder. New machinery, bought at this point in time, would cost more and an equivalent number of labour units, when replaced would require an equally larger sacrifice. Not right now, but latter when replacement is necessary. This fact, that replacement does not take place until much later, causes people to lose sight of the effects of currency depreciation quite easily. And finally, this misconception is helped along by the techniques that are used to calculate the costs of running the machinery, because this is usually done with the help of certain fixed depreciation mechanisms.

However this may be, the mistake which people are about to make is serious, even more serious than if a similar mistake would be made with raw materials. Because this kind of mistake can linger on for years. It leads right from the start to price erosion which shows up only gradually at the expense of new enterprises and of those enterprises that are having their machinery replaced. And in the meantime, any business that makes this mistake will eat into its capital, even if the increased price of the product would allow for a higher calculation. The profit on the product is calculated at too high a level, the dividends paid out are too high, and what is consumed is fictitious income in the true sense of the word. Logic and healthy business policy demand that consumption of *labour units* is calculated at a higher price level straight away.

If we assume that dealers and manufacturers alike stick to the principle described above, again the question remains what it means to have a positive difference between the purchase price and the replacement value of the exchanged goods. We could consider this question in combination with the question is the annual balance affected by price increases? It applies to both areas. Because stock also increases in replacement value through price rises and thus shows a positive difference between purchase price and replacement value - stocks of liquid assets as well as unused labour units tied up in fixed assets. Anyway, this same question, but now in respect of goods and products sold during the year, will certainly come up when drawing up the annual balance. Because it is important to have an idea about the method of calculation right from the start of any exchange, since this has a great influence on the selling price and the whole price policy - in other words, at the point of exchange one has to be aware that profit is not determined by purchase prices but by higher replacement value and, thus, at every exchange one also has to know the increased replacement value - but decisions about the significance of the positive difference between purchase price and replacement value cannot be made until the annual balance; at that point it will have to be decided how much the proceeds, resulting from the positive difference, contribute to the profit of the enterprise.

Let's first have a look at the value increase of stocks and raw materials.

Undoubtedly - that is, for those people who accept replacement principles - the goods have increased in value. But does this increase create disposable income? Certainly not! We can even offer two arguments to base this on. In the first place this increase in value of the capital goods has not come to fruition yet, because exchange has not yet taken place. *No fruition without exchange*, one of the tenets of the theory says. A tenet which in practice has been proven correct since long through its intuitive business policy in which non-realized profits are considered to be undistributable, in other words, are looked upon as non-disposable income and thus not real profit.

But even apart from the fact that the value increase has not come to fruition because of the lack of exchange, it is *in essence* not yield anyway and it essentially does not create disposable income; even if the exchange had taken place, it still would not have created disposable income. Because that value increase does add to the income contained in the capital goods, that income does group and expand, but it is the trunk that is growing, no fruit is being produced; the value increase retains the capital, claims it as soon as it comes about and does not let go it, not even in an exchange. *Because the exchange itself creates an economic obligation to replace the goods at the higher price.* For our central issue here it is theoretically of little importance whether the value increase is expressed in the books and on the balance sheet by putting the stock prices up. Form a practical point of view it is definitely more efficient. Because once the above-mentioned "approved" method for calculating sales has been accepted, it can only be of advantage that in the next period one works with the prices and values that have been adopted in the accounts. But once again: as far as the principle is concerned the method of accounting is not crucial. Nor is it basically important, what name one gives to the account where the capital increase, flowing from the increase in value, is recorded. As long as one makes sure that the name chosen does not cause any misunderstanding and in particular does not create the impression that a profit has been made or disposable income has been acquired.

There remains the final question of what is the significance of the difference between the purchase price and the replacement value of the goods exchanged in the course of the year. The answer is not difficult if one realizes that these value increases are nothing but value increases of part of the stock of raw materials and labour units at the moment of exchange; that part, namely, the equivalent to what has been spent on the exchanged good in raw materials and labour units. If at all possible stocks should be valued regularly as if for the balance sheet; anyway, this suggestion is not totally impossible and is in fact quite often followed up. However, basically the value increase of part of the stock in the exchanged good has the same meaning as that of the whole stock: the value increase is retained by production, it is claimed immediately and that claim is maintained; it will never yield disposable income. This value increase does not yield any profit.

Again, theoretically it is of little importance for the issue under discussion how this sort of thing is recorded in the books. I just want to point out once more that formal enquiry into the size of the disposable income from exchanges normally does not take place until the annual balance. It usually takes the following form: what part of the positive difference between the acquisition prime costs (or previous book value) and proceeds is disposable income or, put differently, what part of the difference is non-spendable and must be considered as capital growth not available for consumption.

As far as fixed assets are concerned we do well to look especially at the problem of asset depreciation when drawing up the balance sheet. What is conveyed by this depreciation? The value of the labour units used up in the previous financial period plus the decrease in value of the still available labour units. Both groups of labour units are affected by the depreciation: those used up on products in the past year and those still available. This depreciation, then, will have to be set on the basis of the higher replacement value. The used up labour units possessed a higher value, so we have used up more capital and in the future the gradual decrease in replacement value - known as the law of economic wear and tear - will also take place at this higher level. The depreciation formula will have to be adjusted to higher acquisition prime costs.

This demand is all the more severe because of the fact that at the same time the replacement value of the left over labour units has increased. The peculiar nature of depreciation techniques threatens to confuse us. Is it really necessary to increase depreciation? one asks, often with a bit of surprise. Shouldn't it rather be decreased or perhaps left off the books for a while, now that the left-over labour units have gone up in value? These questions arise because people are ignorant about what the value increase means. Value increase leads to capital growth which does not create disposable income; this growth has not come out of profitable exchanges and, here too, is immediately tied up in the production process. Admittedly, the actual replacement often does not take place until much later, but the economic obligation to replace exists immediately and is there to stay and the extent of that obligation is determined by the new price. In contrast, consumption of the increased value of labour units leads to larger sacrifices which will have to be covered by either higher product yield or, as losses, by income from elsewhere.

In spite of the different form it takes the above argument shows that the problem is really much the same for fixed assets as for liquid assets. One important question, however, concerning fixed assets has not been discussed yet. And it is a question about labour units: what meaning do price increases have in relation to labour units? not only those used up in last year's sold products or those still contained in the assets but also the *previously used labour units*; the sort of question that seldom needs to be asked about previously used raw materials. Fixed assets are special in that the amount of labour units is piled up in them for many years ahead and that the actual replacement does not take place until many years after acquisition. For our particular problem the effect is that, as soon as depreciation and price increases start, a larger or smaller part of the tool is being used up. This means, then, that the products previously manufactured with the tool or machinery were valuated on the old basis and that the corresponding asset depreciation was also calculated at the old, low level although later on all labour units - including the ones valuated at too low a level - will have to be replaced by more expensive ones. The question arises whether the more expensive replacement should not lead to revision of the former calculations. Mind you, at the moment I am asking this question without thinking of profit policy or benefit policy. I just wonder whether that adjustment is really necessary in order to arrive at a correct calculation of the income over the past year.

Actually, the answer to that is yes. It is a fact that in our former calculations we have estimated the replacement price at too low a level. It should be understood that this is not a question of businesses having made mistakes but of mistakes being caused by depreciation and that they have not emerged until now.

In the meantime, the business is stuck with them. And we can not do anything about it because the products were sold on a different basis and the profits calculated on this basis have been used up. The best we can do is a repair job, but it will have to be done without delay; it is depreciation that causes us to make mistakes and for that reason we will have to repair the situation in the very same year the depreciation occurred. Otherwise disposable income will be entirely out of the question.

This loss undoubtedly is of an exceptional nature and that's why it is possible to cover it with, for instance, reserve capital. If previously disposable income has been saved, it is justifiable to relieve last year's proceeds from the burden of this exceptional loss. But if there are no reserve funds available, the disposable income from the exchanges will be decreased, even through this loss, however exceptional, just as through all the other exceptional losses.

Now that we have had an overview of the significance of price rises for valuation and profit calculation at the point of exchange as well as for the balance sheet, we will be able to look at something that I have purposely avoided so far, although it played a role right from the start of the analysis. I have spoken of price rises, I have talked about value and cost price before and after currency depreciation. However, I left out of the discussion the fact that prices, costs and values before and after depreciation are expressed *in different values of the guilder*. We said that the price rise was due to very special circumstances. Circumstances not tied up with the goods but with the money and in a special way too. Two questions come to mind. Firstly, assuming it applies to normal price rises, are we allowed to apply the general replacement theory also in this case under these exceptional circumstances? And secondly, would not the problem be much easier to solve if we take the changed value of the guilder as our guideline rather than the changed value of the goods?

My answer to the first question would definitely be in the affirmative. The fact that replacement costs have gone up because of the guilder does not alter this line of thought. Even if we would consider - something we really should do - the depreciated guilder as a completely new monetary unit, still called guilder only because of tradition, even if from now on our currency would be in pounds sterling or in dollars, the fact remains true that the sacrifice at exchange is determined by replacement cost - which can only be measured in the new currency. If from then on we would call the new guilders 1/9 we would have a better idea of the problem and in particular we would understand that the difference between the acquisition prime cost in guilders and the replacement cost in pounds sterling is not profit; it would in fact be impossible to figure out. It would probably be much clearer that all we do is give a new quantitative representation of the economic significance of the same good by a new standard. The problem essentially remains the same. One could raise objections against the fact that in my analysis I spoke of an increase in value and an increase in cost price, while in actual fact it was not the value as such that changed but the standard for measuring the value. Quite true! And yet, I did not make the formula invalid because every value depends on its standard. Anyway, I deliberately chose to word things this way so as not to burden our issue with yet another difficulty.

Moreover we have to bear in mind that even without formal currency depreciation the question of price changes is partly in the area of the changing value of money, i.e. the change in the purchasing power of the currency. A general price change of goods is equal to a change in currency value. Thus the problem of currency depreciation is in essence no different from the problem, of currency inflation and this in its turn no different from the problem of general price rises of goods.

But - and now we come to the second question - if this is correct, is it not simpler to push this whole argument from the replacement theory angle aside as superfluous and to argue straight from the point of difference in currency value? If this were possible I would have no objections; for various reasons I would even recommend the method for practical application - if only for its attractive simplicity. But in my opinion it is impossible to build a watertight argument without at some point taking into account the concept of replacement value. Unless one wanted to argue on an exclusively monetary level; but, even if one could reach a solution that way - something I deny - the argument would definitely lose some of its attractive simplicity and lucidity. And I am afraid most people - including most experts - would not be able to understand it.

Business Policy

Up till now I have limited myself to the question of what value *is* and what profit *is* in connection with the consequences of currency depreciation without paying attention, other than as illustration, to the consequences of a business policy based on this analysis, or of one with a completely different outlook. If we want to have a clear picture of the significance of the analysis and the ramifications of the conclusions, we need to face the consequences they have for business and society fairly and squarely.

As for the consequences for businesses I have mentioned it in various places in this paper. Having another systematic look at them, the theory appears to lead to what is called a *conservative* business policy. Part of what other people consider to be profit is qualified as fictitious income and declared non-disposable; it is considered to be capital growth or "reserve capital". Non-advocates of the theory declare the positive difference between purchase price and proceeds to be disposable income. If this difference has increased because through currency depreciation sales prices could be put up, these producers think they are rich with their one-off fictitious profit and what's more, to the economic community they present an image of increasing profits which is misleading. And if they have not put their sales prices up these producers will be using up their capital and will soon experience they lack the capital to keep their business going. Not taking into account what the theory teaches, leads the producers also to an incorrect price policy. Stocks, still bought at old prices, are still being sold at old sales prices or costed in the products at old prices. The stupid phenomenon we remember so well from inflation days is threatening to repeat itself: goods are sold or costed at prices lower than those one has to pay for replacing them. In the shops we see again the same items at different prices; the person who can not take a size 7 in hats, but needs a 7 $^1/_4$ will have to put up with having to pay a few more ("new") guilders than his friend who does take a size 7.

But, one asks, is the "conservative" producer not being threatened by the Government measures against bumping up prices? It certainly looked like it at one stage. However, replacement value theory appears to have gained more approval than people would have thought before the drop of the guilder. All of a sudden many business managers are remarkably capable of handling the concept . . . without having applied it ever before in their business! But let me not poke fun at them; rather, let me rejoice in the fact that people have woken up to the theory. I am pleased to see that the Government too is prepared to recognize that a price rise based on replacement value is not "unreasonable". Meanwhile, however, it is not enough for the businessman to demonstrate his appreciation for replacement theory just by attempting to get higher prices for his products from his customers; he will also have to show in his profit policy that he understands the significance of replacement value. In other words, he must not record seeming windfalls form price rises as profits and spend them and he will have to increase his depreciation charges.

I feel that in this latter area people will have difficulty in accepting the consequences of the theory and therefore a word of warning is warranted.

We should bear in mind that in the propaganda for the current devaluation it is repeatedly said - and incorrectly so - that it's true that costs will be going up because of rising prices of raw materials and subsequently of wage increases, but that interest rates and assets depreciation would remain the same, which would mean we would be way ahead of other countries. Nothing is less true. If we would follow this indication we would give away a considerable part of our production apparatus to foreign customers, as some time ago countries with a high inflation rate found out to their own detriment.

The Consequences for Society

If we ask ourselves what the social significance of the whole issue is, it is clear that we are in grave danger of using up a considerable slice of our national income, a danger which will make itself felt in various ways. The consumer who still receives goods valued in old guilders for his new devalued guilders, uses up with each of those new guilders a bit of national income; rational consumption requires that the consumer be immediately aware that on the same income he must now cut down on consumption. And any business that calculates its profit at too high a level, tempts people, who have a right to those profits, to spend more.

On that score there is a further, more serious, danger. Because if dividends on shares are too high the exchange rate will shoot up, which in its turn - on a larger scale - will create fictitious incomes that, as we know, tempt many a person, and in the long run the majority of shareholders, to socially detrimental expenditure.

People will object that this expenditure also has an advantage, namely that it will stimulate business life and will generate incomes that are based on reality. This is a very dangerous misconception. It is not true that these sorts of incomes are based on reality. These incomes are just as unrealistic as the ones generated by revived business life brought about by injections of purchasing power such as we see applied on a large scale in the US and elsewhere. I know I am going against popular opinion. I do not want to be a prophet of doom, but I am warning against the optimism of many people that let themselves be dazzled by the immediate results of the "Ankurbelung" (post recession reconstruction). It is difficult not to be charmed by something that's happening right in front of one's eyes.

The devaluists have predicted that devaluation will bring a revival of the business economy. If, and in as far as, this revival is to be obtained from increased sales abroad, there is indeed is a case for talking about real progress and I'll be happy if that is achieved; but I think the prospects in this respect are less favourable than people would have us believe. If, however, this revival is not based on a realistic situation, repercussions cannot be delayed. The picking up of the market as result of the large demand from buyers fearing price increases, is one of the consequences of a incorrect price policy and repercussions of this are already visible in some businesses. And if people stay with this price policy things will get a lot worse!

But it has to be understood that sometimes a businessman's price policy only *seems* bad. A period like we have just had offered golden opportunities to lots of businesses to get rid of old and obsolete stock, which, of course, was done at the "old" price! But many a businessman heaved a sigh of relief when he indeed managed to obtain this "old" price.

Currency Depreciation and the Taxman

I have arrived at the last part of my discussion; a few remarks about the consequences of currency depreciation for taxes. Naturally, I will limit myself to the consequences for income tax because it is especially with income tax that my analysis links up.

There are various difficulties here, one of the most serious is the following: that even a logical and economically rational calculation of income need not necessarily be a useful basis for taxation. For one, you only have to pay tax once a year. And secondly, the taxman cannot be sure, that the taxpayer in his spending will stay within the limits of the rational calculation.

Let's give an example. If the taxation department for the time being will not touch certain benefits, for whatever reason, in order to levy tax on them at a later date, it has no guarantee whatsoever that the benefits will still be there when the tax is due to be levied; they may have been consumed in the meantime even though they did not yet rate as rational "disposable" income. Although these things are important I cannot discuss them at this point. Partly because they would take me beyond the parameters of this paper and partly because these problems are there to be overcome - by which I mean to say that the tax department needs to do all it can to take the economically rational profit calculation of the enterprise as the basis for its levy. It is satisfying to see that in this country the taxman is striving towards that goal and we may indeed expect that the tax department, especially in connection with the issue under discussion, will bear in mind what kind of requirements flow from the abovementioned ideas for the levying of tax.

Even with those expectations I still foresee problems. But I do not think they are located in the replacement principle, at least not in the theory as such. As far as I know the tax department has never opposed the theory in principle and I assume, therefore, that it will not refuse to acknowledge valuation and profit determination on the basis of that principle as "good business practice".

As far as the law is concerned, I cannot see any objection against the application of the principle in general and certainly not against accepting it for the consequences of currency depreciation. And yet I fear that the taxation department will not be readily prepared to follow the guidelines indicated above for determining tax levies. I recently heard the opinion of one of the accountants in the direct taxes department which boiled down to the following: for the so-called profits resulting from currency depreciation, the principle of replacement value is the correct basis in *business economics* but the regulations under Art. 14 of the law according to existing jurisprudence do not allow the application of this principle for the *levying of income tax*; the tax owed is on the positive difference between purchase price and proceeds.

I admit that in the legal world one could possibly find support for this opinion, but I don't think the last word has been said about it. Partly because the High Court in the course of time has repeatedly revised its opinion and has shown itself willing to try and adapt its interpretation of the law to what is economically efficient for business, but especially because the matter, in the form in which it is now being presented to the tax department, has never been raised as a fundamental issue. Due to currency depreciation implementation of the replacement value principle has become so crucial, that I am inclined to assume that the taxation department and the High Court will now be prepared to reconsider the matter.

But there is another difficult point. In general - if not totally ruled out by law in the opinion of the High Court - the legal profession has concentrated on the question whether a certain method of value and profit calculation can be considered to be good business practice. The general tendency of the legal profession is as follows: if a method of calculation is not *in conflict* with good business practice it should also be acceptable as a basis for taxation. In these matters the High Court usually put less emphasis on whether the method was sound from a business economical point of view than on whether there was a *customary practice* at all, especially in the enterprise whose calculation techniques were under scrutiny. If this practice is not completely *unacceptable*, the taxation department and the High Court are inclined to acknowledge it as good business practice, apparently based on the thought that usually for the taxation department any method will in the long run lead to a reasonable way of taxation provided it does not change. For Example, too low a valuation will in the long run - sometimes even in a year or so - result in a higher profit. But the taxation department has adopted a more rigid attitude with respect to the levels of asset depreciation because recovery in that particular area is expected to stay out for a while.

No doubt the method described here has certain advantages. It provides the business enterprise a great measure of freedom in its calculation methods and prevents many a conflict between the tax department and the taxpayers about economic problems. However, it creates for the issue under discussion considerable difficulties: it does not provide any guidelines for unusual and influential circumstances and, more in general, for those circumstances influencing value which are irreversible or even adverse. And currency depreciation is such a circumstance. This difficulty *per se* does not necessarily have to stand in the way of correct levying of tax under the new circumstances, but it does necessitate a firm line of action under these circumstances. However, the taxation department and the High Court are after *customary practice*. There would not be any problems if businesses were used to applying replacement theory principles. But apparently in only a few enterprises this practice has been adopted and it seems that now for the first time people wish to apply the principle, but only in as far as it has to do with the influence of currency depreciation. At first it will look as if they will be breaking with an existing custom and understandable the tax department who knows its customers will be inclined to object to this discontinuity in the valuation system. And yet it seems to me that they are not justified in doing that.

I can appreciate that in business the principles of replacement theory are generally not implemented very scrupulously. In every day business life these principles do not play a major role. Nor do they play a major role in the tax department. Moreover, prices have been going down for years now, and other principles have served to solve valuation problems, principles that are in agreement with those of replacement theory; for a long time there was no need to implement the theory. As far as the fixed assets are concerned, we can say that the decline in prices is normal and, further, that replacement theory was applied to the usual depreciation methods also under this normal price movement, without it being stated explicitly. Now, however, this customary practice is all of a sudden disrupted, caused by something exceptional. It becomes necessary just for once to apply the principle of replacement theory to a special case. Now, I do not think that this is an arbitrary deviation but an adaptation to changed circumstances. And it would be very sad, if the taxation department would oppose such a move and thus would claim part of the non-disposable income and spend it. It would be unfair to the taxpayers and economically speaking it would be disastrous.

Business Economics[1]

(Extract from *Bedrijfseconomie*, Vol. II, 1968)

G.I. Groeneveld, *et al.*

Part II

A. III. Replacement Value Theory

1. Replacement value and realization value
2. Valuation, replacement and replaceability
3. A critical look at allocation theory
4. Replacement value considered in regard to the various means of production. Finished products. Organic versus incidental view. The passive means of production.
5. Some observations about the actual determination of replacement value.
6. Replacement value in regard to the various means of production. The argument continued. The active means of production.
7. The value of the complex of the means of production, the industrial enterprise as a whole.
8. Replacement value and reproduction value
9. Conclusion

B. I. The Basic Principles of Costing

Cost and Its Function in Production

1. Definition of the concept
2. The importance of cost for price formation
3. Some critical discussions of the literature

   C.A. Verrijn Stuart. E. von Böhm-Bawerk. Theorists outside reality. First defect: a causal explanation is lacking. Second defect: neglect of the law of continuity. Third defect: identification of the offering price with the value assessment of the producer. Fourth defect: the moment of economic exchange is not recognised.

4. Conclusion from the previous section

---

1 This extract from *Bedrijfseconomie* is a distillation of recollections by Groeneveld *et al.* of Limperg's explanation of replacement value theory.

5. The relationship between cost and price formation needs to be elaborated on three points.

6. Buyers' and sellers' premium and the entrepreneur's premium

7. Rational price differences within the framework of the proposition of an identical market price.

8. Rational price differences which are at variance with the propostion of an equal market price.

9. The factors which determine the level of cost. Stating the problem.

10. General discussion of the economic sacrifice. Sacrifice is the occupation of means. Actual definition of this sacrifice. The valuation of the sacrifice. Measuring the sacrifice: historic cost and economic cost. Some examples: labour of the volunteer and of the owner of the enterprise.

11. The consequences of a price change. The effect of an incorrect calculation on price policy. A look at the years during and after the first world war. Errors in the practice. Errors in the theory: Marshall, J.M. Clark.

12. German theory dealt with as a final section

13. F. Schmidt's theory of the *Wiederbeschaffungswert* and the theory of the "organic balance sheet" and other concepts of German theoreticians.

14. The significance of cost calculation. Preliminary and subsequent calculation.

15. Costs and losses.
    Means of production as assets rather than costs. The difference between costs and losses. The demarcations between costs and losses. Normative conclusion.

16. Costs and "expenses"

17. Conclusion.

A. III. Replacement Value Theory

1. Replacement Value and Realization Value

From the two previous chapters [Vol. II] it follows, as we proposed at the beginning that in production, we are not dealing, in the first instance with a subjective value concept, but with a special form of objective value, namely *replacement value*. In addition, we are dealing with a second value concept, *realization value*. These are not two values of the same good, but two conceptions, two value concepts apparently in conflict with each other.

The concepts will now be defined in more detail in order to better understand them. The *realization value* concept is based directly on *yield* - in terms of *usefulness* for the satisfaction of needs. One therefore uses the term usefulness or satisfaction value in economics.[1]

However, the other value concept, *replacement value*, is also a satisfaction value concept, however. But it is not directly based on yield, nor - and this needs to be taken into account especially - on the lack of usefulness through the loss of the object, but *on the sacrifices which need to be made because of the replacement of the object.*[2]

There are therefore two kinds of satisfaction values:

> *A realization value*, i.e. the value measured in terms of how much the object can satisfy the needs, or produce the means (there)to;

> *A replacement value*, i.e. the value measured in terms of the cost of replacement, in terms of the sacrifices of means to satisfy needs needed to replace the object.

The significance of any good, whether a consumption good or the means of production, can therefore be established from two different points of view. *The* value of that good for the owner, i.e. the quantitative expression of the importance of the good for his well-being, still needs to be established. It is indicated by the *lower* of the two values, because the well-being of an individual is dependent only for that lower value on the possession of the good.

---

1 In Vol. I: *Theory of Value*, Limperg speaks of *satisfaction* value.

2 Limperg adds that one could call this concept, without reservation, a *cost value* but he does not wish to use this term because it can lead to frightful misunderstandings. We add here that Limperg, in later years, did use this term in the material which was dealt with in *Theory of Value*. See *Vol. IB, Theory of Value, Ch. III, Section 5*, p.181.

This is of great importance as far as our problems are concerned. Because in total production, i.e. in industry, it is the contrast between replacement value and realization value which helps to explain the phenomena of commerce. In our opinion, the replacement value of all goods comprising the means of production of the enterprise, that is to say, the replacement value of all capital goods, or in other words, of the capital of the enterprise, determines the value of that enterprise. Realization value, on the other hand, has a special significance for an enterprise and we will get to know this significance. But, generally speaking, the magnitude of the value [of the enterprise] is determined by the costs of replacement.

Before continuing, it is necessary to specify both concepts. What is meant by realization value and replacement value *in production* (in the calculation)?

[Enterprise] *replacement value* is the value which is determined by the *replacement cost in the buyers' market* of an enterprise.

Realization value is to be differentiated into *direct and indirect* realization value. *Direct* realization value is the realization value of a good *when the good itself is sold. Indirect* realization value is what is obtained *through the realization of the product* for which the good to be valued has been used.

When as in the above, we compare realization value with replacement value, we refer to the *indirect* realization value, that is to say, the yield in usefulness by way of a normal exchange of the product in the *sellers' market* of the product.

2. Valuation, Replacement and Replaceability

First of all, we must ask ourselves the question: in an enterprise when does valuation of capital goods (that is, the active and passive means of production) take place?

Two moments can be pinpointed: the moment in which the offer of a product in the market has to occur and the moment at which one wishes to ascertain the outcome of the production process. In practical terms, one can say, respectively, the moment of setting the product's tendering price and the moment of drawing up the balance sheet and the profit and loss account. In this volume, we will only consider the first moment.

It is important to point out that a producer indeed has to arrive *practically every time* at a value judgement and does in fact do so. The problem of value is therefore not only of theoretical, but also, of practical importance. If a producer exchanges or sells a good, he has to know its value. Without that knowledge, he cannot know whether he is acting rationally.

If one accepts replacement value and realization value as two coordinated concepts, which, in other words, are both based on the usefulness of the goods, then it will depend, as we have seen, on the circumstances which of the two determines *the* value of a good for the owner. Therefore we will always have to keep track in particular in what way the well-being of the individual, for whom the value must be established, depends on the possession of the goods. We can, however, find similar circumstances for large groups of cases and we can therefore suggest general guidelines for production.

The importance of the means of production in the production process is determined by the importance for the producer's income formation. It is rarely a question, as we established earlier, of direct satisfaction of the needs for the producer.

From the point of view of replacement value, we also state that the importance of a good can only be considered if replacement is possible, that is to say, replacement in the economic sense. Does it also happen in production that a good is irreplaceable, as it sometimes does with a consumer, for instance, where a relic is concerned?

In regard to goods which we are concerned with in the first place, i.e. the passive means of production, we can postulate the remarkable fact that the *purpose* of the enterprise is replacement. The quicker goods are being replaced, the better. In this case, there must be replaceability. But also for the active means of production one can state that there is replaceability in the economic sense.

If one takes into account what we have said about the broad concept of economic replacement, (the concept of *substitution*[3]), we find that in a regular production situation there are indeed no irreplaceable active means of production.

After all, when is substitution impossible in an enterprise, in an industrial enterprise? When, in other words, is income *totally* dependent on the possession of a certain good in an industrial enterprise? (It is a matter of total dependence; as soon as there is only a relative dependence, substitution can apparently occur).

This total dependence only exists if, with this good, the production process as a whole lapses. When, therefore, the *existence of an industrial enterprise depends on it.* Income in an industrial enterprise is usually totally dependent only on one thing: on the complex of means of production and actions, on the industrial enterprise itself. It is possible that the size of the income steam is dependent on the use and therefore on the possession of a *certain good* to such an extent, that one is *inclined* to consider that good, that means of production, as irreplaceable in regard to the industrial enterprise. This view is however is based on incorrect observation, on a lack of understanding of the essence of the matter. This is because, production, is not a matter of producing one particular good, nor of using one particular means of production, but only of creating an income flow. Every means of production can, in

3 See Vol II, Section 5.

principle, be replaced and every means of production normally has a replacement value.

If it has been the intention when forming the complex to obtain income from using one particular means of production, one can of course speak technically of an irreplaceable good if one wishes; but it is then usually not correct in economic terms because the purpose does not rest in that replaceability. There is reason to speak of an irreplaceable good in the case of the Victoria Springs for the Victoria Water Marketing Company, from which the shareholders derive income. But if the Victoria Springs were to cease producing water, or, if there were more demand for Victoria Springs water than the springs could provide, the managers would no doubt try to show that the Victoria-source would nevertheless in economic terms, be replaceable for the company; in other words, they would do their utmost to replace this means of production by another. Of course it sounds somewhat strange if an enterprise operating certain springs considers those springs as replaceable. But, after all, it is not so different from the Amsterdam Bus Company without buses, the Netherlands Electric Railway Company without electricity running steam engines, a tram company without rails and with buses, or a Penny Paper which costs twopence! Whereas in those cases where the company is *totally* dependent on the possession of one *particular* means of production, which acts as the *initial* means of production, there is indeed a good which is economically irreplaceable and the value of that good will be only its *realization* value. We mention as examples: a concession for the supply of a good or service or a patent for the development of a mine.

However, in an industrial enterprise all means of production are generally replaceable. Only one thing is irreplaceable, the industrial enterprise itself. It is this collectivity which has to be considered continuous. This collectivity is the income producer, the means of production by themselves are not. A means of production may be of great importance for the income stream; however, it will still be subordinate to the collectivity, a replaceable part of the organism, which is like a cell in the industry as a whole. It is the collectivity, the cell, which is the source of income for the owner, however important is the function of a certain means of production in that cell. It is never any of the means of production itself that is the source of income, it is always the complex.

We draw attention to the fact that this consideration is not only important for the phenomenon of value and for many problems in industrial economics, but also because it thus assails the allocation theory of economics.[4]

---

4 For a detailed discussion see *Vol. I: Ch.III, Section 6.*

3. A Critical Look at Allocation Theory

Allocation theory deduces the value of the means of production, i.e. the value of the complementary goods, from the value of the resulting product. This suggests that the means of production have a value in this theory determined by their indirect realization value, a value determined through the ultimate realization of the product, with the result that the surplus value of the good over cost is allocated to one complementary good. To do this, the theory has to consider this good to be irreplaceable. Here, therefore, it is in conflict with our [previous] conception in two respects. Normally, there is no irreplaceable good and one can not therefore allocate the surplus value of the good to any particular means of production. Our theory leaves the surplus value to the *complex* and to the *product*, whereas the value of each of the means of production, therefore of each of the complementary goods, is independent of the value of the complex and of the product, and is determined by its replacement value.

Every hypothesis is admissible, if logical, provided it is not in conflict with the observable facts. And the hypothesis of the irreplaceability of one of the means of production *is* in conflict with the observable facts. Normally, the means of production being complementary to each other, are *all* replaceable in the literal sense of the word, that is not in the broadest sense, the *economic* replaceability, but the technical *replaceability* which can be observed and which also comprises economic replaceability. Since this is so, allocation theory is for that reason alone useless as a hypothesis. It is incorrect and it has to be incorrect because it brings us into conflict with the phenomena of business.

For that matter, allocation theory fails completely in one particular case. This is the case where an enterprise operates at a loss or - to continue the consideration of the product for comparison with allocation theory - if the product stipulates a price which is lower than production costs. Here allocation theory leaves us totally without a solution and it fails, because the value of the product cannot be split up.

And the same applies to the means of production of an industrial enterprise. They, in themselves, can all be completely sound and yet constituting the complex, may not lead to a satisfactory result. For example, when we are dealing with too expensive a product for a certain area. Another striking example is a too unfavourable proportionality of one of the means of production; in this case the unsoundness of the apparatus results directly from the organisation of the complex. For this case too, our theory leads to a totally satisfactory solution. The means of production have a value determined, for each one separately, by their replacement value. Means of production do not have an independent realization value. Their collective realization value is the realization value of the complex, of the industrial enterprise. Thus, the total replacement value of the means of production is higher than their collective realization value. And indeed, in practice that is how it is.

In the usual case of profit arising from production, allocation theory, as we have said, cannot satisfy us either, because it attributes the result of the production to only one means of production. This is so, although each means of production is only one of the links in the production [chain], which together bring about the result - and where none of the links is indispensable if we were to think of a particular *good.* Not that the particular good is indispensable, but as a *type* the link is indispensable. As a type *every* means of production is indispensable. There is therefore no cause at all to indicate any *one* of the *types* of goods as the particular cause of income, and so not of net income either. It is totally impossible to say which part of the realization value created in the product should be attributed to any particular means of production, because all means of production are absolutely essential. If we are to be consistent in our reasoning, allocation theory would have to attribute to each means of production, even to the smallest part of the means of production, the full value of all products to be produced with its assistance. It should be kept in mind that on each of those small parts, *if it were to remain unavailable,* the prosperity of the owner depends, up to the total realization value of those products. But where the means of production become available, they will be replaced. And so it turns out that, for the costs involved, the prosperity of the owner is dependent on the complex of that means of production.

To finish our critique of allocation theory in economics, we will discuss some cases where the replacement value of one of the means of production approaches the realization value of the complex, making it appear as if the realization value of the complex is identified with, or should be attributed to, one of the means of production. This is the case if one or more of the means of production has an exceptionally great influence on the size of the profit. We illustrated this earlier on page 52 with the so-called initial means of production, which demonstrates the concept of economic irreplaceability as an exception.

We expand this reasoning to a few such cases of similar nature to see whether, there too, the theory is indeed valid. We will consider those cases where allocation theory appears to provide a satisfactory solution to the problem. The following cases are perceived as typical.

- A shop whose results are particularly dependent on the shop's location, or, in general, enterprises (or companies) where the *site* greatly affects the results.

- An enterprise managed by an entrepreneur who has exceptional qualities, who manages to obtain particularly good results with the means of production available to him. More generally, the companies where exceptional ability of one or more persons affects the enterprise favourably.

- An enterprise which produces a good whose production requires the use of a patented means of production. More generally, companies where one or more means of production can provide the producer with a more or less strongly monopolistic position in the market.

For a correct general discussion one needs to take into account first of all the reason why an enterprise, as a complex, obtains a realization value above the replacement value of the means of production. In other words, how does such a complex produce profit for the owner?

There may be various causes, operating singly or in combination. These will be discussed later, when we deal with entrepreneurs' premiums.

Here mention of a few aspects will suffice. The most important causes may be: the relatively favourable location, the relatively high ability of the entrepreneur, a monopolistic position and a relatively favourable proportionality. In three of the causes the word "relatively" is used. This is so because an enterprise, operating in a competitive market, only creates an entrepreneur's premium if it is producing under conditions which are more favourable than the so-called marginal enterprise. It should straight away be mentioned in regard to location and proportionality that they are elements of a complex which are not inherent in one particular means of production. Both are relatively favourable only in the framework of a production process. The size or quality of the unit of a means of production are not, by themselves, favourable; they can be favourable only if they work out favourably within the framework of the complex as a whole, if they fit in harmoniously within the complex. Location seems to be connected with one particular block of land, or with one particular area; this, however, is not the case. This becomes obvious if one studies Weber.[5] It is only favourable in the context of the place of origin of materials, the size of the production, the size of the outlet, etc. Therefore, more in the context of the entire complex.

The two other causes of an entrepreneur's profit have to be considered somewhat differently.

Exceptional ability of an entrepreneur, particularly may have a more favourable effect on the results; essentially it only means that he is, qualitatively speaking, different from the average entrepreneur. He therefore has a higher replacement value than the average entrepreneur! We can, however, expect the same favourable result if we replace him by someone of similar ability. Moreover, the most able man, by himself, does not mean anything either unless he is working in a complex which is suitable for him.

---

5 A. Weber, *Über den Standort der Industrien.*

With a monopoly, based on the use of a patented means of production, a monopoly can be so strong that actual real replacement is indeed absolutely inconceivable. If this is so, replacement value can equate to the realization value of the complex, but it nevertheless will continue to exist and the realization value does not transfer to the patented means of production. This occurs because that same patented means of production can encounter in different complexes more favourable or more unfavourable results, and, in addition, exceptional qualities of the entrepreneur, as well as a relatively favourable location, and a relatively favourable proportionality may exercise their influence in favour of the realization value of the enterprise.

In summary, we therefore arrive at the following conclusion. The production unit obtains a price in the market; the *product* has an independent realization value. But allocation from the realization value to each of the component elements of the product (including work units, service units and operating units of the tools which have been used), to any *means* of production is impossible. No producer can therefore become aware of that value. He only becomes aware, in the normal course of production, and specifically when he sets the offering price of the product, of the *replacement value* of the *means* of production.

4. Replacement Value Considered in Regard to the Various Means of Production

Finished Products: Organic versus Incidental View

Assume that the producer offers the finished product on the market and the market price that can be obtained is known.

The question arises whether these goods have a value which is determined by replacement value or by realization value?

Here we straight away are looking at those objects which cause the greatest difficulty, because in this case the replacement value and the realization value are in conflict with each other. In subjective value theory we inevitably run aground on this point. Remember, here too *the same* goods do actually have a replacement value and a realization value. The former is formed by the total of sacrifices which have to be made in order to replace the good; i.e. the total of sacrifices for raw materials, the use of the means of production, labour, etc. - all this *in the buyers' market*. The latter is formed by the realization *in the sellers' market*. We are faced here, in regard to an industrial enterprise, situated between two markets, with the question: which price determines the value of the good? The answer is: the lowest. Which is normally the price in the buyers' market.

However, it can be argued that no sensible businessman will give up the good for that price if he knows that it has a higher replacement value. This is correct as far as it goes. It does not mean, however, that subjective value theory is right when it states that the value of these goods equals their exchange value, which, in turn, would equal their realization value. *Exchange* would then be inexplicable, would it not? It is really remarkable that here the previously emphasized theory of exchange (which, it should be kept in mind, is based on the *difference* in subjective valuation) is, in fact, abandoned. Apart from this, however, it should be stated that the fact that a good is not given up although one is compensated for its value, does not prove the value judgement to be incorrect. We pointed out earlier that giving up a good one possesses, only occurs if a motive exists. In production this can only be the economic motive. This has the result that one does not give up goods unnecessarily for the payment of the replacement value, but only for a higher amount. That higher amount has to provide the profit. The fact that a producer does not give up the product for payment of the replacement value, does not therefore prove that the good as such has a higher value for him. If the same good were *offered* to him, he would at the most pay the replacement value for it. *Giving up* goods is the ultimate means for obtaining income.

Doubt arises, nevertheless, after further consideration, about the question whether the value of the product is not the realization value after all. The question arises as follows: if the producer *knows* that a good can be replaced for $x and if he *knows* that others are prepared to pay $x + y, what then is the value for him of the good, for what amount does his prosperity depend on that good? The answer should be based on the following. If he can sell the good only once or if when he loses the good he misses out *permanently* on the $y, the value of that good is then indeed for him $x + y. But, *generally*, that is not the position in production. It can happen in special cases, but we are not concerned with those. In production, the goods are each individually elements of a continuous flow of goods which moves in one direction. And for those elements of the flow an *incidental* view is not suitable. Indeed, realization value does determine the value of a good incidentally. Because of the action of the law of continuity, the incidental view does not apply in our society, rather, the *organic* view is the one we have to take. That is to say, the view of the importance of a good for the formation of income as an element of that continuous production flow, as an *organ* of the complex. And see here, a new concept contrasting with that of the Austrian school; this school has always taken, in its conception, the good as the object in its incidental relationship to the subject and in its incidental significance for the subject's prosperity.

One has to make a sharp distinction, in economics, between the incidental getting rid of a certain good and the sale as part of production flow. Selling a good does not mean a regretted loss of the good, but rather a means to obtain income; every sale leaves open the opportunity for a subsequent sale at a later date. If the intended sale does not occur, one attempts to bring it about with another member of the market personnel of the sellers' market. The sale forces the seller to replace a good at the moment of sale, in order to provide for a later need of the same buyer. It is not always possible, however, to follow the continuous stream in such a way that one regularly provides for the needs of the same buyers. On the other hand, there are many cases where this happens, but free market competition usually causes mutual shifts to occur in the contacts between buyers and sellers. This, however, does not prevent the flow as a whole, as a collectivity, to continue.

A finished product thus has for an industrial enterprise a value which is determined by its replacement value. This replacement value consists of the replacement value of the components of the product, materials, labour and services which have been used. This is, therefore, the total of sacrifices and this, again, equals the total of *costs* which have to be made to replace the good. The producer comes to the market with this value judgement, or, rather, he ought to come to the market. We say "ought to" because many producers come to the market, regrettably, without a value judgement, or with an incorrect value judgement, as a result of either an incorrect insight or because of other circumstances, which we will discuss later. We need to keep in mind in all of this that the offering price does not infer a value judgement. This offering price is only a tentative suggestion, which von Böhm-Bawerk and others have wrongly identified with a price estimation. We will deal with this more thoroughly when we discuss cost later.[6]

The Passive Means of Production

If we consider the means of production from which products are made, we find in the first place the passive means of production. These, in commerce, are technically the finished products; in that area, the problem of the value of the passive means of production is thus solved by considering finished products.

It is a different matter in industry where, with the assistance of the active means of production, the product is made from the passive means of production, raw materials and auxiliary materials or factory supplies.

---

6 See p. 90 ff.

The producer, in regard to raw materials, does not know the realization value and he cannot even find out that value. When we state this, here we need to keep in mind that it is not a matter of proceeds from the sale of these materials; this, in the normal course of events, would be disastrous, because it has to be done in a market which, for the producer, is not his usual one. It is, however, a matter of a realization value in the sense in which we normally use the word, that is to say, the realization value via the sales proceeds of the final products. Because it is via the products that the raw materials have to fulfil their function in the production process, to provide their *usefulness*. The remarkable thing, in view of the purport of allocation theory and of subjective value theory, is that the producer cannot get to know this. And although one can argue, in terms of economics, that in the final analysis the value of the raw materials is determined by the realization value of the products which have been manufactured from them, the producer will follow a different line of reasoning and he has to do so. He knows intuitively that he cannot determine, from the realization value of the product, the value of complementary goods. He cannot work out the realization value. If he takes the importance of the raw materials into account, he will, in the regular course of events, when the flow of goods is proceeding evenly, i.e. without a hitch in sales, not take the slightest notice of the realization value of the raw materials.

5. Some Observations About the Actual Determination of Replacement Value

Here we interrupt the argument to discuss more thoroughly some important questions.

A trader, as we saw, finds in his stock of goods the stock of *raw materials* as well as the stock of *products*. Here, the difference between replacement value and realization value is determined exclusively by the price difference in the two markets, between which the enterprise is situated. The replacement value is determined by the price in the *buyers'* market, the realization value by the price in the *sellers'* market. The value to the trader is the replacement value and is therefore determined by the price in the *buyers'* market. The replacement contains, at the same time, remuneration for services, storage, etc., being therefore the complementary goods.

It is important to emphasize this, because in the industrial-economic literature and practice one always hears about, in the context of various controversies on the value problem, of "valuation at market price". This is an expression which causes confusion. For that matter, its origin is due to insufficient insight of the subject; no distinction is usually made between the buyers'- and sellers' market. Without that distinction the problem will not be solved. When one says that the value of the stock of a grain dealer is determined by the market price, one has not said anything. Remember, replacement value as well as realization value are determined by the market price. For an Amsterdam grain dealer who has stock lying in storage in the city, there is indeed a difference between replacement value and realization value, unless he is a speculator, that is to say, unless he speculates on a price difference between two points in time in the same market.[7] But if he is a proper dealer, he is, with his business, a link in the production flow; he then deals on two markets. That does not mean two market locations, but two markets with different market personnel. That difference - as we saw before - can arise from a geographic difference. The dealer can act as a buyer in the United States, importing and selling the grain here, in smaller quantities, to local buyers. In the continuous production flow the value of the grain for the dealer is determined by the replacement value, by the price in his buyers' market.

The same has to be said about the value of raw materials for the manufacturer. For him too, the replacement value is determined by the price in *his* buyers' market, i.e. the market in which he will be part of the personnel as a buyer if he replaces the good. Here too, general terms such as market value or market price are meaningless. A manufacturer has a fixed position, it should be remembered, between the markets of the flow of production.

For a trader as well as a manufacturer another controversy occurs in regard to the raw materials, instead of or in addition to the controversy of replacement value versus realization value. It is the controversy of purchase price versus replacement value, a controversy which is of special importance in regard to cost, but which already needs to be discussed at this early stage in regard to the following question: by which moment in price formation in the buyers market is the level of the replacement value determined? We know that the price in the buyers' market determines the replacement value, but we still do not know at which moment. For example, can it be the price at the moment when the good which is in stock was bought?

One might be of the opinion that we do know that moment. Remember, we stated earlier that the replacement value was determined by the price (in the buyers' market), at the moment the product leaves - in economic terms - an industrial enterprise. We saw this when we were discussing the value of finished products. We justified this with the explanation that at that moment the need for replacement came into being. The quantity of raw materials which, in the product, leaves an industrial

7 For a detailed discussion of the phenomenon of speculation we refer to *Vol. IV, The Theory of External Organisation*, in particular *Ch. V, Section 4*; *Vol. VI: B, The Theory of Profit Determination: Ch. III, Sections 7 and 16; Vol. III, Theory of Financing*: in particular, *Ch. IV, Section 5.*

enterprise, is, so to speak, functionally connected by the continuous flow to the corresponding quantity of raw materials which has to be obtained, or be "sucked in", from the buyers' market. This reasoning is indeed correct; it also - once the replacement value concept has been accepted - appears to be obvious. However, we have to take note of what is happening here; the matter is not as simple as it looks. We therefore once again use the illustration of the production flow with the widening of the flow representing stock in an industrial enterprise.

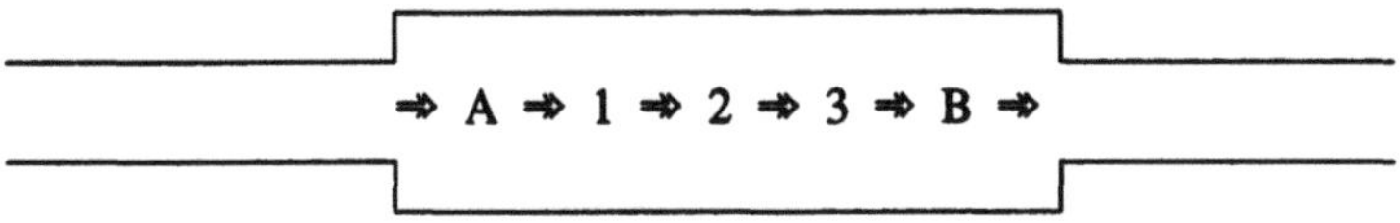

Let us assume that the time which is needed to propel a piece of raw material from A to B is three months. That means that in this industrial enterprise a stock of raw materials is required, that are unprocessed, or in process or in the form of a finished product. The three stages are indicated as 1, 2 and 3 above.

We have assumed, in the discussion to date, that the production flow runs through the enterprise completely regularly. That is to say, delivery to buyers and from suppliers is regular; at least the flow from (order to) suppliers takes place at an absolutely equal pace with the delivery to (order from) buyers. So we followed the continuity principle taken in an absolute sense. When such a flow is assumed, we may think of the relationship between the raw materials particle of B and that of A just as well in the reverse order. If a producer can count on a regular flow out of B, he may anticipate this knowledge three months beforehand and make the purchase from his supplier three months ahead; what is more, he *has to* do this. Because if he doesn't, if he does *not* anticipate an expected flow from B in three months' time, he will not have a product ready later on, when the demand arises in three months' time. This train of thought apparently leads to the peculiar conclusion, that the causal or - if you like - functional relationship between the sold and the replacing raw materials components can be conceived in an order which is the exact reverse of what we have done so far. One can consider this in such a way that the sale of a product at B is not linked to a purchase *at that moment*, i.e. at the moment of sale, but to the replacement by purchase *three months* beforehand - thus at A -, because at that point it could already be mathematically established that after three months the obtained raw materials component would be needed for a product which had to be supplied and because one *had to* anticipate that sale - because the production process would take three months. Seen this way, every purchase is therefore linked with a sale after the time required by the production process; that is to say, seen that way, replacement is ahead of the sale by that length of time. We thus find that we are not saying too much if we state that the situation is not as simple as it seems. Of course, the question now arises: which price in the buyers' market determines the replacement value? The price at the moment of the sale of the product or the purchase price of the raw materials three months beforehand - i.e. the outlay price?

There can be no overall answer to that question. The factors determining the replacement value will depend on the location of the means of production in the production flow.

And the matter does not rest with the two conceptions indicated here. It follows from the replacement value *concept* that it will depend on the circumstances which factors determine the replacement value. Remember, replacement value is nothing but the quantitative representation of the significance of a good, seen from the point of view of the *sacrifices* which have to be made for its replacement. It will depend on the circumstances which sacrifices will have to be made and thus also what the level of the replacement value is and how it is determined.

Even though no general rule can be indicated as to what factors determine the replacement value, the contrast in concepts, set out above, is nevertheless of a general nature. What we *can* indicate is its significance.

If the structure of the production process in regard to continuity were indeed as firm as was assumed in the foregoing, *both* concepts would in fact be correct. One could then not even say that one of the two should take precedence. Both, in themselves, are logical, they are merely stated from a different point of view.

But the practice of production is different. Acquiring means of production and the selling of products are generally not linked so firmly to each other that the latter concept is admissible. It is only admissible when there is *indeed an indissoluble relationship*, as occurs *with purchases which are intended for particular sales*. Those raw materials components are not replaced. But when it is a matter of a *general stock*, which serves as a collectivity in the production process to which one adds or from which one takes away without a mechanical relationship but with a causal tie, only the former concept can be applied, because their replacement does not occur regularly. At least it does not need to occur regularly.

One thing still needs to be mentioned. The possibility that the purchase price determines the value, apparently does not result from the circumstance that at one time a sacrifice was made to the amount of the purchase price, for the piece of raw material which was actually used in the sold product. Not the historical fact as such is of significance for the level of the value of a good, but *the circumstance that the good, when it was acquired, immediately obtained its destination for the benefit of a particular part of the production.* As soon as that destination no longer exists, i.e. as soon as the mechanical relationship does not exist, or is broken, the purchase price too, will completely lose its importance; it has become a historical fact, not important for the determination of value - in the same way that sacrifices made do not determine the value of a product.

Nevertheless, here we can state that it is essential to know the purchase price when determining the level of the replacement value! We needed to discuss this view for the sake of completeness and because it explains certain phenomena in the cost problem.

In general, however, one can adhere to the earlier conception: a sale in the continuous flow of production necessitates replacement and it is the replacement value which determines the significance of a good for the producer. The circumstances at the moment of sale, when the economic relationship with the purchase comes into being, determine the factors, however, which, in their turn, determine the level of the replacement value.

6. Replacement Value in Regard to the Various Means of Production

The Argument Continued

In section 3 of this chapter we argued that a producer cannot, generally speaking, determine the realization value of his means of production and, because of that, the significance of the replacement value predominates in the production process. We did not want to imply that a producer can never be aware of the realization value of a good. He can, as soon as a good is an independent source of income, outside the context of the flow of production. For example, the owner of a security can become aware of its realization value, because it is a source of income which, independent of any production process, can produce income for him. This does not mean that the significance - for the producer that is to say, *the* value - will be determined by the realization value of the security, but in this case *for that reason* it is at least possible that the realization value is playing a part. Here, an industrial enterprise does not need to be the bearer of the realization value, because this "means of production" can have an independent realization value. We will have to take this possibility into account when investigating the value of those means of production in an industrial enterprise.

In the meantime, suffice to point out that there are companies where securities do have an organic continuous relationship in the flow of production, in the production process. For example, a life insurance company where all sources of income are tied together into one source of income. A security then acquires a totally different nature.

Although no more details[8] are provided, we only mention it as an example, in order to emphasize again that the problem of value can only be solved if, repeatedly, one returns to the question: what is the significance of the good for one's prosperity; i.e. in production: what is the significance for the formation of income? The quantitative expression of that significance is the value. And it will only be possible to solve the value problem if one puts that question for each case in particular. Of course, one can distinguish very large groups of analogous cases for which one can generally establish the significance of the good for prosperity. A universal answer for all cases can, however, not be given - it would be in conflict with the value concept itself.

The Active Means of Production

Let us, in the framework of the cost problem, consider for a moment the remaining group, the so-called active, mainly durable, means of production.

Here too, it is again replacement value which generally determines the value for a producer. His income only depends on its possession to the extent of the amount of money he has to forego if he replaces the means of production by another, similar means of production. Also in regard to these means of production, the producer cannot be aware of an independent realization value, because the durable means of production is one of the many indispensable factors in the production process. There can be no allocation. He can only become aware incidentally of the existence of the realization value of such a means of production if the flow of production is broken because the means of production, or part of it, is being missed, and therefore the income, or part of it, may thus be lost. Such a case *can* occur but is of little interest to us. We are ready for it, however, in our argument because in that case realization value can also become important in our conceptualizing. But even then it is only to the extent it does not in this *abnormal* case, exceed the limit to which the replacement value can rise above the *normal* replacement cost. In such a case people, forced by the abnormal circumstances, will be prepared to pay an abnormally high price for the replacement good. But, even though one can become aware of the existence of a realization value, again its value turns out to be the replacement value. In social value every means of production, every "complementary good" really has the realization value of the *entire* complex. Remember, each of the complementary goods is

8 This subject is discussed in detail in *Vol. VI: B, The Theory of Profit Determination, Ch. I, Section 2.*

supposed to be absolutely necessary. Von Böhm-Bawerk[9] has a predilection for using the example of a pair of gloves. Each of the gloves has, as a complementary good, the full realization value of the pair, whereas by itself it has a realization value of zero. But for a manufacturer both gloves, left and right separately, do have a value.

In the normal production process, the matter is very simple. The replacement value of all means of production together is lower than the realization value, unless one is operating at a loss. But in that case one cannot consider that loss as the difference between the replacement value and the realization value of one particular means of production, but of the complex. One then finds that the means of production which, in other industrial enterprises - whether or not in the same branch of industry - can be used profitably, actually produce a loss in the enterprise under consideration. It must be the combination which is the cause.

But this position too, is after all a deviation from the norm. If the means of production has been selected appropriately, it will be an indispensable link in the production process and it will lead, *with* the other means of production, to an advantageous difference for the producer, to the formation of income. Its significance for that income stream is determined by the sacrifices which have to be made for its replacement. In regard to the durable means of production certain peculiarities occur, which we will discuss in detail later on, and of which a few will be considered now.

It should be remembered in the *first* place that, for a production process, it is not a matter of a tool, a means of production as such, but of the technical capacity which it represents for the production process. For example, in regard to a steam engine it is not a matter of the steam engine itself, but of the motive power or the heating which it can produce. If, therefore, the steam engine can be effectively replaced by a combustion engine, the value of the steam engine can also be affected by the sacrifices which have to be made to obtain a combustion engine of the same capacity. As always, it is not a matter of replacement, but of substitution. If a combustion engine is cheaper than a steam engine, the replacement value of the steam engine will no longer be determined by the price of a new steam engine, but by the lower price of the combustion engine, because income depends on the possession of that steam engine only to the extent of that purchase price.

In the *second* place, we again have to remember that a durable means of production is nothing but a stock of work units tied together into a technical unit. Of these work units, a part is used in production every time. With the result that the stock of work units gradually decreases. If we then ask ourselves what value the

---

9 We refer to E. von Böhm-Bawerk: *Kapital und Kapitalzins* II: *Positive Theorie des Kapitals*, 4th ed. 1921, *Vol. I, Part III: Value and Price, Section I, paragraph VI: The Value of Complementary Goods.*

means of production has, the answer will differ depending on whether the stock of work units, present in the means of production, is larger or smaller. A new tool, on that account, has a higher value than an old one, because the stock of work units in the new tool is greater than in the old one. So if we are speaking of the value of a tool, we are concerned with the value of the stock of work units and thus with the replacement value of those work units. Hence, the value of a tool decreases gradually, even though the price one has to pay for a new tool has remained equal to the price which was paid in obtaining the tool the value of which we are assessing. This is therefore not caused by the replacement value falling in regard to the purchasing price, but results from the stock of work units decreasing. When forming a value judgement in respect of a durable means of production one therefore has to make a sharp distinction between the replacement price of a new means of production and the price changes on the one hand, and the gradual decrease in value of the tool as a complex, as the balance of a stock of work units. And one should also keep very much in mind that this has nothing to do with a "market price" of the old tool on a sellers' market of second hand tools.

This last observation brings us to a *third* important point.

Tools fulfil their task in the production process by giving up work units to the product. As such they have a realization value via the realization of the products, which are manufactured with the help of this tool. It can, however, also - as we have pointed out before - have another incidental value, namely the realization value derived from its *exchange*. This is usually the case when the tool can no longer properly fulfil its function in the industrial enterprise. One then speaks of residual value, demolition value, scrap value, etc. Active, durable means of production therefore have *two kinds of realization value:* the realization value via the normal course of the production process, therefore via the realization of the product, and the realization value via the sale of the means of production itself.

This phenomenon is important by itself, but it is also significant because it draws attention to the following phenomenon. If a good only derives its significance from its direct utility value, and so is determined by its realization value, the *highest* realization value, if the good has, or can achieve two or more destinations, will express its value. Remember, the most favourable use produces the highest revenue and, when replacement in the production process is no longer possible, the proceeds will also have been determined together with the use. One then finds the size of the proceeds to be dependent on the possession of the good, also to the highest realization value.

7. The Value of the Complex of the Means of Production, the Industrial Enterprise as a Whole

Let us finally consider the complex, the industrial enterprise as a whole. We have established that this complex is the bearer of the income stream generated and therefore also of the realization value which the complex as a production apparatus derives from the proceeds of the uninterrupted series of production processes which was achieved with that apparatus. Also it is apparently possible, when we know the realization value of the complex, as well as the replacement value of the means of production, to establish the value of the organisation making these means of production into a higher unit, thereby creating a net income for the owner. This organisation apparently has to have a value to the owner equalling precisely the difference between that replacement value of the means of production and the realization value of the whole.

We need to look at this more closely, because a proper insight on this part of the value problem is useful for many other problems.

How can the owner of an industrial enterprise become *aware* of the realization value of the complex? He becomes aware of it via the net income generated with the help of the complex. This, in our society, is known as monetary income. He will not have a clear idea of the *size* of the realization value; there is no call for that, unless something happens.[10] But he *will* be aware that the complex has value for him as soon as it produces a net income, when he can obtain with that complex an *entrepreneur's premium.*

We now will attempt to obtain an insight into the considerations determining the size of the realization value as well as considering from the producer's perspective what price he is prepared to sell the complex. How will he calculate its value? In order to be able to visualise this properly, we will set out a very simplified financial illustration. For the sake of convenience, we assume that all capital components are constant, that is to say, that their amounts remain equal.

Land	$100,000	All assets at replacement value
Buildings	200,000	
Equipment	300,000	
Raw materials + finished product	200,000	
Debtors	200,000	
	$1,000,000	

Income $100,000

10 As in the case of liquidation or fire damage.

Will the producer be satisfied with an amount equal to the replacement value of the capital? No, he will not. By selling the complex, he loses his source of income for good, since the buyer insists on the "competition stipulation". He would want to obtain more, because, with payment of the replacement value of the capital, he will not obtain more than an interest of, say, 5%, i.e. $50,000 annually. His current income from the complex amounts, however, to $100,000 per year. We now find that the entrepreneur's premium, which he obtains from the complex, amounts to $50,000 per year.[11] If he were to be deprived of that income, he would want to be recompensed; remember, the complex is worth to him $50,000 per year above the replacement value. If, again for the sake of convenience, we assume that the producer himself no longer works in the factory, he is supposed to be able to live on his retirement income.

The $50,000 entrepreneur's premium is really a simplified presentation of the total of the proceeds of the products generated yearly. These proceeds can be divided into a part equal to the replacement value of the means of production which have been used during that year, and surplus proceeds. For the sake of convenience, we can leave that first part out of the discussion and will attend to the surplus part of the proceeds.

The question now arises: what is the realization value of a source of income of $50,000 annually. If we assume that generally we obtain interest from debentures, mortgages and the like, of 5%, we have a criterion for comparison, something that is needed for measuring the value of the complex.

If one can count on that $50,000 in perpetuity, in other words, if that income can be considered as everlasting interest, the value of that source of income is obviously $1,000,000. But may one consider that source of income as everlasting? No, definitely not. We know that an entrepreneur's premium, by its nature, *has to* in the long run partly disappear, and for another part is shifted to and fro, with shifts in consumption and flow of production in the short run. Every entrepreneur's premium therefore contains a certain element of uncertainty, and even an element of definite disappearance. The value of that source of income will thus be lower, usually much lower, especially if the entrepreneur's premium is high. That high premium will incite competition, that is to say, it will incite the founding of new enterprises which will appear on the market with the same product, in order to obtain part of the premium.

It is not possible to give a general criterion to determine the reduction of the premium; it differs for each branch of industry and for each enterprise. But we are

---

11 The problem of simply subtracting interest on capital will be discussed in detail in *Chapter B II A: Interest.*

able to give an important indication about the limit *above which* the value of the complex cannot rise. That limit lies at the point where the realization value would exceed the replacement value of the *complex*. Because in fact, the complex, the immaterial part of that complex, the *organisation*, also has a replacement value. If this is so, the value can, again, not be higher than the lower of the two values specified.

How should the replacement value of the organisation as a whole be understood? In the same way as the material means of production: in terms of the sacrifices which have to be made to replace the organisation by another organisation which has the same satisfaction value. It is conceivable that such an organisation can be set up without more, or without significantly more sacrifices on top of those which are needed for the replacement of the means of production. If this is so, the replacement value of the organisation will equal zero. But then it cannot have any value either. If, in an enterprise, the organisation is found to have a realization value, it does not, for the owner, have a significance above the replacement value. And no buyer will be prepared to pay anything for it. Because he will have enough sense to set up an organisation himself which can be founded with so few sacrifices. And we can add that the realization value will have to disappear quickly because of the quickly growing number of these easy to set-up enterprises.

But this is usually not the case. The organisation of an enterprise is usually the result of many years of work. To replace it, considerable sacrifices by many parties are usually necessary. No organisation of any scope can be set up in a hurry. For instance, managers and deputy managers, and the lower echelons as well as the workers need training. Only after years of experience does a manager know how to create the most favourable circumstances. Experience and knowledge have been accumulated from numerous production processes, which for a new organisation have to be acquired all over again. Sales too - and thus again the complex which, in its size and composition, depends on the magnitude of the sales - have not suddenly attained, or cannot suddenly attain the level of those of the profit producing enterprise. These sales, this circle of customers, have normally been built up gradually; only by degrees is the trust created among the buyers, by personal visiting, by the quality of the goods, by advertising, etc. Replacement of an organisation does not mean - as with the means of production - ordering and delivery within so many weeks or months, with a price which has been agreed to beforehand. The replacement of an organisation means founding an enterprise all over again, becoming an entrepreneur all over again.

This is the reason why people are prepared to pay remuneration above the replacement value of the physical means of production. However, who will evaluate accurately the replacement value of the enterprise? This, in many cases, cannot be done accurately, but such an evaluation is nevertheless a basis for the enterprise's value, an amount which can never exceed its replacement value of the complex.

Will the owner of an enterprise be prepared to hand it over to someone else for payment of the replacement value of the means of production plus an amount for how they have been organised? This is possible under the right circumstances. These may even be such that he hands them over below the replacement value.[12] But this does not normally happen, of course, because that would not be in the interest of the owner? He would again have to create a new organisation in order to obtain the same income, with all the trouble and burdens and risks this entails. However, of course he would want *more* than the replacement value.

Would the buyer be prepared to pay the realization value? Ordinarily this will not be the case, because he would then never be able to obtain income from the complex himself. Would he be prepared to pay more than the replacement value (of the net assets or capital)? It is likely he would, because he has the certainty of the existing organisation. The purchase price will therefore lie between the realization value and the replacement value of the organisation.

We are, by the way, not at the moment interested in this transaction. It was discussed because it was the only way to understand reality. Remember, for the owner of an industrial enterprise there is no reason to form a clear idea of the value of the complex during the production process. This value is of no importance for the production process. Whereas it is important for a producer to have continuously a clear idea of the value of the means of production being used - in order to arrive in the market with the correct independent valuation of the product and to obtain the correct proceeds - the value of the complex, which is permanent, is of little importance to him. That question is not of interest to him in the context of the production process, but only in the context of its winding up, its removal, at least for him, as a source of income.

It is also very important to realise that for the owner, an organisation can never have a value which is higher than its replacement value. This value may be unknown or difficult to estimate, but it can on no account be higher than the organisation's replacement value, irrespective of the level of the realization value of the complex.

We state this so emphatically because we want to warn here against a misconception which occurs very often in regard to "goodwill'. Goodwill is the capacity of an enterprise to obtain (in the market) an entrepreneur's premium in its product. The value of goodwill is therefore the replacement value of the *organisation*, of the combination of means of production *and* actions above the

---

12 When continuation would cause a loss greater than giving up the enterprise for an amount which is below the replacement value.

replacement value of the means of production themselves, or the (lower) realization value of the enterprise.

8. Replacement Value and Reproduction Value

In Schmalenbach's *Finanzierungen*[13] one finds an exposition which, for a large part, runs parallel with the discussion in the previous section. Schmalenbach makes a distinction between future proceeds and reproduction value. He defines the latter as the replacement value of the enterprise.

The word reproduction value (in this context sometimes called reconstruction value) calls to mind the term reproduction costs in economics.

The question arises whether one can say that the value of finished products is determined by their reproduction costs; in other words, whether the value is the reproduction value. In social economics, as well as in business economics this concept is often used. And for some goods and some cases the concept seems indeed useful. Because if a finished product has to be replaced, it usually means that it needs to be *replaced by a newly produced good.* An industrial enterprise often has to "reproduce" the good which has been sold. This term is not really entirely correct, because the finished product, in the continuous flow, is transferred to the consumer and the newly produced good goes to another consumer. (We leave the product which has been incidentally destroyed out of the discussion). It is not really a question of reproduction if one keeps in mind that the flow of production continues. But we leave it at this discussion of terms. Of fundamental importance is the difference between the concepts *reproduction* and *replacement* is a matter of principle, because replacement is possible from an existing social stock, whereas reproduction only occurs when a newly produced good is added to the existing stock. Thus, a quantity of grain, for example, which a grain dealer takes to the market as a product, can be *replaced* by the purchase of the same quantity which is available in the stores of other wholesale dealers. For this replacement, this grain does not need to be reproduced; this can only be done at the next harvest. Here arises then a divergence in the meaning of the concepts, which will be of fundamental importance, because apparently, since the price is formed subject to the stock conditions of the moment, there can be a difference in the effect on the price formation when it is a matter of reproduction or of replacement *without* new production. Admittedly, socially speaking, in the continuous flow of production replacement, for the dealer, will normally mean reproduction, that is to say, replacement by newly produced

13 Editor's Note: E. Schmalenbach, *Finanzierungen*, 2nd ed. 1921 and later editions; esp. the section on "The valuation of an enterprise".

goods, but not necessarily so, because consumption does not need to be constant and is, in fact, not constant. This, among other things, will depend on the price. For the individual producer there is obviously a big difference, whether he achieves replacement from present stock or from future production because the replacement price may be different.

The difference in conception is very clear in all cases where the reproduction for the *individual* producer means a difference in time in the availability of the good, whilst it is a matter of immediate availability of the good. For example, the replacement value of a ship is determined by the price which one has to pay for a similar ship at that same moment in the market. That price is strongly affected by the prices of freight which prevail at the moment of the sale. On the other hand, the production costs of a new ship are determined by the prices for labour and materials required for building such a ship. If a short period is needed for the production of a new good, the reproduction and replacement costs will tend to coincide. They usually will not be able to diverge a lot and will affect each other because, if there is a great divergence, one will want to delay replacement. But in all cases where a long period is needed for the manufacture of a good, there can be considerable divergence between reproduction costs and replacement costs, or between reproduction value and replacement value. Very much in accordance with the general design of our conception in regard to the value problem, we are of the opinion that one cannot say in general terms *whether*, in a specific case, *the* value of a good is determined by the reproduction costs. It depends on the question whether replacement is actually possible by reproduction and, if so, whether the replacement from existing stock or reproduction requires a smaller sacrifice. Replacement value always applies, therefore, even though its level is determined by reproduction cost, i.e. *in cases, where replacement consists of reproduction.* Fundamentally important, the significance of the difference should be kept in mind, the difference being hidden in the varying conditions of stock and of the market personnel for the price formation of the good which has already been produced and the good which still has to be produced.

9. Conclusion

In the discussion above we have asked ourselves what is the value of goods at the moment they are sold. This moment, it should be kept in mind, is for our problem one of the most important in the production process, because the producer is forced at that moment - at which he is relinquishing the good - to form an idea of the level of the value [of that good]. However, the technology of the enterprise entails that the producer asks himself that same question at other moments too. Apart from particular reasons which can exist - for example, in the case of fire to determine damages - those evaluations will, in a normal production process, always be connected with a concern to either lay the foundations already *before* the moment of sale, for an evaluation of that moment, or to obtain an insight in the outcome of the enterprise over a certain period. The first concern takes us into the area of cost calculation, the last one takes us into the area of balance sheet problems. With both objectives one will always have to keep in mind that the moments when valuation takes place, are moments on the path followed by the flow of production in an enterprise. We will have to take into consideration, at the same time, that the relationship which exists between a good and the producer, in regard to the above-mentioned objectives, is and remains the same as the relationship we have indicated for the moment of valuation at the moment of sale. *The good has, also at any moment in between, no other importance for a producer than that of a means of production, a link in the production flow.*

B. I. The Basic Principles of Costing

Cost and Its Function in Production

1. Definition of the Concept

We need to start by defining the concept of "cost". This is especially necessary because there is great confusion in the literature about the term "cost" and the concept of "cost". The word is used in all sorts of meanings and for all sorts of problems. If we want to be able to use it, we will have to make a choice.

Linguistically, the word cost [in Dutch, "kostprijs", literally translated: cost price] indicates the price determined by the costs. With these costs are meant the cost of production of a good. We can of course measure the cost of a good or service or action at any moment we wish and we can also do this for any purpose. However, if one wishes to speak of a cost *problem*, it is necessary to keep in mind a specific objective. And with this objective, the determination of the concept and the choice of the term, it is necessary that we, as always, dovetail as much as possible into other economic problems and existing economic terminology, in order to prevent confusion. That is why we use the "cost price" concept in the context of the problem of price formation.

In that problem the offering of a product in the market, is the moment where cost, the amount measured in money of the costs of a product, acquires such importance that one can speak of the moment at which the problem arises. The question then arises what factors determine the costs of the product, which factors determine its cost. In the word cost, for that matter, lies linguistically speaking, the connection with exchange. Remember, one might be able to speak of "costs" at any moment in the flow of production, but one only speaks of *cost*, apparently, if one pinpoints the moment of the exchange.

There is no doubt that, originally, when using the word cost, one was thinking of the total of sacrifices which were made to prepare a good in such a way that it could be exchanged; one was thinking, therefore, of the costs which were *incurred* at the moment of exchange, of what could be called "historical" cost. In contrast with what can be observed about this in the social-economic literature and in practice, we posit that the theory of price formation forces us to conceive cost as the sacrifice made by a producer in the product offered by him at the moment of offering. A producer, in order to act rationally during the exchange, has to know the extent of that sacrifice to be able to compare it with the proceeds resulting from the exchange. We consider the sacrifices, the costs, as a function of the price; only in this context can we speak of cost.

Thus, the "cost" concept acquires its own defined content.

We define cost as the quantitative representation of a sacrifice made during the exchange, in the organic context of production.[1]

This concept completely fits in with the discussion on the value concept in production. They are each other's mirror image. A good, in the meaning of a possession, is a value category; when we give up the good, we speak of it as a cost category.

It goes without saying that, besides this cost concept, there is still room for the other, the old cost concept, which we call historical cost, or rather, the purchase price or production price. It is an entity which no doubt also has its significance, within the problem of price formation as well, but one quite different from cost. We will discuss this again later.[2*]

In this line of argument, as may have been observed, the cost concept and the value concept have thus become identical. This is the case in so far that the size of value and cost is normally the same for a product at the moment of exchange. And indeed it is a fact that value is measured by, and can only exist because of the costs; conversely, costs are measured by the value and they can only exist because of the value. When there is no cost, there is no value; where there is no value, there is no cost either. We are here thinking of the so-called free, non-economic goods.

The cost concept which has thus been created is essential for the problem of price formation, not only because cost, in this sense, has an important effect on price

---

1 Limperg emphasises here - as he does elsewhere - that one only talks about cost in connection with regular production; it is neither relevant for incidental cases nor for the consumer. According to him an incidentally exchanged good does not have a cost price.

2 Here Limperg points out that in business economics literature (e.g. in Simon: *Cost accounting and the organization of factory administration*) one frequently comes across the idea that the cost price of a good does not have one value but several, depending on the purpose for which the cost price is determined. For instance there is a cost price which can serve as a basis for determining the sales price, another one which serves to measure production efficiency and a third one that may be used as a basis for valuation for drawing up the balance sheet. In this kind of argument cost price is an entity "to work with". This concept of having different cost prices for different entities, representing different notions, has been categorically rejected by Limperg, because of methodological and scientific reasons. To avoid misunderstanding and confusion, Limperg thinks one should concentrate on one purpose. And for him that purpose is the producer's valuation in the market, within the framework of market price formation. This way of thinking does not necessarily contradict what is discussed in Chapter III C: integral and differential cost calculation, which fits into the theory of cost differentiation.

* See p.111 ff. [All page cross references within "B. I. The Basic Principles of Costing" refer to actual page numbers in the Dutch text].

formation, but especially for laying the foundations of the entire theory of price formation. This importance will now be discussed in more detail.

2. The Importance of Cost for Price Formation

What importance does cost have in the context of price formation in the market?

Before we can answer this question, we will have to deal with a terminological problem. What is meant by "price formation in the market?". One should not, with the concept "market", think of a technical market, but of the so-called economic market. With the technical market one thinks of a market place. We are thinking of the total suppliers of goods and services, even without their having to meet in person in a market place. The technical market is expanded by the use of letters, telegrams, and phone calls, by using representatives, agents, etc. In an economic market, there is a meeting of supply by producers on the one hand, and demand of consumers or consuming producers on the other hand. When studying the price problem in economics it is a fairly general custom to think of a market where on one side consumers demand as well as buy. For the theory's development it is more appropriate to select a market where producers act on both sides. This is of special importance because there are infinitely more "markets" between producers and producers than between producers and consumers. Moreover, we thus have the advantage that there are individuals on both sides of the market who are operating, or who should operate accurately in order to act rationally. A consumer buys in a hit or miss fashion, in spite of the theory's assumption which presents him as a painstakingly calculating interested party. But the producer must definitely calculate painstakingly. This way, the gaps in the existing theories of price formation can be demonstrated properly.

The theory of price formation, as it can be found in the textbooks of social economics, teaches how from the total of supply and demand in free trade eventually one price is formed, or at least a number of prices within very narrow limits, which together form a general price at which goods are exchanged. The result is - according to the theory - that not all goods offered are being bought and that not all goods for which there is a demand are being sold. All demand and supply whose respective demand and supply prices lie outside those of the so-called marginal pairs, unsatisfied.

In the problem of price formation it is now a matter of investigating what factors determine the market price, - the resultant of all that supply and demand. Remember, the mechanics, outlined above, of price formation only explain the solution of different demand- and supply prices in a general price, but nothing about the factors which determine those supply - and demand prices. The only "explanation" which is given with the analysis of the mechanism is that those prices are the result of evaluations by producers on the one hand, and of consumers on the other. But that is really only another way of describing the question which for us - and really for the price formation theory too - is so very important and we therefore need to acquire an insight into the *producers' considerations in their supply and demand actions (while not considering the consumers. Therefore,* we will now look into producers' evaluations.

3. Some Critical Discussions of the Literature

A notion - one might say in our country the predominant notion which is often put forward - in this regard is that evaluations result from the experiences of producers in the market. Price formation theory of the Austrian school is, in our view, based on this notion.

C.A. Verrijn Stuart

In our country, an outstanding representative of this school is C.A. Verrijn Stuart. In his book: *The Foundations of Social Economics*, the author ponders what happens in the market and what motivates a supplier. He develops the concept of *subjective value.* How is this value determined? By the market prices as they came into being just before. It is the existing market quotations - i.e. the prices at which the exchange took place - which determine the subjective value for a supplier. "This subjective exchange value is based on prices obtained *earlier* by them or by others. These prices create an expectation about the level of the prices which can be obtained at present also, and they will, as long as this expectation is not found to be unrealistic, affect the attitude of the suppliers in the market. However, if these prices cannot be obtained at present, the subjective exchange value disappears as an element from the value judgement formed by the suppliers in regard to the goods they are offering for sale, and this judgement is replaced by a judgement based on the marginal usefulness of those goods for the suppliers themselves. This judgement will then probably be very low, so that the suppliers will be prepared to, as it is called, "sell at any price".[3]

It is striking that Verrijn Stuart in the 3rd edition of his work (1930) revises the above quoted passage to such an extent that the suppliers' subjective value judgement disappears altogether and that they orientate themselves completely to the subjective value judgements of the buyers.

3 C.A. Verrijn Stuart, *The Foundations of Social Economics*, 1920, pp.201-202.

Let us take a closer look at this outline of events.

We do not wish to embark on a detailed criticism of the distinction made by Verrijn Stuart and von Böhm Bawerk between the basis of earlier and present prices. Both authors attach great importance to this distinction because they themselves realize that, without this distinction, they would explain the price from the price. We only wish to point out that in our view this distinction has no significance in this context and that these authors, in price formation theory, are, in fact explaining the price from the price; they are using the price as a basis for the valuation of the supplier in the same market namely the sellers' market. We refrain from further comment because it would lead us too far into the area of the price theory itself.

But the rest should not remain undiscussed, because it deals with the producers' considerations; and these are for us of particular importance.

First of all, attention should be paid to the fact that here the concept of "subjective exchange value" is being used. This adjective "subjective", as has already been pointed out in Chapter I and as has been demonstrated extensively, is as a reflection of a producer's considerations, totally out of place. This becomes apparent from the explanation given by the authors, according to which this so-called subjective exchange value derives from prices obtained earlier, even from prices which have been *obtained* by others! How can this be called a *subjective* exchange value?

If we overlook this and if we assume that it should have been "specific" or "individual" exchange value (which, in the *psychological* value theory of the Austrians is of course not allowed), we arrive at a much more important objection.

It appears, according to Verrijn Stuart, that producers-suppliers do not have their own value assessment. Because their value assessment turns out to be nothing but an expectation of a price *to be obtained.* With Verrijn Stuart, that is even an expectation based on *earlier* prices; von Böhm Bawerk is of the same opinion.

One must realize the stupidity of the producer, as he is shown here by Verrijn Stuart and von Böhm Bawerk: because a price was obtained "earlier", the producer offers his product at a price based on that price! Verrijn Stuart, following in the footsteps of the Austrians goes even as far as leaving out of consideration a change in the market position since those earlier prices! This, at least, Taussig does not do. He too, uses anticipated prices, but he at least thinks of expectations based on the situation in the market at the present moment.[4] This is some improvement, but it is by no means sufficient; we find it to be fundamentally wrong.

There is no question here of a causal relationship between offering price and sacrifice. The action of the producer is completely inexplicable deductively and,

4 F.W. Taussig, *Principles of Economics*, 1921. I, Ch.10.

inductively, the Austrians have observed and reasoned just as badly. Logically, only Taussig's induction can be accepted. Verrijn Stuart's and von Böhm Bawerk's are illogical. But even if Verrijn Stuart did assume that a producer took account of a changed market situation, obviously the nature of his so-called value assessment would still not change. It would remain to be nothing but an anticipated purchase price. That supplier who wants to sell "at any price", is basing his offering price not on his own valuation (of a *producer*, therefore), but on a valuation of a *buyer* (consumer or producer-user). Basically it amounts to the fact that all producers would arrive in the market with supplies which have been made to fit the anticipated bids of the buyers. What remains of a price formation between suppliers and buyers?

The producer's "valuation" according to Verrijn Stuart is nothing but an earlier price, according to Taussig nothing but an estimated future price; with both, a failure of the intention means nothing but a wrong assessment of the *present* market situation. And success means that the producer made the correct assessment. One would say that the person who made the correct assessment should be a prosperous man, that he must make money if his assessment is successful. But it works out quite differently, or it does not need to work out that way, because Verrijn Stuart's value assessment says nothing about the value of the good for the producer.

The fatal effect of the casuistry of this theory becomes apparent especially if one considers from Verrijn Stuart's view what occurs if the supplier finds that his "value assessment" does not fit the assessments of the bidders. The subjective exchange value of the object for the producer then suddenly disappears and marginal utility replaces it. That is to say, direct usefulness or satisfaction value becomes the basis. Imagine the unfortunate producer who has made a mistake in the prognosis of the market situation and who, as punishment, has to be content with "any price" (even with "any acceptable bid"); he would have to do this in actual fact - if the reasoning were correct and direct usefulness were to determine the value for him - because that direct usefulness of 1000 loads of linseed or of a flour mill is in fact nil. A machine toolmaker finds his tools which have been offered for sale suddenly reduced to scrap value, indeed to even less, because "scrap" too, has a marginal value of zero for him. And it becomes almost funny if we continue in this casuistry; the producer has to be pleased if he finds a buyer for that scrap, because the proceeds are then higher than the value which the good has for him; he must have made a profit, since he received more for it than its value. It is a most peculiar reasoning. It is even within itself contradictory. A producer who cannot even sell his good at the anticipated price of Hfl.10, but only at Hfl.9.50 must, according to Verrijn Stuart, value the good at *that* amount and not at a personal marginal value. That price can still be advantageous for him in comparison with its costs.

E. von Böhm Bawerk

Von Böhm Bawerk, in *Kapital and Kapitalzins, Vol II: Positive Theory of Capital*,[5] sets out an argument similar to that of Verrijn Stuart. He arrives, however, at an even more peculiarly formulated conclusion.

He points out that most sales involve "professional producers and dealers", who cannot use the goods themselves. This, according to von Böhm Bawerk, has the result that the norm of a subjective utilization value is cancelled as a deciding element in the value assessment. He does not say why.

We are using the same idea as a starting point in the argument, but we are being consistent; we completely eliminate the subjective element and the utilization value. Von Böhm Bawerk here means *utilization* in the direct satisfaction of needs.

But let us now take a look at his conclusion.

> . . . this, finally, has the result, in these sales, that the limiting effect of the valuation figures of the last seller on the theoretical formula, does not make itself felt, *and that the price level is, in fact, only limited and determined by the value assessments of the buyer'.*

He states a little later that, in the developed market traffic of the four assessments, the value assessments of the sellers are completely cancelled and that it can be said that, for the large social-economic market traffic, the market price is determined *by the last buyer's assessment figure*.

What he says in a footnote on pp.303/4, is also peculiar. He gives an outline of the actions of the supplier who occasionally lets himself be excluded from the market, perhaps at various times, but not in the long run. The good has to be sold.

One should realize what this statement means in von Böhm Bawerk's theory. A detailed analysis of the formation of prices was given beforehand, in which the mechanism worked perfectly and in which the price was explained beautifully from the two opposing value assessments. The entire beautiful argument is being thrown out just like that. Not for an exceptional case; no - although von Böhm Bawerk does not dare to say so - practically for entire price formation! The lovely casuistic structure - which is being built on enthusiastically - is being stripped of its foundations.

It is becoming perfectly clear how von Böhm Bawerk, similar to Verrijn Stuart, but even more so, eliminates independent valuation of the product from the theoretical explanation.

---

5 E. von Böhm Bawerk, *Capital and Capital Interest*, 4th edition, 1921. *Vol. II: Positive Theory of Capital*, pp.302ff: The subjective value of goods for the sellers.

Although one *will* find mentioned by von Böhm Bawerk the element of cost calculation for the producer-*buyers*. It is odd, however, that this does not occur in the explanation proper of the price formation, but totally unexpectedly when he is dealing with the "Law of costs", where he says: "A producer will obviously not give more for a hundredweight of iron than he himself can demand from his own customers as the purchasing price; . . .".[6] With the explanation of the price formation itself such a calculation is not discussed, but with a bit of help one can insert them oneself without impeding the author's argument.

It is also odd that von Böhm Bawerk elsewhere[7] discusses, as a special case, what happens with a purchase with the aim of a resale, in a commercial transaction, therefore. He there ponders on the relationship between two successive markets. How does he see these? Not as an ordinary phenomenon, which applies to all production enterprises, but only for a commercial deal with a resale in an unchanged condition. It is indeed remarkable how he works this phenomenon into his theory, or rather, gets rid of it. He argues as follows: when a trader acts as a buyer in a market, he in fact does not represent his own inclination to buy, but that of the consumers on whose behalf he is buying and he thus arrives in the market with the subjective value assessment of those consumers, based on the marginal usefulness of the goods for them! It is obvious that an extraordinary jump in the reasoning is being made. So there are thus no producers' value assessments! Because every producer represents as buyer the inclination to buy of the next party. The subjective value of these producers suddenly disappears under the table.

Then there is a peculiar gap in the reasoning of this excellent dialectic thinker: von Böhm Bawerk does not realize or does not wish to realize the analogy in this respect between a commercial enterprise and a production enterprise.

If we thus assume that von Böhm Bawerk does acknowledge a calculation for buyers-producers, it is odd that he does not use that calculation for the producer-seller. Because, essentially, the position of a producer in between the two markets in respect of that calculation, is of course precisely the same and it will only depend on the circumstances where, finally, a calculation will form the direct basis for a producer's actions in the market. If beforehand he has a bid from his buyer, or if he knows the price he can obtain, he will let himself be guided in the buyers' market by the calculation. If he has no influence, or little influence, in the buyers' market, he will use his purchase price as the starting point for his offer to the buyer.

---

6 E. von Böhm Bawerk, *op cit.* p.309.

7 E. von Böhm Bawerk, *op cit.* p.300.

The above has shown the conceptions of von Böhm Bawerk *et al.*, and of Taussig about the bases of the price formation in regard to the value estimations of the producers.

What it amounts to is that the producers-sellers do not have any influence on the price formation.

Theorists Outside Reality

With this conception, the question inevitably arises how is it possible that there is *diversity* in the offering prices in the market, when one assumes, as the Austrian school does, that a producer-seller lets himself be guided in his value assessment by the market price he has obtained earlier, whereas, with these authors, value assessment and offering price are identical. We realize that this value assessment, according to these authors, will ultimately have no effect on price formation, but initially, and when there are no disappointments they do affect price formation. And in the framework of the price formation mechanism we indeed find, in the work of these authors, the familiar list of different value assessments from which the general price is the result. Well then, it remains unexplained and inexplicable, how these differences in value assessments arise. They can only be errors, stupid mistakes - stupid, because one can usually find a value assessment in the newspaper -, but they can not be differences which are explained causally. It is therefore completely illogical in the Austrian price formation theory that there can be differences in value assessment. To which should be added this peculiar representation of reality that all producers will know beforehand what value assessment their consumers will come up with in the market, i.e. that they know at least the basis on which this assessment is based.

For price theorists who are of the opinion that a value assessment is based on the anticipated market position of a good in the future - like Taussig, for example - a difference in value assessment can arise because every producer may have a different view of this market position and therefore of the behaviour of prices. What then does this difference in value assessment mean? An *accidental* difference in view; "accidental" because it is not ruled by economic circumstances themselves, but by the view one has of them. If we know, however, that the information about these circumstances is becoming more accurate but especially when we know that the information in regard to the majority of these products will be publicly made known, no basis can be found for a *general* difference in value assessment.

Even more peculiar for a proper understanding of the picture of reality given here, is the following. It follows in any case from the reasoning that, if two producers have the same view of the price movements, that their value assessment has to be the same. This is absolutely in conflict with reality, because these two producers arrive in the market with two different offering prices. This theory is thus condemned because, *if* one wishes to base the theory on what actually happens, that reality has to have been observed correctly and the theory must be based on correctly represented facts.

The reality is that producers arrive in their buyers' market as well as in their sellers' market with different asking prices and different offering prices, which are not identical, but based on *different* "value assessments", their (the producers') *cost.* This is the case, even though the producers know the earlier market price accurately and even though their insight in the market position is the same. And that difference has to be there, because it has its accurately determined economic significance and because it is not accidental. Because *a producer's value assessment is determined by the total of the production costs of his product.* Producers will produce as long as cost is lower than the asking price of interested parties. Every exchange and every production is thus logically explained. On this basis, a producer has to produce because of the effect of the economic motive and he has to leave off producing if that favourable difference does not exist.

Before we discuss in detail the above proposition, the theoretical defects need to be pointed out in the popular price theories outlined above, because, in a critical review, it is not sufficient to demonstrate a divergence from reality.

The most fundamental defect is the application of a reasoning which does not show a causal relationship. An inductive argument is introduced, under the semblance of deductive argumentation, without sufficient induction, however.

A value- and price theory should derive its significance as a theory from deductive argumentation. Argumentation is intended that way and is indicated accordingly. However, for deduction it is necessary *to establish a causal relationship between two phenomena*, an obligatory relationship. One can thus accept the theory of a price formation mechanism. But that causal relationship has not been demonstrated with price formation theory, it has not even - and that is the most serious aspect of the defect - been sought.

What should of course have been done if this causal relationship had been sought? The problem should then have been posited as follows:

With what value assessment *must* a producer arrive in the market when he offers his product for sale?

After setting this problem, one should have, reasoning with the economic motive as a starting point - i.e. the general cause - deduced the "force" which determines this value assessment, in other words, one should have established the *law* which affects price formation from this side.

The problem has not been posited this way, however, no law has been established and no causal relationship has therefore been established between production and price formation. People have said: a producer *will* do this and *will* do that. But what he "will" do is not deduced as a result from a cause. People have not said, therefore: a producer *must* do this or that, because it is a rational action. This is nevertheless essential if one wishes to conduct a *deductive* argument. It is necessary that one somehow deduces the action as *essential* - based on the effect of the general force of the economic motive or, what is here the same, by tracing the economic motive from the other phenomena.

It should be noted that now even the *exchange* can no longer be explained. It is certain that the Austrians with their value theories have tried to demonstrate that the exchange can only be explained when both parties have an advantage. What do we find now? The offering party *values* his good at the anticipated price. If that anticipation turns out as expected he will *not* carry out the exchange according to the theory, because there is no advantage for him! All causal explanation is lacking. The entire theory is thus condemned from the start.

First Defect: A Causal Explanation is Lacking

What has actually been done? It has been assumed that the producer follows a certain line of action. This is an inductive method. It is allowed in order to arrive at an argumentation, provided it is first demonstrated, of course, that a certain phenomenon, in fact, repeats itself so many times and under such circumstances that one can deduce a trend from this. One should have come up with a *law*, a causal and therefore indissoluble relationship between the striving for income by the producer and the way of assessing the value which has been noticed as a trend. Nothing of the kind can be found in the argumentation. And this is impossible because there is no trend, and no certainty exists that the offering price, assumed by von Böhm Bawerk, would result in an advantage for the production. Only when a causal relationship can be established between the price, the value assessment and the income, will there arise a relationship between price and production. Production needs to be explained and one cannot do this on the basis of the criticised theory, which does not use as a foundation an advantageous difference between value assessment and price.

This unexplained so-called trend has been nevertheless used as one of the pillars - really *the* pillar - for the argument. Because with that assumed line of action of the producer the price formation is explained. But then there is of course no question of deduction.

Only thus can it be explained too, that von Böhm Bawerk has designed an entirely different line of arguing for the producer-buyer and for the producer-seller.

Second Defect: Neglect of the Law of Continuity

The second fundamental defect can be considered as a direct consequence of the one discussed above. Because one did not look for the causal relationship between the actions of a producer in the market, and the production process, the entire combination of price formation phenomena is in the air; in the theory under fire the price formation of each good is considered as completely incidental.

The law of continuity is not recognised, or at least not taken into account.

Every offer, every exchange is an isolated case in the explanation; remember, both are ruled only by the consumer's asking price. The transaction has no connection whatever with the production and with the conditions under which production occurs.

Our conception, as set out in the proposition on p.86, establishes a direct relationship between the offering price and exchange on the one hand, and the production costs of the offered good on the other hand, and this conception fits in logically with the theory we have developed so far.

Remember, if cost is in fact the value assessment of a producer, his behaviour in the market is then explained and determined by the conditions under which he carries out production in his industrial enterprise. Events in the market are no longer up in the air, but are closely linked with production which is governed by the law of continuity.

One could suppose that we are exaggerating by saying that no link is established between production and market price in the rejected theory. On the contrary, a relationship is established, but in a way which is totally unsatisfactory for the explanation of production. According to subjective value theory the relationship is as follows. *In the long run*, according to this theory, an enterprise which suffers losses will *disappear* as a producer-supplier and supply will decrease as a result, whereas production, on the other hand, will be expanded if profit is made.

No doubt this reasoning is correct. An enterprise which produces at a loss will indeed disappear in the long run.[8] It is however clear that this relationship between production costs and price formation would only be able to explain large jolts in the price formation, which occur in times of crisis, as a result of over-extension in production, etc., when weak enterprises are being eliminated. However, the *normal* price pattern in a calm development of production in society cannot be explained by this.

If it were true that corrections in the price pattern could only come about by such rough means, if a consumer's value assessment indeed ruled the price pattern to

8 Limperg points out in passing that the notion of loss needs an explanation, because here too there is confusion over the nature of costs. That explanation is given in *Vol. VI: B, Theory of Profit Determination*, see esp. Ch. 1: Section 4.

such an extent that again and again a number of enterprises would be killed off, trade and industry would not have a moment of peace left.

However, the fact of the matter is that the relationship between production and price is quite different. The law formulated by price theorists, according to which production will decrease in the long run if the price does not cover costs, is an incorrect law. It should read as follows: *production is abandoned if production costs exceed the proceeds of the product*, not in the long run, but immediately.

This law is a direct result of the general force which governs economic life. The economic motive forces a producer not to produce if the proceeds of the product do not cover the costs. Because the economic motive is transformed in him into a striving for income. If the proceeds do not exceed the product's costs, no income is formed, but, on the contrary, is sacrificed. A producer who acts *rationally* must therefore abandon production, not in the long run, but *immediately*.

Price formation is, therefore, indeed affected by the limitation of production, but not the way it is assumed in the challenged theory. Among other things, the experience that production costs exceed proceeds can certainly lead to the destruction of the enterprise, i.e. to destruction of the part of the production apparatus which the enterprise or industry uses in society. But that is only one form in which the law is expressed. Normally, the effect is much quicker, more significant, which thus prevents great convulsions. The general phenomenon is far more significant than the specific one, on the one hand because the general one also includes the specific one, and, on the other hand, because it provides an explanation of the concrete phenomena in normal industrial life.

One may object to this that there is a lot of goods produced of which the costs are not covered by the proceeds. Such an observation can be correct, but it is however not proof of the invalidity of the law formulated above. If, *in spite of* the effect of the force formulated in this law, production nevertheless occurs, it proves either that it is believed incorrectly that costs are higher than proceeds, or that another force is at work which - also arising from the economic motive - neutralizes the force referred to in the law or exceeds it. In the first case it is believed that the sale takes place below cost, whereas this is not the case at all. It thus happens that in economics one has taken something for costs which were not costs (for example, work units), or one has used the wrong cost concept (historical cost, i.e. monetary sacrifices made earlier). On the other hand, it often happens that the effect of the law is neutralized by other forces. In that context, one may speak of a trend, because it becomes apparent that in reality (in regard to concrete phenomena) the law's effect will not always be expressed externally, in those concrete phenomena.

We have discussed this particular criticism at length because, in our experience, it is especially at this point that the conception of value and price theorists leads to completely irrational actions which make us wonder where one may find the effect of the economic motive, which is the force controlling all human actions. In the train of thought of these theorists *cancelling* of production does not fit, only the elimination of production, after the production apparatus - in this case the enterprise - is destroyed. They can only think of the *long range* effect, not of an immediate effect of the economic motive in every part of the production process. They never assume in their explanations that a producer will compare costs and proceeds. They will let him compare an earlier market price with the present market price, or a price anticipated in the future with the present price, or perhaps a market price with sacrifices made earlier.[9]

We can conclude the argument with the proposition that a producer has to appear as calculator not only in the buyers' market but also in the sellers' market. And this not only for the theoretical reason set out earlier - that it is illogical to introduce a producer as a calculator in the buyers' market, but not as a calculator in the sellers' market - but also for the practical reason that, for the majority of producers, the prices in the buyers' market are *given* and can be affected much less than the prices in the sellers' market. The normal situation is generally that cost is a given and the sales price has to be determined. A producer in that sellers' market is usually not the helpless possessor of goods which, for him, have no appreciably positive, or even a negative marginal value, but as the possessor of goods which, for him, have an objective value which can be accurately determined in the continuous stream, so that costs and proceeds can be, and must be weighed against each other.

Third Defect: Identification of the Offering Price with the Value Assessment of the Producer

We will now deal with the third defect in value and price theory which is being criticised here. *The producer's value assessment is wrongly identified with the offering price.*

That the value assessment and offering price have to be two very different things, already follows from the theory of exchange. They cannot be the same, because an exchange would then no longer be rational. It has been rightly argued in modern value theory, that exchange would not be economically motivated if both parties did not benefit. If the offering price is in accordance with the producer's value

9 The discussion has been abbreviated at this point. Limperg describes in detail the disastrous effects of the challenged theory when it was implemented. This could be observed in the years during which he raised this matter.

assessment, he would never benefit from exchange. It is clear that there is no advantage - assuming that the offering price indeed induces a buyer to exchange - to relinquish a good at a price which agrees with the value the good has for the seller. One does not need to be a producer for that. Therefore, one can never explain the fact that a producer obtains an income from the exchange.

The situation is actually very different. The prices obtained in the market, and therefore *a fortiori* the offering-price, must normally be *higher* than the value assessment, than the value of the good for the producer. *Next to this*, we find the offering price. The basic difference between the two is that value is an objective given, which is not determined by any action or by any insight of the producer, whereas, on the contrary, the offering price is controlled to a certain extent (only partly!) by the personal views of the person who has to determine this offering price in an industrial enterprise. The "subjective" evaluation of the mood in the market often plays a role here. The effect on the price formation will ultimately not be determined by these somewhat arbitrary offering prices, which, besides, are based on a value assessment. The confusion introduced in the theory, can only be sorted out if one makes a distinction between these two. For the *explanation of the mechanism* of price formation the offering-prices are of significance. But for the *explanation of the level of the price* - as it will be in the long run - the causal relationship with production is necessary: and that relationship is not established via the offering price but via the cost to the producer.

The question might arise in the mind of many whether, if one needs a calculation for the value assessment, the value assessment does not, after all, become dependent on the insight of the producer and whether one therefore does not arrive, after all, at a "subjective" value assessment. That question, however much conceivable, points to a thorough misunderstanding.

A producer as calculator can make *mistakes*. He may, for example, make an arithmetical error. He may even make a faulty calculation because he has an incorrect insight in the technique of cost calculation, or even in the nature of the costs. But those remain errors and difference which have nothing to do with a subjective judgement of the good. It is conceivable that the value of the good for a producer can often be better determined by his bookkeeper than by himself. It is possible, however, that the accountant is of the opinion, later on, that the bookkeeper made the wrong calculation. And it even occurs that two accountants will have a difference of opinion about the way in which the value has to be calculated. But all this relates to a difference of opinion about the calculation method, not about the importance of the good for the producer. Those differences will have to disappear in the long run with an increase in industrial-economic knowledge and insight. The value of the good remains the same.

So there is not only confusion and cause for confusion between price- or value assessment and offering price in the general economy but, there is also confusion and cause for confusion in the practice of industry and in part of the industrial-economic literature. The cause is to be found in the circumstance that, in practice, in the calculation (i.e. here the technical calculation of the offering price) a *profit mark up* is often calculated, sometimes in the form of a separately calculated profit mark up but also by a common mark up for profit with part of the costs. That profit surplus is then usually calculated as a percentage of the "remaining costs".

An example of each of these calculations may explain the technique.

Raw materials	$10	Raw materials	$10
Wages	10	Wages	10
Remaining costs	5		
	$25		$20
		Remaining costs	
Profit 20%	5	and 50% profit	10
Offering price	$30	Offering price	$30

These two calculations are indeed calculations for the determination of the offering price. The second obviously has the disadvantage that it is less accurate and less detailed and fundamentally incorrect. Combining costs and profits is a combination involving very heterogeneous elements of the offering price. The calculation we are dealing with is a calculation of what *is*; it is the calculation which one needs to work out the value. That value is here $25. The remaining $5 is in economic terms an *estimate* of expected profit or of desired profit. Because this estimate is now also presented as if it were exact, it acquires the appearance of being a calculation the same as that of the value of the product. This resemblance is indeed only a seeming one.

Calculating profit in this manner also creates the kind of confusion where, when studying the problem of price formation and the problem of value and costs, one has the impression that not only the formation of the price in the market is determined by the costs of production, but also by the profit added by the producer, in accordance with his own judgement and therefore arbitrarily, to those costs. This, of course, is theoretically impossible - that is to say, in general and in the long run; impossible at least for the cases we are always talking about in economics, when we do not indicate the opposite, namely cases of free exchange and free flow of new production. This can exist without any profit. No production fails to come about (that is to say, needs to fail to came about because of the economic motive), as long as the costs are covered by the proceeds. Here we point out that in the costs are included the work of the entrepreneur and capital servicing.

How should this profit calculation be considered in regard to the theory of price formation? As the result of experience in the market, or as the result of a prognosis of the future market situation?

Here we find what the value theorists assumed as a phenomenon for the *entire price*. On the assumption of a fairly stable profit margin, It is usually indeed a case of management in many companies, calculating with that profit margin as with a fixed given for the offering price. Theoretically, this calculated profit margin is, however, something quite different than calculated costs or calculated value. It can then also be observed that the so-called profit mark-up is often economically speaking a costs' mark-up for management salary and interest loss. This causes even greater confusion.

Fourth Defect: The Moment of Economic Exchange is Not Recognised

Finally, we will discuss a fourth defect of the theory. Price formation theory starts from the assumption that the goods which are being offered *have already been produced*. This is wrong theoretically and in reality.

In practice it is wrong, because a large part of production does not occur *before* but after the exchange. One can say that this is the case for the greater part of industrial production, which occurs *after* the exchange (on order) and therefore after one knows the sales price. For all products which are being exchanged *before* production the situation for the offering producer is in *actual fact* totally different from what the usual price formation theory assumes; price formation has already occurred before production takes place.

Theoretically the assumption is incorrect, not only where it is in conflict with reality but also for the other cases.

Let us first consider cases where production has still to take place. It is understandable that the theory according to which a disappointed supplier who finds his expectation, based on earlier prices, not realised, must sell at any price, loses its foundation. If a producer were always to arrive in the market with goods which had already been manufactured, he would get into a much more dependent position, especially if the good were subject to deterioration or economic change, such as changes in fashion.

But even in the majority of those cases where production actually precedes exchange, the situation is mainly theoretical and normal such, as if exchange preceded. This is because production does not occur incidentally but because of the effect of the law of continuity. The normal course of production is that, even if *formally* there is no order, a producer knows nevertheless that he will sell his products and usually even to whom and at what price.

There will no doubt also be moments when a buyer objects to an asking price and when he buys from another manufacturer. If a large number of buyers acts that way, a manufacturer will have to lower his price. He will, however, not yet be at the mercy of the whims of his buyers (if he calculates a reasonable price!), because those buyers, in their turn, cannot manage without the progress of the continuous flow of production; so even then we mostly have a situation in which theory does not accord with reality. However, once the continuous flow is delayed, or temporarily broken, circumstances may occur which agree with the teaching of price formation theory. Specifically in times of crisis. This, however, applies to *abnormal* circumstances. Production *normally* is geared to the price and not the other way round, even in the process which preceded exchange. If there is a disappointment because of unexpected circumstances, production will not be continued unless the producer knows whether he can be confident again that the proceeds will cover his costs. That is why after such a disappointment, production therefore will again be *omitted* if unfavourable difference between costs and proceeds exists.

However important a correct insight may be in the situation where there are abnormal cases, first the normal situation has to be found; this has to form the basis of price formation theory.

4. Conclusion From the Previous Section

On page 86 we put the proposition: a producer's value assessment is determined by the total production cost of a good. We know that a certain value assessment is at issue here, namely the assessment guiding a producer in his actions in his sellers' market when he decides his offering price.

We criticised the conceptions which prevail in usual price formation theories and we thus came to the opinion that value assessment is one which is based not on the sellers' market prices, but on the production costs of the product. In other words: production only makes sense if the price in the sellers' market exceeds the costs of production and it is therefore necessary that a producer bases his offering price on those costs.

This idea needs to be worked out in more detail in regard to the *value* of the good offered in the market. The value of a good is the quantitative expression of the importance which that good has for the producer's prosperity. What importance does a good which a producer offers, have for his prosperity? Because, in continuous production, the replacement value is usually lower than the sales value, this importance is normally expressed in terms of replacement value. And this, in its turn, is again determined by the sacrifices which are required to replace the good which has already been manufactured, or the means of production which will be required for the product which still has to be manufactured. And also we can thus say that the value of a product for the offering producer is determined by the total of production costs, but not by past production costs. They are either production costs of the product which still has to be manufactured, determined by the replacement costs of the means of production which are to be used for this, or the replacement costs of the finished product, the production costs, therefore, of the replacement good.

This is the normal state of affairs with the value of a product for the producer and this normal situation will, in any further analysis, be accepted as a basis. We know that the value of a good is determined by the smallest of two values we have distinguished, the replacement value and the realization value. Again, in normal circumstances, the replacement value is lower. But in those cases where the realization value is lower, *that value* will determine the value for a producer. We should also understand *this* situation. Because even if it is at variance with a rational situation, it nevertheless occurs repeatedly, more often even than a producer, and all of us, care for. It is important to appreciate that the realization value too, is not the subjective utilization value for the producer and that, even then, the value of a good for the producer is not reduced to zero. Nor is that realization value determined only by value assessments of interested parties. The offers and stocks of the offering producers still affect the market price and therefore the realization value. Therefore, it needs to be kept in mind that the proposition we have put is only correct for normal cases. In abnormal cases, which nevertheless occur repeatedly, price formation will be affected by a value assessment of the producer, which is determined by the realization value, thus by the price of the product in the sellers' market. Only then, in the abnormal case, is a producer's value assessment no longer determined independently, but also by the other party, but never by this other party alone.

We can now determine more specifically and in general *the importance of cost for price formation.*

If we identify cost (i.e. the quantitative expression of the sacrifice in an exchange in the organic context of production) with the production costs of the replacing product, we find from the discussion above, that it is one of the factors determining price in the buyers'- and sellers' market. In the sellers' market it is also one of the factors which determines the price, if the sales price of the product is known, because it demonstrates, for each of the means of production, how high the sacrifice can be if production is to take place at a profit. In the sellers' market it will be one of the determining factors too, if the prices of the means of production are given. Its influence on the price formation of the sellers' market is a direct one, not an indirect one via the destruction of the enterprise, as one might wrongly conclude from price formation theory.

It is essential to establish here how important cost remains in this regard, in abnormal cases too, where proceeds of the product are smaller than its replacement value. This importance becomes no less, even in those cases where production does not precede price calculation, but is dependent on its result. At that moment, cost will prevent production.

And if production has already taken place, excessive cost will have a great significance for price formation as it will prevent a repetition of any unprofitable production. It then affects with full vigour, albeit for a next stage of the production, price formation.

For the rest, it always serves, and always makes itself felt as a measure for comparison besides the offering prices of the buyers.

5. The Relationship Between Cost and Price Formation Needs to be Elaborated on Three Points

Before discussing the root of the cost problem, namely the factors which determine this, we will deal with three points which form an addition to what has been described on p.86 in regard to the *difference* in the "value assessments" of the producers, a difference which is essential because it has its accurately defined significance and because it is not accidental.

For that reason we will discuss the problems of:

- buyers' and sellers' premium and the entrepreneur's premium
- rational price differences within the framework of the theorem of equal market price
- rational price differences which will be at variance with the theorem of an equal market price.

6. Buyers' and Sellers' Premium and the Entrepreneur's Premium

Social-economic theory usually deals with an over familiar price formation scheme. Let us examine this more closely, particularly the case which occurs most frequently of a market with producers on both sides.

The theory of price formation states that, when there is a difference in offering and asking price, supply and demand which lie outside the marginal pairs, will not be satisfied and that the satisfaction of demand and supply within the marginal pairs will take place at the same price (with small differences).

Let us look at an example out of Verrijn Stuart's textbook for a picture of what happens.[10]

Subjective Basis of Exchange of the

Buyers:	Sellers:
A Hfl.20	H Hfl. 7
B Hfl.18	I Hfl. 9
C Hfl.16	J Hfl.11
D Hfl.15	K Hfl.12
E Hfl.14	L Hfl.14.50
F Hfl.10	M Hfl.15.75
G Hfl. 8	N Hfl.17

As Verrijn Stuart demonstrates, the price will finally lie between Hfl.14 and Hfl.14.50. D and K are the marginal pairs still participants whilst E and L are not participating.

The question arises: why is it that producers on both sides arrive with, different asking- and offering prices. Why is it that only part of the producers is "satisfied" and another part goes away "unsatisfied"?

In the line of argument of the subjective value theory this is not really a question. Since we are dealing with "subjective" value judgements[11] we have to accept them!

However, this is not our line of thinking. There must be a cause why A is prepared to pay Hfl.20 for a good and G only Hfl.8; there is a cause which forces N to ask Hfl.17 for a good (his product), whereas H can be satisfied with Hfl.7.

To know that cause - and to know it *well* - is of the greatest importance for a proper understanding of price formation. We find that it resides in the circumstance that everyone finds his value assessment dictated by the cost of his product; buyers, because they can still produce at a profit their product for the manufacture of which the traded good is the means of production; the suppliers, because the offering price of their product covers at least their costs.

10 C.A. Verrijn Stuart, *The Foundations of Social Economics*, 1st ed. p.199; 3rd ed. p.223.

11 *Ibid.* p.199 and p.224 respectively.

If we leave out of consideration the causes which lead to the difference in cost, we can establish that *cost here demonstrates in a new way its significance for price formation.* It opens up a new point of view for the significance of the advantage which, according to the theory of price formation, comes into being because the buyer - as a result of the formation of a unit price - succeeds below his value assessment and the supplier above his value assessment.

Verrijn Stuart[12] called that advantage the "entrepreneur's premium" and "users' premium" whilst sometimes in the Anglo-Saxon literature it is referred to as the "producers" and "consumer's surplus" or "rent" (Marshall).[13]

We now find that this advantage is not an advantage stemming from price formation, the way Marshall and others saw it. Verrijn Stuart even calls it the most general form of business cycle profit![14] It is an advantage in the *production costs*, a favourable difference in cost, which a producer can use in any market.

The expression "rent" is valid for a consumer; his "rent" originates from his greater purchasing power which, with every purchase at the same price, causes him to make a sacrifice which is smaller than his fellow buyer with less purchasing power.

However, for the producer this expression is a total failure. Remember, his lower cost, for example as a result of the fact that his company is larger, makes him arrive in every buyer's market for each of his means of production as a buyer with the highest valuation for his product. If the idea of Marshall and Co. were correct, a producer would receive X times a producers' premium in X buyer's markets + 1 time in the seller's market, thus X + 1 times the favourable difference between his cost and the cost of the marginal entrepreneur.

Indeed, the so-called producers' - and consumers' - premium in price formation, or rather the *buyers'* - and *sellers' premium*, are nothing but reflections of the entrepreneur's rent, the entrepreneur's premium or *entrepreneur's profit.* Entrepreneur's profit is usually defined as the income of an entrepreneur. And one then has the concrete entrepreneur in mind.

In Vol. I, General Introduction, section 17, we have already established that we are of the opinion that in our present society one can no longer refer to a concrete "entrepreneur" concept, but only with the theoretical subject of *entrepreneurial activity*, with which one can combine a more useful concrete concept, entrepreneur's profit.

What, then, is the profit of the concrete entrepreneur? It is the entire income he obtains from the enterprise. Economists who use this concept, indicate that he has

---

12 C.A. Verrijn Stuart, *The Foundations of Social Economics*, 1st ed. p.210; 3rd ed. p.236.

13 A. Marshall, *Principles of Economics*, 8th ed. pp.124ff, 811, 830ff.

14 A. Verrijn Stuart, *op cit.*, 1st ed. p.210; 3rd ed. p.236.

used his capital in that enterprise and that in addition, he uses, his labour. That is the reason why classical economists already split entrepreneurial income theoretically into capital interest, entrepreneur's salary and entrepreneur's premiums. This way, a series of theoretical magnitudes comes into being, because in concrete terms an entrepreneur only obtains a homogeneous income, namely the difference between his production costs and the proceeds of his product. It is assumed that the concrete entrepreneur receives as capital interest an amount of interest in excess of the capital used, equal to the income which he would receive as a capitalist if he lent this capital at a fixed interest. It is also assumed that this concrete entrepreneur receives as entrepreneur's salary, a salary equal to the fixed salary which he would receive as a manager employed by another entrepreneur. If one subtracts these calculated quantities from total income, the real entrepreneur's premium (which is often split into entrepreneur's risk and entrepreneur's premium) remains.

According to our view of an entrepreneur *that* is the real entrepreneur's income. Remember, the entrepreneur's premium is payment *above* the amount the concrete individual would have received as fixed income. It is the added payment which is being received, the premium from the enterprise above what one would receive if one requires a fixed income.

How does this entrepreneur's premium come into being? Simply because in an industrial enterprise in which it is being created, *production takes place in more favourable conditions* than elsewhere, that is to say, than in the so-called marginal enterprise, which produces with costs which are equal to the proceeds of the product.

In the General Introduction[15] we previously indicated that generally many economists make a mistake when explaining an entrepreneur's premium as a risk premium. Accepting risk does not create income. We have already explained in that introduction why carrying risks is not the purpose or means of being an entrepreneur, but the result of linking the size of one's income to the results of the production process. If it were different, the person who accepted the greatest risk should also receive the highest income. This is obviously not the case. He often has the greatest losses. A marginal entrepreneur accepts a greater risk than the person who is standing at the other end of the row of entrepreneurs and risk increases as an enterprise approaches the marginal enterprise. It is therefore indeed illogical to wish to explain, in general, entrepreneur's premium as a risk premium, as a reward for the bearing of risk, even though it is true that profit is often made because one dared to accept risks.

---

15 Volume I: Introduction and Value. A. General Introduction: I. General concepts, sections 17 and 18. Some of the material here is the same as that covered in Volume I, but we have left it on purpose. Both parts of the text aim at explaining a phenomenon which is still being misunderstood.

Entrepreneur's premium can only be explained as a rational income category in terms of the more favourable conditions under which an enterprise carries out production, when compared with the marginal enterprise.

In regard to those more favourable conditions[16], we can categorise entrepreneur's premium into a number of premiums according to the nature of the "condition" from which they arise, i.e. according to the causes.

As stated in the Introduction, we make the following distinction:

a. Business Location Premium

b. Organisation Premium

Business Location Premium is derived from the more favourable conditions created by the relatively favourable location of the enterprise in regard to the natural state and the distance to the supplying and buying enterprises. It is the *Standorts-Praemie*, explained by Alfred Weber.[17]

Organisation Premium is received from the relatively favourable conditions, under which production proceeds in regard to the quantitative proportion of the means of production which are being used (more favourable proportionality), a more efficient organisation of management, a more efficient organisation of labour, etc.

It is mainly these two premiums which constitute an entrepreneur's premium. They in turn, can each be divided according to causes. One can thus speak of a *proportionality premium* in addition to the *efficiency premium* in the narrow sense (namely efficiency of labour). Both kinds of premiums can again be divided into a temporary and a permanent premium. That part of a premium, received by a producer, because he creates or captures a favourable condition before others, but which he loses when others *can* follow his example, is of a temporary nature. This premium which we will call lead or initial premium, (*voorsprongs premie*) will in the long run be eroded. It plays a large part especially in regard to the organisation premium. It is the premium which one obtains if one is able, before one's competitors, to apply new discoveries, put into operation larger equipment, capture new markets, etc. It is also the premium associated with Schumpeter's "new

---

16 Volume I: General Introduction, section 18 mentions *two* general causes: (1) the existence of a monopoly or monopoly type position for the enterprise; (2) the unequal conditions under which enterprises produce and exchange. Market forms and the issue of power are *in these cases* irrelevant.

17 A. Weber, *Industrial Sites*, 1922

combinations".[18] But it is not the only premium, it is not even the real premium; it only exists as long as this lead exists.

The lead premium is of great importance, because it forms an impetus in industry, with all its advantages and disadvantages. When it has stopped, however, a permanent premium remains in many cases; permanent also in a static society (without risk!): the *permanent premium of the establishment site* and the *permanent organisation premium*. As regards the former, it is easy to understand that this can be partly permanent; for the latter this is perhaps doubtful. But there is no reason for such doubt because one only needs to remember the increased efficiency when larger units of the means of production are used. To be sure, a large concern cannot satisfy all needs efficiently and in many industries a small enterprise remains useful and efficient for part of the needs. Albeit that often such enterprises only barely exist, literally as a marginal enterprise on the periphery of the market; a large enterprise can thus have a permanent efficiency premium.

To the extent that the premiums we have mentioned are lead premiums, it is understandable that the premiums are perceived to be risk premiums, although this is wrong. Remember, "having a lead" often means taking additional risk. One can therefore say in every day life that the daring and the spirit of enterprise have been rewarded with this premium. Indeed, it is often found in industry that courage in accepting risk offers a rich reward to an enterprising capitalist and occasionally also to an enterprising worker. But, only if the enterprise *is successful*. That condition of "being successful" means precisely that the source of the premium does not reside in running a risk, but in the relatively favourable conditions under which it was found one could finally produce, *after* running that risk.

It should, besides, be pointed out that a lead premium is by no means always obtained in circumstances when special risks are run. Where a very large factory applies a new discovery and if it therefore has to replace certain equipment with new equipment, such an enterprise keeps its lead premium, without any new risk; or, putting it more accurately, it replaces the old premium by a new one, after the old premium enabled the company to write off completely the old equipment in good time, whereas the competing company was not able to do this and thus stays behind all over again. In this way a lead premium also can therefore acquire a more permanent nature.[19]

---

18 J. Schumpeter, *Theory of Economic Development*, 2nd ed. Munich/Leipzig, 1926, Ch. II, *Das Grundphänomen der Wirtschaftlichen Entwicklung*, pp.100ff.

19 We highlight here the two causes for a lead premium to acquire a more permanent nature: (a) continuity in the relatively larger size of the production units and (b) continuity in modernisation and improvement of the units.

Finally, it should be mentioned that a premium may exist which neutralizes a negative factor in the production, so that, in the end, not even an entrepreneur's premium results. We should mention, as an example, a small enterprise on a particularly favourable business location.

All these causes of the origin of a premium are potential causes for a producer to offer a higher price in the buyers' market, and to offer a lower price in the sellers' market than his competitor. Only when looking at the matter in this way, can one understand the price formation scheme of price theory and understand why it acquires real significance.

There is no question of "*rent*" originating from *price formation*. Even less of a profit caused by the business cycle. The latter is obtained from price fluctuations in the buyers' market. "Rent" is obtained from more favourable conditions of production.

The entire theory of "rent" from price formation is a beautiful example of twisted thinking, originating from vague reasoning, not based on reality, by people who do not know reality.

It is the marginal enterprise which is forced to ask the highest price and to offer the lowest price when playing the market. And with the enterprise at the other end of the line it is the other way around. The former moves with difficulty in the market, struggles with prices; the latter arrives easily at the prices it can afford to ask or to offer, he finds it easy to compete. But a premium does not arise in that way. The premium is formed by the favourable differences between proceeds and costs.

7. Rational Price Differences Within the Framework of the Proposition of an Identical Market Price

Previously, we have always spoken only of the significance of cost in price formation, which is expressed in a uniform price. Price formation is indeed of great importance in economic theory. But it is by no means the only aspect of importance and it is therefore necessary that attention is now paid to price *difference*. One thus avoids one-sidedness. Moreover, through those price differences, cost acquires a much greater significance.

We divide price differences into those differences having a rational place within the scope of the theorem of an equal market price, and other differences which lie outside this scope, and which are really at variance with this proposition. In this section we will deal with the first group.

Of course, theorists also have seen that in real life prices are not as uniform as they assert. This, in itself, does not say anything against the theory; the real point is of course agreement between the economic law, the abstract phenomenon and the trends in actual phenomena. There are many deviations which for the theory are the result of interfering influences, which are only temporary, even though they can immediately come to life again by new interfering influences. Among these interfering influences the theory includes the power factors which prevent free price formation, because they impede the free exchange assumed by the theory. This will not be discussed here, so as not to spend too much time on price formation theory itself.[20] Here we are only developing an addition and a correction to present price formation theory. Our concern is with price differences which arise and are justified even when free exchange and free price formation operate faultlessly.

The "equal price" of price formation theory only applies to *one* market, i.e. a market with the same buyers and sellers. Different markets exist for the same good and in these different markets goods obtain different prices. Think of the price differences of American wheat in America and the same wheat in Europe; and especially of the price differences of the same good in an industry in successive markets, which occur between the various stages (import trade, wholesaler, retailer, consumer).

It is strange that so little attention has been paid by the theory to these divergences. From what does this price difference arise? Essentially from nothing but a difference of *costs*.

1. This is of special significance for the price difference for identical goods in successive markets. Such a series of successive markets arises from the differentiation of the branches of industry and this differentiation finds its origin in a cost difference between the transfer in stages of the original product to the consumer via intermediate independent branches of industry and a direct transfer from the original producer to the final consumer. One finds that by the insertion of an independent industrial branch production costs (calculated from the original producer to the consumer) may decrease. A simple example should clarify this. The wholesale stage in the paper trade, located between paper manufacturers and bookshops, printers, etc., makes it possible to produce greater quantities in specialised factories. The paper market[21] is split by

20 According to Limperg the phenomenon of the so-called "interfering influence" is of great importance and he blames theory for having spent altogether too much energy on analysing a non-existing world. That reality has indeed become part of his own theory and has been set within the framework of the *Theory of the external organisation* in which power relations are discussed. See Part IV: Chapter III C.

21 For the sake of clarity we add the word *horizontal* here: the market between paper manufacturer and wholesaler and that between wholesaler and consumer, being a differentiation in the stages of industry.

wholesalers, into two markets where different prices operate for the same good. Buyers and sellers are therefore split in two. A uniform price will come into being in each market, apart from the "irregularities" mentioned above, but the two uniform prices are not the same. The difference between the two is formed by the *costs* of the marginal entrepreneur in the differentiated wholesale business. However, it is clear that this price difference in no way affects general price formation theory. The theory just does not take the analysis that far.

2. The same can be said in regard to the price difference between goods of the same kind, but of a different quality. Here too, we are often dealing with goods which, from the point of view of price formation theory, are being traded in different markets. There are usually different buyers and sellers for different quality goods. On the other hand, part of the buyers and sellers will usually compete in two or more of those markets,[22] but there is generally a group of buyers and sellers who drop out. There is an interdependence between the price formation in those different markets, because buyers and sellers will shift with the price movement, but price formation in each of the markets essentially refers to different goods.

   It is, on the other hand, important that we realise that in this context too, the price difference is brought about by the difference in costs. When a better quality is obtained through another, more costly processing of a good, the producer will have to make good those higher costs. When, conversely, a buying producer, because of the better quality of a good which for him, is raw material or auxiliary material, results in decreased production costs (for example, by using a smaller quantity, by better technical output, etc.) this producer will be prepared to pay a higher price because of the costs he has saved.

3. Finally, even for goods which are completely identical, there are price differences originating in the same market, i.e. price differences which are connected with a difference in delivery time, instead of delivery and difference in time of payment. It is known that there are different price quotations for "prompt" delivery time and goods delivered at a later date. We thus find price differences for delivery on location, f.o.b. a certain port, from the factory, etc.

---

22 This is *vertical* split in the production stage of the good, the result of specialisation.

And, finally, there are different prices for cash delivery, or in one or more months.

The first differences can apparently be explained from the fact that in economic terms we are dealing here with *different* markets. This becomes very clear when we keep in mind that to a certain extent there are even different technical markets for transactions with "prompt delivery" and "on instalment". The technical organization of the instalment market is often different from that of the other market. But in the instalment market itself there are again different buyers and sellers for the different instalments.

The situation is different for the two other categories of price difference. They apparently originate from the circumstance that payment for other services can be included in the prices of goods, namely *transport* services and *finance* services respectively. These services can be considered, on the one hand, as cost categories for the offering producers; on the other hand they are goods and services on behalf of the various buying producers, which justify separate payment without causing a divergence from the theory of a uniform price.

On the other hand, the question arises, how *identical* prices can be explained for goods *at a different place of delivery*. It is known, remember, that many producers deliver their goods carriage paid at the place of destination, although the costs do differ and although this does result in a difference in the price of the goods, because transport is included in that price.

We will not offer an explanation for the fact that the one occurs (geographic price differences) as well as the other (uniform price in spite of geographic differences of delivery locations). It should suffice that attention is paid to the fact that, if the price is identical when a good is mailed from different mailing places to the same destination, an establishment premium comes into being for the selling producer who is situated most favourably in regard to the place of destination situated. Conversely, when there is a difference in price, this premium comes into being for the buying producer who is located most favourably in regard to the mailing place, if the mailing is done from one place to different destinations. These premiums are reflected in their turn in the various value assessments of the buying and selling producers in the market.

8. Rational Price Differences Which are at Variance with the Proposition of an Identical Market Price

We will discuss two important groups, namely price differences which are related to *quantities* which are involved in one exchange, and price differences which depend on the *use which is being made of goods.*

1. Price differences on account of exchanged *quantities* can show us that even outside the margins indicated by the classic price formation scheme, there is the possibility for an exchange, even in a completely free market. The scheme shows that with certain differences in cost only a part of all buyers and sellers will take part in the exchange, and this, at a uniform price. This is incomplete and not in accordance with reality. This will become clear from the following example.

   1000 kg yarn of one kind can be spun much quicker in one run than 10 x 100 kg of the same kind at different points of time. It is therefore understandable that the person who orders 1000 kg wants to pay less than the person who buys 100 kg. And the supplier should not object to charging the former a lower price, because per unit costs for carrying out this order are lower. The large buyer finds in the lower unit price of his raw material one of the elements of his entrepreneur's profit or entrepreneur's premium and, in fact, part of his organisation premium. The theory[23] also states that large scale production leads, to a certain extent, to lower production costs. One of the factors of lowering cost can be found in the opportunity to pay a lower price for larger quantities, in addition to costs savings which can be obtained in one's own production process. This premium could not exist if a uniform price were to be introduced.

   We will illustrate our argument with the help of Verrijn Stuart's[24] price formation scheme dealt with earlier (on p.97). The marginal pairs are D and K (who, as we saw, were still participants) and E and L (who will no longer participate). They are sometimes also called respectively the marginal pair for the price upward and for the price downward?

---

23 See Part IV: *Theory of the external organisation*, Chapter XI: The issue of the size of an enterprise.

24 C.A. Verrijn Stuart, *The Foundations of Social Economics*, 1st ed. p.199; 3rd ed. p.223.

Verrijn Stuart assumes here that each of the suppliers and buyers arrives in the market for one unit. But this means that a very important element is being kept outside the argument. The *number* of units plays an important part, not only in regard to the general price, but also for exchanges to actually come about. One particular enterprise can buy on a large scale, the other cannot; one enterprise can supply on a large scale, the other cannot. This does not need to lead to a separation in the market, the groups are competing with each other. It is thus possible that G (the buyer at Hfl.8) does *not* "go home disappointed". H offers at Hfl.7 *in case he can find a large-scale buyer.* If only G is such a large-scale buyer, then H benefits perhaps much less from a price of Hfl.14 to Hfl.14.50 (uniform price), if he has to sell to A, B, C and D. G's price of Hfl.8 can be much more advantageous for him. An exchange will come about which would not take place at the uniform price. Because the fact that G cannot pay more than Hfl.8, may be caused, for example, because his factory is located very unfavourably; he depends on his large quantities, his organisation premium. You cannot therefore talk about an isolated exchange, because it takes place under fully competitive conditions.

It is also possible that A (buyer at Hfl. 20) or someone else who would be able to pay the uniform price - and who would, according to Marshall, even obtain a premium! - does not *wish* to pay more than he knows is necessary because of the manufacturing quantity which is advantageous for the supplier. If he has to compete with G he will offer Hfl.9 and he will exchange with H or I (suppliers at respectively Hfl.7 and Hfl.9) if they are able and willing to supply the large quantities. Thus A will succeed *below* the uniform price, which the theory uses as a starting point. In other words, A will see to it that the sellers' premium which, according to the theory of the uniform price, would flow to H, does not cause his organisation premium to disappear. The cause of this phenomenon therefore lies in the *specifically* lower production cost of H or I.

2. Finally, another category of price differences finding their origin in cost differences among the interested parties, so that part of them would be unable to buy at the general market price; their valuation for the good is so low that they would not be interested at that general market price. Under certain circumstances *different* prices would result. These price differences are at variance with the general market price, and are only possible, because the operation of the value assessments of the marginal pairs is being eliminated.

The freight tariffs of a regular shipping line will serve as an example. It is a well-known phenomenon that a distinction in price is often made in these tariffs for the transport of different goods and this difference is sometimes substantial. How does such a price difference arise?

Let us assume that a shipping line uses ships of 5000 tons to maintain regular traffic between two countries. Assuming for the sake of convenience that the ships are always fully loaded with different kinds of goods, for which the tariff has come into being and is being maintained through the operation of free competition. The ordinary tariff is Hfl.40 per ton.

Freight received per trip	5000 x Hfl.40 =	H fl.200,000
Costs per trip		H fl.180.000
Profit per trip		H fl. 20.000

The enterprise discovers (or some other entrepreneur finds out) that in one of the countries there is a product which would make transport to that country worthwhile - that is to say, it could be sold there at a profit - if the freight were no more than Hfl.15 per ton. If this were possible, 5000 tons of this product could be shipped per trip.

It is discovered that, if ships of 10,000 tons are brought into service, the costs per trip will be $250,000. Again for the sake of convenience, we leave out of consideration the question of return freight, because we can also assume that in the reverse direction too, a product can be transported under similar conditions. The shipping line's calculation would now be as follows:

10,000 tons costs	Hfl.250,000
revenue of the 5000 tons existing trade (at hfl.40)	Hfl.200.000
loss (with increased tonnage)	Hfl. 50,000
present trade, with the old tonnage, means a profit of	Hfl. 20.000
fall in income (with increased tonnage and insufficient load)	Hfl. 70,000
5000 tons new trade at hfl.15 (additional)	Hfl. 75.000
more profit (with increased tonnage and full load at two tariffs)	Hfl. 5,000

The shipping line would therefore act rationally if it were to take up this trade. What is it going to do? If it sets its tariff (for *all* trade) at Hfl.15, it will receive for existing trade 5000 x Hfl.25 = Hfl.125,000 less; in spite of lowering the costs per unit (5000 tons = Hfl.200,000 as against 10,000 tons = Hfl.250,000) and in spite of increased trade the line would not earn Hfl.5000 more, but Hfl.120,000 less. This would be crazy. A uniform tariff of

$$\frac{\text{Hfl.}250{,}000 + \text{Hfl.}20{,}000 + \text{Hfl.}5000}{10{,}000} = \text{Hfl.}27.50$$

would make the plan fail. What will the company do? It sets a special tariff for that (additional) trade and there is no price formation law which forces the company to discontinue in the long run this price difference.

Two points are important here.

There is *no* question of a "monopolistic" influence, as is often said, when such price differences for rail traffic are being discussed, although a monopoly position *can* have an effect on such price differences.

We are, indeed, dealing here with a price difference for a completely similar good. Remember, the good here is *transport service*, a service which is completely the same for each of the goods which are being transported. Of course, there can be different transport services, such as transport by weight or by volume, but we are not dealing with such a difference.

The existence of a price difference, as the example shows, is therefore possible. This means that the price is detached from what is called the operation of the price estimation of the marginal pairs. What does such a price difference mean? The enterprise, in setting its tariff, has taken account of what in such cases is called the paying capacity of the good which is to be transported. The supplier, in this case, has set his price lower for part of the interested parties (for the transport services), because the cost of their (to be transported) goods did not allow for a higher price. This means, therefore, *that the offering price has been set at a different level for different destinations of the same good.*

There is no room at all for such a difference in the price formation scheme of social economics and in its theory of a uniform price. It is precisely an axiom of that price formation theory that the mechanism of price formation operates in such a way that, whatever the differences in price estimations - that is to say, whatever the cost of the interested parties - *all of them* are served at the same price. Whoever cannot pay that general price, is sent home "disappointed". The producer of the good which can only bear a freight price of $15, would in Verrijn Stuart's scheme belong to those whose price estimation was below that of the marginal pair downward. Here, on the contrary, he is being received with open arms and one realizes that the costs of the offering producer are having an important effect. We see, on the other hand, that the costs of the shipping company have had a very important effect also. If the costs per ton of the larger ship had not been much lower than those of the 5000-ton ship, the company could not have made an offer.

These, and similar phenomena will be discussed in detail in this volume. At this moment, it is useful to establish from the above that, however valuable ordinary price formation theory is to us, one should nevertheless take into account phenomena which are not being explained by *that* theory, even those which are in conflict with that theory.

9. The Factors Which Determine the Level of Cost. Stating the Problem

We have taken an important step on the road to solving the cost problem. It is, however, only a first step, which has shown the connection between cost and price formation.

We now have to tackle the central problem which we can state as follows: what factors determine a product's cost? This problem will be broken into numerous sub-problems, which will be discussed successively. It is, however, essential that we keep in mind continuously what place this main problem has within the general theory, that we keep looking at it within the framework of the general price formation problem. That place then determines the content of the cost problem and of the cost concept.

This way of thinking shapes the problem, because what matters in the formulation of the problem is the cost price of the product at the moment when, at the place where and during the circumstances under which, it arrives in the market. It is a matter of cost as an element of price formation of the product which is being put on the market.

The concept of cost-price has acquired its specific and definite content from the multiplicity of concepts, which can be conveyed linguistically by that word (cost-price). We can, for example, speak linguistically of the cost of a certain quantity of products, which is larger or smaller than the market unit. Or we can speak of the cost of a product at a point in time earlier than the moment of putting it on the market and in a place different from the place of taking the product to the market; one speaks, for example, of the cost of a product at the moment it was finished: warehouse price, and of the product location factory, location railway station, etc. These are all uses of the word cost price which are linguistically correct and which do not necessarily lead to confusion, because they are within the boundary of the problem. When, however, we speak of *the* cost price, it is a matter of a clear-cut concept which was defined earlier (p.78):

> cost is the quantitative expression of the sacrifice made by the producer in the exchange of his product (within the organic relationship of production).

In order to set out this quantitative expression, one needs to take into account that this sacrifice is a composite. Admittedly, we encounter the product unit which is put on the market, as a single expression of the sacrifice, but that product is actually the result and the resultant of a great many sacrifices, whose magnitude we need to know if we wish to arrive at the quantitative expression of *the* sacrifice in the exchange. We thus see cost as the total of the sacrifices which are made when using means of production in producing the product unit. Finally, in the normal course of events, we can more accurately see *cost as the total of sacrifices when using the means of production for producing the replacement product unit.*[25]

10. General Discussion of the Economic Sacrifice

Sacrifice is the Occupation of Means

We remind readers of the discussion in Vol I: "Introduction and Value"[26] about the *economic* concepts of costs and sacrifice. In our theory the sacrifice concept is not a psychological concept, it should not be seen in the sense of suffering distress. In production it is just a matter of occupying the means which are available for the satisfaction of needs. Thus, in regard to the use of means of production, we speak of a sacrifice as soon as these means of production are not abundantly available. Because the user has the same means of production at his disposal only once, using it means occupying part of the means of production which are available for the satisfaction of needs as a whole (i.e. in a society based on exchange in the production for the formation of income). The use of a certain means of production therefore means the withdrawal from the use for other purposes. Thus, the means of production which have been used, become a sacrifice on behalf of, and thus are part of the costs of, the particular product for which that means of production is being used.

---

25 The actual replacement, as was said above, is not a condition for value determination by the manufacturer. Compare, for instance, Vol. I: B, *Theory of value*, III, section 7b: p.208ff. The replacement of used means of production is, however, the normal state of affairs in the continuity of the production process (p.210).

26 Vol. I: BI, section 14: p.108.

The most telling point is the contrast in conception in regard to human labour which has already been dealt with elsewhere.[27]

Actual Description of this Sacrifice

A second point of general importance is that it is essential to have a proper understanding of what really is the sacrifice that is made in production when one uses means of production in the production process.

We know what *raw materials* are. This is simple. One can say that the sacrifice consists in those raw materials themselves, which are transformed into the product. They are the *passive means of production.*

We also know about the *active means of production.* These can be divided into *auxiliary materials*, which disappear in the production process, without, however, being transformed into the product materially, *human labour*, and the *tools* which we will discuss later.

Of the *auxiliary materials* the physical capacity is applied to the passive means of production. This capacity is also partly physically, but not materially, transformed into the product. One obvious example consists of the fuel used for heating processes. Fuel is not transformed materially into the product, but, insofar as heat alters its quality and form, it is transformed physically. It would therefore be possible in this case, to consider immaterial physical heat as the sacrifice made for the production. But it is apparently here only a matter of words. Whether we consider coal as the sacrifice, rather than the calories it contains, is of no importance economically. To determine the economic significance of the sacrifice, we will have to take into account, however, the circumstance that the calories which were used were contained in that coal, of which the price differs from that of other fuel. We therefore look upon coal which has been used as the sacrificed means of production.

Something similar applies to *human labour* and the work carried out by *equipment or tools*. In regard to the latter we know that no piece of equipment is transformed into the product, nor does material disappear through wear and tear, but that usually only immaterial production capacity is used, or occupied. A *tool* is *the stock of work units* being used up. When we say, therefore, that tools form the sacrifice for production, we mean the immaterial work units which are being used up, whilst the tool, as a technical entity remains completely unchanged.

---

27 Ibid. p.109.

The Valuation of the Sacrifice

A third point concerns the valuation of the sacrifice. So far, only a physical expression of the sacrifice has been made, albeit that we are not tied exclusively to a physical-material expression. However, this does not provide a complete economic expression for our free exchange society. In order to obtain this we have to assess the physical sacrifice at its value and, this is done through establishing the economic magnitude by means of the price, after the physical magnitude of the sacrifice has been determined. The price is expressed in money, i.e. purchasing power. The economic magnitude of the sacrifice is therefore determined by *valuing the physically measured sacrifice in terms of its purchasing power.*

Measuring the Sacrifice: Historical Cost and Economic Cost

The fourth and last point of general importance concerns the problems which are connected with that measurement of the magnitude of the sacrifice in money, which may lead to misunderstanding and indeed have done so in the past causing serious errors in theory and practice.

In the past, it was the generally held and many people are still of that opinion,[28] that, in determining the magnitude of the sacrifice, it is a matter of determining the size of the capital tied up in an enterprise, when it obtained the means of production. This is a totally wrong conception of what actually happens.

This controversy has already been touched on when we were discussing the cost concept (p.78). We disagree with the conception which defined the cost concept as the quantitative expression of the sacrifice when the means of production are being obtained, instead of the quantitative expression of the sacrifice during the exchange of the product.

We will now discuss this controversy in detail. We postulate that is now no longer just a matter of the content of a concept or of the meaning of a word. The word cost can be given this or that meaning, that is not of prime importance. It is now a matter of the magnitude of the sacrifice itself, as that quantitative expression is actually a basis for the offering price of the product, i.e. the exact content of the cost. Which magnitude determines, or is the basis of, the offering price, the sacrifice in money or capital made earlier, or is it the value at the moment of the exchange?

---

28 The last time Limperg worked on this text was 1935. To show that his statements are still relevant we refer to a few more recent arguments against the application of replacement value when calculating either cost price or profit. O. Bakker, *Business Economics*, Vol. III, 3rd imp., Purmerend, 1956; J. Kreiken, *Objective Profit Calculation and the Dangers of Replacement Theories for Business and Society*, Haarlem, 1957; L. van Kampen Jr., *Problems Around the Issue of Secret Reserves*, Arnhem, 1957.

Either the means of production being used for the production, has value for the enterprise, or it does not. If it has value for the enterprise, the use of that means of production also entails a sacrifice and, in fact, precisely the size of the value of the means of production, no more and no less.

It is clear that it is completely immaterial in economic terms, whether earlier on an enterprise has, or has not used capital for the means of production that is being used. Nor is it relevant how much capital was used, at least for the present purpose, namely the determination of the size of the cost of the product as a basis for the offering price.

If the good has a value for the producer, potential capital is tied up in it at that moment up to that value. If the means of production has no value at the moment of the exchange, then no potential capital is tied up in it.

Considerable misconceptions prevail about whether value is known, or whether value should be attributed to a means of production for the producer. These misconceptions are in line with the reprehensible conception in this traditional theory about the size of the cost price.

One of the most telling examples is the following. The owner is made a present of the means of production; this example is not impractical, one only needs to think *of the work of a volunteer*. Does this also indicate that using this labour means that there is *no* sacrifice made by the producer? This conception which frequently occurs is obviously incorrect. The use of the labour of a volunteer means an economic sacrifice on behalf of the product which the volunteer has worked on (in as far as this labour was useful for production). The product costs something, namely the amount of volunteer labour, notwithstanding that the owner of the enterprise obtained that labour for nothing. The sacrifice of volunteer labour in the product should therefore be valued, measured in money, if the manager wishes to know the correct cost of the product. Here is another illustration of the mistake which is made, if one thinks of value measurement as a calculation of the capital which was used earlier in the means of production: if we assume that a *means of production has increased or decreased* since it was obtained. One may assume that in general the means of production was obtained in exchange for a sacrifice in money matching the value of the means of production at that moment. When it was obtained part of the capital of the enterprise was therefore used in that means of production, the size of the former matching the value of the latter.

If the value - for whatever reason - is found to have changed at the moment when the size of the sacrifice has to be established in the product to be traded, there can be no doubt about the answer to the question which value determines the size of the sacrifice. *A value which held good in the past, can not have anything but historical significance.* Only the value at the moment at which the sacrifice is made during the exchange, can obviously determine the size of the sacrifice and therefore become a function of the offering price.

The contrast made here between the value applicable at the moment the means of production were obtained and the value at the moment in which the sacrifice is made during the exchange, also applies irrespective of the theory of the replacement value. And it equally applies when the value of a good is determined by its sales profit (ie profit on realization). However, the contrast assumes an even greater importance within the framework of the replacement value theory, where in a society based on free exchange the value of a good for a producer is generally its replacement value. Thus the replacement value theory strengthens the conception according to which the historical cost or purchase price[29] is *not* a function of the offering price, because we find that the value of a good is determined by the sacrifices which need to be made for its replacement - and not for its purchase.

The conception which is generally held and which differs[30] the one we advocate ascribes to the phrase cost price the meaning of the historical details, in industrial economic theory as well as in social economic theory. We therefore interpret the word differently. Historical features no doubt have a real significance in addition to the features of cost as we use that term. That given shows, in comparison with the proceeds of the product, what has been gained or lost in production, starting from the amount of acquisition - i.e. from laying them in stock - of the means of production. Producer and bookkeeper see "reality" in this notion. This is only a historical reality, however.

It may seem as if, for example, a producer had made a profit in the exchange, whereas economic reality may be that he did not make a profit but a loss in that exchange, or perhaps made less profit than historical cost-based calculations would reveal. It is therefore expedient to label the two concepts (which both represent a certain reality) with different words. This can be done by speaking of *historical cost* and *economic cost*; however, the word cost has to be set aside later for the concept which indeed indicates the *costs*, the *sacrifice* in the economic sense, as it fits into the framework of the greater problems of costs, of value and of price formation. Historical cost can then be called the *purchase price.*

---

29 This term, introduced on p.278, is preferable and will be used hereafter.

30 In 1935 Limperg observes fundamental differences between the "generally held conception" and his own views. But he also establishes that this generally held conception is gradually becoming a "fairly widely held opinion" and that within the system of thought he promotes one can detect a significant change in ideas which, however, has not yet touched the fundamental concepts. Therefore the other opinions still need discussing. Although it is now 30 years later, the editors see no reason to omit this part of the discussion. Certain sections have been shortened, leaving untouched some of the more "famous" illustrations.

Some Examples: Labour of the Volunteer and of the Owner of the Enterprise

The difference in conception, however, far exceeds a difference in terminology, a difference in the use of a word. We demonstrate this with the aid of some examples.

Initially, we refer back to *volunteer labour*, not because it is so important, but because it is so simple and so clear.

We assume that in an engineering works a certain machine, or one or more parts of a machine, are made by a volunteer. The bookkeeper records accurately the raw materials which are being used and the wages which are being paid for the manufacture of the machine. When the machine is finished, he adds up the amounts and in all sincerity tells the works manager that this total is the "cost" of the machine. If, on the basis of the purchase price established accurately by the bookkeeper, the manager sets his offering price, the result will be that he gives the buyer the volunteer labour for nothing. That this is incorrect in economic terms, is obvious. If a present is to be given, this should go to the manufacturer - who, as against that present, trains the volunteer and incurs costs elsewhere - and certainly not to the buyer. At first sight there seems no real damage, but a closer look shows that such an offering price, which has been calculated at too low an economic level leads to too low a revenue.

Admittedly, it is only a matter of losing profit, and no loss is being suffered. But it is essential to realize the further consequences. Next time the same machine is ordered the offering price is asked for in advance. The manufacturer consults his accounts and there finds the previous purchase price. All other factors having remained the same - he repeats his previous offer. But he no longer has a volunteer. The result is that labour now has to be paid for in the usual way. The machine becomes a losing proposition or, if this time a correction is carried out in regard to the calculation of labour, a higher price will have to be asked for the same product. The calculation set out here will not be conducive to a good relationship with the buyer, nor help to obtain a correct picture of the results of the production and of the way the enterprise operates. The incomplete accounts provide different cost prices under equal circumstances.

A different and more important example. No monetary sacrifice is made either by the owner or by the enterprise for labour performed by the owner of an enterprise, i.e. the members of partnership. No sacrifice in labour made by these persons therefore is expressed in the purchase price. The practical consequences in regard to the calculation of the so-called cost prices will here be the same as in the cases of volunteer labour.

In the rest of the discussion many more, and very important differences between the cost price and so-called "reality" will be discovered. It is essential that one understands that this "reality" is *not* economic reality.

11. The Consequences of A Price Change

We now need to discuss the *consequences of a price change* and the resulting differences between purchase price and economic cost price. We are here dealing with errors which are of a different nature, as will be seen later. But they have in common with errors discussed earlier, that they arise from the wrong conception about the nature of cost and about the rational basis of the offering price. As a striking example we select enterprises where the prices of the raw materials show strong fluctuations. We choose for that purpose an oil factory and a cotton mill (spinning and weaving).

If an oil manufacturer, expecting a price rise, has bought a supply of oil seeds to process in the future, and if the price falls, the price of oil, as we know from experience, and as can be explained economically for that matter, will also go down. What should the manufacturer do about his purchase price? He cannot do anything. Were he to set his offering price on the basis of that purchase price, he would find that there would be no buyers.

It can also happen of course, in spite of complete accounts and all, that a producer cannot find buyers at a price which leaves a profit margin above his economic cost. But in this example he completely loses the apparatus of the calculation made on the basis of his accounts. If the accounts had been correct and had therefore the cost calculation been correct, the producer would have been able to differentiate between the cost of the product, calculated on the basis of the replacement value of his stock, and the loss he has suffered because of his premature purchase, his failed "speculation". The word speculation should not be understood in the usual disapproving meaning, but only as indicating a transaction aimed at obtaining an advantage from successive price differences in the same market.

The Effect of an Incorrect Calculation on Price Policy

Here we come to the heart of the problem. The challenged calculation and methods of bookkeeping lead to a situation in which loss through speculation or stock losses e.g. "cyclic losses" are marked down as production costs and which - in the case of price increases - stock profits or speculation profits, c.q. "cyclic" profits are subtracted from costs none of which have anything to do with production costs, i.e. with the cost price of the product being offered. If the manufacturer had not created stock, or if he had formed it at a later date - assuming this to be technically possible - he would have arrived at a different purchase price for the same product.

In practice we often find that managers with a lot of common sense do intuitively what theory, on the basis of careful reasoning, indicates as correct.

However, here we have to state that a correct calculation, free from purchase prices, occurs far less frequently than one might expect, in view of the importance of the problem. A correct calculation occurs most often in those industries where price fluctuations of raw materials are many and considerable. In those industries one acts, in principle, in an economically correct way; although calculation on the basis of the purchase price is nevertheless evident in many companies. When prices fall in the buyers' market one is, however, forced to put these aside, whereas, when prices rise, one believes one can gradually afford to obtain a greater profit margin. This leads to a totally wrong price policy.

It is worth while illustrating this with an example. In practice one does not often have an opportunity to observe accurately the consequences of such an incorrect price policy. If, in general it is the lack of economic insight that causes an incorrect price policy in an industry, it often happens that the producer, who wants to adhere to the correct price policy, is persuaded to go along with others.

If, in an industry, in spite of a price rise of raw materials in the buyers' market, the majority calculates incorrectly, and therefore sets the offering prices too low, the individual who does make the correct calculation and who therefore arrives at a higher offering price, cannot find buyers for his product. On the face of it, he cannot compete. The others, of course, if they sell below cost regularly, will not be able to keep going and in the long run they will, have to give up, but the correct calculator cannot wait for this. Anyway, it happens (and one often finds this in the retail business), that casualties will be replaced by new entrepreneurs who, in their turn, because of incorrect calculation, will cause this so-called *price erosion.* Virtue - which here means, the correct economic insight - is therefore not always rewarded in business, unless one is able to impart this correct economic insight in a wider circle; a generally healthier price policy then exists and the individual producer then has a better chance to maintain a correct price policy.[31]

We assume, in another, elementary example, that we are dealing with a branch of industry with a number of enterprises all making the same kind of product and all relying, for their raw material, on the purchase by *one* enterprise, for example, a trust (which makes it therefore possible to assume, in the previous phase of the industry, uniformity of conception in price policy). Among the producers there is one who forms stock, all others buy progressively as they need the raw material. The stock represents one month's sale. So manufacturer A who keeps stock on hand is with his purchases always one month ahead of his competitors. Whereas the latter

31 To get an idea of the developments that made this correct economic insight popular in broader circles in our country, see S. Kleerekoper: *Handbook of Comparative Business Economics*, 1956, Chapter XIII, esp. Part C.

immediately transfer to the trust the demand for their product into a demand for raw materials, manufacturer A does this too, but he replenishes his stock with it. *All* manufacturers thus transfer to the trust the demand for their products, but A supplies the good he has received only in the product of the following month, whereas the others process the raw material into the product of the same month. There is obviously only for A a problem of choice between a calculation on the basis of the purchase price or on the basis of replacement value; the others have no stock and the two concepts, for them, coincide. We also assume that A calculates on the basis of the purchase price and that during a long period there will be an increasing demand for the product, subsequently changing to a decreasing demand.

The increasing demand for the product is transferred to the trust by all manufacturers. We assume that this trust is limited in its production. The inevitable result is then a price rise of the raw material. All manufacturers without stock are forced to immediately increase their prices for the product. Manufacturer A does not do so, having a stock of which the purchase price is lower. His stock will be sold quickly, of course. The other manufacturers have had more trouble. Their representatives initially report that A's offers are at lower prices and that they are therefore unable to sell. But this offer will soon finish and the increased demand will force up the price. Then the other manufacturers will be successful in achieving their turnover again. All manufacturers make the same profit. Now the downturn comes. The demand is decreasing, that is to say, the same quantity can only be sold at a lower price. The decreased demand again makes itself felt in demand for the raw material of the trust, which also decreases its price. All manufacturers experience difficulties in selling, but manufacturer A most of all. Because he still has expensive stock and he offers his product calculated on the basis of the purchase price. His representatives return with the message that they cannot place the good; the other manufacturers profit from the increased opportunity to sell and in the end A too has to lower his price. And this continues. Again and again A runs behind the price trend with his offering price. The end is a continuously increasing deficit, without his having made a surplus during the favourable time. If he had calculated with the economic cost price, he would have been compensated for the value increase of the stock in his product and that profit - which would have been only phantom or fictitious profit - could have been reserved for the times in which he would make a loss on his stock. He would not have used up the profit made because of the boom!

A Look at the Years During and After the First World War

This theoretical example can be observed often enough as a phenomenon in practice, although it rarely appears so strikingly that it is clearly visible for outsiders too.

Yet, during war years[32] and during its aftermath, we had the opportunity to observe the phenomenon also from the outside, because in those days it occurred so generally and to such an extent, and indeed in two ways: because of relatively increased demand in regard to supply and to production, and because of the weakening of the currency. This last factor obviously operated in exactly the same way as the price increase which was the result of a changed relationship between supply and demand.

What was happening at that time? In the first place, initially, practically everyone determined the size of the sacrifice on the basis of the purchase price, but gradually opinion prevailed that this basis was incorrect and that economic cost had to be the basis. Then, consumers and authorities objected to the exorbitant profits made by the possessors of stock if they took the increased prices in the buyers market into account. That does not mean, of course, that all price increases were based on these considerations. Because it is also a fact that many producers and businessmen charged their regular customers the price increases only reluctantly and there were many for whom the principle of calculation on the basis of replacement value, was not accepted, not even in the long run. In some shops one saw the most peculiar phenomenon that one and the same article was for sale at two different prices. Shop keepers, wholesalers and manufacturers offered articles from old stock at a price lower than the purchase price of the goods which they had already in stock from earlier consignments. People were generous to their customers and they even boasted about it because of all the money they made. But when the downturn came many people became victims of the incorrect system. The cause of the collapse for many lay precisely in that system. They thought they were rich and consumed an income which, for a great part, consisted only of "phantom profit" and, as a result, they lacked a buffer to break the drop in price. Because, with the theory of the replacement value as a basis of economic cost, another important principle is connected - namely that *profit resulting from a price rise*: profit from a boom, therefore - is *not* to be identified with profit from production.[33] People who identify cost with the purchase price, have to consider the profit made in a sale of stock, as profit from production. And they thus make a great mistake which can only be avoided if it is realized that the sacrifice made in the exchange, becomes greater through a price increase. In the exchange a profit is made only if, and insofar proceeds exceed the higher replacement value. One can hardly overestimate the practical significance of this truth. If one has this insight, one also understands that there is a large difference, in economic terms,

---

32 Reference here is to WW1. It is the editors' considered opinion that the entire line of argument is still valid today.

33 See Vol. VI: B, *Theory of Profit Determination.*

between book profit, made on stock, and profit which comes into being in the exchange. The former is profit caused by a boom, which will be lost sooner or later. Let us assume, for the sake of convenience, that there is stock of a constant size. One will be aware that this stock, because of the law of continuity, will be continually replaced. The production apparatus is not complete as long as stock is not replenished. If one sees a price rise in the buyers market, the value of a stock also rises. And if one expresses this value rise in the accounts, one records a profit which, when a price decrease occurs, will change into a loss. That profit was obviously made outside the production process; it was not made by the production and not during an exchange. That profit therefore does not form income, if one looks beyond the arbitrary limits formed by the annual accounts; when the amount of income which may be consumed is determined, this profit should not be included in the calculation. It should be reserved.[34]

This conclusion, which is extremely important for industrial practice, can only be accepted when the correct theoretical insight has been acquired about the nature of the sacrifice which was made in the sale - i.e. about the nature of cost.

Errors in the Practice

We have been able to observe all this very clearly in the years during and after the war. It was, however, only a symptom of the phenomenon which regularly occurs. But we will not go as far as F. Schmidt, in ascribing to this phenomenon the cause of the economic boom.

Schmidt, whose views we will discuss later, states: "Business cycles - a miscalculation!"[35] We think this remark an exaggeration, the result of an incomplete view of events. But we are certain that the incorrect conception of the nature of cost and of the sacrifice in the exchange does not help to stabilize business cycle fluctuations and therefore also results in harm for society as a *cause* of these fluctuations. If all producers were to increase their prices immediately, as soon as a boom starts, on the basis of the replacement value and if they did not consider the book profit thus made during the exchange as profit - if they were not to consume this profit, that is - they would naturally have a more inhibiting effect on a price increase and exaggerated expansion.

Finally, the phenomenon is not limited in practice to general business cycle fluctuations. In nearly every product individual "business cycle" fluctuations occur

---

34 See further Vol. VI: B, *Theory of Profit Determination*, esp. sections 12 & 16.

35 F. Schmidt, "Business Cycles - a Miscalculation!", *Zeitschrift für Betriebswirtschaft*, 1927. *Ibid.*, *Business Economics and Business Cycles*, Ch V-K. 3, pp.97ff, Berlin 1933.

and these give rise to the same phenomenon. And, separate from those real fluctuations, price fluctuations are the rule with numerous products. We find an obvious example in all those products of which the market position is affected by variations in the size of the harvest. All enterprises which trade or process such products, are continuously faced by this theoretical problem in its practical significance. And we are able to observe that the difference in conception about the significance of purchase price and economic cost sometimes is the basis for a difference in management policy and that it therefore completely dominates the difference in the characteristics of the various companies. Theoretical examples provided have shown this connection, practical experience confirms this. As a result, we find companies whose management policy (price policy) is based on the principle of economic cost whilst other companies still adhere to the principle of purchase price. The former follow price movements in the buyers market, the latter are guided by the purchase price and thus lag behind.

The error, i.e. starting from an incorrect basis for management policy, is scientifically partly a remnant of the company's position in times of a more isolated exchange.

In the past, when a merchant obtained his wares from foreign countries and when he gradually used up his stock by transporting and selling to his customers by degrees, exchange to a far greater extent had the nature of an isolated exchange. Price movement in the [buyers] market made itself only gradually felt. We find this characteristic of trade - industry at that time did not play a significant part as yet - even expressed in the accounts and in the method of drawing up a balance sheet. Every lot of goods was considered in isolation. When a balance sheet was drawn up no profit was calculated; the balance of the account of a lot which had not yet been entirely sold, was transferred simply to a new account. For calculating profit one knew therefore only the difference between purchase price and proceeds. This was possible, and, in the circumstances, it was correct. There was no general market. A merchant isolated, so to speak the stock, and he could usually consider that stock as practically untouched by a price movement in the market.[36] Practically there was no replacement value. When the stock was exhausted, new stock was fetched from distant lands and the same isolated exchange process started all over again. That situation has therefore thoroughly changed. Most goods are traded and quoted in

---

36 Limperg draws a general picture here of the pre-replacement-value era and links it up with the pre-industrialisation era. However, we should not close our eyes to the fact that there are earlier traces of developments in business and price politics that definitely do point to a connection with price movement in the buyers' market. For example, at the time when the guilds were important, there was the adaptation of the weight of a loaf of bread to the price of grain.

technical markets.[37] Sellers and buyers take note of these quotations and both groups are affected in their value assessment of the goods in stock by new price quotations. This also meant that one can buy for those prices at that moment in the market. A value assessment is formed under that influence; a social value judgement comes into being in optima forma, the replacement value makes itself felt automatically. This change in thinking among people in business takes place gradually and is especially fostered by the consequences of war.

For that matter, we do not need to look for a historical explanation of faulty conceptions. It is understandable that a business man who has no economic training, regards the difference between purchase price and proceeds for as profit or loss, because he thinks in terms of hard cash.

Errors in the Theory: Marshall, J.M. Clark

More serious, however, is the fact that nearly all theoretical economists have adhered to old conceptions, which were re-enforced by the dominating influence exercised by subjective value theory on price formation theory. Social economists, ignoring the replacement value concept, have accepted the common parlance about cost, so that their theory defines it only as the purchase price. It is amazing that these theorists have not considered the question of what the size of a sacrifice in exchange means for a producer. All the more amazing, because this theory logically leads on to that. The fight against the old cost value theory should have led, following the road of logic, to the result that a sacrifice in exchange cannot be expressed by the purchase price.[38] That purchase price, it should be remembered, is essentially nothing but the old cost value concept in which one expresses what sacrifices were and have been made to produce a good. Subjective value theory has rightly objected to the conception that the value of a good would be determined by that historical given. That means however, that the *producer's* sacrifice can not be measured by that given either. It is crazy that a *consumer* should form his valuation economically correctly, but that one assumes that a producer still values according to - or compares with - the rejected cost value concept.

We have to state that social economics has confined itself to registering the observed actions of individuals and has not been concerned with specifying what these individuals with a proper insight of the events should do on the basis of the economic motive. We should not start from an assumed incorrect view, even though

37 Present economic markets enable buyers and sellers to gain knowledge of prices and price developments of most goods with the help of modern business-economic observation techniques.

38 See also: Vol. I:B, *The Theory of Value*: Ch II, Section 5d "Cost value and labour value".

we should of course take into consideration, when explaining events, the fact that many individuals act differently because they have the wrong conception of events, or because economic circumstances force them to actions different from what one might expect. The theory has not exposed the error which has been made; on the contrary, it has sanctioned this error, among other things by inductively drawing the conclusion from often superficial observations, that certain actions are systematic.

This error is general. Even with an author such as Marshall, who, along with others, has attempted to penetrate to the heart of the matter in regard to production, we find the same misconception: he only considers the purchase price.

In his book *Industry and Trade*,[39] Marshall speaks about "cost of production" whilst differentiating between "money cost" and "real cost". This contradistinction resembles the one made by us. But Marshall has something quite different in mind and he finally comes to the conclusion that for a producer the money cost forms the basis for his actions and not the real cost. He illustrates this by speaking about child labour and he points out that, even if that labour is paid for at the full market price (for adult labour) the work which has been done is rarely worth its "real cost", because the satisfaction of needs created by this child labour, does not make up for the "social cost", made in the form of harming a child's life "spent in grievous and depressing toil, and without an adequate education to prepare for the duties of after life." Here Marshall introduces concepts of social cost and social value, which, however, are completely different from the concept social value and social costs which we are using. We have in mind the quantitative expression of the value (of the sacrifice), measured by means of the (social) market price, without considering the usefulness which, from a social point of view, one can ascribe to a good *outside the market*. Apart from this, Marshal is of the opinion that a producer will let himself be guided in his actions by the amount of "expenses" or "money cost" and he there follows the customary way of thinking.

Only among those American authors who can be considered as industrial economists, does one find a conception which is somewhat similar to ours. J.M. Clark, for example, has recognised the significance of replacement value, without seeing or accepting, however, the consequences.[40]

---

39 A. Marshall: *Industry and Trade*. London 1919. Book II, Ch. 1, p.183.

40 See, for instance, J.M. Clark: The Economics of overhead costs. Chicago 1923, pp.13 and 39.

12. German Theory Dealt With as a Closing Section

In what follows the theory of F. Schmidt and of the German financial statements theorists is discussed in detail. This discussion is an extension of what we dealt with in Part 1B, *The Theory of Value*, and in particular the part which deals with, and criticises Schmidt's theory of the replacement value (*Wiederbeschaffungswert*). The initial repetition runs into a discussion which cannot be omitted in the body of critical considerations about the various value theories.

13. F. Schmidt's Theory of the Wiederbeschaffungswert* and the Theory of the "Organic Balance Sheet" and Other Concepts of German Theoreticians.

A very important and decisive step in the right direction was first taken in Germany by the industrial economists. Their theory carries the mark of its origin: the problems of inflation. It originated, moreover, in circles which were orientated towards accounting problems rather than towards economics, as is generally the case in Germany and one can say that in the literature dealing with calculation and the balance sheets which appeared after the first World War, the new German concept opened new vistas. The significance of the replacement value concept has been recognised by practically all German industrial economists. The most consistent advocate of the replacement value concept was F. Schmidt. His two most important books in this field are *Calculation and Price Policy* (Berlin, 1930) and *Organic Current Value Accounting*.[41] (Leipzig, 1929, 3rd ed.)

There are two reasons for looking more closely at the German Concepts. The first is that in Germany so much attention has been paid to the problem and that it was tackled for the first time in a more general way. The second reason is that it will be useful to point out the difference between our concepts and those of the German industrial economists, particularly those of Schmidt, because they appear to be similar. We are going to state our three main objections to Schmidt's theory and to those of the other Germans.

The most fundamental objection is that a new value concept is introduced incidentally, without its basing it on a general value theory or without using it as a basis for a general value theory. Errors are found in business policy as well as illogical ideas on price policy in general and specifically in that of companies; in

---

41 The first edition of this work appeared under the title of *The Organic Balance Sheet within the Framework of the Economy*. Leipzig 1922.

* [Literally: replacement value, but as Limperg disagrees with Schmidt we will use the German word.]

particular a different price policy and a different business policy are suggested without a theoretical explanation. The theory of the (*Wiederbeschaffungswert*) is not a value theory. It is an artificial construction in order to arrive at a price policy and a finance policy and it provides a course of action for drawing up the balance sheet of the company. As such it has great merits, especially for the past, for the period of inflation, even though it was conceived too late. But it misses out on the illuminating moment which true theory needs. It shows up the mistakes a different policy can lead to but it does not explain why the value of goods is determined by their replacement costs. It has no connection with, neither does it attack the economic value theory in general; it leaves it undisturbed. It therefore has the character of an artificial construction as well as being of an incidental nature. And Schmidt erects this construction on the basis of the consideration that his theory serves as an attempt to solve all immediate problems as regards the accounting system of the company, "in order to maintain the relative value of the company",[42] or because of the assumption that its relative position (i.e. that of the normal company) has remained the same in the national economy,[43] without further explanation why this requirement is necessary.

Our theory of replacement value is a value theory which goes right to the core of the problem, the concept of value. Hence, it is not offered incidentally as a *production* guideline, but it explains why the consumer as well as the producer must, in certain circumstances, accept replacement costs as the quantitative representation of the significance of the product. We then continue to build upon this analysis of the value concept as a basis and the next decisive moment is the analysis of the cost-price concept where the cost-price, as a quantitative representation of the sacrifice which occurs during the exchange, is based on the value of the good. This sacrifice cannot be greater or smaller than the value of the good. We thus find a logical basis for the rational behaviour of the producer, that is to say, for his price - and business policy. The result is that, among other things, the producer also retains, as Schmidt calls it, his (relative) position in the production structure. We emphasise the word result; the fact that this result is useful, we have also shown. However, the value-judgment is still not explained.

The second fundamental objection against Schmidt's theory is that it is essentially a theory for a time of price-increase and specifically for the period of inflation after the first World War. It is not a sound basis for a period of deflation.

---

42 F. Schmidt, from the Preface, *The Organic Balance Sheet within the Framework of the Economy* (added by the editors).

43 F. Schmidt, *Organic Current Value Accounting*, p.30. This was quoted by Limperg.

Here the incidental nature of the theory shows up very strongly.[44] The theory of Schmidt and his supporters was developed during the inflation, that is to say, it arose out of the difficulties which arose through the decrease of the purchasing power of money. His requirement, that the relative place in production be maintained, arose from this. This also explains his introduction of the so-called Organic Balance Sheet, which is the Balance Sheet of the company as the organ of a society bound together organically. Such explanations are, however, not based scientifically and sometimes lead to completely arbitrary and definitely erroneous conclusions. As an example we refer to Schmidt's discussion of the price change of fixed assets in his book, *Organic Current Value Accounting*.[45]

Apart from this, it is understandable and fortunate that the experience of the inflation period in Germany led to some intensive thinking and it is also plain that the phenomena during such a period are shown up very clearly.

However, with this problem it is not a matter of change in the purchasing power of money, but of [specific] price-changes; the change in monetary purchasing power (which is Schmidt's starting point) is *one* of the causes of price-changes. Schmidt's theory therefore narrows our horizon, it limits analysis in an arbitrary and irrational way.

Our third objection against the German views is that the value problem was considered too much - and dealt with too much - as a balance sheet problem. Schmidt is in this respect one of the least guilty. It is Schmalenbach and other theorists who were very much oriented in this direction. We remind readers of the dispute over the static, dynamic or organic balance sheets. This dispute is probably a result of the fact that industrial economists in Germany were oriented strongly to the *techniques* of accounting.

If the value theory is especially linked to the periodical balance sheet of the company, it presents a serious hindrance to its proper development; this perspective causes various dangers which we will point out.

How did German theorists come to see the valuation problem as a balance sheet problem? To be able to analyse this we need to examine what usually happens in a company's accounting system. When drawing up the periodical account of the business results, usually annually, one splits up the presentation of the outcome over two successive periods.

If one considers all transactions which occurred over a certain year - the entire production and all exchanges of that year - as one entity, one will be able - this is how

44 In spite of Schmidt's assertion to the contrary, in the preface to the 3rd edition! "Everything I have stated applies to any value-change ..."

45 F. Schmidt, *Die organische Tageswertbilanz*, 3rd ed., pp.181-3.

the reasoning goes - to determine correctly the end result of all transactions, the resultant of all individual exchanges, if one values correctly the goods which one possesses at the beginning of the period and those in possession at the end of the period. Looking at the training of accountants and at business practice too, one even has the impression as if the outcome were determined really only *during* and *by* drawing up the balance sheet. This, in practice, is indeed often the case because of an incomplete accounting system and because of inadequate insight in the requirements of the company; the situation in actual fact is quite different. With each exchange there is either profit or loss and it is necessary to value, with each exchange, the goods which are being exchanged in order to be able to distinguish, with each exchange, between the profit or loss caused by the business cycle and profit or loss which occurs in production. The valuation problem and the cost-price problem are not balance sheet problems but price-formation problems which must be solved therefore for the exchange taking place during the period. They are not problems which are connected with the balance sheet that is to say, connected with the goods which were *not* exchanged. Of course the same mathematical result must be obtained along these two different roads if one is in agreement about the value-, cost- and profit concepts, specifically if one therefore also applies the formation of reserves out of profit made on stock. But the method is fundamentally different.

In Germany - and here in the Netherlands too - long before the first World War - there was a theoretical and practical problem whether stock on the Balance Sheet ought to be valued at its cost-price or at its market-price. Cost-price at that time was what we now call historical cost or purchase price; as regards the market-price no distinction was made between the purchase- and selling market, which caused confusion for those companies which do not produce goods, that is to say for wholesale- and retail firms. No definite solution of the problem was found. Both systems had their advocates but the practical solution was usually a compromise: the lowest of the two prices was chosen. This was not done for any theoretical reason but because this was considered to be safe. Thus the lowest profit was calculated which was in accordance with what was done by careful producers. It seemed to be a confirmation of the theory. In actual fact, however, there was a lack of insight among accounting theorists as well as among business practitioners. The idea was to avoid recording a profit which had not (yet) been achieved so as to remain on the safe side. As regards fixed assets, the situation was much simpler, or so they thought. Where fixed assets were concerned, it was not a matter of the market-price, that is to say, of a sales-price. The cost-price (historical cost) was always the basis for valuation, of which part was depreciated annually for wear and tear.

Whilst they thought they were home and dried,-they did not realise, how utterly wrong they were. In Germany, inflation served as an eye-opener; other countries, however paid no attention to this problem. Only in the Netherlands, already before the first World War - and therefore entirely independent of the effects of inflation, but rather on principle - it was pointed out that the market-price of the purchasing market decides the costs of production. Here we point out that this view was stated actually separate from the *balance sheet problem*, as part of the cost-price problem.[46]

An outline of the development in Germany will be given just because in this sub-section we wish to show how the new ideas arose out of the balance sheet problem.

The careful method of drawing up the balance sheet which we have described and which was even prescribed legally, did not prevent the producer (in time of inflation) from going rapidly downhill. This was in spite of the fact that he appeared to calculate according to the safest method. He did not calculate profit on stock but he did calculate, with every exchange, a profit if historic cost was exceeded. He was careful in his fashion when drawing up the balance sheet, but he was reckless when calculating profit where the transactions concerned occurred repeatedly, whereas stock, after all, plays a part only once a year when profit is calculated. One can already see the fundamental error which is made if the value problem is dealt with as a balance sheet problem. Initially, this error was not perceived. It was only observed that more and more "operating capital" was needed. One ran aground, one had to borrow money, increase capital because more and more was needed to finance stock which, physically, remained at the same level. Gradually, it was also found that when fixed assets (viz. tools) were being renewed - whilst the level stayed the same - they cost far more than when purchased originally. The unpleasant discovery was made that, when a depreciated asset was being renewed, far more money was needed to buy a new one. One began to wonder whether depreciation was being calculated correctly; that is to say, whether in the cost-calculation of the product enough cost representing the use of work-units coming out of the asset, was being calculated. Very slowly it dawned upon them that the calculation was indeed incorrect and that there was no profit on the sale of the products because the calculation of the sacrifice at the exchange was based on historic cost which was much below the replacement value of the asset. When, finally, it was realised that this meant impoverishment one then had to accept the fact that the problem could not be solved with a different

---

46 Limperg refers here to one of his own articles: "Cost price", *Accountancy* (Dutch journal), 1918. May we add that upon consulting earlier volumes of this journal it confirms the statement concerning the point in time. This journal - which is under the Limperg's editorship - also provides an insight into the development of replacement value theory and cost price theory.

system of balance sheet valuation. If the fixed assets on the balance sheet were valued at a larger amount, the depreciation for used-up work-units admittedly increased, but the apparent value-increase of the remaining work-units was greater and therefore led again to the calculation of a financial increase, in fact, a profit.

This erroneous view is giving way gradually to the correct way of thinking. This is important because it is to be feared that conditions similar to those at the time of inflation will occur wherever devaluation takes place.[47] Prices will rise in accordance with increased replacement value. As regards fixed assets, one must accept the fact that wear and tear during the years before devaluation of the monetary unit, had been calculated at too low a level.

These are our views on German theory which dealt with one aspect of the replacement value problem.

14. The Significance of Cost Calculation

After our digression about the problems of establishing and measuring the size of the sacrifice, physically as well as in money, we should, in addition, look at two other problems of particular importance.

In this section we will pay attention to the calculation a producer has to make for the exchange. Cost is determined, as we have seen, by the total replacement value of the means of production which have been used. In industry this means in practice that the value of the means of production which have been sacrificed, needs to be calculated.

This *calculation* is always necessary, even though in some industries it sometimes, by way of exception, happens that there is no question of an offer in the strict sense before exchange. Exchange then takes place without the buyer knowing the price beforehand. This cannot happen anywhere as a rule, because it is always an unpleasant situation for a buyer to have to hear afterwards what price he has to pay. It nevertheless occurs in the case of operations or transactions where the costs are difficult to calculate beforehand, such as repairs, installation of equipment, furnishing, wiring, etc. In those cases too, however, the nature of the calculation remains the same. Technically it is changed to the extent that in this calculation, which is carried out afterwards, one usually has at one's disposal the data to determine accurately the physical size of the sacrifices, whereas with a calculation before exchange, it is often necessary to make an estimate, either because the physical size of the sacrifice is not precisely known, or because the price of the means of production cannot be

47 Limperg used this part for his lectures (for the last time) in the spring of 1935.

determined with any certainty, because the product, at the moment it is offered, which should be the moment of calculation, usually has not yet been manufactured. The price of the means of production is perhaps known at the moment of offer, but it can change during the time which passes between the moment of offer and the moment of exchange. A cautious producer will eliminate this risk as much as possible by asking for a fixed offer. But this too, is not always possible.

What is so remarkable is that the actual calculation - the calculation which precedes the offer - often has the nature of an estimate; it is therefore often called, specifically among those producers for whom it contains many uncertain elements (among builders of dikes for the department of dikes, etc. plant installation, buildings etc.), *budgeted price*. Its nature, however remains similar to that of the calculation of a merchant who offers coffee. With this budgeted price too, one is dealing with a calculation as the basis for the determination of the offering price. For that matter, even in the case of a coffee merchant there is an element of estimate in the calculation, even though this is not so important that one speaks of a budget in technical terms. Remember, in his company too, sacrifices are made for which he cannot determine the magnitude with certainty and accuracy every time with every exchange and for every quantity of the product offered by him. The quantity of coffee may be known accurately, as well as the price and perhaps the transport costs, and the like. But he does not know precisely the size of the sacrifice in the labour of his staff and of himself, the cost of storing in his warehouse, lighting and the like. Here too, he has to make do with an estimate. How this takes place and especially on what bases this estimate has to founded, will be discussed in Chapter IIIC, section 37: Standard Costs [of Volume II of *Bedrijfseconomie*].

We therefore should state here that cost, as much as value, has in most cases, the nature of an estimate in practice. This nature of cost of course creates an element of *uncertainty* in company policy, specifically in price policy. Nevertheless, a lot depends on the calculation being correct. The offering price depends on this and therefore the proceeds of the product and thus also the results of the exchange, the amount of profit. It is necessary, of course, that the estimate is carried out correctly, but it now becomes also, in regard to that estimate, a requirement of good business practice that this calculation, this estimate, is checked, that it is tested as soon as data are accurately, or more accurately known. An efficient accounting system - that is to say, a system specially equipped for that purpose - is an essential instrument for this. But it is also necessary that a manager pays special attention to this verification of his estimates and that he realizes that checking a calculation not only means the prevention of errors in subsequent calculations, but also an inducement to examine the causes of these errors and thus a search for faults in the company. When one considers the great importance of this task for a manager, one would expect that continuous attention would be paid to this in practice. However, if one observes practice, one will often find that capable managers neglect this important element in their management and that they set greater store by rate intuition than exact knowledge. One cannot generalise in this matter, of course.

Preliminary and Subsequent Calculation

Since the need for verification is obvious, we will devote a few words to this element of the calculation. The most common form of this check is the check carried out periodically, with the aid of the accounting system on the magnitude of the cost factors. For costs such as administration, lighting, so called general costs, a check can be carried out only periodically for an entire group of exchanges. This is usually very efficiently done with the aid of the figures of the customary accounts. There are, however, many cases where a check can be carried out efficiently only by making a verification calculation, which follows the former closely. In a heterogeneous production, specifically piece production, a general check of the administration is not sufficient. Examples, again, are buildings, installation of equipment, and the like. In a properly run company a special calculation is made after the end of the production. If this calculation exists, it is differentiated in a *preliminary calculation* (i.e. a calculation on behalf of the offer) and a *subsequent calculation* (i.e. a calculation which serves to verify the estimates which were necessary in the preliminary calculation). However, a subsequent calculation essentially exists also in all other cases where a verification of the calculation on behalf of the offer occurs, even though no formal calculation is drawn up. A subsequent calculation is economically an indispensable complement of practically every preliminary calculation, as a basis for the offering price.

This distinction in preliminary and subsequent calculation has led, by the way, to two misconceptions, one of a theoretical and one of a practical nature.[48] It is a theoretical misconception that those two calculations were seen as the expression of two cost concepts. In this context, a distinction was made between prospective cost and retrospective cost, that is to say, cost which provides a prognosis of costs which are to be expected and cost which is an expression of the costs in production. It is believed that one can thus create a synthesis for the antithesis which we indicated between cost and purchase price. Remember, for prospective cost one may and one often has to detach oneself from the accounts, from the facts, the monetary costs,

48 Limperg's discussion of these two misconceptions has been included in abbreviated form.

from the historical costs. For retrospective costs, however, one needs to adhere to reality, namely the history as one finds it accurately recorded in the accounts.

Here one finds misunderstanding and a confusion of concepts. In regard to prospective cost we wish to point out that the cause of disengaging oneself from the historical purchase price was not to be found essentially in the circumstance that a prognosis is made of future costs. This only applies to production which will take some time in the future and in those places where no stocks of the means of production are available. This is only so in some cases. The problem arises from the question whether it is a matter of the monetary sacrifices or of *economic* sacrifices in a broad sense. It is then a problem whether the purchase price rather than economic cost, based on the replacement value, determines costs, irrespective of whether there is a stock of the finished product rather than means of production. There is also a misconception in regard to retrospective cost. With the subsequent calculation too it is neither a matter of the purchase price nor of the monetary sacrifices which have been made. Both calculations must rest on the same basis. In order to determine the result, obtained in the exchange, one cannot compare two results which have been constructed from different factors. The same cost concept has to be the basis of both calculations.

From this arises an often occurring practical misconception. Retrospective cost as subsequent calculation loses this way all significance as a check of the prospective cost as preliminary calculation, because they are constructed on a different basis. What good does it do if, for stressed concrete, one has calculated the cost beforehand, on the basis of the current market price (on the basis of the replacement value, therefore) and if, in the subsequent calculation, one calculates the cement used from stock at the original purchase price? One thus obtains data which cannot be compared, which cannot be used as a check on each other.

Calculations as we described them, are merely technical aids to determine the size of the cost, of the sacrifice. Calculations, made at different points in time, can *differ in accuracy* because of a difference in available data, but they cannot lead to a *different cost price.*

15. Costs and Losses

Means of Production as Assets Rather than Costs

Finally, we need to answer another question if we wish to obtain a proper understanding of the nature of cost and knowledge of the content of cost. When does the use of the means of production (and services) result in *costs* and when in *losses?*

This question is extremely important. Remember, costs are elements of the cost-price and therefore of the offering price of a product, therefore also of price formation. Losses are no such thing. Without running ahead of an analysis of the difference between the two, we wish to point out, solely in order to emphasize the importance of the problem, as an example, that it obviously does make a difference whether one considers a raw material and the use of labour which have turned out to be useless, as a result of a worker's incompetence, as production costs. These costs have to be calculated thereby increasing the offering price, or they represent losses that have to be covered out of profits that were made elsewhere.

Before answering this, another question needs answering: when are material goods that are being used as means in the production process, to be considered as capital and when as costs?. The question can also be put as follows: when does possession of goods become a sacrifice for production?

At the start of our analysis of value- and cost concepts (see p.78 in original)*, we argued that value and costs are two concepts for quantitative expressions which are each other's mirror images, but which cover each other in size when applied to the same good, at the same moment. The two concepts belong merely to different conceptions. Where goods are thought of only in terms of their significance for the formation of a producer's income, this determines the value and the good is considered as a bearer of value, as an asset. If, however, one asks about the size of the sacrifice in the exchange, that is to say the sacrifice made by relinquishing the good, one speaks of cost and the good is perceived as a good bearing costs.

When is the first, when is the second conception applied?

A conception depends in the first place on the framework of the problem in which the good is considered. In the theory of financing means of production are, for example, usually considered as capital goods.

Here, the cost problem is relevant to us and we need to ask at what stage of the course travelled by the means of production in the production stream, this means of production *can* be considered as a cost bearer? Will this not be until be the exchange? No, it will be much earlier, usually during the purchase. We wish to state this more accurately: it can be from the moment the means of production is an essential element in the production process, from the moment it is an essential possession. At that moment the means of production can be considered, therefore, as a cost bearer, as a sacrifice in the production process.

Thus, we know stocks of goods,[49] the same as stocks of work units with buildings and equipment. There is here the technical necessity of buying work units which will be used only in later years in a certain product. But that entire stock of work units is already in use in the production process right from the start. A sacrifice can be considered as the work units for one product unit which is taken up *and* the work units which are to be used in a year's time. In other words, only the work units which have been detached in the production flow can be considered as cost bearers, whereas the stem from which the work units are being detached continues to be considered as a capital good. Alternatively the entire stock of work units can therefore be considered as a sacrifice in regard to a series of production processes stretching over the years, and therefore that entire stock of work units, that is the entire equipment or building, can be considered as a cost bearer for the production processes of a series of future years.

The latter conception is not the customary one, but it is correct. The customary conception is the former, that is to say, the building, the equipment is considered as a capital good, the used up part is considered as cost. So in this conception there is a progress, a slow change from capital good to cost bearer.

In the second conception capital good and cost bearer are standing next to each other from the start as conceptions which complement each other, whose application depends on the problem. In the cost problem the good which has been obtained is a cost bearer from the start, in the finance problem, it is a capital good.

The difference in conception can perhaps be best understood if one looks at the presentation of events in the accounts.

The primitive presentation is as follows: equipment is a possession, depreciation is an expression of the costs. The other conception: the item equipment is the total of the sacrifices for a series of production processes which is sometimes split up, when a balance sheet is drawn up, into a group of sacrifices of the past and a group of the future.

What is the importance of this distinction which, at first glance, may seem a bit pretentious? The importance lies in a sharpening of the theoretical insight and thus in the correct solution of a number of problems which, without this insight, will not result in a correct solution. Thus, insight is sharpened in the practice, where some of those problems cause great difficulties. The problem of valuation for the financial statements thus acquires a totally different aspect, even the nature of financial statements themselves changes. Generally speaking - and certainly for the problems which we are dealing with in this volume - the significance lies in the fact that right

---

49 In a brief note Limperg explained that we are concerned here with needed stocks, not speculative ones purchased outside the production stream and then stored. In the latter case the

from the start, that is from the moment of acquiring the means of production, c.q. from the moment of possèssion being essential a connection is made, with the sequentially arranged sacrifices, between the uses and unused, work units intended for future use, between latent and effective production capacity. That production capacity too, which is intended for the future and which is for the moment still latent, is from the start a sacrifice in the production, for present production too, which, no more than future production, could be carried out without being tied up as stock in the means of production. The work units intended for future use should be considered, already at this time, as cost bearer and they can therefore affect the cost of the product right from the start.[50]

The Difference Between Costs and Losses

We will now discuss the difference between costs and losses. Here too, the two concepts initially do not contain a contradiction, but only a difference in conception. In the traditional accounts no difference is made even between costs and losses. The balance sheet and the profit and loss account of a factory are the most telling example of this. On the one hand, the used raw materials, paid wages, interest and the "expenses" are entered in the "profit and loss" columns and, on the other hand, the proceeds of the products. Costs and losses are here taken to be completely identical and the final balance of the "Profit & Loss account" is called net profit. The costs of all exchanges which have taken place in the past financial periods, have been put together and set as a whole against the proceeds of all these exchanges. One, nevertheless, speaks of profits and losses. And the profit balance, the "net profit" or "net loss" indicates the resultant of the profits and losses which have been incurred together with all exchanges. People are so used to this form and this way of expressing things that no one realizes this peculiar mixing up of the concepts "costs" and "loss" which here takes place.

If, however, one looks at only one exchange by itself, no one would think of calling the costs of this exchange "loss"; in this case no loss is put against profit (here to be called, by way of differentiation, gross profit), but one speaks without exception of costs and proceeds and only the *difference* between the two, the outcome of the exchange, is called profit or loss.

A sacrifice in raw materials, in labour, etc. for a certain product will not be called, neither theoretically nor practically, a loss, no more than the proceeds of the product will be called a profit. Only when the *combined* sacrifices made for the

---

means of production can only be regarded as capital goods.

50 As for the way they influence, see a.o. "the cost category equipment" (B II, sect. 197 ff.), "the problem of combined costs" (B. III A, section 10), "the capacity costs" (B. III D).

manufacture of a product, exceed the proceeds, does one speak, for an individual product, of a loss. Originally, this custom in accounting was an innocent confusion of terms and a change in conception; innocent, because it had, in this case, only a formal consequence. But one should realize that here, in fact, two different conceptions are being expressed. The first conception is that the goods and services which are indicated as *costs*, are still considered in their function of constituent elements of the product; in this conception the sacrifices are therefore still constituent factors of the product causing one to expect a profit, an income in the future, by means of the exchange, from the favourable difference between cost and proceeds. If we follow the second conception, and if those sacrifices are indicated as *losses,* one behaves, in terms of economics, in a very odd manner. One then considers the used means of production as lost, that is to say, as being sunk. It is apparently only the producer's good luck which, unexpectedly, throws a "profit" in his lap to the amount of . . . the entire proceeds of the product!

It is not as crazy as that, however, and with some effort we can give a more rational content to this formal conception. The new interpretation entails that one no longer considers the means of production themselves which have been used (therefore that one no longer considers the content of the sacrifices), but that one sets out a mathematical picture of the components of the loss or of the profit which is the result of the exchanges. One can thus consider each of those quantitative expressions as a *part* of the quantitative expression of the result of the exchange and the combined (gross-) losses and (gross-) profits as a *specification of net profit* or of *net loss.*

This distinction in conception in a certain sense is a continuation of the distinction between value bearer and cost bearer. There are three concepts which show the continuation as follows:

1. An asset is the means of production, considered in relation to its significance, its value for the production process as a source of income or as a fractional part of that source (in which we differentiate categories of capital goods);

2. This same good is then considered as a cost bearer, as a sacrifice in the production process, as a constituent element of the product (where, now, we differentiate categories of costs);

3. Finally, we find the quantitative expression of the sacrifice as part of, as a specification of, the outcome of the production process (where income is split up and where we differentiate categories of gross losses and gross profits).

The transition from 1 to 2 does not refer to a change of the economic position of the good in the company, but only to a continuation in the economic conception: the means of production was first looked upon as a value bearer in regard to the production process, then as sacrifice in the production process.

The Demarcations Between Costs and Losses

The fact should, however, now be recognized that this conception is not as innocent as one might think. This formal blotting out of demarcations between costs and losses actually leads to confusing consequences when we abandon questions of a formal nature and when we are concerned with the questions having a material significance.

One immediately finds that this way of presenting things shows the following dangerous aspect: it means that any differentiation between costs and losses is abandoned in the accounts as well. No matter how difficult it is in practice to draw a sharp demarcation - we are surely all agreed about the importance of the difference and thus about the value of that differentiation, if it is kept in mind that *costs are constituent elements of the price, and losses are not.* Any business man neglecting this differentiation must, as a matter of principle, inevitably make mistakes.

As we asked at the beginning of this section, when do the used means of production become costs, when losses? Essentially, an answer to this question can be speedily given: if the use is effective, if it does not lead to a squandering of the used means of production, we are dealing with constituent elements of the product and with cost factors which, by means of cost price and offering price become constituent elements in the price formation. If the use is ineffective, if it is in vain, it is no more than waste and it becomes a loss. As simple as this statement is, the problem of application, which we will discuss in detail at a later stage, is very complicated. The nature of the difficulties we will mention briefly, because without this knowledge, the content of cost cannot be determined properly.

It is not difficult to see that it is hard to answer the question whether, and to what extent, the use of productive capacity is effective. First of all, it is often extremely difficult to work out whether, and to what extent, there is waste in the technical sense in that use. Even if these facts can be established, this is by no means the end of the story.

Technical waste is often unavoidable and less avoidable in one company than in another company; technical waste need not be economic waste. For another reason too, not every technical waste should be considered waste in economic terms: when preventing technical waste for the company in question costs more than that waste, obviously no waste occurs in economic terms, there is no waste. On the contrary, preventing technical waste would in that case precisely become economic waste, and turn into a loss.

However, for the problem of the importance of cost in the context of price formation, it is sufficient and decisive if we know that the sacrifices made in the production, can be considered only as cost factors as long as these sacrifices can still be considered as constituent elements for the formation of income. As soon as it has been established that these sacrifices are ineffective for that purpose, they can no longer be considered as costs, but they have to be indicated as losses and they must therefore not be calculated as the basis for the offering price. And when this has been established, it is obviously also necessary in the accounts, that they are no longer considered as costs, as constituent elements of income, but are indicated as losses. If it has been established that any sacrifice was ineffective, i.e. made in vain, effective statistics require - for the accounts to truly serve as an instrument of observation - that those sacrifices do not remain linked with sacrifices of which it has been established or of which at least one can be confident that they are indeed sacrifices which are effective for income formation.

It is very important to establish that the decision regarding whether a sacrifice is effective or not, is not only often technically difficult to make, but is also often, because of its nature, arbitrary. Because, for a cautious and pessimistic producer, it will be established earlier than for an incautious, optimistic, speculatively inclined producer that a sacrifice is totally or partially wasted. For a cautious producer, the moment of change will have arrived before it has been established that a sacrifice is ineffective or in vain; he will decide that a loss has been incurred, when he is convinced of it, perhaps already when he fears it, or when he assumes the possibility exists. This arbitrary nature is not so much of importance in regard to the uses of means of production and services on behalf of production processes which have been completed, but more in regard to future production uses. The former can be checked more or less accurately, the subsequent calculation may be more or less correct, but the method is essentially exact and the result of the calculation need not be subject to subjective considerations. It is apparently a totally different matter where sacrifices are concerned, which are made totally or partly for future production processes.

One will realize how important but also how difficult and arbitrary the decision is here.

It is important if, for example, one thinks of the volume of the stocks of work units, enclosed in buildings and equipment for a remote future. A manager has to ask himself again and again to what extent these work units are still useful for the future. In practice he does this every year when the financial statements are drawn up. The problem of valuation for the balance sheet is nothing other than the problem of a separation of costs and losses between past and future. And it will therefore have to be considered each year again whether, and to what extent, the stocks of work units are still constituent elements for future production. Because if they are not, it may be presumed they have been lost in the past.

Apart from being important, the decision is also difficult and arbitrary, so that, in this context, one can speak of a "balance sheet policy"; which is strongly influenced by subjective considerations because the more confidence there is in the future, the less quickly one will decide to degrade the sacrifices from the category of costs to that of losses and one will therefore more likely be prepared to make sacrifices and, on the other hand, less willing, in sales policy, to accept a loss, be more tenacious in regard to adhering to the offering price which should cover costs.

The above shows too, how the demarcation between costs and losses grows fuzzy. Not formally, however, in view of the nature of things; not theoretically, because the distinction has been determined objectively. But we are dealing in practice with cost as calculated by a producer. And we find that the demarcation is fading as a result of the circumstance that the exact difference is expressed only after the exchange and that no one can draw the dividing line for the future with certainty and accuracy.

The fading of the demarcation becomes even clearer than in the examples set out above, if one considers the sacrifices which cause only immaterial results, such as experiments, advertising campaigns, organisation cost. These sacrifices appear in the balance sheet as an "asset". Here, one did not acquire an asset which derived its replacement value from the social value which, in most cases, provides an important objective element for the manager's decision (compare the value of the organisation). Here a manager is practically entirely dependent on his own assessment regarding the future. It will depend on this assessment whether it is deemed economically justified to consider the sacrifices made in an advertising campaign as costs of subsequent years. To what extent the demarcation fades is clear if one realizes that the result of the decision is that sacrifices for advertising are not only "promoted" from losses to costs, but even - as a result - are entered in the balance sheet as a "possession".

There is an even more telling example of the fading of demarcations. It is even possible that the deficiency of a financial period, that is the resultant of losses and profits incurred on the exchanges and services which took place during that period, can revive as costs, if one considers the production processes of that period in their connection with those of succeeding years. If a new company incurs a loss during the first year or years, this need not be a cause for disappointment. A producer may have been aware, right from the start, that for several years he will have to make an effort to conquer the market and that only after some years he will have obtained a sufficient volume of sales for his company to be profitable. If this is so, he will consider the result, in economic terms, of the first and second, and perhaps the third financial period - in which losses were incurred - as the costs of the production processes of, for instance, 4 or 5 years. Since we are speaking here of purposeful actions, this conception may not only be admissible, but it may also be economically rational. We emphasize the word *may* be, because it is a matter here to get to know conceptions, concepts. A very telling example of this conception we find repeatedly in the life insurance industry, particularly when we observe the item "organisation costs".

Normative Conclusion

The conclusion that the demarcation between costs and losses may entirely fade away, is important, for theory as well as for the practice. But it is also a dangerous conclusion and this only for the practice. It provides a refuge for any optimist in industry, whose company's results are not what he and others expected, as well as a refuge for a swindler for ripping off investors. It is necessary and useful that the nature of this fading is known, but one should be very careful in practice in using this knowledge. One should rather be on the side of caution, not count more than necessary on the future and use as a guideline for company policy that the postulate applies that *only a sacrifice which is made purposefully may be considered as a cost element.* And another postulate needs always to be kept in mind that *once it has become apparent that a sacrifice has been made partly or wholly in vain, it should no longer be characterised as a constituent element of income formation.* The sacrifice which has been made then needs to be considered as a loss. It is then a requirement of proper management policy to acknowledge the existence of this loss as quickly as possible, because it is useful that the useful as well as the useless effect of the sacrifices which have been made are established as soon as possible.

16. Costs and "Expenses"

Finally, we need to say something, in the framework of this discussion, about the distinction between costs and expenses.

All those sacrifices which are made on purpose, but which have remained without useful effect, are expenses in the true sense of the word. It is incorrect and confusing for an economic discussion, if, following common parlance, we call part of the costs expenses, although they have been incurred on purpose as much as the others. This word expresses the intuitive insight of many industrialists who consider all sacrifices for which he obtains no immediate result, as expenses. This view is of course incorrect. Cost precedes results. The sacrifices which have been made are only expenses if a result is not forthcoming, that is to say, if costs have been incurred in vain, wrongly, without results. We therefore do not speak of expenses when we are dealing with salaries, rent, lighting and heating, but of costs. Only that part of the costs which results in a loss, forms expenses; but this applies as much to those sacrifices for which an immediate result in the product was obtained.

17. Conclusion

The analysis set out so far shows clearly that the significance of cost for price formation is a far more complicated problem than one would expect from becoming familiar with the usual price formation theories. One has the impression in these theories, as if cost is an accurately determined given, which provides producers with an easily manageable guideline for their actions. The opposite is true. The difficulties in these theories are elegantly and ably skimmed over, difficulties which exist on the side of the people offering their product, whilst concentrating on the problems of demand, specifically consumers' demand. The price formation theory urgently requires review if it is to explain what actually happens in the market and if it is to provide a useful basis for other theories, specifically those dealing with the business cycle. The need for a review of price theory will be felt again and again when we continue the analysis.

4. JULIUS AUGUSTUS FRITZ SCHMIDT

(A) Schmidt and the Background to his Organic *Tageswertbilanz*

(i) Schmidt's Professional Activities

Elsewhere we have commented in detail on Schmidt and his *Betriebswirtschaft* theory (Clarke and Dean, 1986 and 1989). Relying inter alia on Schwantag's [1951] observations some points raised there will suffice here.

Schmidt's early professional life is instructive. A summary appeared in the Report of the Second (Het) International Accounting Congress in 1926:[1]

> Professor of Business Administration, born on March 13, 1882 in Wahrenbruck, a district of Halle. He had nine years of practical experience in the retail business, wholesale, manufacturing, bookselling, insurance, overseas import and export; during that time he spent one and a half years in New York and half year in Buenos Aires. From 1906 till 1909 he studied at the Leipzig Handelschochschule (School of Economics) and at the Universities of Leipzig and Besançon. Between 1909-1910 he was teacher at the Höhere Handelsschule (College of Business and Commerce) in Dortmund. From August 1910 until April 1912 he was research assistant, till April 1913 lecturer of business administration and since then professor at the academy and later at the University (of Frankfurt am Main). Visiting appointments: 1912 Cologne, 1922 Mannheim, 1925 Vienna. [p.379][2]

As a trained economist, who taught commerce at the Universities of Leipzig and Besançon it was not unexpected that his writings would exhibit a strong recourse to the current economic thought, particularly marginalism, Irving Fisher's work on indexation, and an acknowledged indebtedness to Ricardo for his replacement cost notions (Schmidt, 1923 and 1926). This did not mean that Schmidt uncritically accepted the current economic ideas. The words of Schwantag [1951, p.3] are apposite, "The book [*Domestic Payment Transactions*, 1920] is complemented by the description of cash payment transactions [which] are covered and also questions of monetary theory are dealt with. Schmidt's criticism of the quantity theory of money is put forward here."

---

1 Schwantag's biography, reproduced as *Appendix A* in Clarke and Dean (1986), covers both this early period of Schmidt's career and subsequent events.

2 This is a translation from the original German contained in the Proceedings, *Het Internationaal Accountantscongres* [1926].

Although Schmidt's work has received increasing attention recently, it has been frustrated by language barriers. Reference to Schmidt has been restricted primarily to his contributions in *The Accounting Review* (1930b, and 1931) and *The Harvard Business Review* (1930a). Yet Schmidt has been described by those able to pass through the language barrier as the progenitor of the ideas underlying replacement value theory (MacDonald, 1977, p.246) and as the developer of the "first, full-fledged theoretical framework dealing with inflationary accounting" (Mattessich, 1982, p.351). Perceiving Schmidt's organic notion, Mattessich (1982, p.354) described Schmidt's theory as a "genuine current cost system", and as having the aim of maintaining *relative* material values in the economy. It would also have the side benefit of mitigating the cyclical nature of economic activity. Schmidt considered indexation mechanisms such as *Indexbuchführung* and *Goldmarkbilanz* to be *partial* solutions (1924, pp. 80-121). In his opinion they failed to analyse firms and their related accounting in the context of the market economy, particularly in its depressed post-war state. In this respect they lacked an organic, holistic perspective. Clearly, he perceived accounting as an integral facet of any theory of economic equilibrium (Schmidt, 1921, pp.36-7). This perception of accounting as part of the theory of the dynamic economy is evident in the following extract attributed to "Schmidt, 1921":

> The firm does not operate in a void, but, is rather, part of the whole market economy. . . . A business manager without a clear conception of the source of his values, profits and losses would be as inconceivable as a captain without any knowledge of the current or a pilot who knows nothing about wind and weather conditions. (Isaac, 1950, p.126)

Schmidt, thus, can be seen to have proposed his organic current value accounting in a deliberate attempt to place the theory of the firm, and accounting for a firm in the context of a dynamic economy. The fundamental organic nature of this part of Schmidt's accounting theory is well captured by Schwantag [1951]:

> The main (academic) result of (Schmidt's early) studies is the conception of organic current value accounting *as a theory of relations of values in business administration*, derived from the relations of values in the economy. The title does not nearly indicate the contents covered in the work. Schmidt is neither only concerned with problems of accounting theory nor with problems of the practical preparation of the balance sheet. Rather he wants to analyse the substance of the production process of the firm from an economic point of view. The starting point is the practical experience of the effects of inflation and the fall in productivity resulting from the war and post-war period, which had lead to the disruption of the currency, the wear and tear of the stock of fixed assets and to the weakening of physical and productive working capacities to an unprecedented extent. Against this background of the economic situation of the time it was obvious that the measure of economic figures formerly held to be fixed - the money unit - was flexible in reality and that this flexibility had to be taken into account when measuring. There is hardly

> a contemporary expert in business administration who has not commented on the question of how the effects of inflation could be eliminated from accounting for the firm. But to realize that money as a measure is not fixed in general and that this causes fundamental problems for the relations of values in business administration as the basis of the disposition of firms as units of production - like private households as units of consumption - and that the solving of these tasks of disposition is of critical importance for economic equilibrium, is the unparalleled achievement of Schmidt. (pp.5-6)

This organic theme is apparent also in the extract from Schmidt (1929a), *Das Prinzip der relativen Werterhaltung* (The Principle of the Relative Maintenance of Value), reproduced at the end of Schwantag's [1951] biography. Schmidt's concept of the *maintained firm* entailed the retention of its relative capacity to *satisfy* consumers' needs, its relative share of the market for its production, its relative overall size in the productive fabric of the economy. Schmidt's firm was perceived as "a cell in a living organism which is a market economy" (De Motte Greene, 1937 p.77) and thus only one of the collection of economic means to an end. It was not an end in itself.

(ii) Schmidt and the 1920's *Betriebswirtschaftslehre*

Noted Austrian accounting historian, Seicht (1982, p.47), describes and places Schmidt's organic theory in historical perspective:

> F. Schmidt has extended and systematized the theories of Kovero (1912) and Fäs (1913). Schmidt, by his organic current value accounting wants to calculate the sales result based on current values in the sense of an operating profit for cost accounting purposes. Therefore expenditures have to be valued at replacement costs at the respective sales date and the assets of the balance sheet at their replacement costs at the balance sheet date.

It is also evident from the translated material that Schmidt was cognizant of the views of classical economists, in particular Ricardo (1817) and Carey (1837), who suggested that the replacement costs of factor inputs were relevant for businessmen contemplating action. This is clearly evident in Schmidt's acknowledgement of his indebtedness to these classical economists in his [1923] and [1926] works. In the [1923] article Schmidt noted Ricardo's belief that the "determinant for the price of any good is not the actual expenditure on behalf of that good, but the costs involved in the reproduction of that good".

Schmidt was one of a number of German academics in the 1920s pursuing the theory of business economics or theory of the firm. He was recognised as the intellectual leader of theorists advocating an *organic* theory of the firm. Schranz's (1930) overview of "modern German accountancy" theories indicated the scope of the

German modifications to conventional practice. Schranz's overview included descriptions of the static concepts of Schaer (1890), Hügli (1894), Nicklisch (1912) and Osbahr (1912). Explanations were given also of the *dynamic, monist* approach originating with Schmalenbach and of Schmidt's *organic, dualistic* theory. With respect to the latter Schranz noted:

> The organic balance sheet of Schmidt and his adherents is, as a matter of fact, the balance sheet of inflation times. It endeavours, to establish principles which *obtain also in the time of diminishing currency value*, that is, in the time of inflation. The organicists emphasize the principle, that only the *value of objects* must be included in the balance. It is only permitted to distribute profit, if the distribution *does not disturb the substantial reserves of the enterprise*. For the determination of results ... values on the day when the balance sheet is constructed must be employed . . . profit derived from the sales is given by the difference between this current replacement price and the selling price. The difference between the acquisition price and the selling price . . . is to be excluded from the calculation of the income, for this difference only causes a change in the value of the business assets. We carry over the difference - as a correcting item - to the account of the enterprise's own capital. In this way we have shown the fluctuation in the purchasing power of the enterprise's own capital. In preparing the balance sheet, *we must reckon with the same values*, viz., *the current values of the day of the statement.* In this way we obtain the correct figure for the profit arising from sale, and we can eliminate the acquisition price differences. With the employment of the organic process, production and consumption can be immediately followed with precision, and the disparities between production and consumption, manifested in economic crises, can be excluded. Economic crises are, in great part, attributable to the circumstance that the enterprises do not publish a faithful picture of themselves, but give false data in consequence of incorrect calculations of profit. (1930, p.166, *emphasis added*)

Schranz's explanations invite several observations. He seems to give Schmidt the role of leader in this field of thought, the others the role of "adherers", as being attached as followers of his central theme.[3] Similarity between Schmidt's ideas and contemporary arguments for replacement prices is beyond dispute. "Profit" can be distributed only if "substantial reserves" are not disturbed, he explained; profit on sales is calculated as the difference between the current selling price and the measure of the current cost of inputs, the "current replacement price" in Schmidt's scheme; and "value changes" in fixed assets are not income. Each is a feature of modern CCA proposals. Although discussed in more detail in *chapters 5* and *6*, the following extracts, taken mainly from Schmidt's [1926] seminal paper,[4] illustrate that similarity:

---

3 Schneider (1981, pp.137-8) confirms Schmidt as that movement's leader.

4 Originally presented at the Second International Accounting Congress [Schmidt, 1926]; then published in *Zeitschrift für Betriebswirtschaft*, Vol. 3, 1926 (pp.813-25, 906-29), and

[O]nce it has been admitted that in an individual sales transaction profit can only be what exceeds present acquisition costs of the input factors a later use of original acquisition costs in the profit and loss account would mean stating fictitious profits, namely holding gains, as profits; or fictitious losses, namely holding losses, as expenses. The provision set aside from individual sales for the replacement of the input factors would later in the case of fictitious profits, be partly declared as distributable without it being so; or the amount set aside from individual sales for profit distribution, because it is not needed for the replacement of the input factors, would in the case of fictitious losses later be added to capital, although the firm does not need that amount. (Schmidt, 1929a, p.265; cited in Schwantag [1951, pp.7, 8])

Business profit can only be that which exceeds the amount necessary for the maintenance of a firm's assets.... *In terms* of physical qualities it is only possible to increase the assets of a firm through turnover. Turnover, however, can involve either the transformation of goods into money and of money into goods (equation = goods ⇛ money ⇛ more goods) or of money into goods into money (equation = money ⇛ goods ⇛ more money). In the first case we are dealing with turnover of trade and manufacturing whereas in the other instance we have an example of speculative turnover. [Schmidt, 1926, p.384]

Reproduction value accounting is based on the concept that the assets of a nation and of a firm do not consist primarily of money but of goods . . . it tries to avoid the damages caused by the assumption that all assets are money . . . most of the inaccuracies of traditional balance sheet concepts result from this biassed conception of accounts. . . . The leading principle of the current value accounting approach is the maintenance of the firm in its real (physical) state . . . the firm can only generate a profit if the sales proceeds . . . are higher than the cost of replacement or reproduction at the date of sale. . . . *Profit is only that part of sales profits which exceeds the current acquisition value (replacement) of costs* . . . current value accounting . . . has to trace every single item through the sales accounts . . . by initially recording on the goods or merchandise account the incoming input factors at a cost value. . . . When the respective goods are sold the sales proceeds have to be compared with current acquisition value and not with the historic acquisition value. [Schmidt, 1926, p.407]

A balance sheet which is based on replacement values informs the entrepreneur about the value of his individual assets in the buying market at the date which the balance sheet is drawn up. If there are no omissions the total sum is the amount at that date which would have to be invested to rebuild the firm. [Schmidt, 1926, p.403]

A considerable portion of Schmidt's work contrasts with the ideas of some of the contemporary European business economics theorists; not only with Limperg (see *chapter 5*) but also many of the French writers of the 1920s (see *Appendix I*). His theory was operationalized into cost accounting as well as external financial

---

eventually included (almost verbatim) in Schmidt (1929a, pp.54-90). Also included in this volume.

accounting, a point overlooked by Edwards and Bell (1961); the French theories, we are told mainly were not (Wasserman, 1931, pp.8-9, notes 26 and 27).[5] Schmidt's accounting was proposed as a means that would be for the good of the economy; in contrast the French did not, in the main, allude to macro considerations. In this regard, the impact of the post-war inflation on Schmidt's thinking should not be overlooked. Of particular significance were the immediate pressure of German's precarious economic state following the war, and the crippling prospect of war reparation payments to be exacted by Britain, the U.S.A. and France (Bresciani-Turroni, 1937, pp.274-82 and Holtfrerich, 1986). In contrast the French did not have the same kind of pressure - they were to be reparation recipients. Reparation payments were a means by which French industry would be restored. For Germany, restoration and maintenance of industry were critical to the making of the reparation payments.

(iii) Schmidt's Published Work and Essential Features of *Organic Accounting*

In contrast to Limperg (*chapter 3*), Schmidt's *published* writings are large in number and substantial in content. Also his works gained international recognition; as noted in *chapter 2* some even appeared in Dutch in 1923, in English (1929), and his magnum opus, *Die organische Tageswertbilanz* (1929) was published in Japanese in 1934. Added to this his ideas were exposed internationally at the Second and Third International Accountants Congresses in Amsterdam, 1926 and in New York, 1929. There can be little doubt that the main features of his works could have been expected to have been known by leading European business economists. Voigtländer's [1952] bibliography, of Schmidt's works, attests to the extensive nature and potential accessibility of Schmidt's writings.

The essential features of Schmidt's organic theory are as follows:

(1) He believed any business or accounting theory should be consistent with the theory of economic equilibrium. He attempted to integrate the theory of the firm with a theory of accounting, an approach he described as *organic*. Specifically his theory was based on the "principle of relative maintenance of value", necessitating that a firm retain its relative capacity to satisfy customers' needs, its relative share of the market for its production and its relative overall size in the productive fabric of the economy.

---

5 The ideas of French theorists in the mid-to-late 1920s need to be documented in the Anglo-American literature. This would help historians better understand how *European* inflation accounting thought developed.

(2) Assets are to be shown at their costs of replacement as at the balance date.

(3) Contrary to the received wisdom, Schmidt understood exactly the effects of changes in the general level of prices. His examination of this issue was extensive (1922a; 1922b; 1924 pp.80-149; 1926 pp.394-8; [1927b]; (1929 pp.68-71); 1930b pp.236-8). Schwantag [1951, as translated in Clarke and Dean, 1986] suggests "that Schmidt wants to analyse the substance of the production process of the firm from an economic point of view . . . (taking account of) the effects of inflation and falling productivity . . . it was obvious that the measure of economic figures formerly held to be fixed - the money unit - was flexible in reality and that this flexibility had to be taken into account when measuring". In essence his organic system was a form of stabilized accounting, a point not lost on Sweeney who described Schmidt as "the German authority . . . (on) the subject (of stabilization)" (1935, p.199).[6] Schmidt in fact suggested a type of gearing adjustment nearly fifty years before the 1975 Godley and Cripps U.K. proposal emerged.

(4) Business profit can only be that which exceeds the amount necessary for the maintenance of a firm's productive assets [Schmidt, 1926, p.384]. . . . The leading principle of the current value accounting approach is the maintenance of the firm in its real (physical) state . . . the firm can only generate a profit if the sales proceeds . . . are higher than cost of either replacement or reproduction at the date of sale [Schmidt, 1926, p.407]. As implied by the argument in (3) above Schmidt was prepared to modify his replacement cost basis for capital maintenance in the case of speculative assets which were financed by loans. This issue is dealt with in Tweedie and Whittington (1984, pp.28-30) and Mattessich (1982, p.496).

(5) Changes in the values of fixed assets are not regarded as profit; the increases or decreases in values are recorded in a special capital reserve account (*Wertberichtigungskonto*).[7] Again this principle is modified in respect of speculative assets.

(6) Although Schmidt recognized the distinction between general and specific price changes and their differing impacts on a business, he rejected the *incorporation* in the accounts of general price changes in deference to specific price changes. However, this has to be considered in the light of his suggestion that firms should match their monetary assets and liabilities, a strategy he described as the "identity of values in the balance sheet". Balancing amounts of monetary assets and liabilities would protect the entity against changes in the value of money. This could be achieved, he argued, by financing real assets from owners' equity and nominal assets from debt capital (for detailed discussion see Clarke and Dean, 1986, p.77)

(7) Schmidt's work introduced ideas not held by many of his contemporaries in the German *Betriebswirtschaftslehre*. A considerable portion of his work contrasts with the ideas of some of the contemporary European theorists - this point was overlooked by Edwards and Bell (1961), but noted in the more recent

---

6 This point has been questioned by Graves (1990).

7 Schmidt used the following synonyms to depict this capital adjustment account; *Wertänderungskonto, Vermögenswertkonto, Wertberichtigungskonto*. The adjustment account corresponds to the more recent Current Cost Adjustment Reserve within the CCA system.

evaluations of Schmidt (e.g. Coenenberg and Macharzina, 1976; Mattessich, 1982, 1984; Tweedie and Whittington, 1984 and Filios, 1985).

(8) Schmidt's terms "Betriebsgewinn", or according to Mattessich "Umsatzgewinn" and "Spekulationsgewinn" (1984, p.521) or "Konjunktur-or-Marktgewinn" (1982, p.354), were synonymous with Edwards and Bell's "current operating profit" and "holding gain" respectively.

(9) Throughout Schmidt's works, argument and examples are couched in terms of economics applied to commodities, from the perspective of the wholesaler, retailer or consumer. This shows Schmidt's perspective of an integrated commercial environment in which his accounting was to function. Contrary to the view proposed by Limperg, it alludes to the integral part Schmidt perceived accounting to have in any complete theory of the firm and the economy.

Whereas each of Schmidt's contributions to the literature generally contain succinct statements relating to the substance of his organic theory, the focus on each occasion, understandably, was on the "essential features" of it. Identification of the salient features serves as a necessary backdrop to an informed reading of the following translations of his work (section **B**) and to comparisons with Limperg's *Bedrijfseconomie* (*chapters 5* and *6*, pp.277-301).

(B) Biographical Data and Other Translations of Schmidt's Ideas

(1) Karl Schwantag, "F. Schmidts wissenschaftliches Werk" (The Academic Work of Fritz Schmidt), *Abacus*, September 1986, pp.90-99; translation of original which appeared in *Zeitschrift für Betriebswirtschaft*, January 1951, pp.1-14.

(2) Dr. Voigtländer, "Bibliographie: Das wissenschaftliche Werk von F. Schmidt" (Bibliography: Fritz Schmidt's Academic Work), *Abacus*, September 1986; pp.99-102, translation of original which appeared in *Zeitschrift für Betriebswirtschaft*, January 1952, pp.182-5.

(3) Fritz Schmidt, "De winst van de onderneming" (Enterprise Profit), *De naamlooze vennootschap roermond*, 15 February & 15 March 1923, pp.302-4 and 332-34.

(4) Fritz Schmidt, "Gewinn und Bilanzwert" (Profit and Balance Sheet Value), *Proceedings, Second International Accountants Congress*, 1926, pp.381-419.

(5) Fritz Schmidt, "Indexziffern" (Index Numbers), in H. Nicklisch, *Handwörterbuch der Betriebswirtschaftslehre*, 1927, pp.274-82.

(6) Fritz Schmidt, "Ist Wertänderung am ruhenden Vermögen Gewinn oder Verlust?" (Do Holding Gains or Losses Represent Profit or Loss?), *Zeitschrift für Betriebswirtschaft*, 1928, pp.1-19.

The Academic Work of Fritz Schmidt[1]

Karl Schwantag

When Fritz Schmidt died about a year ago at the age of 68 he left behind an academic life-work which, in scope and depth of insight, only few academics are able to produce. When Schmidt, in 1906, took up his studies at the School of Economics in Leipzig, business administration legitimately could not be called a science. A century after its initially meagre starting point relating to the techniques of trade, a body of knowledge was erected which - no matter if it is regarded as an independent science or as part of an integrated business science - was clearly recognizable in its scope and structure and was firmly established, although not completed since this would signify the end of every science. Our insight into economic relations, as well as that of the methods of efficient practical economic management, has been enriched by his approach. One of the great architects taking part in that construction was Fritz Schmidt.

Schmidt's publications truly reflect the development that our discipline has taken from business techniques via systematic compilation and classification of methods of business administration to the theory of business administration within the framework of the economy. In his work *three stages* can easily be discerned:

- the *first* in which Schmidt deliberately limits his task to the clear recording and description of business organization forms and methods (1907-18);
- the *second* in which he advances, in important sectors of business administration, to the theory (1918-36);
- the *third* in which, in the process of consolidating the works of the second stage, he puts forward the theory of business administration in a consistent form. He did not have the privilege to finish these later works.

---

1 On 1 February, 1950, now almost a year ago, Dr rer. pol. Dr oec. h.c. Fritz Schmidt, retired full professor of business administration at Johann-Wolfgang-Goethe University in Frankfurt/Main, founder and editor of this journal, *Zeitschrift für Betriebswirtschaft [ZfB]* from 1924 to 1950, passed away. The following article by one of his students is published by the editor and publisher in his memory. The next number will carry a complete bibliography of Fritz Schmidt's academic work as supplement to this article.

[This article is translated from *ZfB*, January 1951, pp.1-14. The complete bibliography which follows was prepared by Dr Voigtländer and published in *ZfB*, January 1952, p.182-5. For the translations we are indebted to Walter Thanner and Thomas Junge; for checking consistency in translations we are grateful to Angelika Dean (née Schulz) and Sonja Wienker. Any errors and omissions and the use of English accounting terminology remain our responsibility.]

The following appreciation is based only on those articles which were fundamental in the development of knowledge. Numerous articles in which Schmidt discussed current economic and business problems, the development of auditing and *trusts* and the organization of academic studies of economics have to be neglected here, although they influenced practitioners quite considerably.

I. Recording and Classification of Material

a. *Works on the Stock Exchange System*

Schmidt's *first publications* deal predominantly with questions of the stock exchange and banking system. In addition, we find those from the field of trade: "Goods traffic in Bookselling Through a Mediating Agent" (1926), "Organization of an Argentine Textile Import business" (1910), "The Valorization of Coffee" (1909), "The Production of a Catalogue" (1910). In contrast to these articles, which obviously originate from occasional suggestions, the publications in the field of the stock exchange system are systematic preparations for the publication of his first book. Published in journals: "The Commodity Exchange of Le Havre" (1909), "Exchange Rates of Argentina" (1909), "Pricing on the Stock Exchange" (1910), "The Cotton Trade in Le Havre" (1910), "The Commodity Exchange of Paris" (1910), and "The Time Bargain Settlement Office of Le Havre" (1912) are the results of living abroad in Argentina and France; and "The influence on Prolongation of a Change of Practices in German Securities Trading" (1912). As a result of these research activities the book *Liquidation and Prolongation in Security Dealing* was published in 1912, with a second unchanged edition appearing in 1923. Schmidt describes the character of the work in the foreword: "Due to its emphasis on the individual firm, the only goal of this book is systematically to describe business techniques in their most important detail, although sometimes legal and economic problems are covered".[2] The book is intended to serve the practitioner, and in addition to that, "to bring a complex field of precision engineering of economic life forward to the economic expert".[3]

This deliberately limited task is fulfilled by the book exemplarily. For this reason, even today, it is the standard work for the business administrator* looking for an exact description of the technique of these two stock exchange transactions.

---

2 F. Schmidt, *Liquidation and Prolongation in Securtiy Dealing*, 2nd edn, Stuttgart 1923, p.iii.

3 *Ibid.*, p.iv.

* *Business administrator* and *business economist* are used synonymously.

An interesting example of academic work in this kind of publication is the *method of presentation.* In the first part the fundamentals of liquidation are outlined in the following order: goals - methods - results; followed by a second part which describes the execution of the liquidation at the stock exchanges of European countries. The same structure - only slightly modified - is used for the description of prolongation. It is noteworthy that Schmidt in the two basic parts of the work, after a description of empirical particulars, extracts what he regards as generally valid results. This already shows his pronounced academic inclination.

Schmidt again deals with problems of the stock exchange system in his article "The Formation of Stock Exchange Prices" (1918) which subsequently is followed by publication of the book *The Stock Exchange and its Transactions* (1st edn, 1920; 2nd edn, 1922 by Gloeckner's Handelsbücherei). Despite its (late) year of publication this work can still be counted as the first stage of Schmidt's method of working. "Its main task is . . . to categorize systematically the variety of phenomena of the stock exchange, which in a modern economy, . . . is totally indispensable" thereby enabling the reader "to come to a correct and just judgement of the very complex phenomena of stock exchange activity".[4] The work today still deserves much attention, although some details are now outdated. With that publication and the article "Arbitrage" in the *Concise Dictionary of Political Sciences*, (4th edn, 1923), Schmidt's research in the field of the stock exchange system concluded. He never took it up again.

b. Works on Banking

Of particular importance for the academic development of Schmidt are his research activities in the field of bank management and banking operations - of payment transactions. The first publication in a journal on the whole field is "French Joint Stock Banks" (1907). It is followed by "Exchange Rates of Argentina" (1909), "The French Mortgage Bank System" (1910), "The French Local Authority's Bank" (1910). As a result of that research work during the first world war he wrote the book, *Cashless Payment Transactions in Germany and their Advancement* (1917). Its goal is a "systematic and complete description of the existing channels of payment" in order to "come to a fair judgement of the performance of the involved intermediaries".[5] This publication is also limited to a systematic description of the organization and methods of the channels of payment and the organization of the intermediaries of payments. Here also the systematic description of individual facts is

---

4 F. Schmidt, *The Stock Exchange and its Transactions*, 2nd edn, Leipzig 1922, p.ii.

5 F. Schmidt, *Cashless Payment Transactions in Germany and their Advancement*, Leipzig/Berlin 1917, p.v.

followed by general results found by comparison of the outlined forms and by proposals for the improvement of the organization.

II. The Breakthrough to Theory

The *second stage* of Schmidt's research work is characterized by a substantially enlarged depth in its objectives. Not only the systematic description of technical procedures as such - which, however, as we have shown have been complemented by Schmidt who was such an outstanding conceptual thinker, his task now evident almost everywhere, is to provide general conclusions; certainly systematically registered empirical facts still remain the starting point for further research but now classified practical knowledge serves as the first step of a generalizing - theoretical - delineation of the essentials. The later works of that period even relinquish the description of single facts totally.

a. Payment Transactions

The first book to mention is *International Payment Transactions and Exchange Rates* published in 1919 (2nd edn, 1922). This work, as well as the last-mentioned, is based on preliminary studies over many years. In some chapters it also is an extremely profound systematic description of the international payments media, of the technical and calculation basis of foreign exchange dealings, its methods and organization. But beyond that, in its sections on the balance sheet system of international payments, on prices of the payment media, the short- and long-term fluctuations of exchange rates, their dependence on arbitrage and the economic control of exchange rates, it advances towards a theory in the best sense of the word. Above all it lays the foundation for a *new theory of balance of payments*, and in connection with that, a theory of the *formation of exchange rates*. Thoughts about the primary dependence of exchange rates on the balance of payments and about their secondary dependence on the balance of Receivables and Payables - which in its part is composed of the trade-, service - transactions, capital transfers and the balance of (short-term) borrowings which lead to a tertiary dependence of the exchange rate on the price level of goods - are also and especially in comparison with the latest (economic) publications in economics, still today of high academic merit. Due to direct deduction of theorems from a thorough analysis of the technical requirements, his thoughts have a special appeal and are of high educational value. This is not impaired by the fact that some details today are only of historical value and that important problems, especially those of government controlled international payment transactions, are not considered since they were not topical then. It is a great pity that the work could not be edited again in a new, up-to-date form.

In order to present a full coverage of the payment transactions system in 1920 Schmidt published the second substantially extended edition of his book, *Cashless Payment Transactions* under the title *Domestic Payment Transactions*. The book is complemented by the description of cash payment transactions. In this all of the domestic payment transactions are covered and also questions of monetary theory are dealt with. Schmidt's criticism of the quantity theory of money is put forward here. As well his statements on the question of money creation by paper- and deposit-money, are of lasting value. Incidentally, these arguments have been repeated in an extended form in his later works.

Apart from pertinent articles in the *Concise Dictionary of Political Sciences* 4th edition, "Clearing", "Cashless Payment Transactions" and "Postal Cheque" and a later concise description of payment transactions in the compilation, *The Civil Servants' University*, Schmidt did not express himself on these subjects again. His intention, contained in the course of the 3rd edition of the *School of Economics*, to publish another book on payment transactions unfortunately could not be realized.

b. "Organic" Current Value Accounting

In contrast to the aforementioned publications of books which were based on previous articles (in journals), Schmidt's most important work, *The "Organic" Balance Sheet Within the Framework of the Economy*, comes out without any preliminary publications. The first edition was published in 1921; a second, extended version in 1922; a third, substantially enlarged in 1929 and in the year 1934 a translation into Japanese was published. With this work Schmidt achieved tremendous success. The second edition already contains in the bud almost all the ideas, the extension of which occupied Schmidt till the end of his life. There is no doubt that the starting point can be found in his *Payment Transactions*. Being beyond the scope of narrow business administration, in this work he advanced from the individual phenomena of the firm or between firms to a general economic theory. In *Organic Current Value Accounting* - as the work is entitled from the 3rd edition - he extracts a relation between the values of the firm based on an analysis of the economy. That Schmidt has studied economic theory in preparation of this work is shown by his minor publication, *Fundamentals of Economics* which was first published as a small volume by Zellenbücherei in 1920, and the second edition in 1922. This book does not claim to enrich economic theory in an academic sense. It is a first orientation about basic economic relations for the educated lay person. As such it is distinguished by conciseness, preciseness and elegance of presentation. Although, according to present scientific standards, some of the basic theorems - like for example, Ricardo's theory of wages, the dependence of the saving ratio on interest rates, the theory of over-production as the cause of business cycles - are outdated. They either have been relinquished or at least have been complemented by Schmidt in later publications. The book even today could still serve its purpose and it definitely represented then, the present state of research. Unfortunately this small volume in the first edition was published under the title *Fundamentals of Economics in One Hour* - and not *Theory of Economics* - because in the same series other books like *History of the World, History of German Literature, History of World Literature* (the last two small volumes by the remarkable poet Klabund), and *Chemistry* have been published with the same appendix (to the title). This stirred up a certain animosity from exponents of the theory of economics which could be hardly less justified with any other business economist than Schmidt. Indeed, all his works provide evidence of the high importance he attached to economic facts and to the findings of economic theory for business administration. In connection with Schmidt's academic works this publication is worth mentioning because it shows, to a large extent, that he must have studied contemporary economic theory. After all it is common knowledge that the shorter and more concise, an actually extensive subject can be described, the more intensive must have been the author's preliminary studies.

From an academic point of view the main result of these studies is the conception of *organic* current value accounting as a *theory of relations of values in business administration*, derived from the relations of values in the wider arena of economics. The title does not indicate the contents covered in the work. Schmidt is neither only concerned with problems of accounting theory nor with problems of the practical preparation of the balance sheet. Rather he wants to analyse the substance of the production process of the firm from an economic point of view. The starting point is the practical experience of the effects of inflation and the fall in productivity resulting from the war and post-war period, which had lead to the disruption of the currency, the wear and tear of the stock of fixed assets and to the weakening of physical and productive working capacities to an unprecedented extent. Against this background of the economic situation of the time it was obvious that the measure of economic figures formerly held to be fixed - the money unit - was flexible in reality and that this flexibility had to be taken into account when measuring. There is hardly a contemporary expert in business administration who has not commented on the question of how the effects of inflation could be eliminated from accounting for the firm. But to realize that money as a measure is not fixed in general and that this causes fundamental problems for the relations of values in business administration as the basis of the disposition of firms as units of production - like private households as units of consumption - and that the solving of these tasks of disposition is of critical importance for economic equilibrium, is the unparalleled achievement of Schmidt. By that he anticipated findings which were only achieved by other economists many years later in the wake of the large world-wide depression in 1930/32 and which found their most precise expression in Keynes' *General Theory of Employment, Interest and Money,* published in 1936. What Keynes declared as the effect of liquidity preference, of disinclination for investment or consumption, namely the disproportion between workable input factors, demand for consumer goods and demand for producer goods, had been recognized by Schmidt as early as 1922, when he determined the cause of depression as being the insufficient inclination of producers to invest resulting from fictitious losses, the origin of involuntary unemployment as defined by Keynes. There is an analogy also for boom periods.

It is true that the discussion about the substance and the causes of business cycles has not been finalized to this day. This is proven by Haberler's work *Prosperity and Depression,* published by the former League of Nations and now edited by the United Nations, which provides a survey of the present state of business cycle theory. In discussing the theories of overinvestment it is pointed out:

> *Wrong accounting procedures*: There is also another factor which tends to increase the demand for consumer goods. Accounting is more or less based on the assumption of a constant value of money. Periods of higher inflation have shown that this tradition is very deep-rooted and that long and unpleasant experiences are necessary to change habits. The effect is that durable production goods - like machinery and factory buildings - are entered into cost accounting at their actual acquisition costs and are depreciated on that basis. When prices rise this procedure is wrong. The higher replacement costs should be substituted for the historical acquisition costs. However, that does not take place, or only to an insufficient extent and only after prices have risen considerably. That results in depreciation charges which are too low, paper profits* arise and the entrepreneur is tempted to increase his consumption. In such a case capital is treated as income. In other words: consumption exceeds current production.[6]

The footnote* added by Haberler is particularly interesting:

> These paper profits are also capable of enhancing the cumulative power of the upswing because they encourage creditors and debtors to borrow and to lend more. They promote an optimistic mood which is predominant during the upswing and as a result credit expansion is likely to be accelerated. This phenomenon is exactly reversed in the downswing of the cycle. See the excellent analysis of that phenomenon in E. Schiff, *Capital Accumulation and Capital Consumption During Business Cycles* (1933), especially chapter IV, pp.113-134; also F.

6 Haberler, *Prosperity and Depression*, 3rd edn, p.55.

Schmidt, *Business Cycles in Industry - A Miscalculation* (1927), who has tried to build up a complete theory of business cycles on this factor.

The footnote reveals that Schmidt's *Theory of Business Cycles from the Viewpoint of Business Administration* (Berlin/Wien, 1933) apparently did not come to Haberler's attention either during the writing of the first edition in 1936 or during the further editions, as an earlier edition of Schmidt's work with the referred title *Business Cycles in Industry - A Miscalculation!* is quoted in a book of Schiff which was finished in 1932. At least it is shown that Schmidt's ideas meanwhile have been generally accepted as an important contribution to the theory of business cycles.

Economic theory of the past 20 years was able to make substantial progress due to the perception that the economic process can be explained only after an *analysis of the behaviour of the planning of economic entities - firms and households*.

> Since it is oriented to the future such a causal analysis which also aims at explaining a concrete historical economic process, necessarily has to start with the analysis of the economic plans of individual planning subjects, e.g. in the free (exchange) economy with which we are dealing, analysis of the economic plans of households, private firms and of the government. This is so because each disposition which is realized is the result of a certain economic plan or calculation.[7]

To the extent that this conception becomes accepted the immediate practical importance of the accounting system of firms for the development of the economic process will become more and more clear. The importance of the actual behaviour of firms, to the extent that they differ from that which is assumed in the conventional theoretical models of thinking, has been shown especially in the research works of Hans Möller.[8]

Now, perhaps it may be argued that the basis for business dispositions really is not the balance sheet nor the profit and loss account but cost accounting. But in cost accounting the claims made by Schmidt regarding the evaluation of costs and profits and by that, with regard to his profit concept - with certain modifications and refinements which in particular Schmalenbach contributed to[9] - would be common knowledge in business administration. To that now we can reply in Schmidt's own words, "If once it has been accepted that in an individual sales transaction profit can only be what exceeds present acquisition costs of the input factors a later use of original acquisition costs in the profit and loss account would mean stating fictitious profits, namely holding gains, as profits; or fictitious losses, which are holding losses,

---

7 Erich Schneider, *Introduction to Economic Theory*, Part II, Tübingen 1949, p.1.

8 Hans Möller, *Costing, Sales Policy and Price Policy*, Vienna 1941.

9 E. Schmalenbach, *Costing and Price Policy*, 6th edn, Leipzig 1934, and *Control of the Economy Through Prices*, Vol.I, Bremen/Horn 1947.

as expenses. The provision set aside from individual sales for the replacement of the input factors would later, in the case of fictitious profits, be partly declared as distributable without it being so; or the amount set aside from individual sales for profit distribution, because it is not needed for the replacement of input factors, would in the case of fictitious losses later be added to capital, although the firm does not need that amount. *It is impossible for me to understand this dualism in the attitude towards the profit term. The economy as well as economics would have to be void of any logic if that shiftability of terms were possible.*"[10]

What was proven logically here by Schmidt meanwhile has turned out to be *practically* necessary. The consistent and systematic short-term and yearly statement of income developed from cost accounting, but which at the same time is part of the profit and loss account [one of the annual financial reports], has been called "*organic profit and loss accounting*" in the rules and guide-lines for cost accounting and the recently published guide-lines for accounting by the study group of business administration of industrial associations. The application of these rules eliminates all distortions due to tax and commercial laws and is aimed at reporting the correct operating profit only. It has been shown elsewhere[11] that *organic* capital accounting also is implied in it, at least imminently; and if you want to calculate correct costs of interest it has to be prepared in the context of the total balance sheet. The fact that tax authorities still disapprove balance sheets and income statements based on current values rather supports the correctness of current value accounting than speaks against it. How far the criterion of an accounting, which is correct from the point of view of business administration, is from their thoughts, the numerous valuation laws which are conditioned by mere tax purposes - for example the discretionary valuation for certain fixed assets - have demonstrated well enough. But, as soon as the statement of income is introduced as appropriate in general, it will be impossible also for tax authorities in the long run to disapprove of such a correct accounting method. Therefore we can by no means agree with Schmalenbach that the dualistic balance sheet concept should be dropped because the endeavours of the dualists have not been successful.[12]

Our portrayal up to this point has primarily dealt with the appreciation of Schmidt's theorem of the sales profit as the relevant amount for business dispositions and for distribution - of which holding gains as they are unrealized speculation profits have to be clearly distinguished - now only a few words need be dedicated to the

10 F. Schmidt, *"Organic" Current Value Accounting*, 3rd edn, Leipzig 1929, p.265, emphasis in the original.

11 K. Schwantag, *Interest Rate and Capital in Cost Accounting*, Frankfurt am Main, 1949, p.54.

12 E. Schmalenbach, *"Dynamic" Accounting*, 8th edn, Bremen/Horn 1947, p.110.

other, hardly less important propositions. From the consideration of the fluctuations of productivity which can be caused as well by changes in the marginal productivity of the production factors, as by a change in the technical horizon, he derives the principle of the *relative - not the absolute - maintenance of values.*[13] Thus holding gains are kept separate from sales profits, since the latter which differ from gains resulting from changes in the value of money, in that they are realized. Further the *principle of the identity of values in the balance sheet* means that a protection of the firm against the effects of changes in the value of money, affecting the nominally fixed assets and liabilities, can be achieved by financing real assets from owners' equity and nominal assets from debts. The parts in Schmidt's writings concerning the connection of the reproduction and the discounted present value are of special importance, and should be obvious for anyone in practice who has ever had to calculate the whole value of a large firm afresh.

The fact that, in a certain way the correctness of current value (organic) capital accounting has been acknowledged, in principle - at least in this case - denominating opening balance sheets (after the war) in Deutschen Mark is mentioned here but it cannot be taken as evidence of a general acceptance of Schmidt's ideas. However, this instance proves, that if changes in values occurring in the economy are strong enough, an adjustment of the balance sheet in the sense of *organic* (current value) accounting can become inevitable.

The ideas which Schmidt developed in his *organic* current value accounting were followed up subsequently in numerous articles and contributions to compilations. The most important ones are:

Contributions:

The Firm in the Framework of the Economy, in: *Outline of Business Administration*, Vol. 2;

Profit and Balance Sheet Valuation, in: *Second International Accountants Congress* (1926);

The Valuation of Fixed Assets in Financial Statements: *International Congress of Accounting* (1929) [subsequently reproduced in *The Accountant*, 16 November, 1929 pp.619-26];

The Factors of Industrial Capital Requirements, in: *Capital and Capitalism* (1931).

13 [For more information on this point see the translation from Schmidt (1929a), "The Principle of the Relative Maintenance of Value", at the end of Schwantag's biographical note.]

Articles:

Profit and Fictitious Profit of the Firm (1922);
Balance Sheet Adjustment with Index Figures (1922);
The Profit of the Firm (1922);
Revaluation of Balance Sheets to a New Currency (1924);
New Goldmark Balance Sheets and Goldmark Accounting (1924)
Value of the Firm and Capital Evaluation with a Goldmark Balance Sheet (1924);
The Adaption of Firms to their Economic Situation (1926);
Profit and Balance Sheet Valuation (1926);
Rising Depreciation Charges (1927);
Is a Value Change in Assets a Profit or Loss? (1928);
The Distorted Profit and Loss Account (1928);
Balance Sheet and Taxes (1928);
The Importance of Replacement Value (1930);
Is Appreciation Profit? (1931);
Nominal and Real Balance Sheets (1937).

Most of the articles in German are published in *ZfB*[14] and are contained in the 3rd edition of his book.

c. *Cost Accounting and Price Policy*

It has been emphasized already that the valuation principles for the firm, developed by Schmidt, apply to all forms of accounting not just for the balance sheet and the profit and loss account for which they are described in *organic* current value accounting. Therefore it is suggested that the significance of its particularities, for cost accounting should be delineated. Schmidt did it in the book, *Replacement Prices on the Day of Turnover in Cost Calculation and in the Economy* which was published in 1923. Here, only some theoretically important supplementations and enlargements which the work contains, when compared with *organic* current value accounting, are pointed out.

In connection with the supplementation of the theoretical foundations, the introduction of the *circulation model* has to be mentioned, which after its initial development by the *Physiocrats*, for a long time had not been used for the description of the economic relations between macro-economic current figures. With that

14 Further: F. Schmidt, *Balance Sheet Value, Annual Profit and Balance Sheet Revaluation*, Berlin 1924. A complete list of all of Schmidt's publications with an exact specification of the source is to be published in the next number of this journal. [It is reproduced at the end of this article.]

Schmidt picks up an approach which has become typical of the economic theory of the last decade.[15]

The theoretical importance of Schmidt's circulation models lies in their application not only in explaining the relations in a stationary economy but, after an introduction of data variations - especially the circulation of money and the changes in productivity - in using them to carry out an analysis of the repercussions of the change of macro-economic figures on the micro-economic values of the firm. The improvement of this method, which was not fully developed at the time of the first publication, was one of the main objectives of Schmidt's later works, in particular the unfinished *General Business Administration.* Of importance also are the critical comments on the different possible methods of *index calculation* which later have been developed further in the article "Index Numbers" published in the *Manual of Business Administration* [1927].

Also worthy of attention is the lack of any comment on the problem of the dependence of *costs* on the *degree of employment* although Schmidt already had referred to it in the second edition of *Organic Current Value Accounting*. There he adopts Schmalenbach's definitions of costs. As his own idea the postulation emerges that the firm concerned should *combine the production factors in such a way that all of them cross the threshhold of degression at the same time*. Moreover progressively increasing costs are already called "degenerated proportional or degressive". The book does not deal with cost accounting techniques. Price policy is described but not its dependence on output and inputs and by that on the degree of employment; rather only the repercussions of the principle of current value in a situation where costs are assumed to be fixed, are analysed. Price formation of the monopolist is dealt with in the chapter, "Dangers and abuses in cost accounting and price policy".

Schmidt does not consider the problem of costs and the degree of employment in detail before publication of the article, "Cost Calculation and the Degree of Employment" in 1925. He deals with price policy again and more extensively in an article, in 1929 ["Price Policy"]. Both publications, as well as the articles "The Just Price" (1922), "Sliding - Scale Prices in the Price Policy of Companies" (1922), and "The Theory and Practice of Decreases in Prices and Wages" (1930) were preliminary work for "Cost Calculation and Price Policy" published in the first edition of *Handelshochschule* [College of Commerce] in 1930 and in an extended reprint as a book in the same year. Having been written as a textbook this work contains a description of cost recording and apportioning, and remarks on the tasks and forms of calculation (whereby the fixing of unit *profit* is mentioned in particular), and on the short-term operating account. In particular the chapters, "Cost Calculation and the

15 For example Böhler, Erik Schneider, von Stackelberg, Waffenschmidt.

Degree of Employment", "Price Policy", "The Dynamics of Price Policy" and "Adaption of Operations Through Price Policy" are theoretically interesting. Here Schmidt coins the term *graded* cost calculation, in other words a cost accounting which places side by side total costs as well as a breakdown of costs in categories for various product quantities per unit of time. Such a cost calculation shows the minimum cost from the total cost of all the units and the cost categories referring to each unit. The price policy should be based on the optimum costs of a unit rather than on the average costs. "The price policy of a businessman aims at achieving the most favourable operating results through full employment. This can be achieved by either influencing the quantity of the products and the means of production upon the prices of cost components and goods, (in other words the profit margin), or by influencing the prices of products (cartels) upon the quantity. Consequently means of price policy are the fixing of prices of the products as well as the quantity of the products and means of production for an individual firm or a whole industry. Limits to price policy are in the first place the estimations of consumer demand, and secondly the costs of the products and their cost components".[16] With regard to the question, dealt with by Schmalenbach, as to whether regulated prices (cartel prices) should be kept inflexible in, or adapted to, the course of business cycles, Schmidt supports the latter opinion since "every stabilisation of prices deprives the world of its regulating power and hence is absolutely to be rejected".[17]

Schmidt also examines the problems in determining the *lower limit for prices* and comes to various conclusions for each of the following situations:

1) Surplus production industries:

   (a) Choice between winding-up and reduction through continuing operation,
   (b) Continuing operation and temporary closure;

2) Normal situation of markets and operations; and

3) Over-employment.

The lower limits for prices are: in the case of *1a*, the proportional allocated costs plus yield from net realization value minus the yield from the future value of maintained assets of a material and immaterial kind; in the case of *1b*, the proportional unit costs minus the additional costs for idle time and restarting; in the case of *2*, the average unit costs during full-employment; in the case *3*, the average

16 F. Schmidt, *Cost Calculation and Price Policy*, Berlin/Vienna, 1930, p.114.

17 F. Schmidt, *ibid.*, p.120.

unit costs during full-employment for the quantity of full-employment and for the excess production, the average unit costs during full-employment plus the additional costs of over-employment.

It appears that Schmidt attempted to solve the problems of price policy based on their dependence on costs and degree of employment, quite originally, even though not in accordance with the form supported by the majority of the other cost and price theorists.

Other published works by Schmidt in this area are the following articles "Principles of Price Policy" (1933), "Incentive Pay" (1935), "Rationalization, Price and Wages" (1936), "Cost Planning, Capacity Utilization and Export" (1936), "Profit of War and Armament" (1937), "Differential Return or Output Bonus" (1940), and "Depreciation During War" (1941).

These publications were published in the *ZfB*. It would be going too far to consider the content of these articles in more detail here, they are worth reading over and over again, however they do not contain essentially any new theoretical viewpoints.

As the last major publication in this field, "Cost Calculation and Price Policy" was rewritten for the second edition of the *Handelshochschule* in which an interesting chapter on *state price policy* was included. Regrettably the remarks on the dynamics of price policy and the adaption of operations through price policy, which had been in the first edition, were not included in the new edition.

d. *Theory of Business Cycles*

As well as the last edition of *Organic Current Value Accounting* and *Cost-and Price-Policy*, the book, *Theory of Business Cycles from the Viewpoint of Business Administration* published in 1933 is a further development of the ideas which in the bud were already contained in the fundamental publications of the years 1920 to 1923. Schmidt first developed these ideas further in an article in the *Zeitschrift für Betriebswirtschaft* with the title "Business Cycles in Industry - A Miscalculation!", published in 1927. The work then was published as a separate publication, and as supplement to the *School of Economics* (1st edn), under the same title. Finally in its 4th edition, which was substantially enlarged, it was entitled *Theory of Business Cycles from the Viewpoint of Business Administration.* Its importance has already been pointed out above. Careful analysis of the statistical data, as well as comments on other theories of business cycles and the detailed representation of economic changes in market situations together with the parts on cyclical trend analysis and business cycle policy, make the book one of Schmidt's most valuable works. A shortened version has been incorporated in the 2nd edition of the *School of*

Economics under the title "Economic Fluctuations in Business Administration and Economics". New material provides an instructive analysis of the economic fluctuations in the years 1933 to 1938 due to government interference.

Articles on this subject include: "Business Cycles in Industry - A Miscalculation!" (1927), "Business Cycles and Job Creation" (1935) and finally the contribution, "Balance Sheets and Business Cycles" to *The Balance Sheets of Firms, Festschrift to Julius Ziegler* (1933).

III. The Consistent Theory of Business Administration

The essential works of the third stage of Schmidt's life-work are: "Introduction to Business Administration" (published in the 2nd edition of the *School of Economics*), the first volume of the "General Business Administration" (published in the 3rd edition of the *School of Economics*), an article "Capital Formation from Sales" in the *Zeitschrift für das gesamte Kreditwesen* (1949) and his last publication " "The Firm in the Cycle of the Economy" which came out as the first article when . . . this journal resumed publication after the war. He did not live to see it.

Already the "Introduction . . ." contains a *general theory of business administration from the current value perspective.* After a description of the object of the analysis and the method of economics and its development and classification, he deals with the relation of government and business, of economics and economic practice. Subsequently, economic principles of management based on scientific operating methods and the integration in the economic process, the market as an instrument of the economy are discussed and a theory of business profit is presented. As basic terms of an economy based on sales and private capital, the substance of expenditure and costs, the acquisition value, holding gains and losses, proceeds and the production factors are discussed. An analysis of the firm within a (circular) economic process - hence the model of a stationary economy - is followed by an analysis of the factors changing the economy and the dynamics of economic changes. Consistent theories about individual branches of the course of operation are derived from a general economic theory. This gives the paper an internal consistency which makes it stand out amongst most other theories of business administration. That Schmidt, however, did not regard this publication as a satisfying keystone of his work is shown by the first volume of his new *General Theory of Business Administration* in which the structure is even more systematic and in which the sequence of ideas is even more consistent than in the first edition. It includes the chapters: "Economy and Economics - Economic Methods - The Business in the Cycle of the Economy - The Dynamics of Economic Changes - The Changing Factors of the Economy", within which the general economic expositions are concluded. The time necessary to draw conclusions from these expositions was not granted to Schmidt.

In his last paper: "The Firm in the Cycle of the Economy", Schmidt summarizes the most essential findings of a busy life as a researcher in title and content on only a few pages: "The Business as a Unit of the Economy - The Organic Approach - The Stations of the Cycle - The Sales Economy - The Property and Capital Economy - The Personnel Economy - The Circulation Equation in a Synchronous Economy". These brief headings of the individual chapters reflect the quintessence of his findings and the way they developed in Schmidt's long struggles to find solutions to problems. Schmidt concludes his life work with the words:

> The inquiries so far have shown that in the circulation of assets through the economy and through businesses, goods and money are intertwined like woven fabric. As a conferrer of purchasing power, money is like a magnet from which the flow of goods is attracted and forced in the direction of the consumer. The circulation equation results from the circulation of incomes . . . Every change in the flow of goods or purchasing power means a change in costs and prices. Thereby the way is open to findings which disclose the field of general market changes to managers and provide the basis for management dispositions in good times. A practitioner needs such universal principles of business operations and management in order to - in the disorder of isolated phenomena and the wrong opinions that stem from various agitations and ideologies - put a clear arrangement in his dispositions which correspond with the regularity of the economic process.

The Principle of the Relative Maintenance of Value

> Based on the knowledge that the natural and harmonic principles of a free economy, regulated through competition and the point of maximum profit, bear the tendency to always adjust to the individual business so that it offers the consumers the highest degree of satisfaction, it basically requires only an examination of the effects of these principles on the business in order to create the foundations for the extension of an organic accounting system. As the highest principle for the organic examination of a business the principle of its relative maintenance of value stems from this. Maintenance of value of a business does not mean protecting fossilized establishments which barely meet the demands of consumption anymore, rather it means maintaining each business at its relative value, i.e. to the degree to which it serves the satisfaction of consumers" needs in each case. This is the first meaning of the attribute *relative,* though there are still other meanings.
>
> The maintenance of value is relative also in regard to the total production. If total production falls [as in Germany after World War I] the size of the individual business has to quantitatively fall too; the business only has a claim to a relative share of the reduced production and its assets have to fall below their replacement values - to the level where the assets are needed for production and turnover. If an increase in

production takes place, *ceteris paribus*, the circulation of the economy allows a proportional augmentation of the individual business in which assets will increase above replacement value as they are not enough for production and sales.

A precondition of the demand for the maintenance of value of a business is the maintenance of that degree of internal economy which allows it to produce at costs which are below the market price by at least the entrepreneur's remuneration and normal interest plus the risk surcharge.

F. Schmidt (*Organic Current Value Accounting*)

****

Bibliography: Fritz Schmidt's Academic Work[1]

Dr Voigtländer

The titles of books are marked with an asterisk (*).

I. First Publications

*1. *Accountancy for the Commercial Operations of Municipalities Using the Example of a Power Plant*, Berlin (Springer) 1914.

2. "Book Trade through Negotiation of an Agent", *Zeitschrift für Handelswissenschaft und Handelspraxis (ZHH)*, Vol. 1, 1908-9, pp.162-70.

3. "Valorization of Coffee", *Jahrbuch Nationalökonom*, new series, Vol. 38, 1909, pp.662-70.

4. "Organization of the Specimen Section of the Telegraphic Circulation of an Overseas Import Transaction", *ZHH*, Vol. 2, 1909-10, pp.319-24.

5. "Organization of an Argentine Textile Import Business", *Deutsche Handelsschullehrer Zeitung*, Vol. 7, 1910, pp.157-61, 169-72.

6. "Transactions in Wool at Le Havre", *ZHH*, Vol.3, 1910-11, pp.128-30, 251-5, 329-30, Vol. 4, 1911/12, pp.49-51, 363-5, 395-6.

7. "The Production of a Catalogue", *ZHH*, Vol. 3, 1910/11, pp.352-6.

8. "Principles of Classification", *ZHH*, Vol. 4, 1911/12, pp.96-100.

9. "Average Percentage on Stock-Taking", *ZHH*, Vol. 7, 1914/15, pp.285-7.

II. The Stock Exchange System

*1. *The Carry-Over (Prolongation) Dealing*, Munich (Beck), 1912.

*2. *Liquidation and Prolongation in Securities Dealing: A Systematic Description of its Technique*, Stuttgart 1st edn 1912, 2nd edn 1923, 283pp.

*3. *The Stock Exchange and Its Transactions*, Leipzig 1921, 2nd edn 1922.

4. "Arbitrage", *Handwörterbuch der Staatswissenschaften.*, 4th edn,Vol. 1, 1923, p.916-20.

---

1 [Translated from *Zeitschrift für Betriebswirtschaft (ZfB)*, January 1952, pp.182-185. This listing was prepared by Dr. Voigtländer and is a follow up to Karl Schwantag, "Fritz Schmidt's Academic Work", *ZfB*, January 1951, pp.1-14.]

5. "Exchange Rates of Argentina", *ZHH*, Vol. 2, 1909-10, pp.54-6, 147-51.

6. "The Commodity Exchange of Le Havre", *ZHH*, Vol. 2, 1909-10, pp.420-7.

7. "The Commodity Exchange of Paris", *ZHH*, Vol. 2, 1910-11, pp.289-321.

8. "The Time Bargain Settlement Office in Le Havre", *ZHH*, Vol. 5, 1912-13.

9. "The Influence on Prolongation of a Change in Practices in German Securities Trading", *ZHH*, Vol. 5, 1912-13, pp.205-8.

10. "On the Theory of Exchange Rates", *Zeitschrift für handelswissenschaftliche Forschung* (ZHF), Vol. 11, 1916-17, pp.93-124.

11. "Formation of Stock Exchange Prices", *Deutsche Handelsschullehrer Zeitung*, Vol. 15, 1918, pp.125-7, 133-6, 141-4, 151-3.

12. "The Formation of Stock Exchange Prices", *Zeitschrift für Sozialwissenschaften*, new series, Vol. 9, 1918, pp.375-94, 520-49, 635-58.

13. "The Control of Current Exchange Rates. A General Theory", *Weltwirtschaftliches Archiv*, Vol. 13, 1918, pp.531-79.

14. "The Relation of Counter Rates in Foreign Payment Transactions", *ZHH*, Vol. 11, 1918-19, pp.232-42.

15. "Exchange Rates and Their Control During the World War and in the Transition Period", *Weltwirtschaftliches Archiv*, Vol. 14, 1919, pp.210-74.

16. "Arbitrage and Exchange Rates", *Schmollers Jahrbuch, new series*, Vol. 43, 1919, pp.203-62.

17. "The Dependence of Exchange Rates on Interest Transactions and Differences in Interest Rates Prevailing in the Market", *Schmollers Jahrbuch, new series*, Vol. 43, 1919, pp.743-69.

18. "Balance Sheet Idea and Exchange Rates", *Zeitschrift für Sozialwissenschaften, new series,* Vol. 10, 1919, pp.125-54, 285-302.

III. Banking

*1. *Domestic Payment Transactions* (see Section IV, "Payment Transactions").

*2. *Balance Sheet Value, Annual Profit and Balance Sheet Revaluation*, Spaeth and Linde, Berlin 1924 (Bücherei für Bilanz und Steuern Vol. 11).

*3. "*Balance Sheets of Commercial Banks*" (together with Prof. Kalveram) in Das Buch des Kaufmanns, 6th edn, Vol. 2, pp.511-20, Stuttgart 1922.

4. "French Joint Stock Banks", *Zeitschrift für die gesamten Staatswissenschaften*, Vol. 63, 1907, pp.710-11.

5. "The French Mortgage Banking System", *Zeitschrift für das gesamte Staatswesen*, Vol. 66, 1910, pp.73-107.

6. "The French Local Authority's Bank", *Die Bank*, Vol. 1910, pp.628-36.

7. "Argentine Banking", *Zeitschrift für das gesamte Staatswesen*, Vol. 67, 1911, pp.96-113.

8. "Provincial Clearing Houses in Cheque Transactions. II", *Bank-Archiv*, 1917-18, pp.79-81.

IV. Payment Transactions

*1. *National Payment Transactions*, 2nd rev. edn, Leipzig 1920. (First published as *Cashless Payment Transactions in Germany and their Advancement*, Leipzig 1917).

*2. *International Payment Transactions and Exchange Rates*, Leipzig 1919, 2nd edn 1922.

3. "Clearing", *Handwörterbuch der Staatswissenschaften*, 4th edn, Vol.1, 1923, p.18.

4. "Cashless Payment Transactions", *Handwörterbuch der Staatswissenschaften*, 4th edn, Vol. 2, 1924, pp.330-61.

5. "Postal Cheque", *Handwörterbuch der Staatswissenschaften*, 4th edn, Vol. 6, 1925, pp.984-8.

6. "Payment Transactions", *Die Beamtenhochschule*, Vol. 4, pp.323-90.

7. "Improvement in Cashless Payment Transactions", *Die Bank*, 1918, pp.15-23, 110-17.

V. The Organic Current Value Accounting

*1. *Fundamentals of Economics*, Leipzig 1919 (Zellenbücherei 24).

*2. *The Organic Balance Sheet within the Framework of the Economy*, Leipzig 1921, 2nd edn 1922; 3rd edn *Organic Current Value Accounting* 1929; 1934 Japanese Translation, 4th edn 1951.

3. "Organic Accounting", *Handwörterbuch der Betriebswirtschaftslehre (Hdw. d. Bwl.)*, Vol. 1, 1926, column 1346-51.

4. "The Firm within the Framework of the Economy", *Die Betriebsverwaltung*, Grundriss der Bwl. Vol. 2, pp.68-95, Leipzig 1927.

5. "Profit and Balance-Sheet Valuation", *Het Internationaal Accountantscongres*, Amsterdam 1926, pp.378-419.

6. "Principles of Valuation", *International Congress on Accounting*, New York 1929, pp.493-511.

7. "The Factors of Industrial Capital Requirements", *Kapital und Kapitalismus*, Vol. 2, Berlin 1931, pp.116-33.

8. "Accounting Theory", *Die Handelshochschule*, 2nd edn, 1937.

9. "Profit and Fictitious Profit of the Firm", *Zeitschrift für Aktienwesen*, Vol. 32, 1922, pp.50-6.

10. "Balance Sheet Adjustment with Index Numbers (Goldmark Accounting)", *Zeitschrift für Aktienwesen*, Vol. 32, 1922, pp.474-82.

11. "De winst van de onderneming" ("The Profit from the Business"), *De naamlooze vennootschap roermond*, Vol. 1, 1922-23, pp.301-4, 332-4.

12. "Revaluation of Balance Sheets to a New Currency", *Zeitschrift für das Gesellschaftswesen*, Vol. 33, 1923, pp.381-7.

13. "New Goldmark Balance Sheets and Goldmark Accounting", *Zeitschrift für Betriebswirtschaft* (*ZfB*), Vol. 1, 1924, pp.2-34.

14. "The Value of the Firm and Capital Evaluation with a Goldmark Balance Sheet", *ZfB*, Vol. 1, 1924, pp.209-20.

15. "Accounting Theory", *Mitteilungen des deutschen Hauptverbandes der Industrie*, Vol. 6, Teplitz 1925, pp.430-6.

16. "The Adaption of Firms to their Economic Situation", *ZfB*, Vol. 3, 1926, pp.85-108.

17. "Profit and Balance-Sheet Valuation", *ZfB*, Vol. 3, 1926, pp.813-25, 906-20.

18. "The Profit-Sales Ratio", *Archiv für das Revisions- und Treuhandwesen*, Vol. 23, 1927, pp.79-83.

19. "Depreciation Increased by Saved Interests", *ZfB*, Vol. 4, 1927, pp.816-39.

20. "Is a Value Change in Assets a Profit or a Loss?", *ZfB*, Vol. 5, 1928, pp.1-19.

21. "The Distorted Profit and Loss Account", *ZfB*, Vol. 5, 1928, pp.81-99.

22. "Accountancy and Taxation", *ZfB*, Vol. 5, 1928, pp.561-75, 641-59.

23. "The Importance of Replacement Value", *The Accounting Review*, Vol. 5, 1930, pp.235-42.

24. "The Accuracy of Balance Sheet Figures and the Leader Principle", *ZfB*, 1935, pp.385-407.

25. "Nominal and Real Balance Sheets", *ZfB*, 1937, pp.309-13.

26. "Is Appreciation Profit?", *The Accounting Review*, Vol. 6, 1931, pp.289-93.

VI. Works on Accountancy and Price Policy

*1. *Replacement Price on the Day of Turnover in Cost Calculation and the Economy*, Spaeth and Linde, Berlin 1923.

*2. *Fictitious Profit, Calculation and the Balance Sheet*, Teplitz-Schonau 1924.

*3. *Cost Calculation and Price Policy*, Spaeth and Linde, Berlin 1930.

4. "Inflation and Accounting", F. Schmidt, G. Strutz and R. Fischer (eds), *Inflation and Business*, Berlin 1923, pp.1-39.

5. "Index Numbers", *Hdw. d. Bwl.*, Vol. 3, 1927, column 274-82; Vol. 2, 1937, column 352-60.

6. "Cost Calculation and Price Policy" in *Die Handelshochschule*, 1st edn, Vol. 1, pp. 1474-1567 (2nd edn, 1937).

7. "Profit Margin and Price Policy" in *RKW, Kostenaufbau, Kostensenkung, Preisgestaltung*, Leipzig 1932.

8. "The Trade Margin" in *Festgabe für Prof. Hellauer zum 65. Geburtstag*, Frankfurt am Main 1936.

9. "Adequate Price", *ZHH*, Vol. 15, 1922/23, pp.150-4.

10. "Sliding - Scale Prices in the Price Policy of Companies", *ZHH*, Vol. 15, 1922-23, pp.218-24.

11. "Fictitious Profit, Cost Calculation and Accounting", in *Mitteilungen des deutschen Hauptverbandes der Industrie*, Vol. 4, Teplitz 1923, pp.383-7, 869-74, 905-11.

12. "Cost Calculation and the Degree of Employment", *ZfB*, Vol. 2, 1925, pp.378-82.

13. "Price Policy", *ZfB*, Vol. 6, 1929, pp.641-66, 731-54.

14. "The Theory and Practice of Decreases in Prices and Wages", *ZfB*, Vol. 7, 1930, pp.699-702.

15. "The Basis of Depreciation Charges", *Harvard Business Review*, Vol. 8, 1930, pp.257-64.

16. "Decrease in Price through the Obligation to Labour Service", *ZfB*, Vol. 8, 1931, pp.222-4.

17. "Flexible Wage Policy", *ZfB*, Vol. 8, 1931, pp.766-78.

18. "Principles of Price Policy", *ZfB*, Vol. 10, 1933, pp.513-23.

19. "Incentive Pay", *ZfB*, Vol. 12, 1935, pp.15-33.

20. "Profit of War and Armament", *ZfB*, Vol. 14, 1937, pp.1-11.

21. "Performance and Wages", *Rhein-Mainische Wirtschaftszeitung*, Vol. 2, 1936, pp.49-51.

22. "Differential Return or Output Bonus", *ZfB*, Vol. 17, 1940, pp.1-14.

23. "The Absorption of Surplus Profit", *ZfB*, Vol. 18, 1941, p.1.

24. "Profit in Mercantile Affairs, Taxation and Pricing Law", *ZfB*, Vol. 19, 1942, pp.1-15.

25. "The Unification of Balance Sheets", *Der praktische Die Betriebswirtschaft*, 1943, pp.1-15.

26. "Performance Depreciation According to Productivity", *Wirtschaftszeitung*, 1947.

27. "Principles and Methods of Price Regulation" (paper presented at the 3rd Deutschen Betriebswirtschaftstag) in *Der praktische Die Betriebswirtschaft*, 1938, pp.1-20.

28. "Rationalisation, Price and Wages", *ZfB*, Vol. 13, 1936, pp.914-16.

VII. The Theory of Economic Cycles

*1. *Business Cycles in Industry - A Miscalculation!*, Berlin and Vienna 1927.

*2. *The Theory of Business Cycles from the Viewpoint of Business Administration*, 4th rev. edn, Berlin 1933.

3. "Accounting and Business Cycles" in *Festgabe für Julius Ziegler: Die Bilanzen der Unternehmungen*, Vienna 1933.

4. "The Theory of Business Cycles from the Viewpoint of Business Administration" in *Die Handelshochschule*, 1st edn, Supplement, Berlin 1932, (supplement) (2nd edn, 1937).

5. "Business Cycles in Industry - A Miscalculation!", *ZfB*, Vol. 4, 1927, pp.1-29, 87-114, 165-99.

6. "Miscalculation as the Reason for Business Cycles", *Vierteljahreshefte für Konjunkturforschung*, Vol. 1, Erg. H. 4, 1927, pp.3-27.

7. "Business Cycles and Employment Creation", in *Der praktische Die Betriebswirtschaft*, Vol. 6, 1935, pp.537-54.

VIII. Papers on the Complete Theory of Business Administration

1. "Introduction to Business Administration" in *Die Handelshochschule*, 2nd edn, 1937.

2. "General Business Administration, 2 Parts" in *Die Handelshochschule*, 3rd edn, 1948-52.

3. "Capital Formation from Sales" in *Zeitschrift für das gesamte Kreditwesen*, 1949, p.176.

4. "The Firm in the Cycle of the Economy", *ZfB*, Vol. 20, 1950, pp.3-10.

IX. Papers on Trusts and Taxation Theory in Business Administration

1. "The First German Congress on Audit and Trusts", *ZfB*, Vol. 13, 1936, pp.505-7.

2. "The Required Audit for Public Companies", *ZfR*, Vol. 7, 1930, pp.207-11.

3. "Annual Statement of Accounts in Company Law Reform", *Archiv für das Revisions- und Treuhandwesen*, Vol. 27, 1931, pp.202-15.

4. "Company Accountancy and Auditing", *ZfB*, Vol. 9, 1932, pp.169-72.

5. "Proportional Company Taxation", *Wirtschaftsprüfer Zeitung*, 5 January 1949.

X. Papers on General Economic Problems

1. "The Economic Situation of Coal Mining in the Ruhr Area", *ZfB*, Vol. 6, 1929, pp.300-3.

2. "Combat or Preservation of Unemployment", *ZfB*, Vol. 7, 1930, pp.401-8.

3. "Support for the German Car Manufacturing Industry", *ZfB*, Vol. 7, 1930, pp.462-3.

4. "Deflation Crisis and Emergency Decrees", *ZfB*, Vol. 9, 1932, pp.1-16.

5. "Revitalization of the Economy", *ZfB*, Vol. 9, 1932, pp.577-604.

6. "The Third Economic Plan", *ZfB*, Vol. 10, 1933, pp.1-11.

7. "The Social Economy Company Policy in Crisis", *ZfB*, Vol. 11, 1934, pp.273-84.

8. "Fundamentals about the Problem of Short-Term Credits", *ZfB*, Vol. 11, 1934, pp.415-26.

9. "Non-Durable Economic Goods and Shortage of Raw Materials", *ZfB*, Vol. 14, 1937, pp.185-6, p.432.

XI. Papers on Matters of the University and the Profession

1. "The Endowment of Research and Teaching in Economics" in *Protokoll der Generalversammlung in Jena* ... 1925 (Vereinigung der sozial- und wirtschaftswissenschaftlichen Hochschullehrer), pp.31-42, Hamburg 1925.

2. "The Future of Business Administration" in *Die Zukunft der Betriebswirtschaftslehre, Festgabe zum 70. Geburtstag von R. Stern*, pp.147-59, Berlin, Leipzig and Vienna 1925.

3. "The Teaching of Business Administration at German Schools of Commerce", *ZfB*, Vol. 10, 1917-18, pp.89-94.

4. "The Graduate in Business Administration and the Graduate in Economics", *ZHH*, Vol. 2, 1925, pp.305-8.

5. "The Training of Business Engineers at the Technical College in Berlin", *ZfB*, Vol. 4, 1927, pp.641-3.

6. "Economics University Training in the United States", *ZfB*, Vol. 7, 1930, pp.846-51.

7. "The Training of the Business Trustee" in *Der Diplom Kaufmann*, Vol. 10, 1930, pp.482-90.

8. "The Graduate in Economics and University Reform" in *Der Diplom Kaufmann*, Vol. 10, 1930, pp.522-9.

9. "The Advancement of Economic Teaching and Research", *ZfB*, Vol. 10, 1933.

10. "Economics University Reform", *ZfB*, Vol. 11, 1934, pp.158-70.

11. "The Reorganisation of Economic Studies", *ZfB*, Vol. 12, 1935, pp.210-17.

12. "The Advancement of the Auditor", *Der Wirtschaftsprüfer*, December 1933.

13. "The Auditor and Tax Consultant", *Wirtschaftsprüfer - Zeitung*, No. 37, 1947.

14. "The Economic Assessor", *Wirtschaft und Finanz Zeitung*, 1949.

15. "The Economic Assessor", *BFuP*, 1950, pp.241-6.

XII. Editor

1. *Studies on Business Administration and Financial Management.*

2. *Economic Theory and Practice.*

3. *Journal for Business Administration*, Spaeth and Linde, Berlin 1924-44; Gabler, Wiesbaden 1950.

4. *The College of Commerce*, 1st edn, Berlin 1927; 2nd edn, Berlin 1937, 3rd edn, Wiesbaden 1949-52.

XIII. Co-editor

1. *Compendium of Business Administration*, Gloeckner, Leipzig 1926-30.

2. *Research and Practice in Business Administration*, 1948-50.

Enterprise Profit*

Fritz Schmidt

I. Introduction

Since the outbreak of WW I in 1914 social economics has seen a lot of changes and every country engaged in world trade has had its share of them. Whether neutral or involved in the war, whether conqueror or conquered, all have been badly affected by value changes such as did not occur during peaceful times of development. The countries that were able to maintain a stable gold value are least affected,[1] other countries show shifts of varying degrees in the buying power of their means of exchange. The erosion of the means of exchange is worst in those countries where, just to eke out their existence, they opted for a certain kind of taxation. This particular form of taxation, characteristic of times of crisis, is the unlimited issue of uncovered bank notes whose increase in number has reduced the buying power of money to the low level of today. In a country when the buying power of money goes down the prices of real assets go up by the same amount, whether due to artificial increase of monetary tokens or to a decrease in production. The more radical such shifts are the more interesting they are for economic science: the "sick body of world economics" reveals many ailments which in times of a balanced economy and stable money had remained hidden. This shows that the economists in a country with an unhealthy monetary unit arrive at new insights much more easily than those in a country where those value changes were relatively small. In Germany the unprecedented shifts in value in balance sheet items and profit and loss accounts of enterprises have led to investigations which will be of lasting influence for the theory of business profit and accounting theory; also for later, when values will have returned to their normal level.

For a long time now the valuation problem has played an important role in accounting theory. Closely connected with it is the theory of correct profit determination. Even in normal times profit was an unstable entity, considerably

---

1 Although in those countries the buying power of money also went down by 75% to a 1/4 of that in 1913, only to rise again to 5/7.

* [This article by Fritz Schmidt was translated from the Dutch journal, *De naamloze vennootschap roermond*, 15 February and 15 March 1923.]

influenced by the economic situation. Often the profit margin was intuitively adjusted through the formation of *secret* reserves in prosperous times - that way reducing profit - while at other times the cancellation of those reserves bumped the result up. The whole approach was without any guiding principle and in fact still is: even in Germany the accounting problems, that resulted from the changing monetary value of goods, are only beginning to be solved.

Value changes of real assets also occurred in times when the means of exchange were very stable in value. Those value changes came about because consumers' value valuations of a good changed or the production costs in the enterprises of the producers changed. Times of inflation cause the issue of uncovered banknotes, prices tend to rise, in fact, market value tends to go up in general, because every consumer's income increases gradually without being accompanied by increased production of economic goods. Consequently all buyers have to pay more for the same commodity, when they want to buy it, otherwise the increased income will enable the other buyers to attract all the commodities. That is why there is a general rise in the price of goods. That can even happen in countries where the gold standard is maintained, for instance, if they are trying to cope with a gold surplus, because, after all, gold is a commodity which goes down in value when it is on offer in excessive quantities.

II. What is "Business or Enterprise Profit"?

a. How Does Business Profit Come About?

If we want to clarify what the concept "business profit" means we will have to try and do this in the light of the purpose of the enterprise. In other words, we will have to find an answer to the question: Why are there always people available who are prepared to tie up their capital and labour into setting up and running a business? They take that decision in order to make a profit on the turnover of their business. A dealer buys or rents suitable premises, equips himself with the necessary goods and makes sure he has sufficient current assets to offset necessary expenditure.

All this is first and foremost capital investment, regardless whether the means for it come from the entrepreneur's private income or whether they are acquired through one of the many forms of credit. The enterprise can exist on the condition that it has some capital at its disposal. And one can only make a real profit by selling the stocks of goods one has available as soon as possible at a good price, i.e. with gain. Obtaining such gains in trade is possible because the valuation by the buyers of the various goods differs from place to place and from time to time. In countries where they grow plenty of grain the price will be lower than in countries where supplies are insufficient. So the merchant does not only do himself a service when he buys grain in countries with large stockpiles and takes it to countries that have a shortage of grain, but he also does the consumer a service. In this way he bridges the distance between two markets. Similarly he bridges the time gap between production and consumption: he buys during harvest time in the producer country, carefully stores the purchased stockpiles away and then sells them to consumers during the course of a whole year until the gathering of the new harvest.

In the manufactured goods trade the goods stream is more spread out because production takes place continuously. There the merchant's stocks are likely to be constant all year round. That's why they are often called "*iron stocks*".[2]

We find the same sort of situation in an industrial enterprise. The only distinction between a business enterprise and an industrial one is that the latter does not buy finished products but manufactures products from raw materials and with labour and technology. The finished products of such a factory in their turn often form the basic products for further processing industries. Usually the proportion of enterprise capital tied up in permanent means (or base capital) is considerably larger in industry than it is in business. However, here too, success of the enterprise depends on whether total production costs will be lower than the amount received through selling the product.

A manufacturer who would want to manufacture goods that in their new form would yield less than the cost of the materials he consumes to manufacture the good, will lose part of his capital on each commodity he produces. And if he insists on continuing in this fashion, he would soon be forced to file for bankruptcy. This suggests that every entrepreneur needs to organize his books in such a way, that at any moment and for every transaction he is immediately able to see what the difference was between costs and proceeds. Where this difference turns out to be a negative amount he will have to make some adjustments to the situation, because in the long run manufacturing and trading are only viable when sales proceeds exceed production costs.

However, there are large problems in drawing up the operating accounts of an enterprise. Normally of all goods the enterprise acquires only that value is recorded in the accounts which the factor inputs have on the day of acquisition. For instance, purchased goods, any wages that were paid, any buildings or machinery that were purchased, are recorded at prime cost price. At the time of recording these costs

2 Strictly speaking "iron or base" stocks are that part of the stock in hand that a business enterprise needs to have as an absolute minimum to keep the business running without any interruptions.

normally coincide with the market value of the commodity(s) concerned, but this market value is subject to change. This can even happen when the monetary unit is stable, although the changes will then be less noticeable; however, they will be very noticeable indeed in a country with increasing inflation or deflation. So every time the collective goods and claims of the enterprise change in value, the question arises whether or not these changes are part of profit. The easiest answers to this problem are to be found in the sales figures for the end products. If the purchase price of one unit of a certain commodity is Hfl. 100,- and if, after having been stored for 3 months, at the time of selling, the same commodity cannot be purchased for less than Hfl. 200,- then, without any effort on the part of the enterprise, the commodity has undergone a value change of Hfl. 100,-. When this commodity is sold for Hfl. 220,- one has to check whether the entire difference between the purchase price and the sale price constitutes a real profit.

And indeed, this is not the case. Calculated that way an entrepreneur could pay out a profit of Hfl. 120,-. If he did that, however, he would not be able to purchase the same amount of goods as before with the remaining Hfl. 100,- left in the business, or rather, he would only be able to purchase half of what he purchased initially. So if one goes by the actual stock in hand the business would have deteriorated in quality. The profit that could have been paid out without eating into the stockpile was only Hfl. 20,-. If a merchant, totally unaware of the situation, sold the goods, purchased at Hfl. 100,-, for Hfl. 120,- because he added a Hfl. 20,- profit onto the purchase price, he gave part of his stocks away for nothing. At a Hfl. 200,- purchase price, Hfl. 120,- only allows you to replenish 6/10 of the stocks you sold; in other words, you sustained a loss in the transaction whereas you expected to make a profit out of it. How on earth is it possible that serious merchants could ever calculate in such a manner? I am sad to say that as a rule they do! This has happened because in merchant accounting they are accustomed to offset the sales price against the purchase price and to look upon the difference either as loss or as profit. In reality, however, like in the above case, the commodity, during the time it had been stored, i.e. without having been sold, had gone up in price in the market where it had been obtained. This value increase (for this particular enterprise was concerned) came about completely independent of the actual turnover. The stocks have changed in value and the merchant has just made the mistake of not taking the nature of this value change into account.

If one sells the goods at a value below the one they had on the day of sale in the buyers' market, you are giving part of your capital away. On the other hand, it is also possible that during the time the stock is in storage, their market value goes down; in that case, however, you cannot do anything about it and it would be wrong to want to to want to sell them for Hfl. 100,- (because that is what you paid for them) plus a profit allowance/surcharge on top of that, especially if you can replenish stocks at Hfl. 50,- per commodity. That way you could keep up your stocks at a minimum proceeds level of Hfl. 50,-. Everything above that would be real profit/actual profit which you could put away without weakening the financial position of the enterprise. Calculating the way he is used to, the merchant would offset a purchase price of Hfl. 100,- against a sales price of, let's say, Hfl. 70,- and so arrive at a loss of Hfl. 30. We call this a *fictitious loss* (*schijnverlies*), a phenomenon similar to the one that occurs when stocks in hand increase in value and so produce a *fictitious profit* (*schijnwinst*). Both phenomena can seriously endanger the valuation and the welfare of the enterprise. If one pays out fictitious profit as real profit, the enterprise will be weakened and its capacity will go down. During the war [WW I] Holland lived through such a period, in which steeply increased prices caused just such fictitious profits. At the moment the country is going through a time of fictitious losses, equally disastrous for the economy, because the post-war crisis, caused by the decrease in value, is worsening because entrepreneurs are holding production back, guided as they are by their miscalculations, that delude them into thinking that continuation of production will cause even greater losses.

However, if these losses are only fictitious losses, such as occur when the value in the buyers' market goes down, for instance, this might lead to unemployment and production stoppage, which are not justified economically. Based on previous purchase prices price levels are kept higher than is really necessary and that is the reason why the turnover is smaller than it actually should be. These facts also tell us that this problem not only concerns the entrepreneur; it is also in the national economy's interest that merchants and industrialists calculate correctly, i.e. in a way that eliminates the occurrence of fictitious profits and losses. When we try to gain proper insight into the nature of fictitious profits and fictitious losses it appears from the examples that time and again it's a matter of the influence the price change has on the unsold parts of the capital, which for the sake of brevity, we will call "dormant capital". The goods enter the business at a different point in time than when they leave. The price changes in the buyers' market that occurred during the time that the goods were stored up in the business premises have nothing to do with the sales profit, because these changes also occur when one is not selling. It is a change in capital value which under all circumstances must be recorded separately from the turnover figures, in other words, not as actual profit. What we showed for stock also counts for all other elements of the costing price, which play a role especially in industry. If the manufacture of a machine needs 100 hours of work the manufacturer wants to be paid for these 100 hours work when he sells the commodity, regardless whether in the meantime, the monetary value of those hours of work has doubled or halved, the physical replacement of labour needs to be considered. Only if the businessman thinks in this way will he be able to buy another lot of 100 hours of work and continue his production uninterruptedly. Only what is acquired over and above the value is real profit which also can be distributed. Of course, this is similarly applicable to other costs such as depreciation and interest which we will discuss below. From these investigations we may draw the logical conclusion that a correct calculation is only possible if one keeps the value change of the dormant capital separate from the actual sales profits, and if this is recorded separately in the accounts. At the same time it is also clear that the entrepreneur has a twofold task within the national economy. On the one hand he is a capital distributor in which capacity he has the task of investing a part of the national capital in such a way that it will increase in value, on the other hand he is a capital investor, who has to act promptly as soon as he realizes that one market has an abundance of relatively cheap goods and another has a shortage with relatively high prices. The entrepreneurial striving for capital growth can produce results in two ways. If they succeed in investing their capital in goods that on average increase more in value than other goods, they will become comparatively richer. But they will also achieve this, when they sell goods which with every sale yield a high interim profit.[3] It is not always possible to combine these two advantages: certain turnovers only go with very specific goods, which don't always provide one with a high interim profit as well as a relatively large price-rise.

b. *The Sales Profit [or Turnover Profit]*

We can only speak of real sales profit, if the total monetary value of the cost elements of any good, calculated according to the price at the moment of the exchange, is lower than the proceeds.

This is in agreement with the old formula, already used by Ricardo, which more or less goes as follows: determinant for the price of any good is not the actual expenditure on behalf of that good, but the costs involved in the reproduction of that good.

It is very interesting to note that it was precisely a traditional economist who, having lived through a period of inflation, wrote these words. So far, however, his message has not exerted any influence on accounting practices. Fictitious profit will

---

3 [The difference in price in the buyers' market and the sellers' market. The term "*omzetwinst*" (sales profit) has been used here and elsewhere for the same concept. The term "*handelswinst*" (trade/business profit) has not been employed because in this particular case it might cause misunderstanding. Establishing standard terminology for business economics is urgently needed.]

occur every time when, during a sales period the market price for the cost elements of the traded goods has gone up, and when in his calculations the merchant still works with the purchase price of these cost elements. Similarly fictitious losses are inevitable if in the merchant's accounts, the fact that the price of the cost elements went down between the day they were obtained and the day on which their sale took place, is not taken into account. Real sales profit in an enterprise derives only from the fact that in comparatively cheap markets (as a service to the consumers) ready-made goods or separate cost parts are obtained, which in the sellers' market, because of higher valuation by the consumers, have a higher value. This difference in value is the sales profit. Consequently the acquisition cost and the sale price of the one day must always be compared with each other and the difference between the purchase value of the cost elements and their price on the day of sale must be entered in the books separately as "value change of dormant capital".

c. *Value Changes of the Dormant Capital*

The property of an enterprise usually consists of two kinds of values. On the one hand there are real assets such as blocks of land/sites, buildings, machinery, stocks in various stages of processing, tools, packing materials, etc. On the other hand the enterprise has to have supplies of money at its disposal to finance running costs. Besides these there usually are financial assets. In other words, property consists of real assets and financial assets or: concrete capital and capital control (N. Polak's definition).

It is important to have a clear picture of these things because the changes in these two kinds of values are opposite in character. If the price of the goods goes up the buying power of the money goes down; so while the real assets of the enterprise tend to rise, the value of the money, in terms of goods, goes down. And when the price of the goods goes down it is precisely the other way round. This tells the entrepreneur that as a capital owner he would do well to invest as much of his capital as possible in real assets and to limit the amount of financial assets as much as he can whenever goods are going up in price. While, on the other hand, it is better to have fewer fixed assets and more financial assets when the price of goods is going down. However, the entrepreneur is not entirely free to do as he likes. In order to have a continuous turnover he must at least keep some stock behind. Without a building and machinery it is difficult to keep up production. If ever he should want to turn all the business assets into money it would mean the liquidation of the enterprise.

Every increase in the exchange value of the "dormant capital" of an enterprise also adds to the money value of the owner's capital, because the outside capital stays the same. If in an enterprise the owner's capital equals the sum of the real assets and if the debts (to third parties) equal the financial assets (currencies and claims) on the credit side of the balance sheet, it is in equilibrium which even major changes in the buying power of money will not affect, as long as the enterprise is able to make real "sales profit". Whether the exchange value of the fixed assets is multiplied by ten or plunges to 1/10 of its value, after transferring this value change to the home capital there will always be enough left to enable equally large stocks as before to be kept. A decrease in exchange value of fixed assets goes hand in hand with a decrease of the cash values required for the turnover, because if a commodity of Hfl. 1000,- was sold on credit at the old price, one would at the end of the credit term receive the Hfl. 1000,- back and could pay off Hfl. 1000,- worth of bank debts.[4]

Is the purchasing power increase one wins on the credit side what one loses on the debit side (through having to pay back with stronger money)?

If one wants to end up with a correct profit calculation, any changes in the money value of the dormant capital arising from a price change, must be recorded separately. When the real assets go up in price, the change must not be processed via the account that indicates the sales profit, i.e. not via the profit-and-loss account, but via a special account, called the "adjustment-of-capital account" (*rekening voor prijsverschillen*); that is to say, if one does not want to record the amount directly into the *capital account*, as the general property account. In any case, such a value change has nothing to do with the turnover. A value increase of real assets (because of rising prices) means an increase of dormant capital, whereas a value decrease means a decrease in dormant capital. Up till now people were want to process this value change via the profit-and-loss account, with the result that any value change of dormant capital was also paid out as profit, although this had a weakening effect on the enterprise; on the other hand decreases in value were recorded as losses, which were not what they were, because the enterprise still had its old stocks of real assets.

Although perhaps not in an altogether logical fashion, the mutations of the real assets had been given expression. However, following this accounting system, one form of value increase of dormant capital remained entirely hidden. When an enterprise in times of inflation and rising prices of the real assets doubled its normal stocks in hand by obtaining large amounts of credit from the bank, it would also acquire an increase in value on the larger stock. This should be shown on the profit-and-loss account or rather on the capital account.

---

4 At a new sale of an equal amount of goods a new claim is put in of only Hfl. 100,- because in the meantime the price of the commodity has decreased by 9/10 to 10% of its original value. This is offset by an equally diminished need for credit at the time of purchase. Thus the money values adjust themselves to the real assets when there is the right distribution of capital. After all, the reduced purchasing power of the money and the claims (and of the money values on the credit side in general) is balanced by the fact that debts to third parties on the debit side are paid with money that has less purchasing power.

Things would look entirely different, however, if in times of deflation and falling prices of real assets the entrepreneur would turn all his stocks into money and would store it until he were able to buy double the amount of goods for it. Such capital gain would not show up in the accounts. And it would be very difficult to find a way in which the results of this successful *distribution of capital* could be shown in the books. The only possibility would be to determine, after having established the real sales profit, how much the market value of the entire capital on the day of balance, after deduction of the undistributed profit and after calculating the change in current value of the *real assets* would exceed the value at the start of the calculation period - in terms of money with the same buying power. Anyway, the entrepreneur should be aware of the fact that this is a way of adding to his property.

III. Today's Merchant Accounting and Its Shortcomings

The old-fashioned merchant accounting method, as it has been used for centuries, only calculates the entire profit of the enterprise, in which the sales profit together with the price changes of the concrete capital (i.e. of the real assets) are expressed in one amount.

The profit-and-loss account absorbs all value changes as if they were all the same. In times of stable purchasing power of money this method is reasonably acceptable, because the value change of the "dormant capital" only has a slight influence on the profit. When, however, as happened in Holland during the course of the war, the prices of all goods on average become four times as high, this increase, i.e. three times the value of the initial capital, will have to emerge gradually as profit. If this fictitious profit is then paid out as dividend, one actually carves up part of one's capital. This explains why in times of inflation there is a lot of capital growth, because the amount that was withdrawn through profit distribution has to be fed back into the enterprise, wherever that is needed for continued functioning. In Germany this way of calculating has led to the situation that the best companies annually pay out high percentages of profit in paper marks on their share capital which still dates from the time that the mark was hard currency. But as a rule they decide at the same time to double their capital and in that way demand a multiple of the paid out dividend from the shareholders. And the proceeds of that capital growth usually only serve to supplement the business capital, which was left weakened through the distribution based on the miscalculated profit, but not for expansion of the enterprise. On the other hand, in a period of falling prices the enterprise, as a result of an incorrect method of profit determination on the profit-and-loss account, will also record decreases in value as losses and as a result pay out less profit than it acquired from sales. But that is also wrong, because it leaves capital in the business that is no longer needed.

The merchant intuitively realizes the danger of equating sales profit with "profit on stocks": he refrains from recording non-realized profit, as it appears from the value increase of his assets, as straightforward profit. That is the reason why he is accustomed to feeding the fixed capital into the balance sheet for the purchase profit only. This does indeed prevent the increase in exchange value of buildings, machinery and what have you from emerging as profit. But depreciation is also done at this lower purchase value and that means, of course, that depreciation, to cover the costs for replacing obsolete equipment etc., during years of higher prices, will be insufficient. A fall in prices, however, is usually booked as a loss. Furthermore, the method of recording all real assets according to their purchase value cannot prevent the occurrence of fictitious profits and losses, that is to say, if they come out of value changes of stock, because the stockpiles are continuously replaced in proportion to the turnover. When a particular level of "iron stock" at the beginning of the year is recorded as representing Hfl. 100.000,-, it is possible that the same stock at the end of the year is in store at a higher price, for instance, as much as Hfl. 200.000,-, without having increased in quantity at all. If one wanted to look upon the difference of Hfl. 100.000,- as profit, as is the custom, it would be a fictitious profit, because the stock pile hasn't really changed and if one pays out the difference as profit, one can only maintain half as large a stock pile from then on, unless one wants to supplement it with credit. If, however, the value of iron stock in our example would have gone down by half, to Hfl. 50.000,-, this drop in price would have been recorded on the stock account as a loss without it actually being a loss: the old stock is still available and represents a turnover of the same size as before.

Mistakes of this nature can only be eliminated by showing the price changes of the goods in stock separately as what they really are, namely, changes in the money value of the capital. Technically one could achieve this by making an entry on the stock account whenever there is an increase of value. This procedure debits this value change from the stock account and credits the "capital value change" account or, in short, the capital account. When stocks decrease in value the records should show the opposite: the stock account should be credited and the capital account should be debited.

But not all firms have an opportunity to operate with iron stocks. Only very few concerns are able to carry a constant quantity of goods of the same kind.

If any fluctuations show up, however, the adjustment of the final stock figures must lead to an incorrect outcome. Therefore, you can only eliminate the influence price differences have on the value of the stockpile, by looking at each case individually. It has to be established how much each value change has contributed to each separate entry from the day of entry until the day of issue.

This may apply to many cases but not to all, because every entry by itself is too small. One is then forced to combine several entries into one arrangement, which can only show an average result.

The simplest procedure is if the figures of the changes in the monetary value of the "dormant capital" caused by price changes are combined with the calculation in which for each element of the costing price the purchase price is compared with the value on the day of purchase and the difference determined. Those differences are collected and are recorded monthly or annually as one entry in the relevant capital account.

From the previous discussion it is quite clear that not only do you have to keep an eye on the merchandise stock and the equipment stock as to their value movements, but you also have to watch all cost elements necessary to make a product or to turn over a commodity. In the same way the value movements of labour costs have to be observed and the differences recorded in the capital account. Depreciation amounts have to be treated in a similar fashion and they must in no way be calculated based on the purchase value of the plant, but rather on the current value the plants have during the relevant production period. The total amounts that have been written off could be considerably higher than the initial costs because of inflation and the resulting increase in market value and that is why it is better to enter the depreciation in a "fund for replacements" account. Otherwise it could happen that the machines account in times of considerable increase of the replacement costs and a concomitant increase of the amount of depreciation would go into the red, if it was not decided to draw some logical conclusions from above current value calculations and to introduce this current value for all plants. If plants undergo value changes they must be calculated via the capital account. The merchant is perhaps not desperately keen on these current value accounting methods, because he does not care for the public knowing the exact value figures of his assets. As long as fictitious profits are avoided in drawing up the profit calculation, it is for the time being not absolutely essential to display on the balance sheet all aspects of the capital property down to every detail. Only when doing the profit and loss calculation the change in current value of the dormant capital must remain strictly separate from the sales profit, otherwise one cannot determine the correct amount of profit. Every entrepreneur should, if only for internal use, draw up a complete "current value balance sheet" on which every credit entry is shown with the value of the day on which the balancing was done; these balances show, in an entirely different manner than was used up to now, what values the entrepreneur has combined in his enterprise. They will induce him more than ever to distribute capital correctly and not to part with any of his property unless at a price that will enable him to obtain an equal amount of goods in his buyers' market and will leave him with a reasonable profit into the bargain. Only calculations including the current value for profit and loss accounting and end-of-period balancing provides the merchant with the right criterion for his *withdrawals*. Unless he knows the current value he cannot determine whether the attainable purchase price really includes true profit.

Because these things have only slowly dawned upon Germany, most entrepreneurs, because of the strong shifts of all nominal values, have thrown their capital away without realizing, let alone wanting it; the old trading practices made them calculate wrongly and moreover the State with its legislation for the prevention of usury urged them to stick to the old incorrect way of calculating, even after the entrepreneurs had realized how mistaken they were. Finally, when the mark took its latest plunge [1922/23], even the State had to admit its untenable position and in a new regulation recognized most of the afore mentioned principles. Economic life will not permanently benefit from this insight unless entrepreneurs hang on to these new methods of calculating, also in times of only minor value fluctuations, because even minor changes in the purchasing power of money and related prices for all merchandise can still have an important influence on profit. Anyway, a correct profit calculation will undoubtedly give the entrepreneur a much better idea of how his business is going, than is the case right now with this random mixture of "change in the monetary value of the capital" and "sales profit".

Profit and Balance Sheet Value[1]

Fritz Schmidt

Contents

---

1 Translated from *Het Internationaal Accountantscongres*, 1926 pp.380-419. Subsequently this article appeared in *ZFB*, 3, 1926 pp.813-825, 906-920 and then as part of the 3rd Edition of *Die organische Tageswertbilanz*, 1929 pp.54 - 90. *Tageswertbilanz* literally, today or present day value accounting, is translated hereafter as current value accounting.

I. Introduction

The fact that the term "profit" is put at the beginning of this investigation is well justified. The issue of balance sheet values can only be decided on the basis of a conception of this term. It will be demonstrated that balance sheet valuation is totally dependent on the conception of what is the profit of a company. To many this term is by no means as clear-cut as it first appears.

Above all, regarding often quite difficult problems, in deciding on solutions, the point of view upon which those solutions are taken has to be stated. For one thing we can argue on the basis that the *firm is to be viewed as an individual entity.*[2] Assuming this, we need to determine which purposes profit accounting[3] has to serve; to what extent the firm by its nature requires net worth (asset) accounting; and which requirements have to be met by it from the point of view of the management, owners, creditors and employees of the company. Besides that it is also necessary to investigate to what extent the laws of individual countries, which impose strict regulations, have to be considered in profit accounting. And we have to see to what extent these are compatible with the firms' requirements. However, at this point it is already clear , that looking at the firm in isolation can hardly lead to a full comprehension of its conditions of existence, and accordingly, cannot lead to the formulation of a[n adequate] profit concept, since the firm is not a totally independent unit, but can only be fully understood as part of the economy. It can only exist in that context like the cell of the human body, in and with it.

Regarding the firm as part of the economy we have to look for a profit concept which is applicable regardless of the economic situation. It has to be a notion of profit which can, regardless of the date of its determination, actually be distributed; a concept which if applied for the income statement that refers to the profit also reflects the development of values corresponding to the respective economic situation. We shall only recognize if we have chosen the correct profit concept by investigating whether it is possible that *all* firms can use it without being mislead, in all economic situations conceivable within the economy. *In short, the profit concept which we have to look for has to be in total harmony with the basic laws of a (free) market economy.* Although it will not be attempted here, there is no way of avoiding discussion of these basic laws.

---

2 [Editors' note: in the original this phrase was highlighted with capitals. This and subsequent phrases appear in our translation in italics.]

3 [*Erfolgsbilanz* in the Murphy and Most's 1959 translation of Schmalenbach's *Dynamic Accounting* is described as "Results Accounting" or "Results Balance Sheet". Hereinafter it is translated as Profit Accounting.]

For this reason it is impossible for us to accept something as true without questioning it just because it is common practice. Also, when dealing with this out-and-out theoretical question, there is no reason being *diverted* from the pure search for knowledge by any considerations regarding technical feasibility. There is every reason to believe that if we succeed in finding the correct profit concept, a practicable way of determining that profit will appear. Even if the perfectly correct determination of a theoretically defined profit should turn out to be impossible, we would have gained very much by knowledge of what is the right thing, because this would enable us methodologically to turn to approximation procedures. Such procedures in fact are frequently used in all applications of theoretical knowledge. We can also, even where the exact recording of expenditure is possible in principle, turn to such average calculations in order to save expenditure. Notwithstanding large problems associated with an exact calculation of this particular concept, [i.e. profit] it is important to recognise that theoretical results cannot be disproved by pointing to those problems. That this happens quite frequently is one of the main causes of the lack of mutual understanding in our science. A profit concept is only then theoretically disproved if it is shown that its attributed effects on the firm and the whole economy are different and adverse.

II. Theory of Business Profit

1. Basic Terms

Business profit can only be that which exceeds the amount necessary for the maintenance of a firm's assets. By that a clear distinction between assets and profit is made while their definition is the main task of the *investigation*. Furthermore the question arises how can a firm achieve an increase over its opening balance sheet's assets. This will be discussed in more detail later on. At this point it must be stated that it can only be achieved by business activity constituting turnover. *In terms of* physical quantities it is only possible to increase the assets of a firm through sales turnover. Turnover, however, can involve either the transformation of goods into money and of money into goods (equation = goods ⇛ money ⇛ more goods) or of money into goods and goods into money (equation = money ⇛ goods ⇛ more money). In the first case we are dealing with turnover of trade and manufacturing in the other instance we have an example of speculative turnover. For the purpose of profit accounting it is essential to define the terms "*capital*" and "*assets*" - used here synonymously - although in economics frequently only the physical means of production are regarded as capital. Capital or assets of a firm can be:

- The stock of physical assets including money, or
- The value of all physical assets including money, denominated in abstract units of money.

The first kind of capital is referred to as the *real-capital* of the firm, whilst the second is *abstract or financial* capital. For determining profit of a business the definition of capital used as a base is very important. In the case of real capital, profit only arises when the physical assets have been increased between the beginning and the end of an accounting period. In the case of abstract capital, profit only arises, irrespective of the size of the stock of physical assets, when the value denominated in abstract units of money has been increased. As may be demonstrated, this is even possible when the physical stock of assets remains constant.

The term "profit of the firm" is used here synonymously with "income". Also, for the calculation of the income for taxation purposes two kinds of income are relevant: One, the theory of sources: being income from employment and investment income requiring maintenance of the physical stock of assets and the other, income from the increase of the abstract capital with the addition of consumption (= wear and tear) during the accounting period. As well as profit, the contrasting loss is taken into account as is its counterpart a decrease in assets. Negative income and negative profit can only result where consumption from a stock of assets or borrowing is possible.

2. *The Origin of Profit within the Firm*

a. Manufacturing (Operating) Profit from Production

The economic task of industrial production is to transform goods which are relatively cheap, in their respective markets, into products which, due to their relative scarcity, are relatively expensive. The difference between factor input costs and the value of the end products - saleable products - constitutes the increment value which makes the origin and permanent existence of industrial production possible. It is the function of the entrepreneur everywhere to identify differences in values and to reduce them by his operations, but always only to the extent that he still earns at least a normal profit for his activities. If, for example, he finds out (i) that certain resources and certain kinds of labour necessary for their processing are relatively cheap due to their abundance and (ii) he also has the know-how to transform these factor inputs into new products which are highly esteemed by consumers and consequently are highly priced, i.e. higher than their cost; then it is worthwhile for the entrepreneur to put his capital and his labour time in this kind of production. If, on some occasions, due to the abundance of similar producers, there arises a relatively strong surge of demand for input factors of a certain kind, the price of these factors would rise and the end products then saturating the market would result in a fall in price. This would result in a quick decline in the increment value which could even, if the costs were higher than the sales prices, turn into a decrease in value.

Relating to business management such a decrease in value results in a loss from sales and in the present case this would be a penalty for producers who, because of poor management, transformed too much input into saleable products. *Therefore the entrepreneur has a vital interest in constantly pursuing the development of the margin of profit between the market for his input factors and for his saleable products. If this margin increases he will expand production in terms of quantity*; if it decreases he has to cut his output. Even for the marginal firm, it is necessary for the satisfaction of demand at the most unfavourable costs, that the business must always yield at least an average interest rate plus the entrepreneur's remuneration if production in this firm is to be continued. Production with costs higher than the selling price would result in a loss for the whole economy as well, since it means the product contains input costs which in their original state, or if they are transformed in other goods, are valued higher by their consumers and therefore satisfy their needs to a greater extent.

All industrial production takes *time*. For this reason there has to be a certain time span, sometimes quite long, between the incoming of input factors and the outgoing of sales products. But to be aware of the development of the margin in due time, in order to be able to make quick decisions the respective date of the decisions has to be considered. This means that we have to compare input costs with selling values as of the same date. Then, at the beginning of a production process we will have to appraise to what extent these values are likely to change from now till the [future] sales date.

b. Trading Profits (From Trade *in Different Markets* and *Change in Location*)

The function of trade is to sell finished products. However, the finished products of a certain firm or market can be input factors for another industry which further processes them. In any case trading companies do not change the merchandise which they trade. This is the cause of frequent reproach against trading firms for being unproductive and their activities being disadvantageous for the ultimate consumer. By investigating under what circumstances trading companies intervene this misconception will soon be cleared up. The goods of a national, as well as of the world economy are distributed quite differently in specific areas. Therefore in certain production areas there are markets in which the quantity of goods supplied greatly exceeds the demand of consumers or other buyers in those areas. This must entail in those areas, market prices that are relatively low. On the other hand there are, for some reason or another, areas in which the supply of the particular goods is far below the quantity demanded. Consequently prices will rise to a relatively high level there. *The margin between markets is the reason for trade.* The trader buys, in a market with a surplus, as many goods as he can profitably sell in a market with a shortage of those goods. The direction in which trade goes is from the producer to the consumer with the opposite being the exception. The amount of turnover is also determined by the margin between prices in both markets. Suppose that the quantity of goods taken out of the buying market were to create a shortage there, while it would lead to a surplus supply in the selling market; then prices in the buying market would rise above those in the sales market. In this instance the profit margin of the trader would turn into a trading loss and *overkeen* traders would be punished with losses from turnover till an equilibrium relation between the two markets was restored. Besides the locality, the time factor is also important. Between buying and selling there is often a haulage distance across continents. If the trader constantly wants to keep abreast in his business, he continuously has to keep track of the development of the trading margin taking into account all costs of trade and he has to increase his business if the margin widens and decrease it if it shrinks.

c. Speculation Profit from Current Value Differences over Time

While, in the turnover process in industrial production and trade the entrepreneur can attribute the cause of his success to the fact that he can sell his goods at a price which enables him at the same moment to buy or produce more goods of the same kind, the intention of the speculator is different. He wants to make more money from money by investing it in those goods, which in the course of the investment period, increase in value. This is why we need to investigate how in an economy it is constantly possible for goods to gain in value. The cause lies in the nature of fixed and working assets. With regard to fixed assets we notice that certain items, like land, can be used continually since they are never used up. An entrepreneur will decide only to use them when he can be sure that the cost of usage is less than the resulting yield. In view of the scarcity of capital he prefers those fixed assets which promise the highest value difference over time, because against the background of capital scarcity, it is impossible to use all the goods which are usable. Those yielding the highest profit have to be used for the economy as far as the quantity of capital available allows. The same is also true for depreciating assets, like machinery and buildings, as well as for pure circulating assets, e.g. inventories, materials and even the demand for labour.

Normally all of these goods are available in larger quantities than *are actually used*. The last available portion of capital sets the limit for their employment. The quantity of assets of a firm is adequate when it is so determined that the products yield a constant return on the invested capital during the time the items are fit for use. Speculation with assets is rare as they are usually owned by the companies. Speculation predominantly takes place in the market for saleable products, the capital market and in the market for entire companies and their shares. Not every saleable product has unlimited chances of an increase in value. In general these exist only during the time needed for the turnover process. In industrial production an extended storage of goods, after production, would not normally lead to an increase in value. Whereas, during the production period, the value of the input factors which a product contains will experience an increase resulting from differences in the market prices for input factors and saleable products. In the case of merchandise an indefinite storage of the goods could hardly bring about an increase in value although this will occur if, for example, after the harvest natural products are supplied to the market intermittently. In this process the speculator, controlling the available capital, has the task of distributing the whole harvest over the year of consumption. It happens because, following the harvest, the supply available in the market goes far beyond the needs of the consumers. If at this stage producers wanted to sell all their harvested goods it would lead to extremely low prices. Now the speculator, furnished with investment capital, will try to assess in the course of the consumption period (a year), how prices of the product will develop after a considerable portion of the available goods has been consumed. As supply decreases prices will rise. The speculator will intervene when, by force of selling pressure, the actual price of the goods has decreased to the extent that the difference to the assessed future price offers him a speculative profit. This speculative profit has to be at least as high as the average interest which the capital invested would earn because the future speculation profit is the source of return on investment. In an opposite way it is also possible to use an expected price fall for speculative purposes. In that case the speculator is bearish and today sells goods which he does not yet own hoping before the day of delivery to be able to buy them cheaper than the selling price. On the other hand the modern form of trade payment is made on the day of delivery. In this form of time bargain, at best, payment of a margin serving as security can be considered. Besides a bearish forward speculation with postponed payment and delivery there is spot speculation. It happens, if the owner of real goods at a certain date comes to the conclusion that their value will drop in the future. In this case the speculator, by selling his goods, will stick to money which he can invest profitably in an interest earning way. Later, after the price drop of the pertinent goods has taken place, from his accumulated stock of money, he can buy back a larger quantity of goods. The last example demonstrates very well the economic function of speculation. *Speculation regulates the relations between the market for money and for goods*. When the supply of capital in the form of money is so high that the price for its use, e.g. interest, is lower than the profit which can be earned from trading or storage of goods, money will flow in all the sectors of the economy where this higher profit is on offer. On the other hand when the profits from trading and intermittent supply of physical goods in general or even only in specific sectors of the economy fall below the yield of money capital, e.g. interest, the influx of money capital must turn into a drain, as the owners of real goods, in case of sound economic thinking, sell them and do not buy them back. Instead, they keep their capital in cash and cash at banks, thereby making a higher profit. Then, as a result of the lack of demand, the prices of real goods will also drop and with each drop prospects for the owners of real goods to get a normal yield, increase. As a result of these considerations it can be said *that speculation provides for a* balance between the yields from money capital and real capital.

From the viewpoint of the balance sheet one of the main issues is that of the *form of profit from speculation*. If a speculator, in order to buy real goods which he hopes will increase in value, takes a loan for which he has to pay interest, then his yield consists in *that price increase* which exceeds the *contractual* interest. In the case of a deliberate holding of the proceeds in form of money from the sale of real goods *the profit of the speculator is the interest for the cash at bank as well as the possible increase in money value*. In both cases after the settlement of the business and the distribution of the profit he has at his disposal the amount of money with which the speculation started. In the first case he can pay back his loan and the principle of maintenance of the firm is thereby observed. *But only the realized speculation profit is distributable*. In the context of buying real goods with borrowed money this means: it is only possible to distribute the increase in value of the real goods which exceeds the amount of the loan and the interest after the business has been settled by selling the real goods purchased for speculative purposes. Before that, the speculative profit is still tied up in the firm. Therefore final profit calculation can only take place after the speculation has been settled and, at the latest, it has to be done when the initially borrowed money is paid back. Also conceivable and quite common in practice is the form of speculation with borrowed money in which several of these transactions are *rolled over*. One buys real goods on credit, sells them and buys again. In this case the profit from speculation resulting from the increase in value of the real goods is tied up until after the last sale of goods, i.e. until after the final redemption of the speculative loan has been made. In the meantime only transaction profits originating from price differences between the buying and selling markets would be distributable. *If* calculation of the profit from the whole transaction is the aim, it follows from that that corporate accounting not only has to account for goods valued at current values in the buying market bought from owners' *equity but also for those bought with borrowed capital.* The calculation of the real speculative profit, which is compensation for the function of distributing goods over time, will have to take place only after the final repayment of loans. Certainly it has to be recognised that also turnover, as far as it is not mere arbitrage between purchase and sale, takes time as well and therefore trading profit can also be profit from speculation if it is financed with borrowed money.

III. Value, Price and Their Change

1. Subjective and Objective Value

All value is based on the valuation of goods by individuals operating in *the economy*. In this connection all valuation which is not based on an adequate income, i.e. on real purchasing power, is irrelevant because only the determination of the buyer to spend a certain part of his income for goods can produce effective demand in the market. The individual valuation of single goods differs from person to person and even different quantities of the same goods will be valued differently by one and the same person. This is so because an increasing supply leads to the saturation of personal needs which causes a very high valuation for goods which are indispensable in satisfying basic needs, while those going beyond that point are valued at a relatively lower level. The consumer directly only values goods which he consumes but indirectly he also values the assets necessary for the production of consumer goods and the depreciation amounts which have to be compensated for in their price. The producer-cum-trader has the task first of all to assess subjectively from the viewpoint of his firm the prospective return of his input factors. Anyone who engages in economic activities to earn a profit will in this connection value the input factors necessary for his firm, at least as high as to ensure that he gets a normal interest during the time of production or turnover. Otherwise it would be more profitable for him to abstain from production or trading. The subjective assessment of suppliers of input factors, especially of suppliers of labour, is influential as well.

The *objective value* and *price*, which, for all goods of the same kind in the same market are identical, are derived from the total of the subjective valuations by the consumers and entrepreneurs making their decisions regarding input factors. Even in the case of an extreme shortage of bread if a consumer with high income is prepared to pay a large part of his available income for bread, in order to satisfy his hunger, he is still able to buy the quantity he needs relatively cheaply at the normal market price if there is ample supply. This is because it is not his valuation which is relevant, but that of the consumer, with the lowest income and a correspondingly low valuation, to whom the last unit of the offered quantity falls. If producers want to sell the total supply they have to be content with the price which this marginal consumer is ready to pay. The same situation prevails in the market for input factors which directly often is not relevant at all for the consumer. For them, the valuation of an entrepreneur who is operating under the most unfavourable conditions and just manages to earn an average interest on his capital invested in the input factors, is relevant.

Objective price and value always tend to be identical. It is only that we are accustomed to accept occasional incorrect valuations of individuals, or of whole groups, as deviations between prices and values. In the long run they cannot last and are just signs of poor economic thinking on the side of the valuing people. Theoretically important is the *term "price level"*. It has to be regarded as an average of all prices, a notion which in practice is very elusive, since different individual items do not easily allow calculation of an average. As a makeshift, a general index which considers the movement in prices of a considerable number of very important goods, is calculated. Theoretically, it would be more accurate to compare *all goods* being produced at times, with the share of the *total* income allotted to them within a certain production period. If it were possible to divide the income of a production period by the total quantity of homogeneous kinds of goods produced during that time we would achieve an *ideal general index.*

a. Normal Price Change

Normal price change is the difference between price levels on the buying and selling markets; it is, simultaneously, the source of profit from turnover.

Among firms necessary to satisfy consumer demand in an economy which is in a fairly normal state, this difference will be sufficient to enable those producing at the highest cost, still to earn a normal yield (interest). Competition among entrepreneurs ensures that firms with a more favourable cost structure also make excessive profits. A second kind of "normal" price difference is the margin between prices at the date of purchase and sale in the speculation market. This market attracts only as much purchasing power as is necessary to secure a normal interest profit for this economic function. Both the above discussed price differences have to be constantly existent in an economy to keep it going. If they were not present there would be no incentive for production, trading and distribution of that production. There has been no era in economic history where these price margins did not exist nor where they did not effectively work.

b. General Price Change

General price changes are to be regarded as those which influence all prices in an economy, at the same time irrespective of whether the influence is totally identical for all goods or with certain differences resulting from special price changes which have to be discussed later. General price changes, which also can be called *changes in the price level, inevitably occur, either when an increase or decrease in the* quantity of goods or an increase or decrease in the available amount of income has taken place between the two turnover periods being compared.

The most common cause of general price changes is known as *inflation.* It makes itself felt such that in addition to the incomes generated by the circulatory flow of economic activity, purchasing power is added which is mainly generated by the government expanding amounts of central bank money. When this additional purchasing power in a period reaches the same amount as the natural level it causes a doubling of prices on average. Recent past [the hyperinflation period, 1922-23] has demonstrated what consequences a continuous series of such creation of income (spending power) can create.

The counterpart of inflation is *deflation.* It would be present if a part of the natural income is destroyed between two turnover periods in the economy. This can result from the withdrawal and destruction of a part of the circulating bank notes. Then the same quantity of goods is faced with reduced incomes and correspondingly the price level will fall.

When income is unchanged general price changes can also occur by virtue of variations in the quantity of goods. When for some reason there is a general *increase in the productivity of the economy*, in such a way that the output per worker and machine is doubled, then a double quantity of goods would be met by an unchanged income level and the price per unit would have to be half. Real life, of course, rarely shows such drastic changes; rather they take place gradually. But when we compare the state of productivity a century ago, with the present, we clearly see the large increase in the productivity of the economy. On the other hand, a *decrease in productivity* is possible as well. The war and post war periods have, for very different reasons, brought about such falls in productivity which meanwhile could be compensated for the most part. A decrease in the quantity of goods must result in the rise of the price level when accompanied by an unchanged income level because more units of income are allotted proportionately to each unit of quantity. *Special attention has to be paid to the fact that productivity and income changes can occur in combination* either with a boosting or with a compensating effect. In the post-war period there has, in general, been a combination of a decrease in the quantity of goods and an increasing level of income thus providing duplicate reasons for price increases. *Furthermore it is of special importance that there is no form of currency which is able totally to prevent general changes in the price level*, for, even if *"hyperinflation"* can be avoided there are still productivity changes which are induced by technical progress and even the most cautious central bank policy cannot always prevent minor changes on the income side and especially because, even the value of gold can fluctuate considerably.

c. Special Price Change

Finally, we have to *consider special price changes*. They affect only individual goods and individual markets without influencing the average of all prices, e.g. if prices drop in particular markets there must be increases in the prices of other goods of the same size or otherwise the average would be changed. So we assume that the total quantities of goods and income are unchanged, and only the allotment to different markets is changed. The most important cause of special change in value is a change in the structure of the needs of consumers. This is most obvious in the markets for fashion articles. If the consumers' preference shifts from one sort of cloth to another this will result in a strong demand for the highly valued commodity and a sharp decline in demand for the one which was in vogue hitherto. Would not an entrepreneur want to take these changes into consideration? Those who, regardless of the lower valuation, put articles of the old sort on the market would receive such low prices that their production cost would no longer be covered. On the other hand since excessive demand would push up the price very much, considering the small supply, the few suppliers of the favoured article would earn very large profits. In practice firms will try to rearrange their production programme according to the different market situations they face. After that has been realized sales of the older article will be made at profitable prices but in lower quantities whilst an increased quantity of the article which is favoured by current fashion will be produced and sold. As profit certainly depends on it, it is particularly important for a firm to identify such changes in market situations as early as possible in order to rearrange production as soon as possible.

Special price changes can also be a function of costs. In individual firms more rationalized production can reduce costs per item. If this production procedure spreads to a greater number of manufacturing firms the competitors in the market will reduce their prices as well. As far as this can generally be observed in firms an increase in productivity would result in a general price reduction. However, we have to take into account also that there are firms which, despite rationalisation over several decades, show an increase in costs. For example, this is true for coal mining, which due to the gradual exhaustion of the easily accessible layers, has experienced increased expenses. A widening of the demand for natural resources which are only available in limited quantities would produce the same effect. In this case, the rising price would have to make ineffective that part of demand which cannot be satisfied from the existing reserves.

d. Money Value (Purchasing Power)

Among the value terms which are of special importance for the balance sheet "money value" must also be mentioned. Wrong and erroneous conceptions have caused quite an amount of unwholesomenesses with regard to operating (cost) accounting.[4] This became fully evident only after periods of inflation although, to a lesser extent it has always been present. The fact, that in the pre-war period in countries with gold bullion standards it was generally taken for granted that money was unchangeable, is evidence of a certain mental inertia in practice and science. Even when it was theoretically understood that this was not true for gold bullion standards, it was very rare, however, that conclusions were drawn from such insight. Nowadays, also for those researchers who were lucky enough to work in countries spared a note inflation, it is clear that money units even of the most stable currencies are constantly subject to certain changes. The yardstick of such changes is the *general index*. Indeed such measures exist for the most important areas of the economy but as they are only based on a selection of prices for goods we always have to be aware that they contain serious errors. In most cases price changes of capital goods are considered only in an inadequate way. After all the figures of the countries with a gold bullion standard also show very considerable changes over the last few years. In any case this makes it certain that it is inadmissible cost accounting to base everything on a [stable] money unit. If that happens in times of inflation when real assets are unchanged, the resulting accounting figures must show an increase in assets which is purely fictitious. If, in addition, this fictitious increase in assets is regarded as distributable profit, it will lead to the most dangerous dispositions of money and fallacies for the entrepreneur and the whole economy. Similar distortions will occur when, in the case of a rising money value (deflation), e.g. falling prices for real goods constituting the assets of a firm, a decrease in the total assets of the firm will be reported. It is of the

4 [Editorial note: *Betriebsrechnung*, has several possible meanings: manufacturing account, operating account, business account; hereinafter operating (or cost) account(ing).]

greatest importance that cost accounting considers any change in the value of money units over time. This is equally important for the owner and manager of monetary capital. For both the owner and manager the value of a money unit on the date of granting and redemption of a loan is not negligible. The efforts of Irving Fisher, to create a dollar currency with a unit which constantly has the same purchasing power, show that the problem has been perceived in the United States. There we can also see the first attempts to incorporate the level of the general index for redemption figures of long term loans.

IV. Balance Sheet Values

Having discussed "value" and "price" in principle, we can now investigate *which kinds of balance sheet values ought to be considered.* After that has been pointed out we will have to look into the problem of what possible balance sheet values suit the purposes which may be stated for the balance sheet.

1. Acquisition Cost Value (Historic Cost Value)

The cost value of an asset is the price which has been paid at the date *of acquisition.* As a rule it is the value at which an asset is included in the operating account. As such it has the distinct advantage of being relatively tangible and traditional accounting without objections has relied on it in the past as the main balance sheet value. Considering all its flaws it could be assumed that its predominance in the balance sheet is mainly the result of more or less mechanical imitation rather than careful consideration. The cost value of an asset is its price in the buying market. On the acquisition date it is a true [objective] value based on the price level on that day of acquisition. But the day after that, already the market situation can have considerably changed and *the cost value then is only of historical significance.* Even if one takes the view that the cost value only has to indicate the amount of money the firm spent on the acquisition date it cannot be used as a yardstick for measuring profit from actual sales since the previous discussion has shown that the value of the money unit at the date of acquisition by no means is necessarily identical with that as at the selling date.

2. *Replacement - Current Acquisition or Reproduction - Value*

The replacement value of an asset is the price at which the respective asset can be acquired in the buying market at the actual or hypothetical *replacement date.* Consequently it is a price which is subject to daily changes and its continuous determination certainly requires various technical provisions and probably can cause costs as well which perhaps constrain its determination to certain dates at which important settlements have to be made. It is important to point out *that the replacement value is a cost price which cannot include any sales profit.* Although, in certain cases, it is a sales price as well, because it informs us of the price for which an asset can be sold in the buying market and by this allows us to compare it with the price in the selling market. Of course, this is, as a rule, only true for finished products. Many input factors cannot be sold again individually after they have entered the firm and become unfinished goods (work in process). That is particularly true for costs of labour and material which have been transformed.

a. Replacement Value at the Balance Sheet Date (at Financial Year End)

A balance sheet which is based on replacement values informs the entrepreneur about the value of his individual assets in the buying market at the date which the balance sheet is drawn up. If there are no omissions the total sum is the amount at that date which would have to be invested to rebuild the firm. Of course, in this connection it has to be considered, that as a rule, a considerable part of the assets which are on the books and which would also have to include intangible assets such as patent rights, advertising expenditure and client goodwill, could be replaced totally but would have to be stated at a discount on the cost value according to their wear and tear. Such a balance sheet based on reproduction values is of the greatest importance for the assessment of the economic situation of a firm because its total sum is the only value suitable for an assessment of the profitability of the firm. In this connection the historic cost value totally fails because, even if depreciation charges are made, only in very rare cases is it still present in the full amount. The reproduction value in the balance sheet shows *what is*, the acquisition value indicates *what was.*

b. Replacement Value at the Time of Sales

The replacement value at the date for which the balance sheet is drawn up is eligible only for those assets which are still in the possession of the firm at that date. But the sales process of the firm requires a large number of goods to pass through the firm during the accounting period. For these sales items, forming only a part of the profit and loss account, there is also a current value which ought to be considered. As a reference date for its determination we will have to consider the *date of sale* or the *date of replacement*. The sales date is the day when a finished, marketable good turns into money; the day when buyer and vendor agree upon the price and enter into a purchase agreement. This *replacement value at sales date* shows the entrepreneur the prices at which he could, at the sales date, replace the input factors which the sold product contains. If selling prices are lower he probably would not put those goods, resellable in the buying market, onto a sales market. As far as this reverse sale is not possible a sales price which is lower than the replacement value plus interest for the intervening period must at least have, as a consequence, that further sales of the same kind will be stopped. If production is to be continued the firm has to put aside out of the sales proceeds an amount, which is as high as the replacement value at the sales date, to enable it to continue production. For this reason profit from sales is only that which exceeds the replacement value of input factors. The purchase cost value of input factors does not mean anything for the ascertainment of sales profits, for it is very unlikely, after a sales period of a certain length, that the input factors which were contained in the products could be replaced at their (historic) cost value. This means replacement value at the sales date must be the basic [necessary] value for profit and loss accounting. Only this value can inform management of a firm whether its production or trading is still profitable at a given moment or whether excess profits suggest an extension of capacities is required; or if it is necessary to cut down because of a lower profit margin.

c. Replacement Price at the Replacement Date

It remains to be investigated, if perhaps the *replacement costs at replacement date*, can provide a secure foundation for accounting. It is unlikely to so do because at the stage of the sales process at which the entrepreneur has to assess cost values and potential profits, the date at which product input factors have to be replaced still lies in the future and the values can only be estimated - they cannot be calculated exactly. Further, it is totally up to the entrepreneur whether he determines actually to replace the sold input factors. He might determine to keep the sales proceeds in money for some time. But even if it were possible at the time of sale to ascertain the good's actual replacement value, that value might not be used as the basis of value in the balance sheet because that particular good is no longer in the possession of the seller. At the very most it is justified to make a depreciation for the short time which would be inevitable to transform the amount of money in goods, even of a different kind.

3. *The Sales Value*

The normal selling price of economic goods contains a profit element. It is one of the oldest principles of accounting to state profits only after they have been realized. For all products still remaining in the firm such profit has not yet been made and it is difficult to determine in advance how much it will be. If we already wanted to show unrealized profits in the balance sheet, we would face a problem by virtue of the fact that such future profits are not distributable, without having first realized those profits by selling the respective products. Also, this would be difficult in case of the fixed assets of the firm.

The selling price is mainly important for profit and loss accounting purposes. There, all sold articles are recorded at their selling prices those prices, being continuously registered in the accounts. Here the selling price is indispensable because it has to be compared with the cost value in order to determine the operating results which are the difference between the two values. In connection with the firm as a whole we find special selling prices, depending whether we use the yield as a basis or regard them in the light of liquidation, with the winding-up of the legal business entity.[5]

4. *Balance Sheet Value of the Whole Firm*

In order to determine the balance sheet value of a firm as a whole one can use very different procedures. In principle it is either the *addition of the values of the individual assets of the firm or the assessment of present value (capitalised income value).*

a. Value of the Firm as the Total Sum of Individual Reproduction Values

In practice the balance sheet, which in most cases is based on the cost values of individual assets, those values often also being garbled by hidden reserves, in practice cannot provide a reliable value of the firm. At the date of drawing up the balance sheet, what has been paid for an asset in the past, often many years ago, is no longer important in order to value an asset. Rather only how much one would have to pay at present is important. Accordingly, here it is the *reproduction value of the firm, that is the addition of the replacement values of its individual assets including the intangible*

---

5 [Editors' note: it is interesting to find reference by Schmidt to exit (selling) prices as an alternative valuation base. A leading German academic, Seicht [1982] notes this was *not* unusual. Detailed examination of Seicht's views and others is provided in chapter 2 of this anthology.

assets, which will be most important. This total value shows *the amount of capital, necessary at the date of drawing up the balance sheet, to reorganise the firm in its present form.* In this way we arrive at the cost of production for the whole firm at the date of drawing up the balance sheet and the sum of capital which it represents at that date. Of course this sum is not necessarily equivalent to the value of the firm as a whole because, it is possible that the firm yields a profit which is higher than normal interest on the reproduction value. In this case the owner will sell his plant only under the condition that he is also paid for the higher discounted present value. Nevertheless the *reproduction value of the firm* retains its great importance because *the discounted present value of the future income stream can be determined only by using it as a case.* In order to know how much the profit is, it is necessary to know the value of expenditure incurred by the operating process. It is represented by the reproduction value or replacement costs of the input factors.

A special way to arrive at a valuation for the whole firm from the sum of its individual assets is provided by a dissolution balance sheet. It is relevant in practical settings in situations where the firm is unprofitable and its profitability cannot be increased by improvements or reorganisation. Then the liquidator has to sell the individual assets as best as he can. The liquidation balance sheet, therefore, *is* based on selling prices but those applicable in a special market. The regular sales markets of the firm are eligible just for the finished products and often, not even for them, if the marketing organisation has already been dissolved at the sales date. Also the sale on the regular buying market is only possible in exceptional cases because property, plant and equipment are in most cases adjusted to the special needs of the firm and it is not easy to find someone else with exactly the same needs. Moreover, most of the machinery and equipment is reduced in value by wear and tear so that the liquidator has to sell it in the second-hand market. If, in addition, there is economic pressure pushing for an immediate sale, then as a rule only part of the *current* acquisition value, i.e. the reproduction value of the firm, will be secured by the sale of all individual assets for liquidation purposes. As this is a balance sheet which takes its guide-lines from a market which is totally different to regular markets of the firm it can only be applied in the special case of liquidation.

b. Firm Value as the Discounted Present Value of the Whole

The fundamental structure of the discounted present value (of the whole firm) as a balance sheet item is totally different. *The basis of the* discounted present value is profit. The net profit of an economic year has to be discounted at the nominal interest rate at the date for which the balance sheet is drawn up assuming sufficient provisions for risks have been subtracted from the profit. Another procedure used to make provisions for future losses is to take a higher than normal interest rate for discounting. This is discernible by looking at the market value of the firm's total shares on the stock exchange. The income which the shareholder receives in the form of a gross return is, as a rule, for industrial shares considerably higher than for gilt-edged securities. The difference compensates approximately for the above-mentioned risks. The assessment of the discounted present value of a firm, of course will not be based exclusively on present and the immediate past figures but also will take the future development of the firm into account. Of course, the interest rate used for discounting will have to be the present interest rate exclusively because, in case of a potential sale of the whole firm, the total sales value has to be paid at the present time or at least must be agreed upon. But it may well happen that the firm yields higher or lower profits in the future. Although the buyer may be convinced that he will make more profit by applying new production techniques it is still unlikely that he would pay the whole additional profit, for he is responsible to the vendor. When profits are exceptionally high at the present time, one has to consider the risk of competitors introducing the same production techniques, thereby forcing profits back down. Therefore we will have to distinguish between a discounted present value at the date of drawing up the balance sheet and a discounted present value taking the future development of profits into account.

Despite the great importance of determining the discounted present value in order to assess a firm's economic situation it is relatively rare to find such calculations in practice. As a rule they are reserved for conversions, mergers and the like, and then, often they are based on incorrect income figures. Reductions in inaccuracy are attempted by basing the valuation on the profits of a number of years, instead of one year, hoping to balance out abnormal fluctuations. Technically it would be no problem to record the surplus of the discounted present value over the reproduction value in the balance sheet. The only thing is that such deviations might by no means appear as profit or loss.

A specific discounted present value is the *reconstruction value of the firm*. Its determination becomes important when the regular profit and loss statement shows that the total profit is not enough to pay at least normal interest on the reproduction value of the firm. Then the entrepreneur has to consider whether to transfer his firm to a different production or trade yielding larger profits. That means he has to assess a future profit and to subtract the reorganisation costs from the resulting discounted present value in order to arrive at the reorganisation value. In this way one can make calculations for different kinds of reorganisation in order to find the most profitable form of future activities. Of course the necessity to assess almost every factor will also provide ample opportunity for errors.

V. Accounting Methods in Theory

As we now turn to examine accounting methods we would like first to discuss those which the German business administration theorists developed from a theoretical point of view. *The origin of these theories, however, is primarily due to the inflation period* which made it absolutely clear how inadequate, accounting methods which hitherto had been practised, were in times of large fluctuations of prices. *What, for this reason, has been accepted as necessary and important with regard to the handling of value changes in the Balance Sheet must quite naturally also be valid for those value changes which appear, although at a lower level in times of so-called stability of the currency.* For the last decade, fluctuations of the price index in the United States which is a country with a gold bullion standard, range between 100 and 300. Of course accounting methods developed theoretically in the first instance, have to be applicable in practice. Where they differ from the common practical methods a detailed explanation of the material reasons has to be given. As limited space does not allow me to discuss all the details in full we have, to some extent, to refer to the essential literature which characterizes the different types of balance sheets.

1. Reproduction Value Accounting (lit: Balance Sheet Based on Reproduction Values)

What has to be depicted in this connection I have dealt with in detail in other places.[6] *Reproduction value accounting is based on the concept that the assets of a nation and of a firm do not primarily consist of money but of goods.* For this reason it tries to avoid the damages caused by the assumption that all assets are money. We will have to prove later that most of the inaccuracies of traditional balance sheet concepts result from this biassed conception of the accounts being represented from the point of view of money. The leading principle of the current value accounting approach is the maintenance of the firm in its *real* (physical) state. The most important consequence is that the firm can only generate a profit if the sales proceeds of outgoing products are higher than the cost of replacement or reproduction of the same goods at the date of sale, regardless of what amount of money has been paid in the past for their acquisition. The money paid at that time is sunk (left) in the product. *Profit is only that part of sales profits which exceeds the current acquisition value (replacement) of costs. Besides that speculative profit presents a special problem.*

6 See Schmidt, *The Organic Balance Sheet Within the Framework of The Economy*, 2nd ed., G. A. Gloeckner, Leipzig, 1922. Schmidt, *Replacement Price on the Day of Turnover in Cost Calculation and the Economy*, Spaeth & Linde, Berlin, 1923. Schmidt, *Balance Sheet Value, Annual Profit and Balance Sheet Revaluation*, Spaeth & Linde, Berlin, 1924.

When we first base our considerations on a firm which is totally dedicated to selling, using no outside capital and which sells its products for cash, then the balance sheets for two years for comparative purposes, have to be based on replacement costs of the individual assets in the buying market. If the firm's stock of assets were identical in real terms at both dates then a mere change in the value of the assets during the time between both balance sheet dates would not result in any profit or loss, whereas in a balance sheet which is based on money value any such change would be recorded as profit or loss. If, for example, the value, in money terms were to double, then we would record a 100% profit. But to distribute it one would have to sell half of the firm's real assets. A mere comparison of two current value balance sheets still would not be enough to provide full *information* because it rarely happens that by the end of any year, the assets are exactly the same as one had at the beginning. Therefore current value accounting, if it is to be correct, has to trace every single item through the sales accounts, for example, by initially recording on the goods or manufacturing account the incoming input factors at a cost value of 100 money units. When the respective goods are sold the sales proceeds have to be compared with the current acquisition value and not with the historic acquisition value. If the current acquisition cost value of the input factors is now 200, a sales profit can only be made when we get more for the product than its current acquisition value, that is more than 200. With that the question arises does the difference now of 100 money units between the acquisition value and replacement value matter. They are *holding gains*. In this connection we can leave undecided the question whether their cause is a value change on the side of the money or of the goods themselves - thus whether it is a *general* or *specific* price change. These holding gains[7] have to be eliminated from the profit and loss account by either directly transferring them to the capital account or by establishing a special account which could be called a revaluation account. These gains cannot be distributed, for if one wanted to distribute those 100 money units it would have to be taken out of the real stock of assets. When, in the opposite case, we assume a *decrease in value* for instance from 100 down to 50, then this also does not mean a loss has arisen because the firm still owns what it had originally, e.g. the same stock of goods. If someone offers 60 for the goods which could be replaced at any time at the cost of 50 money units the firm will sell them at a profit because afterwards it has the same goods and a surplus of 10. Holding losses have to be offset directly to the capital account or transferred to the revaluation account. *The value adjustment account together with the capital account*

7 [Editors' note: Literally the phrase, "Ist Wertänderung am ruhenden Vermögen Gewinn oder Verlust" translates "Do money value changes applied to your dormant capital create profit or loss?". It corresponds to, as Schmidt (1931) used the term in the Anglo-American literature, "Is appreciation profit?", or in modern usage, "Are holding gains profit?"]

indicates in which direction the value of business assets has changed and gives essential indications for the correct disposition of capital. This has as its main task the proper selection of the date of acquisition and of the sales date and also in the economy, has the important function to adjust the value of goods in each case to the ratio between supply and demand.

Another consequence of current value accounting is that depreciation rates for the wear and tear of real assets are not calculated on the basis of the historical acquisition costs but on the current acquisition value. As a result each production period contributes to the replacement of real assets to the extent of their wear and tear. When we, according to this concept, imagine the total assets of a whole nation, as stated in individual balance sheets, then at the end of each year only that which has been produced as real goods in the course of the year *in excess* of the employed input costs could be reported as profit. With such a profit concept a large task would be accomplished. In particular the balance sheet would be shaped into an instrument indicating the amount of possible consumption of a nation without resulting in a decrease in that nation's real assets. What is true for the whole is effected by current value accounting also with regard to the assets of individual firms. Harmony between the whole economy and the individual business can only be established in this way. At this point an objection may be raised that it will by no means be possible in every situation in an economy to maintain the stock of assets in total. Current value accounting would also meet that condition because, if one day a certain kind of goods were abundant, as plant capacities in times of crisis as a rule are, then that abundance would indeed depress their value lower than current reproduction value. If the result is measured on the basis of the depressed historical reproduction values a profit would be possible but not a total replacement after the abatement of the abundance has caused the current acquisition value to rise to its old level. This is the principle of the relative maintenance of the firm which in this case affects value changes of assets in stock as punishment for wrong capital dispositions.

Special difficulties with regard to current value accounting arise from speculation. *Active speculation is based on money which is borrowed short or long-term in order to acquire goods of any kind*: perhaps to buy securities on the stock exchange hoping that their price increase will exceed the interest payment. This opportunity will be best seen in times of a rising price level because, whereas *all* commodity prices rise, the total amount of debt can only increase by interest as the debt itself is fixed by law to its nominal value. Let us suppose that prices generally rise from 100 to 200 money units between obtaining the loan and the resale of the acquired goods. Then the difference between acquisition and selling price, which is 100, minus interest, is the speculation profit. Following the final settlement of the transaction such a profit then is realized and potentially distributable. As long as the resale has not yet taken place, speculation profit cannot be distributed because it has not been realized, even if the value of the goods increases. It is tied to the goods and is equivalent to the difference between historical acquisition - and - current acquisition value. *Therefore it is possible also to report in the balance sheet goods which were acquired for speculative purposes with their current acquisition value.* Only in case of the redemption of the loan are they subject to a special settlement which also distributes that account as profit. In the case of goods which are financed from owners' equity this would be transferred directly to the capital account as holding gains. By that, also, the *kind of speculation profit is characterized. It is mainly a change in value over time and not a sales profit, because purchase and sale take place in the same market* in contrast to the turnover process which takes place in a buying and a selling market: with the resulting profit being the margin between them. *In times of a general increase in value (of goods), e.g. the decrease in the value of money, the speculation profit of one party is at the same time a loss of assets for the other* because, although the creditor gets back the same nominal amount of money no longer has he the same purchasing power. Strangely enough this is often ignored by the owners of capital so that they do not include it in their accounting. But recently it seems to be a growing insight. When inflation was at its highest stage creditors used to demand a substantial increase in the payable interest rate for the prospective inflation. This was intended to offer an indemnification for the lower purchasing power, in form of an inflation premium. Recently it has been agreed to redeem long-term loans after adjustments based on a general index. In consideration of the changed purchasing power, and with regard to a fair compromise, it would be nothing but positive if this became a general custom.

In any case the creditor has to realize that when he gets 100 money units and maybe 10 units of interest after one year, while the purchasing power of money as in the present example, is only half its original value, that interest is by no means profit as it is not even sufficient to make up for the loss of half his purchasing power. In that business deal the creditor did not make any profit but rather suffered a loss of 90 money units. If that insight were generally accepted the determination of interest rates would have to be changed considerably because the interest rate would have to include an inflation premium or a deflation discount depending on the tendency of the direction of the change in purchasing power.

To the extent that speculation money is also used to finance sales transactions, on the basis of current value accounting all sales profits which exceed the current acquisition value of the goods can be distributed. It is also possible to distribute speculative profits periodically, but in doing so, one has to be aware that it is only possible through borrowing additional money. In other words, in this case, the value increase in goods which is to be distributed, has to be taken out of the existing income of others in order that it can be paid.

2. *Acquisition Cost Accounting with an Index Adjustment*[8]

Another form of accounting which has been adjusted for theoretical consideration is the balance sheet based on acquisition costs and adjusted by a general index. *It is based on the view that the assets of the firm, as well as of the economy, lie in money or money's worth* which, in a more primitive version is also characteristic of the simple balance sheet, customary in practice, based on (historic) acquisition costs. But it has been realized that this money value is subject to changes and thus this indexed form of accounting tries to compensate for these effects. Let us suppose that a firm has been established with a capital of 100,000 money units. In case that money loses half of its value, then when the next balance sheet is drawn up all the acquisition costs have to be stated on the basis of the devalued money as at the new balance sheet date, e.g. the balance sheet total has to be 200,000 money units before we can talk about profit. If, in the example the value of money were to double, meaning that the general index would go down from 100 to 50, then every amount exceeding 50,000 units of money in the final balance sheet would be profit. To the extent that operating assets do not remain in the firm just as they were, but are exchanged in the course of the *business* process, a revaluation of their acquisition costs with an index adjustment as at the acquisition date has to take place.

This form of balance sheet with indexed adjustments, for which Schmalenbach and Mahlberg became the major advocates in Germany during the hyperinflation period, has several disadvantages. For one thing its basic assumption that the assets of a firm only consist of money and assets expressed in money-value is wrong. They consist of a variety of goods and derive their value not only from the general price level but also from their specific situation in their relevant markets. For this reason even adjusted acquisition costs can only take changes in the general price level into account; but not those in the special market of the goods, which, apart from general

8 For more detailed discussion see Schmalenbach, *Balance Sheets Denominated in Goldmark*, published by Springer, Berlin 1925.

Schmalenbach, *Fundamentals of Dynamic Accounting*, 3rd ed., G.A. Gloeckner, Verlag, Leipzig 1925.

Mahlberg, *Balance Sheet Technique and Valuation During Periods of Currency Fluctuation*, 3rd ed., G.A. Gloeckner, Leipzig 1923.

Walb, *The Problem of Fictitious Profits*, published by Walter Momber, Freiburg, Breisgau 1921.

changes, have been rather considerable. Consequently this method of accounting does not provide the entrepreneur with the necessary instruments to make the specific dispositions needed for transactions of specific goods. Goods which rise in value faster than the general index will show a sales profit that is too large, because the subtraction from (sales) proceeds for the change of value will be insufficient; while others with an increase slower than the general index will show too small a profit and, by virtue of that, sales transactions are easily directed into wrong channels.

Moreover, there is the grievance that this kind of accounting is hardly capable of distinguishing distributable from, as of yet, unrealized speculation profits. Every general decrease in purchasing power necessarily makes itself felt as a speculation profit involving monetary liabilities (the face value of which are unchanged) whilst again the actual change in value of the special goods may differ from the index. However, there would be ways to link the distribution of speculative profits resulting from that accounting method with the redemption of the money debts. Balance sheet adjustment, according to an index, certainly is an improvement over mere (historic) acquisition costs accounting but it is still affected by the above-mentioned shortcomings.[9]

3. *Net Worth ["Static"] and Income ["Dynamic"] Accounting*

For present accounting theory it is a very controversial question whether the purpose of accounting is to determine value (net worth), or whether it is to state the profit of a production period, or whether we can expect it to do both.

All experts agree that it is necessary both to determine the value of the net assets of firms and their profit. But disagreement is evident when it comes to the question which of these purposes is more important. A quite common view is that it is impossible to achieve both at the same time with the same accounting statement. Whoever agrees with that, naturally for current accounting purposes, has to make a decision as to what he thinks more important: either the determination of profit or of the value of net assets. Schmalenbach adamantly advocates the priority of income/or profit and loss accounting, and based on a point of view that the main purpose of a firm is to generate profit from sales and not to invest capital, one can agree with him. But when it is a question of alternatives I take a rather different view, namely that we have to do both.

---

9 [Editors' note: The section on indexed adjustments is indicative of the development of Schmidt's 3rd edition of *Die organische Tageswertbilanz*. This limited reference to indexed adjustments was retained in the 3rd edition, verbatim, not withstanding that a new section of the 3rd edition (pp.292-304) discussed index adjustments in detail. For further details of what was contained in these three editions see *Appendix III*]

We have seen that quite different figures can be taken as the profit of a firm. *If it is based in principle on original or acquisition costs, which are adjusted according to an index*, then, by regarding the difference between acquisition costs and sales prices as profit, we have to admit that such a movement can only be used for profit accounting purposes. Although in doing so, of course, the question remains can this method, even with adjustments, after all, indicate profit. By no means can it lead to a net worth financial statement because there is a consensus of opinion that the outdated acquisition costs do not represent the value of individual assets nor of the assets as a whole because at the date the balance sheet is drawn up, the value may be totally different. If the profit, which is based on acquisition costs were correct, one could at least use it to calculate the present value of the firm as a whole. But even that is unlikely, since even advocates of (historic) acquisition cost accounting prudently do not calculate the present value of the whole firm from the profit of a single year, but from the average of a number of years. Consequently they mistrust the profit calculation of any single year. Further, it has *to be taken into account*, that when profit calculation is based on the difference between (historic) acquisition costs and sales proceeds, each value change between the respective dates actually has to take effect as profit or loss, at the latest, when the goods are sold. By means of an index adjustment, however, the general changes in the price level can be eliminated. But, especially in the case of long-term assets, holding gains or losses which may originate far back can appear as a profit or loss item in an accounting period which has nothing to do with that period. As a result the income statement doubtlessly will be distorted. At least it is right that someone who calculates profit and loss in this way also has to be an advocate of the incompatibility of Balance Sheet and Profit and Loss accounting.

The situation is different with regard to a *balance sheet based on reproduction costs* where profit is calculated on the basis of current acquisition values. Thus profit is only the margin between the buying - and selling market. Speculation profits can be included in the calculation as normal profits, insofar as they do not result from a general change in the value of money. But they are only distributable where they have been realized. As far as they only represent an increase in purchasing power, and correspond to that lost by the creditor due to nominal accounting, they are not normal profits from business operations but holding gains which, via the monetary claim, are appropriated to only one of the contracting parties as profit. Profit which is calculated in this way provides for the maintenance of the firm and can be distributed in full. In my opinion this is the real profit from business operations. If that is true, then it is bound to be the right base for the calculation, via discounting, of the present value of the firm as a whole. Then, indeed, the present value of the whole can be higher or lower than the reproduction value of the individual items but that means nothing other than the profitability of the reproduction value, which represents the value of the invested capital and is fixed to the firm, can be higher or lower. *But the balance sheet based on reproduction values is already a sort of net worth financial statement because it establishes the invested capital.* Further, if due to the total elimination of holding gains and losses we recognize it as the only base for the calculation of the operating profit, it is exclusively capable of reporting the true profit and thereby also the present value of the whole. Above all it is an inseparable fusion of net worth and profit and loss accounting which, as such, means a considerable advantage but which derives logically from the principle of the maintenance of the firm.

It has to be acknowledged, as it is for the property tax balance sheet, that a liquidation balance sheet besides that, is a net worth financial statement not connected to the profit and loss statement. A property tax balance sheet often comes very close to a balance sheet based on reproduction values in particular when the tax authorities know their business. Finally the reorganisation balance sheet is a discounted present value balance sheet for specific purposes based on an estimated profit.

VI. Accounting Methods in Practice

Accounting methods used in practice are mainly characterized by the fact that all are based on an incorrect idea that the unit of money is invariant. Of course, certain experiences did shake that belief somewhat, but they did not lead to forms of correction which were logically clear. Attempts to find some form of correction all have in common that they are not based on a clear insight into the problems, but more on a certain feeling for what is right, therefore leaving much scope for individual arbitrariness. Above all, only in rare cases has the influence of holding gains and losses been separated from the *real* sales profits. One used to regard holding gains and losses indiscriminately as operating profits or losses as well as true sales - or speculation profits. Here we want to describe primarily the methods which are common in the German law and practice.

1. Balance Sheet of the Sole Proprietorship and of the General Partnership

§. 40 of the German Commercial Code states that all assets and liabilities have to be reported at the value they possess at the date for which the balance sheet is drawn up.

If only read in its literal sense we would have to deduce from it a mere current value balance sheet. However, interpretation in a legal sense has lead to an acknowledgement that the "current value" is only the permitted upper limit and that it is therefore admissible to state lower values. Apparently this is based on the view that a lowering of balance sheet asset values cannot impair creditors of the firm. However, this interpretation means a legally admissible window-dressing which also can be called trade custom.

Strangely enough there are also views, which although accepting the current value principle, are guided by a current value concept against which the greatest objections have to be made. Those views embody *current selling values*. If we wanted to use this value especially for the sales products of the firm then we could report a sales profit which could be distributed already for the inventory at the balance sheet date which is expected to be realized only in the future and perhaps, in case of a change in the market situation, will not be obtained at all. These objections certainly have contributed substantially to discredit the idea of current value accounting. If a current value is eligible as a balance sheet value then it can only be a current acquisition value which does not yet contain a sales profit. Furthermore practitioners are afraid of current value accounting because the techniques of bookkeeping, according to their opinion, forces them then to report any change in values between two balance sheet dates as profit or loss. But they know from long experience that in times of a fast upswing in business activity the general change in the level of prices would have to produce holding gains which could be distributable only if a part of the indispensable assets were sold. In the opposite case a crisis with its general decrease in values would lead to large losses which, in view of the unchanged quantity of assets, with good reason, one would not want to accept. This clearly demonstrates that a balance sheet which reports all holding gains as real operating profit in times of large changes in values can become very dangerous. In the version which I developed these dangers are avoided by transferring all holding gains and losses directly to a capital account or a subaccount thereby influencing the determination of distributable profits. This separate account then, also shows whether the selection of the assets was fortunate enough to at least achieve an average development in values.

In reality German sole proprietorships and general partnerships do not usually prepare balance sheets based on current values but *balance sheets based on acquisition costs*. They are satisfied with stating all their assets at the value in money which they paid at the point of acquisition. Where there is wear and tear certain parts of the acquisition values are depreciated. This generally accepted accounting view regards the total difference between the acquisition costs and the selling price as the profit of the firm. It does not take into account that a change in price taking place in the buying market between the acquisition and sales date appears as distributable profits, able to be distributed only when assets are sold. In case of falling prices between acquisition and sales dates the decrease causes a loss, although the respective amount could be taken out of the firm, without reducing its real assets. Actually this implies that the firm is regarded as a large speculation, in which, at a certain date owners' equity and outside (borrowed) capital have been invested. In that case every increase in that capital, as far as it is shown by sales, constitutes profit and every decrease constitutes a loss. It neither takes into account that the money which certainly was infused was transformed into assets then, nor also that the value of money can be subject to considerable changes. While it is bound to and could reflect company operations, by virtue of the fact that this form of accounting produces very uncertain profit and loss accounts in which even the preparers, lacking trust in the system, falsify it and so turn it into a caricature of reality. Every change in value produces fictitious profits and losses which have been so devastating in the countries experiencing inflation.

2. *Balance Sheet of the Public Stock Corporation*

What earlier was described as trade custom of sole proprietors has been explicitly specified for public stock corporations in §. 261 of the German Civil Code. It is dominated by the concept of the *balance sheet based on acquisition values* as it has been characterized above. Hence it follows that profit is the realized difference between acquisition costs and sales price. But besides that price falls of saleable products which have occurred since their acquisition have to be reported as a loss. Consequently, here the principle of current value is adapted to take price falls into account. The sole proprietor also used to take the same precautions but according to the principle of current value he is obliged to do it. As a result of this accounting method holding gains appear only insofar as fictitious profits when the products have been sold. In contrast, a decrease in value of saleable products has the effect of a fictitious loss even when the products are still possessed by the firm. The more correct form of current value accounting distinguishing between sales profits and holding gains and losses would also show this decrease in value, but as change in value via the capital account, and not as an operating loss. A balance sheet adjusted with the general index would at least eliminate the influence of general changes in the value of money from the calculation of operating profit.

Incidentally, with regard to all German balance sheets practitioners and interpreters of the law agree that the required values set upper limits which can be undercut. This conception results in a policy of hidden reserves being extensively applied. Therefore, what is shown in a German balance sheet, only in rare cases, gives reliable information about the value of assets employed in the firm. Basically, there is also reason to distrust whether the profit which has been established, is correct because a large build-up of hidden reserves will put pressure on it, and at a later date, when the undervalued goods are sold, excessive sales profits appear. All these customs have made the balance sheets a sphinx, the mysteries of which even the guardians of the Temples often cannot unravel. Certainly it would be conducive to the economy if soon we could have realistic balance sheets forming a sound base for management planning and giving a true picture of business activities.

Prof. Dr. Schmidt found it quite interesting to hear quite a number of objections here which are made rather frequently (laughter). The speaker of course cannot prevent anybody from drawing up his balance sheet as he likes. When a tax authority or bank insists on having prepared a balance sheet according to its principles, for Heaven's sake, let them have it. (laughter) When three experts have to prepare a balance sheet without knowing about the others the speaker is sure that three different results and probably also three different valuation principles will occur. That is true for all balance sheets in the world. There would have to be notes here we used the acquisition costs, there the current prices, there we have utilised hidden reserves etc. That cannot be the idea of the balance sheet in its ideal sense. If it shall serve any purpose, and if the public is colour-blind to such an extent that they cannot stand daylight, then a dark balance sheet should be prepared for them. But the speaker for himself would not`t have one prepared. One cannot break customs which are thousands of years old. The speaker, of course, does not expect any accountant to do that. But an accountant who does not know what the correct value for his balance sheet is not a true accountant! (applause)

Index Numbers[1]

Fritz Schmidt

Organisation

I. Concept

Index numbers are indices of shifts in value. They measure either the shifts in value *of a single kind of good only*, or of a *group of goods* or of the *totality of all economic goods* which exist in an economy in a certain period. Consequently it is a matter of individual numbers in the first case and average calculations in all others.

II. Fundamentals of Value Shifts

The value basis of the index calculation is nearly always the market price. Market prices develop from supply and demand on the free market. Demand is determined by the amount of purchasing power at the disposal of the buyer at a certain time. Purchasing power is income in money terms which ultimately stems only from the costs in the turnover process, inclusive in these costs being the entrepreneuers' profit. The income of people not directly involved in production is taken from income that directly originates from these costs., e.g. through taxes from which the civil service is paid. Thus there is no more income for purchases in a certain financial period - besides the remainder from the previous period - than the costs that have occurred in this period. Under certain "laws" this maximum income of the production period has to be spent completely on the purchase of the goods that have been produced in this period.

---

1 Translated from H. Nicklisch *Handwörterbuch der Betriebswirtschaft* 1927, Vol. 3.

However, if this happens the producers have the same amount of money from sales as the income that was available in the previous period. This money is the maximum amount of costs that can be spent in the following period. Thus one production period is firmly connected to the next. The costs, incomes and prices are the same as those in the previous period as long as no shifts in the described circulation model occur. In other words, the price level, the median of all prices of an economy, tends to be stable.

Shifts in Prices can be:

1. Shifts in individual prices while the median price and the circulation model remain unchanged. One reason for this is a shift in the demand structure of income recipients. Some goods rate higher in this valuation, others lower, while the national income and the quantity of all goods remain the same.

2. Shifts occur in the circulation model itself.

   (a) The quantity of goods changes while the national income is constant, i.e. the productivity of the economy increases or decreases. If the productivity increases, the same national income faces more goods than before, consequently less income is allotted to every quantum [of goods] and the prices per unit would fall. If the productivity decreases the same national income faces less goods, thus more income is allotted to every unit of goods and prices would increase.

   (b) The quantity of goods remains stable while the total income changes. This is only possible through inflation or deflation. Inflation means the creation of artificial income - income that has not originated from costs in the same production period, - through bank notes or deposit money and thus to increase the purchasing power of the incomes in such a way that more income than costs are allotted to every unit of goods. Deflation would mean that the government collects a part of the incomes through taxation and destroys it so that the goods face less disposable purchasing power than the required expenditure. Consequently [either] the prices of goods have to increase or decrease.

   (c) Shifts in productivity and income can also occur at the same time and can increase or neutralise each other in their effect on the individual prices. The inflationary period [following WWI] was a period of simultaneous increase in income and decrease in productivity, hence there was a double reason for an increase in prices.

III. The Methods of Index Calculation

1. The most common method is the *quantitative absolute value index.* One determines the prices at a certain time as the base and equates it with the number 1 or 100. All comparative prices at other times are consequently expressed as a portion of the cardinal number through additions to or substractions from 1 or 100. If the comparative number is under 1 or 100, it means a decrease in the compared prices. If the index number increases it shows an increase in prices.

2. The *chain index* is normally determined in the way where the standard prices of each period are not those at a standard time that often is long ago, but the prices of the respective previous period. Which are equated with 1 or 100 for the purpose. Consequently the changes in prices are expressed as additions to or substractions from, the standard price of the previous period. A figure +9 would show that the prices of the last period are 9% higher than those of the previous period; the figure -7 characterises a decrease by 7%.

3. The *weighted index* leaves the quantitative absolute basis and considers shifts in productivity and consumption potential. If, for example, the price of a dwelling required a third of all income at a certain time, its value is still rated as one-third in the index calculation even if a much smaller portion of income is allotted to it. A considerable shift in the standard of living is considered in the way that the composition of basic goods is adapted to the new situation. It is clear that many problems occur at this point, though experienced index specialists like Irving Fisher and E. Kahn assure us that, generally, unweighted indices show comparatively few mistakes in comparison with weighted ones.

IV. The Kinds of Indices

1. *The ideal general index.* A general index marks the median changes of *all* prices in a certain economic period. It would only be determinable if it is possible to determine the sum of all goods and of all purchasing incomes. Even then it would hardly be possible in the case of a shift of the kinds of goods amongst each other to do justice to the quantitative and qualitative effects of

effects of this shift in the stock of goods. In this context it is important to state that such a general index as a median of all figures has to comprise not only all circulating goods but also *all valuable parts of the national wealth.* Also the general index would be an asset index in which the consumer goods would have a comparatively small significance. In practice great difficulties would impede the determination of such an index. Therefore one is very hesitant before undertaking attempts in this direction and usually confines oneself to indices with a smaller range. However, one should stress at this stage that only the ideal general index which in practice is hardly ever completely determinable can give a detailed picture of the median shift in value and thus in the purchasing power of money.

2. In practice the determination of the *wholesale index* is not based on the median of all wholesale prices but on the prices of a limited number of selected goods. These prices are comparatively easy to collect and - if one is aware of the limited range of the fundamental figures - this index can be of valuable service : in particular it has the advantage of fast calculation. Every country with a developed economy usually determines wholesale indices. The British magazine *The Economist* first published these indices in 1864. In Germany Soetbeer first calculated such indices retrospectively back to 1847. Nowadays the *Statistische Reichsamt* [the former bureau of statistics of the (German) Reich] publishes a weighted wholesale index that is based on 38 goods. In addition to this in times of inflation, a number of leading economic magazines have developed their own indices, in particular the *Frankfurter Zeitung* which met an urgent demand for *faster* calculation. [emphasis added by Editor].

3. The *retail index* attempts to determine shifts in value of retail goods, i.e. consumer goods. Here again from the outset the correct selection of the standard goods is crucial, since the totality of all retail goods is impossible to comprise. In Germany Jastrow and Calwer have started with the calculation of a retail index. Since 1920 also the *Statistische Reichsamt* determined a retail index retrospectively to 1913/14.

4. The *cost of living index* is closely related to the retail index. It intends to include price shifts of goods which are particularly relevant for living. The necessities of life are in the foreground while it is very difficult to comprise the other goods of life correctly. According to Morgenroth, one starting point of the calculation is:

(a) The physiological nutritional needs of an individual person or a standard family.

(b) The daily ration for the augmentation (survival) of a human being, e.g. a sailor (Calwer). During the war this calculation became faulty because even a sailor could not receive the normal ration. Thus a so-called "small ration" had become the basis for the calculation.

(c) The standard requirements of a working-class family are estimated and become the base for the calculation.

(d) One starts from statistically recorded real household budgets and follows their changes in the price and quality as well as quantity.

In all cases of calculation with the cost of living index it is very difficult to record in time and correctly the qualitative and quantitave changes in basic goods of an individual and of the average budget. However, the real quantities and qualities need repeated verification.

5. From the point of view of business administration as well as economics the determination of *a productivity index* would be necessary. It would need to show how the productivity of an economy develops in various periods, whether it is increasing or decreasing and to what extent. This index could then indicate to what extent price changes of goods and hence of the general index are to be traced back to such changes in productivity.

6. An *inflation or deflation index* would be effective in the same way. It would have to show to what extent incomes have been artifically increased or decreased. If that were known the rest of the changes in value of the goods could be allotted to the productivity.

7. *A net asset value index* would have to record the changes in value of all capital goods with a long service life. It would be a general index exclusive of goods having a short service span and could give information about value changes on the capital market. In practice some newspapers have developed an index of shares and bonds that can be useful for investors by means of market rates.

8. *A gold-mark index* had particular significance in the inflationary period when the conversion of balance sheets was done according to this standard [voluntarily prior to 23 December 1923 - then *mandatory*]. The price of gold in units of a *paper money currency* can be chosen as the basis. Also the exchange

rate of gold standard countries has often been used. Meanwhile it has been realised that both bases can be considerably distorted in inflationary periods because gold and currency prices run ahead of domestic inflation. The safest gold mark index would still be *the ideal general index*. [emphasis added]

9. *The company index* is of great significance to the operating (cost) accounting, in other words the determination of the median value changes of all assets of a company. Since these goods can be quite different, each company has a differently structured index which can show similarities only for companies of the same industry.

10. The last index of significance to business administration is the *current value of goods* which is hardly an index anymore because it represents only an index number of the value change of the individual good. It is the *most exact index* of value changes of the individual good. Even though it cannot be determined without effort, it can in fact be exactly recorded in most cases, because in the course of time, such numbers are determined within the economy again and again. This index can also be extended as an index of current replacement values and current sales values.

V. The Significance of Index Numbers for Business Administration

1. A company is interested to follow continuously the purchasing power of money because its disposition of goods and money is influenced by it. The ideal general index is most suited for this, though it is not completely determinable. In any case it should not be overlooked that on this index also the changes in income and productivity as well as the influences of glut and shortage of goods on the value of goods have an effect.

2. The answer to the problem for the more or less maintenance of the assets of a company in comparison with the median of the national wealth is of great significance. In this case also the general index is the best measurement. It shows how much the value of a certain quantity of goods has changed from the starting year to the year of comparison. If there is an increase in assets - after the deduction of increases due to profits - beyond the index increase, then the additional value is to be attributed to an overrelative increase in value.

3. The retail and even more the cost of living index is a useful basis for the wage policy of a company as well as the employees' representatives. However, it is

an error to believe that only the needs of consumers for goods of living could determine the wages in an economy. Above all the development of productivity is also decisive. If, following periods show a better productivity which can be measured through the productivity index the real wages have to be increased even if all other circumstances remain unchanged. Conversely the wages in money have to stay behind the cost of living index if productivity decreases, in other words if less goods are produced for distribution. Therefore the cost of living index always needs correction though the productivity index if it is not to provide a wrong measurement for the wage fixing.

4. Calculation, prime cost calculation and price policy of the company also require a foundation in index form if value fluctuations of cost units occur during production periods. Here an operation index can be considered which, however, bears the danger that its median does not correspond with the cost components of the individual good. Therefore the changes in the current aquisition value of the individual cost components are better used as an index in this case.

5. To the productivity policy of the company, above all the productivity index is important. If it is specially determined for the individual company it can show to what extent it was able to keep up with the pace of the general productivity development. Besides the productivity in real goods there is also one in value. The general index as a measurement can provide information about its development. It shows to what extent the company has maintained itself at the average value level.

6. The last years have demonstrated that index calculation can play a considerable role in tax policy. Thereby the government tends to use the general index; temporarily it was believed the cost of living index was preferred in order to allow the companies to participate in the general impoverishment.

7. In the foreign exchange policy of the company a consideration of the general index on the one hand and on the foreign exchange index on the other is of significance. Under normal circumstances one chooses the currency for investment of surpluses which combines great security with the prospect of value increase.

8. For the speculative activity of the company, which can be the selection of the capital investment in certain real goods on the one hand or the choice between the investment in real goods or money on the other hand, the current value of

individual goods compared with the general index and - in the case of investment in money - the general index compared with the nominal value of the money - can be used as a measurement.

Bibliography

"Essay on index numbers" by Morgenroth, *Concise Dictionary of Political Science* (a comprehensively general literature is provided there) -

Fisher, Irving, *The Purchasing Power of Money*, Berlin 1916.

Hofmann, *Index Numbers at Home and Abroad*, Karlsruhe 1921.

Kahn, *The Index Numbers of the Frankfurter Zeitung* [Frankfurt Newspaper], *Die Wirtschaftskurve, Vierteljahresschrift* [The Economic Curve, Quarterly Journal], Frankfurt.

Mahlberg, Balance Sheet Technique and Valuation During Periods of Currency Fluctuation, 3rd ed. Leipzig, 1923.

Schmalenbach, *Fundamentals of Dynamic Accounting*, 3rd ed. Liepzig 1925, Goldmark Accounting, Berlin 1922. *Two Lectures on Fictitious Profits*, June 1922.

Schmidt, *The Replacement Price on the Day of Turnover in Cost Estimation and the Economy*, Berlin 1923, (pp 12f.); id., "Balance Sheet Corrections Through Index Numbers", *Zeitschrift für Aktienwesen* 1922/23, [Journal on Shares].

Zizek, *Fundamentals of Statistics*, 2nd edn. München 1923; i.e. *The Statistical Median*, Leipzig 1903.

Do Holding Gains or Losses Represent Profit or Loss?[1]

Fritz Schmidt

1. Introduction

By holding gains or losses, we mean here any change in the market value of a firm's assets. Since accounting is used for cost calculation and since the assets of a firm represent the balance of accumulated costs, then prices within the acquisition market of the factor inputs have to be used as a measure of changes in value. The extent of any holding gains or losses depends upon the moment of entry in, and exit of, those assets from a company. Every inflow implies a corresponding outflow, and vice versa. This is in line with the exchange principle of the market economy. When an asset is sold, its change in value is no longer relevant for accounting purposes. However, variation in value of the asset acquired in counterpart to the sold asset begins to be included for accounting purposes.

Changes in the value of goods are measured by referring to their market price, while money value changes and changes in the value of financial assets are measured by using a general index representing an average based on the variation in the value for all goods for which such a variation can be measured in monetary terms. This is because money is a common means of exchange. If one wants to keep constant the value of money, then money should represent over time an unchanged purchasing power in the market for goods. This will only be possible if the quantity of money changes in a way that is proportional to the average changes in the value of goods.

The question of whether holding gains or losses, that is a change in value in real terms of dormant (fixed) assets, represents, for the firm or even the economy as a whole, a profit or a loss, a revenue or a "negative revenue", is not only a matter of interest to accountants, but is as well a fundamental aspect underlying general economic theories. Depending on the way in which this question is answered, all basic economic concepts in financial management change. Examples include those of profit and loss determination, going concern value and a firm's market value in the stock exchange, price and cartel policies, balance sheet valuation, balance sheet and fiscal laws, financing sources, and price and interest rate determination. These

---

1 [This article is a translation of "Ist Wertänderung am ruhenden Vermögen Gewinn oder Verlust?", *Zeitschrift für Betriebswirtschaft*, 1928, pp. 1-19.

differences are even more easily observable in economic and macroeconomic theories due to the fact that it is obvious that concepts like the pension, the rate of interest, market value and price, as well as economic yardsticks, such as the normal rate of return and in its harmony as a starting point for any economic changes, revenue and capital, and also profit distribution, all will have to be considered very differently, depending upon whether one understands the national production as being only the output in real goods for a given period of time or as the change in the level of wealth between two given points of time. Whereas, it appears certain that there are time periods where all existing real assets can show a value increase or decrease. We can even say that, depending upon the position one takes on these premises, a very different economic theory will emerge. For that reason it is undoubtedly very valuable, in fact even necessary, for the economic science as a whole to, at last, give to this fundamental question all the attention that it deserves. Everyone who claims to be a "researcher in economics" has to take a position on this question before he can attribute this title to himself. Technical arguments and details, that often provide so easily a way out in the field of business economics, are not appropriate at all for this question. These kinds of technical problems must and can be treated separately.

But the practitioner also cannot afford to ignore this question, to describe it only as a vague and non-operational theory lying way below where the real problems are. The profit figure reported at the annual general meeting will depend on the way in which the question is answered. His general business dispositions, as well as his pricing and cartel policies, will be very different, depending upon whether holding gains are considered as a profit. So will wages policy. This decision is also of great importance for taxation purposes. This becomes even clearer to practitioners when, in application of current laws on profit generated by the sale of entire companies significant increases in value for acquisitions made before war time or under the restrictive valuation methods of the first "Goldmark balance sheet" period appear as realized profit and are, consequently, taxable revenues.

Current value accounting clearly responds negatively to the question asked in the title of this paper. Conversely, the proponents of historical cost accounting (with or without the realization principle and with or without adjustments based on conservatism or the lower of cost or market principle) answer the question in fact positively, at least for those numerous situations that are not corrected, by virtue of a confusion of basic principles. The evidence for rejecting such value changes as profit can be demonstrated in different ways. Firstly theoretically, as I have tried to show within a general framework[2]; secondly, practically, that is the effects of either

---

2 See for instance *Organische Bilanz* [Organic Accounting], Leipzig, 1922; *Der Wiederbeschaffungspreis* [Replacement Value], Berlin, 1923; *Bilanzwert, Bilanzgewinn,*

interpretation and their durability over time are analyzed in different economic circumstances. And, thirdly, by exploring in what direction all the adjustments (resulting from theory and practice) to pure historical cost accounting are made. Should these adjustments occur in line with those of the current value system, then the proponents of a "current value"-based profit calculation would differ from those proposing adjusted historical costs only in one respect. That is, the former would do systematically and with full understanding of the basic concepts underlying their decisions, what the latter try to achieve only through ad hoc adjustments based on wrong theoretical premises but valuably helped by better experiences.

Already in the first edition of *Organische Bilanz* (p.124), I expressed the point of view that holding gains cannot be profit as follows:

> Changes in value between actual and replacement costs have the character of a change in value of capital, conditional on the respective market prices of the goods. Logically, they are capital rather than revenue in nature; they are simultaneously an increase or decrease in capital value and expenditure or revenue.

That was the time where criticisms and rejection of current value accounting were the strongest. It is important to realize that the *practical* measures adopted by most of the critics resulted in the reliance on the same basic principle. It seems, according to all the available evidence, that the time has come to reconsider and question the whole problem of profit and loss accounting, and, one could even rightfully argue, economic theory as a whole. This idea constantly reemerges, as the following statements prove more or less clearly. If business economics wants to be recognized as a science, that is to provide also general, basic and theoretical principles, apart from merely technical aspects, then researchers in this area have to take a position on this question.

The fundamental principles of current value accounting are circular theory, exchange equilibrium and market laws. One would have to disprove these principles or demonstrate an error in their deduction in order to claim that holding gains or losses can be designated as revenue. This is already refuted by the simple terminology, as what is presently already in the form of capital cannot be at the same time a yield of this same capital. The value of capital, applied to existing assets, is inseparably linked with the capital itself, it is just a different way of representing the real assets. The fact that changes in value due to speculative gains on external liabilities are considered as distributable profit after realization of the object of speculation is not an exception to economic laws. Rather it represents a distorted

---

Bilanzumwertung [Balance Sheet Value, Profit Accounting and Balance Sheet Revaluation], Berlin, 1924.

prescription of the law that considers nominal money as a fixed measure. The fact that the legal principle is wrong can be observed by its effect on the investor, who loses in terms of purchasing power on average the equivalent of what the speculator gains in private, as opposed to public, profit. Another proof in favour of current value accounting and the separation of the change in assets' value from profit is provided by the effects created by historical cost accounting on the shape of economic (business) trends, effects that I have already presented in earlier writings[3]. All my previous work is an attempt to refute theoretically and practically the character of profit or loss attached to holding gains or losses.

2. Review of the Literature on Adjustments of Value Changes

We want here essentially to extend the support of the third abovementioned direction of research, that is trying to determine how far the proponents of historical cost accounting, through their adjustments, implicitly acknowledge the current value system. In support of this purpose are many arguments, of which only the most important ones, will be presented here. The *lower of cost-or-market principle* cannot be used as a proof, since even if the price increases, the values (in the balance sheet) remain the same. Indeed, applying the market price as the lower price could give the impression of working with a current value system, except that it is misapplied, since the decrease in value, due to the lack of a separate account [of the change in value], reduces the profit. Nevertheless one can find in this aspect some signs indicating the existence of a certain feeling for the difference between a change in value and operating profit. Probably, it was also assumed that the realization principle would keep separate the notions of value change and profit.

An in-depth discussion of the limits of the lower of cost-or-market principle is presented by Montgomery in *Auditing, Theory and Practice*, 3rd ed., 1923. In this book, the evidence on the strong variations in the purchasing power of the American gold dollar, adduced by a leading authority in economics [Fisher], stands out. The profound significance of his discussion shall only have been totally understood with the work of Schmaltz[4], in explaining in particular how Montgomery defends the idea of not considering holding gains as profit, since the value increase in assets is not distributed, but leads to the creation of a valuation or an appreciation reserve. This reserve increases as long as the assets' value increases, and decreases when the assets' value decreases, that is, decreases in value of assets are deducted from the reserve

3 See *Industriekonjunktur - ein Rechenfehler!* (Business Cycles - an Accounting Miscalculation!), Berlin, 1927.

4 *Bilanz- und Betriebsanalyse in America* (Balance Sheet Analysis and Firm Activity in America), C. E. Poeschel, Stuttgart, 1927, pp.77ff.

and, therefor, this does not necessitate a corresponding decrease of profit, as in the principle of the lower of cost-or-market value. This is also illustrated by the application of the principle of *iron stocks or base stocks*, where assets appear always in the balance sheet with an unchanged and low value. The same basic idea is found in the work of Schmalenbach and his disciples. Since the normal base stock amount always appears in the balance sheet with the same value, any change in value would also not appear in the profit and loss account. Worth noting at this point is that the American experts in this area only apply the principles of the lower of cost-or-market rule and acquisition value principle, after substantial adjustments. An example is the US Steel Corporation's balance sheet. But it is remarkable that also the American tax law refuses to recognize these paper profits and still adheres to the nominal point of view. Further research in the foreign literature would provide us with similar evidence.

The difference between distributed and non-liquid gains appears in the German literature as early as Simon [1910].[5] In particular, he refers to the legislation of some South American countries, where only realized profits can be distributed as a dividend. Further, his example of profit generated by the value increase of a piece of unsold land (still in the balance sheet) proves that he sees holding gains as a form of undistributable profit.

Rehm[6] describes (p.370) as "cyclical" gains all changes in value of investments, changes that should not be taxed, but also not be accepted as a tax deduction when they are negative. Had he applied the same reasoning to operating revenue, he would have arrived at the same conclusions as current value accounting. If he omitted this last point, it is because he, as with most of the proponents of historical cost accounting, believed that the application of the principle of realization would alone prevent such gains resulting from value changes in fixed assets being distributed. On p.645 he mentions very clearly the difference between operating profit and unrealized annual profit. He says:

> The main difference is the following: 1. Operating profits or net profits are not affected by changes in asset value that are caused by circumstances lying outside the normal operations, and not by the operations themselves. Only the capital value (net worth), and not the profit, is affected by any asset value increase not generated by current operations, such as gains from financial investments, lotto gains. The same applies for asset value decreases not generated by current operations, such as the destruction of fixed assets through fire, flood or other extraordinary elements . . . Consequently it is possible to report an

5 *Die Bilanzen der Aktiengesellschaften* [Corporations' Balance Sheets], 4th ed., Berlin, 1910, pp.334ff.

6 *Die Bilanzen der Aktiengesellschaften* [Corporations' Balance Sheets], München, 1903.

annual profit even in the case where operating losses occur, when for instance the asset value increases substantially and this increase in asset value is realized before the end of the accounting year, etc.

Had Rehm applied the same reasoning for all types of assets and had he not considered the difference between acquisition price and selling price as the basic measure for operating income, so he would have to have been close to the current value system.

Also in the work of Schmalenbach[7], even though he rejects the current value system and the concept of profit based on current value, one can find numerous hints towards current value accounting. He starts the paragraph on the influence of the fluctuation in value of real assets on the determination of profit as follows:

> Income accounting is concerned essentially with two different values, *acquisition value* of the expenditure and the *going concern value of* the output. Through them, the cost accounting principles of private companies are linked with the cost accounting of the economy. Had there been in the economy no value fluctuation of real and financial assets, then only the private companies would be concerned with the notions of acquisition value and going concern value. As a matter of fact the value of things does not stay constant; neither for the time period during which they are retained by a firm. First of all we look only at the changes in value of real assets. These changes cannot be ignored by firms, at least when the cost accounting system applies the basic principles of comparability, caution, etc. The most significant value to have an impact in the cost accounting system of a firm, through value fluctuation of real assets, is the *time value*.

Further, he says:

> We have suggested earlier, that in general a transaction is only totally completed when the invoice is mailed. In cases where a transaction overlaps over two or several accounting years, only the already incurred expenditures are taken into account at the end of each year. However, when the value of real assets change, so do the numbers up to a certain level. One can observe then not only an *operating profit, but also an extraordinary profit,* not only an *operating loss*, but also an *extraordinary loss* and, frequently, a combination of operating profit and extraordinary loss or vice versa. In this context the previous viewpoint (a transaction is only totally completed when the invoice is mailed) is not automatically valid; at least one can say that several methods compete with each other.
>
> One principle that does, basically, consider extraordinary profit as operating profit, and that sees it as a transaction only when the invoice is mailed, is the *realization principle.* It relies on the premise that one can talk of a profit, *also an extraordinary profit*, for instance a profit due to a favorable economic cycle, only when the transaction is completed at least to the point where the invoice is mailed. Opposed to that is the *time*

---

7 *Dynamische Bilanz* (Dynamic balance sheet), 4th ed., Leipzig, 1926.

value principle, that states that extraordinary profits are to be considered as realized profit even before their realization.

Schmalenbach is thinking here of a current value system that is, in our opinion, untenable. His chief idea is to prove that any holding gain is an extraordinary profit, that, according to the current value principle, would be considered as a profit if sold before its complete realization. This is opposed to our view that holding gains can never be a profit and can only be paid out as a repayment of capital. Should changes in the value of fixed assets be included in the operating income, Schmalenbach's view of current value accounting (with no differentiation between operating profit and holding gains) could indeed become very dangerous, because paper profits (or losses) become bigger than according to the realization principle, by which only value changes of sold assets are treated as profits. In particular, Schmalenbach wants to use acquisition value to establish the balance sheet. He sees in that system the same advantage that a current value balance sheet has with the separation of operating income and holding gains, that is, that the change in value of an unrealized asset has no influence on operating income. Further, he has no major problem with including depreciation based on current value in the profit and loss account, he only sees as a problem some technical difficulties and the arbitrariness of the people doing the operation. However, he makes the situation more complicated in the sense that he considers the contribution of each asset to the going concern value of the firm as the current value, from which the depreciation amount is determined. This is untenable since in determining profit and loss, that value arises only because of the expiration of the time between acquisition price and selling price. The cost value of the firm is equal to the current (acquisition) price of each asset on the market, because operating income can only be determined by a comparison between the value of assets and the returns from operations. When Schmalenbach considers the depreciation of current value as the theoretically most correct one, he implicitly takes a position on the question of whether a change in value can be regarded as a profit. *In his view, a change in value of the worn out part of a machine is then not a profit or a loss, but a cost;* so he accepts to some extent our basic principle. Similarly, his fear that the change in value of an asset could appear as a profit, only by virtue of an incorrectly oriented current value accounting system seems to indicate that he is not willing to recognize this change in value as a profit or a loss, just as organic current value accounting does through singling it out in an account, termed "adjustment in value".

My view regarding the treatment of speculative reserves are totally similar to Schmalenbach's (pp.199ff), at least as long as they are financed by debt. Profit is in that case equal to the change in value between the acquisition day and the day of sale, but only after settlement. Before that, the change in value has to be transferred (because of its non-realization) into an account for adjustment in value; in Schmalenbach's view, value changes are also separate from operating income, since assets are valued in the balance sheet at acquisition price. Schmalenbach's interpretations of the tied reserves of a firm, the so-called primary reserves, iron or base stocks, are also perfectly in accord with the notion of current value accounting. So says Schmalenbach:

> If one understands correctly the nature of these base stocks, so the physical level of inventory should not vary over time; one can compare them to an organic body, whose cells are continuously renewed, even though one cannot claim that at any time the organic body has been replaced by another.

This sentence accords with the basic principle of current value accounting. However, it has to be extended to all real assets of a firm, to which the speculative reserves financed by external capital belong only under certain conditions. Schmalenbach uses here another method of computation differing from current value accounting. He wants the base stocks to always show the same amount in the balance sheet and so achieve the same objective as current value accounting, which isolates the change in value of inventories between the acquisition day and the day of sale. For instance, following Schmalenbach, if the acquisition price of inventory increases during a period, the profit at the end of the period will, by virtue of the use of the initial, relatively lower, fixed value of inventory, be reduced by an amount equivalent to the difference between the normal value and the current, higher, replacement price. *This does not mean anything other than a singling out of the change of value of base stock and separating it from the profit figure. At this point, Schmalenbach should, if he accepts the consequences of his own views, acknowledge openly the basic principle that a change in value is not profit, even through sale.* Under some circumstances, the precise method of current value accounting may show some minor differences with the method using fixed normal values, but these are rather due to the techniques of base stock valuation rather than defects in the theory itself. When Schmalenbach explicitly (p.209) acknowledges the identity of base stock accounting with profit determination based on current (acquisition) value, he refutes his own explanations, where any changes in value are always considered as profit, even if it is shown as an extraordinary profit, and in particular the statement on page 179 on fixed assets:

> If such a profit or loss arises from disposal of fixed assets, then it is certainly a profit or a loss; there is no reason why these extraordinary profits or losses should not be named "profit"; rather than being only regarded as a mere growth of net worth.

However, concerning the base stock, which is in many ways comparable to fixed assets, Schmalenbach would have had to claim the contrary, had he wanted to maintain his propositions. It is obvious that in the case of the sale of fixed assets, a real operating profit is achieved apart from the assets' book value, just as it applies for operating goods.

Schmalenbach, however, rejects the principle "change in value is not profit" in another way, that is through his notion of a stabilized value of money. He accepts totally the idea that, even in the times of the *Goldmark* currency, considerable changes in the value of money are possible and must be reported in business bookkeeping. This view is exemplified by the following statement (p.218):

> Accordingly, the re-introduction of gold currency does not free us in any way, as we see, from the necessity of money value adjustments, if one is concerned with providing a fairly exact bookkeeping; and, *a fortiori,* neither in a time where much stronger fluctuations in the value of gold are expected; and the value of gold is threatened by fluctuations to a much greater extent than before the war. . . . In these circumstances the bookkeeper has to be cautious with regard to money value adjustments; thus, this question will have to stay a major topic in the bookkeeping and accounting literature.

In order to measure the monetary amount of depreciation, Schmalenbach, after an analysis of the various indexes and currency exchange rates, proposes the wholesale index, since an optimal, general, index that would measure exactly the average of all changes in value does not exist. Further, he acknowledges that current value accounting, as I propose it, represents an adjustment to the value of money, as shown in the following quote (p.219):

> This method, consisting in making business operations occurring at different points of time comparable via time value adjustments, is the oldest of the exact expedients in the inflationary times, and was already applied during the war, chiefly for the computation of the monthly income statement; maybe not always as a conscious money value adjustment, but nevertheless with the effect of such an adjustment.

So far a complete agreement exists between Schmalenbach and myself concerning the view that changes in value cannot be regarded as a profit. However, a difference of viewpoint is observable in another comment by Schmalenbach (p.231):

> General index and special index. (The latter being an average current value of each asset of a firm.) By special index one generally understands a commodity trade index (*Warenhandelsindex*), that picks out a particular type of good, such as food, clothing, or import good, which represents the evolution of prices for them. A general index neither includes all goods, but considers the selected goods as being representative of all goods; this procedure is chosen by virtue of its simplicity (in terms of work involved) and its reliability, with the hope

> that any differences arising were not too important. While it is assumed that the wholesale index is a true measure of the value of money, the special index, conversely, is simultaneously *a function of the change in the value of money and the change in the value of goods*. The special index is applicable in cost accounting whenever changes in value of money and goods are to be corrected at the same time.

The above quote shows a fundamental divergence between Schmalenbach and myself concerning the perception of changes in the value of money and goods. According to Schmalenbach, the general index (which he prefers) is representative of all goods. Fluctuations in the level of this general index can only arise because the value of *all* goods has, *on average*, changed. Thus, a change in the index level can only occur through a change in the *current value* for each individual good. *Consequently, each change in the general index level is the expression of the general change in value of goods, as well as an indication of the average change of all special indexes.* As a matter of fact, the general index indicates only the average change in value of goods, while current value accounting considers the individual change in value of each asset; however, the sum of all changes in the value of assets of the national economy must perfectly match with changes in the general index, at least if the latter is calculated correctly. It is also perfectly illogical to consider the general index as a *measure of the change in value of money* only, as Schmalenbach does, *since the general index is, as well, a measure of the average change in the value of all goods. An adjustment to profit and loss accounting, based on the general index, as proposed by Schmalenbach, refers to the entirety of all assets existing in the national economy as well as the correction based on all changes in current value. This only applies when current value accounting uses the general index to adjust financial (monetary) assets for money value changes.*

With this conception, maybe Schmalenbach only wants to point to the possibility that the current value of each asset does not always have to evolve exactly in parallel with the average value of all goods (incorporated in the general index). This is an obvious fact, proven by experience. In any general price-level change, some goods adjust more slowly than, while others exceed, the average change, and the sum of all above-average changes in value must be perfectly equal to the sum of all below-average changes in value; otherwise the measure of the average change, the general index, cannot be correct. The almost untenable dichotomy presented by Schmalenbach is also evident in his book *Dynamic Accounting*, in which he deals with real asset value change and money value change in two separate paragraphs. But one can see in both cases how things overlap, and that the results do not match perfectly, because two different measurement systems have been chosen to measure the same things. Were the balance sheet and income accounting two different things, then they should absolutely be adjusted using the two measures, in order to eliminate the total value change. That has so far never been wanted nor attempted, but the conceptions in the literature do not so clearly acknowledge that this double adjustment approach would be an impossibility. The view that changes in the value of goods and of money are two completely different things is unfortunately very confusing in current balance sheet theories.

From a technical point of view, Schmalenbach's proposed index-based adjustment of the balance sheet and the income statement is that the decline of money value, measured by the general index, appears as a deduction, that is, as a cost in the income statement, and as an increase of shareholders' equity in the balance sheet. This is actually exactly similar to the treatment of the value adjustment account in organic current value accounting. The simplest form would be to prepare periodic accounts on a nominal basis, with the addition of one account for value adjustment of equity, on the debit-side of the income statement, with a corresponding account for capital or value adjustment on the credit-side. The amount should be such that the purchasing power of capital remains the same. Overall, Schmalenbach, and also Mahlberg, who represents in fact the same basic ideas, have to agree that holding gains cannot be either profit or revenues, as clearly emphasized by the indication of their procedures. The difference between current value accounting and index-based accounting would essentially be that the former considers real assets as dormant, while the latter considers the capital as being dormant. In any case Schmalenbach puts himself in a contradictory situation with his index-based adjustment when related to his previously quoted proposition on profit based on the sale of machines (p.179). He cannot say that this proposition is based on the assumption of a stable price level, since it is included in the paragraph on the influence of fluctuations of fixed assets in the determination of profit or loss, as well as in another of his statements, in which he explicitly recognizes that "extraordinary" profits and losses coming from the increase or decrease in the value of assets, that is dormant assets, are in fact authentic profits and, consequently, revenues. At this point, the difference between the theorist Schmalenbach and the practitioner Schmalenbach is obvious: since the latter wants to keep changes in the value of a machine separate from the profit and loss account, via an index-based adjustment. With the current value system, I subscribe here entirely to the practical balance sheet adjustment approach.

Schmalenbach takes a position on current value accounting in the following paragraph on fluctuations of the value of money (p.269):

> The current value concept is quite useful for money value adjustment in emergency cases; however, it can only be partial. Loss of money value due to debtors, cash balances, closing accounts, gains in money value due to creditors, etc. cannot be recorded as such. If one wished to measure them using index-based accounting, then a systematic computation

> method would be more practical. Further, current value accounting is also related to current value in situations where one would rather use a different method. The correct amount for base stock can only be obtained through index-based accounting. Anyhow the resulting profitability ratios require an index-based method, and methods without indexes provide finally incomparable numbers.

On the same page Schmalenbach continues with his statement on an accounting system where iron stocks keep the same value over time, a statement in which he acknowledges formally a kind of holding gains adjustment. Schmalenbach considers both current value accounting and base stock accounting as non-systematic adjustments. The latter form is correctly referred to as non-systematic on the grounds that it concerns only the inventories, that is only one type of asset. But current value accounting requires a systematic adjustment, that is without exception, of all the holding gains, since it includes all value changes in respect of all assets.

By reading the above quotes from Schmalenbach one could believe that the concept of current value accounting is inappropriate for monetary items in the balance sheet. This is absolutely not the case. As long as financial items are identical on each side of the balance sheet, changes in the value of money compensate and there is no reason to report them in the profit and loss account. The value change of the excess of liabilities over monetary assets represents the growth in financial value due to this excess of debts. This amount, after settlements and deduction of costs, will become an authentic speculative profit. However, when the monetary items on the assets side exceed liabilities, then the depreciation in money terms from this excess would create a reduction in the value of this excess that could only be measured by a general index, because the general index is in fact the current value of money. This decline in value can be charged to the profit and loss account. The general suspicion manifested by Schmalenbach and Mahlberg (*Der Tageswert in der Bilanz* [The Current Value in the Balance Sheet], pp.50ff, Leipzig, 1925) towards current value accounting lies essentially in the fact that they understand it as the value of current operations, while in my view only the current value of acquisition comes into question as a cost value.

Mahlberg, a co-founder of *Goldmark* accounting involving stabilization or equalization of financial values accounting measured by a general index or any similar general measure, correctly writes, referring to an increase of cash inventory from RM10,000 to 12,500, with an index increase from 100 to 125 (p.72): "This surplus on the assets side is not profit, so we have to create a fictitious account on the liabilities side, an account creating no legal liability towards the third parties." Indeed Mahlberg initially refers, with an exaggerated reserve, to an adjustment entry in account X, and later he names this account "account for compensation due to cyclical fluctuations" and the nature of the entry "a money value profit". According to him (p.75), this account compensating for cyclical fluctuations should be an "additional part of the capital", that is exactly what the account for changes in the value of capital is in the current value system. By the way the principle of neutralization of value, which is necessary to the operations recently expressed by Mahlberg, is identical to the idea of base stocks, because the individual value changes of assets, not the average money value change, is kept separate from the profit and loss account. This is, in fact, the principle of current value accounting, mixed with a money value accounting of all monetary items. If money value adjustments applied to debt-financed speculative investments and to the value of assets are included in current value system, then I can see no difference with the current value accounting, to the extent that it is not influenced by the calculation method used. Totally inexplicable to me is the following sentence from Mahlberg (p.74):

> It is still necessary to underline emphatically that money value profits are in fact real profits to the outside world; we do not know whether a loss can be compensated by a later profit, because we know in advance neither the life period, nor the index level at liquidation.

If Mahlberg wants to consider adjustment values (based on the general index) as distributable authentic profits and revenues, he would then be in contradiction to several of his own statements, including the above-quoted ones; further, if he does not want this, and I am inclined to believe so, then he represents the principle that holding gains are not profit.

Walb also has taken a position on the question of profit determination, not only in his comprehensive work on profit accounting (Berlin, 1926), but also on various occasions prior to that book. An important point here is that he proposes as an ideal solution to use a general index to adjust the value of the various accounts in the balance sheet and profit and loss account so as to preserve the same economic efficacy of the initial capital value, that is to preserve the purchasing power of capital. This preference diverges from the opinion (made on p.354) that the neutralization of real assets, such as basic inventories, through a stabilization adjustment is in fact a calculation using the average value of money, while the part which is suppressed in the income statement by virtue of the neutralization process represents undoubtedly individual value changes of assets, as current value accounting separates it by transfer to a value adjustment account.

Considering his views, Walb is likely to be categorized in the group of people for which value changes of initial capital represent neither profit nor loss, even though a clear-cut separation in the concepts is not observable. The adjustment procedures expressed do not allow any other interpretation. In particular Walb emphasizes very strongly the money capital approach of today's accounting, in which he sees as a characteristic of the present. At this point, it would be worthwhile noting in addition to what has been said that this view is to be found only among businesspeople, but not among private individuals, farmers, etc. None of the latter would ever think about considering the value change of land, a share, etc. as profit or loss, or revenue, and this even when the asset is sold.

If the money capital approach of accounting, in its advanced form, is the more advantageous and the more correct, so could it claim to be of universal validity. I would go further and say that while businesspeople use a particular method for calculating revenues, they should also bear the particular consequences of this incorrect, in my opinion, nominal calculation (see my work: *Die Industriekonjunktur - ein Rechenfehler!* (Business Cycles - an Accounting Miscalculation!), Berlin, 1927).

Besides the aforementioned proponents taking value changes into account in determining a firm's income, mention could be made of many others, whose work shows that they desire to separate changes in value from profit through the current acquisition price system or a general index system. Among the proponents of the first method (through the current acquisition price method), I would mention both Geldmacher *(Wirtschaftsunruhe und Bilanz* [Economic Troubles and Balance Sheet], Berlin 1923) and Findeisen (*Der eiserne Bestand* [Base Stock Inventories], Berlin, 1923), where the former wants to use current values in the income statement, while the latter would use the notion of base stocks. Ter Vehn *(Gewinnbegriffe in der Betriebswirtschaft,* [The Notion of Profit in Business Economics], *ZfB*., 1924, p.361) is in favour of the second method (adjustment via a general index) and it is accepted that most of the contemporary economists belong to one of these two basic schools of thought regarding the elimination of value fluctuations from profit accounting. If this is so, then it is more than time to draw the consequences of the basic shift in business economic thinking.

3. The Methods for Separating Holding Gains from Profit

Based on the existing literature in business economics, it is possible to summarize the various adjustment methods proposed by these different authors. The representation is at the same time an argumentation since it is a matter involving uniform thinking about the separation of holding gains from profit.

First of all we can deal with calculation methods that undertake a *systematic and complete* elimination of all value changes from the profit calculation. In contrast to this it will be shown that there are some other approaches that involve adjusting only non-systematically and incompletely the different accounts in the balance sheet and the income statement. Further, the approach of the *methods for measuring the adjustment differs. One group of adjustment methods wants to measure and adjust the value change of tangible assets, while the other group follows the basic idea that all assets of a firm are parts of an abstract capital, which is represented by the capital account and its sub-accounts. In this latter case, an artificial measure of value change, under the form of a general index,* has to be developed, in order to be able to adjust at all. So the *capital amount to be adjusted, as well as the measure itself by which one calculates, are abstract and indirect.* Both are determined from various individual values. At least one can mention that, once the calculation method exists, the adjustment procedure does not present any particular difficulties, even if it is important to note that, in fact, there does not exist a perfectly reliable general index that really represents the correctly weighted average of all changes in value, and that such an index will never exist, due to the very important inherent difficulties in terms of index computation.

The first of the methods of systematic adjustments to be dealt with here is the *current acquisition value* method. This method fits perfectly within the construction of the income account for each sale. Apart from the acquisition value, the current replacement value at the day of sale has also to be determined for each factor input and the difference between the two amounts, representing the change in value, is to be recorded in the value adjustment account, if one does not want to transfer it directly into the proper capital account. The proceeds themselves are equal to the current value at the day of sale as long as they were paid in cash. Concerning debtors one could take into consideration the value change of the purchasing power by one of the two following methods, either by comparing the current proceeds with the equivalent value of the costs at repayment day, or by making an adjusting journal entry on the debit side of profit and loss account for the change in value of the debt. Any change in value of cash balances on the assets side would be dealt with in a similar way. But in fact an important portion of the assets side is offset by amounts on the liabilities side, the value changes of which can be compared directly to those on the assets side, especially when the money value amount is approximately equal on both sides. If debts are repaid unilaterally with non-cash items, then the change in value (as a speculative profit) associated with the speculation goods is to be transferred from the value adjustment account to the profit and loss account. In current value accounting all holding gains or losses have to be transferred to a value adjustment account and at the same time to a profit or loss account as costs increase (or decrease), when the items have been sold. This change in value can only be treated as profit in case of speculation. Otherwise the value change stays for ever in the value adjustment account, even if the underlying asset has already been sold. The writing-off of realized speculative profits is necessary because the corresponding liability values are, as the result of the finalization of the speculation, paid back out of debts and correspond (as part of the capital) again to cash amounts, that are available for any better form of investment. If the firm is either sold or liquidated, the profit on sale at that time can be measured as the sum corresponding to the replacement value of all assets of the firm. All anterior value changes (previously entered in the account for value adjustment) are included in this amount, and they still in this case, do not appear as a profit, because no pending speculation is dissolved (settled) on this occasion.

The second systematic and complete adjustment of changes in value is the *indexed accounting method*, which takes the entire capital as the starting point and considers as profit only the part left over after adjusting for the purchasing power parity at the end of the period. The simplest way would be the comparison of the two capital amounts, one at the beginning and the other at the end of the period, where the two current values of capital (at the date they are established) would have to be first measured. The current values of the two capitals should then be adjusted for purchasing power parity through a general index adjustment, so that for instance if the purchasing power had decreased by 20 percent, a profit could only appear for the portion of capital value appreciation above 25 percent. The average value change is thus separated from profit. Apart from the adjustment method, other, more detailed procedures exist, which especially in inflationary times, do not always produce the same result. For instance regarding the index used to bring the balance sheet to its current value. The index is generally applied to the acquisition value as a starting point. For this reason the use of a unique index is difficult, since the acquisition of the different assets can have occurred at different times. To solve this problem, sophisticated methods were developed, from which Schmalenbach gives vivid examples in his book *Dynamische Bilanz* (Dynamic Balance Sheet). On the top of that is the difficulty of determining the correct index. However, it is in no circumstances permitted to doubt that the intention of the adjustments is to eliminate value changes.

Both the current value system and the index-based method are often in more *primitive forms*, referring only to one type of assets or one group of assets. Adjustments based on the notion of *fixed inventories or base stocks* belong to the subject of current value adjustments. The basic idea here is that an inventory-related profit can only be achieved when the base portion of this inventory has itself been received. This idea applied to inventories is the same that is used in the current value system for all assets. According to this technique, the quantity of goods corresponding to the inventory is recorded at the same value in each balance sheet, irrespective of what the acquisition value or current value is at the date, when each balance sheet is prepared. Consequently the value change occurring between the acquisition and the complete realization of the goods cannot appear as a profit. One difficulty is due to the fact that the normal value of fixed inventories will rather be set as low as possible, so that the current value cannot so easily sink below the normal value, because otherwise, the resulting balance sheet would not be acceptable. For that reason initial acquisition value must be, at the beginning of the process, lowered. This reduction in value could in fact happen by reducing the capital value, but it is, in most cases and following tradition, rather charged to the income statement, as Walb (*Die Erfolgsrechnung* [Income Accounting], already quoted earlier) suggests it in one of his comments (p.373). In the latter case, the profit of the first period, during which the normal price is set, is falsified to an amount equivalent to the value reduction. Further there is also the necessity to change the normal quantity (or inventory) when economic conditions require it. For this reason Schmalenbach has created the concept of "tied, but variable" inventories, in which he wants only to set the same quantity in the opening and closing balance for one period [but the quantity can change from one period to another]. Major difficulties or changes will necessitate a major change in the organisation and the kind of reserves (inventories), because then normal value has lost its effectiveness. Finally Walb also suggests (p.379) that differences appear between current value accounting and mere quantity accounting only when a price change occurs between the day of sale, for which current value accounting compares the cost value and the corresponding revenues, and the day of the replacements (of the sold inventory). When the fixed inventory system is used, any price change of inventory would go into the income account, while, under current value accounting, a price change would also go into profit accounting if, as I think is correct, it represents the value change in money between the two dates, at least as long as one is talking about the money amounts of personal capital. As a matter of fact, the measure is in the first case the price variation of the "no-longer available goods" and in the second case the value change of the "really available money".

In a certain sense, the realization (or neutralization) principle, relative to acquisition or normal prices, is a primitive form of the elimination of dormant capital. It works to an extent in this direction as long as dormant assets are not sold. The prudence shown by several writers, among others Schmalenbach, Mahlberg, Geldmacher and Sewering, with regard to current value accounting is probably due to their belief that keeping the acquisition values for consumption and depreciable goods of a firm is the best way to prevent assets' value changes from affecting profit accounting. It is then overlooked that with the current value accounting system as well, no part of value changes affects the income account, since all value changes are only charged to the capital account. For that reason, we can find quite often the combination of value adjustment for operating assets and the principle of historical cost accounting applied to fixed assets. Problems do occur, though, when the whole firm is sold, because in that case all value changes of fixed assets appear as profit. Further, the reliance on historical cost accounting makes it more difficult to ascertain the true measure of depreciation and the measure of capital yield. But, more importantly, this approach fails to consider that pure holding gains have to appear as profit when they are realized through sale.

Also index-based accounting can be applied unsystematically and incompletely. This happens when it refers only to some, but not all, assets. When acquisition value is adjusted through an index in order to determine the value of the depreciation amount, or when the change in value through indexation is separated from profit, in the case of the sale of an asset.

In order to show the internal relationships of the particular, highly developed, adjustment methods, current value accounting with adjustment of fixed inventory on the one hand, and index-based adjustments on the other hand are both applied using a simple example. For this example, it is assumed that the current value of operating assets has changed at the same rate as the general index, which we know represents the average of current values of all items.

The Technique of Profit Determination According to Different Balance Sheet Theories

Profit and Loss Account

Assumption: Operating inventories do not change either in quality or quantity during the phases A, B, Ca and D.

A. Trading Account with Acquisition Values

Initial inventory	500	Sales revenues	600
Transfer (purchases)	600	Sales revenues	800
Transfer (purchases)	700		
Profit	300	Ending inventory	700
	2100		2100

The profit includes 200 as representing the increase in value of base stock between the day of acquisition and the day of sale.

B. Trading Account with Current Values

Initial inventory	500	Sales revenues	600
Value change	100	Sales revenues	800
Transfer (purchases)	600		
Value change	100	Ending inventory at current replacement value (acquisition value of ending inventory=700)	
Transfer (purchases)	700		
Value change	100		
Profit	100		800
	2200		2200

The change in value is transferred to a capital or a value adjustment account.

C. (a) Trading Account with "Normal" Base Stock Valuation

Initial inventory	500	Sales revenues	600
Transfer (purchases)	600	Sales revenues	800
Transfer (purchases)	700		
Profit	100	Ending inventory	500
	1900		1900

Because of the addition of the principle of a fixed value for tied inventories, the value change of inventory does not appear as a profit in the profit account. The problem becomes more difficult when the level of inventory varies.

Example: Ending inventory is zero; with the sale of the ending inventory equal to 800.

C. (b) Base Stock Accounting when Ending Inventory is Zero

Initial inventory	500	Sales revenues	600
Transfer (purchases)	600	Sales revenues	800
Transfer (purchases)	700	Sales revenues	800
Creation of a reserve for increase in value of fixed inventory (800-500)	300		
Profit	100	Ending inventory	0
	2200		2200

If inventory has doubled (in quantity) between the beginning and the end of the period, then the additional part is to be recorded at an amount based on the last acquisition price. The accounting system becomes very difficult when the quality of fixed inventory changes.

D. Trading Account with Index-Based Adjustment

Initial inventory	500	Sales revenues	600
Transfer (purchases)	600	Sales revenues	800
Transfer (purchases)	700	Ending inventory, at	
Profit	100	the indexed value	500
	1900		1900

The index value is 100 at the beginning of the period and 160 at the end. Current value: Ending inventory = 800. Therefore, the adjusted ending value is 800 x (100/160) = 500.]

4. Summary

When there is some kind of unity in opinion with regard to the basic question of eliminating from income accounting all holding gains, since they are unrealized and speculative, then the question of how these gains should be recorded in the bookkeeping is only a matter of secondary importance. From a macroeconomic point of view, if we refer to all assets of the national economy, the sum of all changes in value in a particular period must be the same, no matter whether a general index or current value system has been used to determine these value changes, given that the variation in the general index must represent the average variation of *all* assets. Consequently, for the economy as a whole, the sum of all profit adjustments (up or down) must be exactly equal for the two methods. In both cases the national product would be increased or decreased by the same amount. However, I have tried to explain the important meaning of this adjustment in my work on *Die Industriekonjunktur - ein Rechenfehler!* (Business Cycles - a Miscalculation!). The index-based adjustment would suffice to account for the fluctuations in the economy on the revenue side. This method would have the advantage in the sense that it could be very simply implemented through adjustment of the capital account. From the point of view of correct operating disposition of course, and also in the interest of the recording of, in some cases, distributable profit and of the exact adjustment of each particular firm to business cycles, the current value system alone would provide correct results. It would be worthwhile, though, if both methods could be freely applied, because both, although using a different approach, aim to correct the same thing, that is the sum of value changes of goods, but not changes in the value of monetary assets in the economy. No national economy, even if the monetary assets and monetary liability items were equal, would have so much money as would be necessary as a basis for these adjustments. The wealth of a national economy consists essentially in physical assets (and not in financial assets), among which there are, in proportion, only a few tangible monetary assets.

Let us leave aside the computational (technical) aspect in making the decision on this most important question, the solution of which would be so exceptionally salutary for the whole economy. Let us attempt to create a unified front of economists under the statement: "Holding gains in a firm and in the economy are neither profit nor revenues". Then the way would be free for an efficient discussion regarding the calculation technique, which today hides this most important aspect. Then proponents of current value accounting, the neutralization concept, and fixed inventory accounting could all examine the problem together with the proponents of index-based adjustment accounting and, in a common attitude, carry through the fundamental recognition of the necessity to adjust the profit and loss account and cost calculation. Then all those accepting the basic principle should also accept the statement that the current practice in balance sheet accounting as well as the prescriptions of commercial law and fiscal law need to be modified, in order to avoid major economic damages. Further, when the view exists, that money value change is nothing but a mirror of the value change of all goods, then the debate on adjustment methods will most likely occur more calmly. Then, the problem to be faced is no longer a monetary problem, but each particular model of operating accounting can be tested in practice.

Looking at the current state of the literature and knowledge in business economics, I think one can easily conclude that the majority of experts would agree about the statement that "holding gains are not profit". I know of no expert in this area who currently does not apply unreservedly the rule "holding gains are not profit" in *his practical propositions*. There are some, though, who still support the untenable principle, even though their deeds contradict it. *That is why it is necessary to achieve a decision, if one wants to avoid the science of business economics receiving the reputation that its members argue on technical details while neglecting what is fundamental and general.*

5. LIMPERG AND SCHMIDT: SIMILARITIES AND DIFFERENCES

(i) Summary

As alluded to in *chapter 2*, initial translations of some of the works of both Limperg and Schmidt allow the following speculations: (i) Doubts are cast on Limperg's proposition that his and Schmidt's basic ideas differed, (ii) Limperg's harsh criticism of Schmidt, for being "incident specific", having only a "balance sheet emphasis" and thus not being "part of a general theory of economic activity", appears to be unjustified. From material provided in *chapters 3* and *4* similarities are certainly evident in their respective theories of business economics: There was unanimity that non-monetary assets were to be recorded at their replacement values; and any increases in replacement "values" or "prices" were not income and therefore should be recorded in a special *capital* account. Their concepts applied to both property and profit and loss accounting; and their preferred systems of accounting were part of a wider comprehensive theory of business economics. Although similarities exist disparities also are evident. Unlike Schmidt's symmetrical treatment of increases and decreases in replacement prices, Limperg "did not admit to symmetry of capital accretion and impairment" (van Seventer, 1975, pp.74-6). Schmidt's reasoning, we are told, was "substantialistic" whilst Limperg's was not (van Seventer, 1975, pp.74-5 and 1969, p.8). And whereas adjustments for general price level changes were not part of either Schmidt's or Limperg's mechanism, Schmidt explicitly sought to capture general purchasing power changes through the balancing of liquid assets and liabilities (his "identity of values principle", see Schwantag [1951, p.9]). Finally, although both described their theory in *organic* terms, they had different notions of organic accounting in mind.

(ii) Similarities and Differences Expanded

Recourse to primary sources provides the basis of our analysis. The aforementioned similarities and differences are now examined, with recourse, initially to Schmidt [1923]:

> However, if these losses are only phantom losses, such as occur when the value in the buyers' market goes down, for instance, this might lead to unemployment and production stoppages, which are not justified economically. Based on previous purchase prices, price levels are kept higher than is really necessary and that is the reason why the turnover is

smaller than it actually should be. These facts also tell us that this problem not only concerns the entrepreneur; it is also in the national economy's interest that merchants and industrialists calculate correctly, i.e. in a way that eliminates the occurrence of fictitious profits and losses. When we try to gain proper insight into the nature of fictitious profits and fictitious losses it appears from the examples that time and again it is a matter of the influence the price change has on the unsold parts of the capital which for the sake of brevity, we will call *dormant capital*. The goods enter the business at a different point in time than when they leave. The price changes in the buyers' market that occurred during the time that the goods were stored up in the business premises have nothing to do with the sales profit, because these changes also occur when one is not selling. It is a change in capital value, which under all circumstances must be recorded separately from the turnover figures, in other words, not as *actual profit*. What we showed for the stock also counts for all other elements of the costing price which play a role especially in industry. If the manufacturer of a machine needs 100 hours work the manufacturer needs to be paid for these 100 hours work when he sells the commodity, regardless whether in the meantime, the monetary value of those hours of work has doubled or halved, the physical replacement of labour needs to be considered. Only if the business man thinks this way will he be able to buy another lot of 100 hours of work and continue his production uninterruptedly. Only what is acquired over and above the replacement value is *real profit* which also can be *distributed*. [p.303]

If one wants to end up with a correct profit calculation, any changes in the money value of the dormant capital, arising from a price change, must be recorded separately. When the real assets go up in price, the change must not be processed via the account that indicates the sales profit, i.e. not via the profit-and-loss account, but via a special account, called the adjustment-of-capital account (*rekening voor prijfsverschillen*); that is to say, if one does not want to record the amount directly into the *capital account*, as the general property account. [p.332]

Because these things have only slowly dawned upon Germany, most entrepreneurs, because of the strong shifts of all nominal values, have thrown their capital away without realizing, let alone wanting it; the old trading practices made them calculate wrongly and moreover the State with its legislation for the prevention of usury urged them to stick to the old incorrect way of calculating (costs and then prices), even after the entrepreneurs had realized how mistaken they were. Finally, when the mark took its latest plunge (1922/23), even the State had to admit its untenable position and in a new regulation recognized most of the aforementioned principles. Economic life will not permanently benefit from this insight unless entrepreneurs hang on to these new methods of calculating, also in times of only minor value fluctuations, because even minor changes in the purchasing power of money and the related prices for all merchandise can still have an important influence on the calculation of profit. Anyway, a correct profit calculation will undoubtedly give the entrepreneur a much better idea of how his business is going, than is the case right now with this random mixture of "change in the monetary value of the capital" and "sales profit". [1923, p.334]

And in 1926:

> Business profit can only be that which exceeds the amount necessary for the maintenance of a firm's productive assets [p.384]. . . . The leading principle of the current value accounting approach is the maintenance of the firm in its real (physical) state . . . the firm can only generate a profit if the sales proceeds . . . are higher than cost of replacement or reproduction at the date of sale. [p.407]

The essence of Limpergian thought (as recorded in Groeneveld *et al.* Vol. II, 1968), is captured by the following:

> [During the post World War 1 period in Holland] Shopkeepers, wholesalers and manufacturers offered articles from old stock at a price lower than the purchase price of the goods which they had already in stock from earlier consignments. People were generous to their customers and they even boasted about it because of *all* the money they made. But when the downturn came many people became victims of the incorrect system. The cause of the collapse for many lay precisely in that system. They thought they were rich and consumed an income which, for a great part, consisted only of *fictitious profit* and, as a result, they lacked a buffer to break the drop in price. Because, with the theory of the replacement value as a basis of economic cost, the most important principle is also connected - namely that *profit resulting from a price rise*: profit from a boom, therefore - is *not* to be identified with profit from production. People who identify cost with the historical purchase price, have to consider the profit made from a sale of stock, as profit from production. And they thus make a great mistake which can only be avoided if it is realized that the sacrifice made in the exchange, becomes greater through a price increase [subsequent to a good being acquired or manufactured]. In the exchange, profit is made only if, and insofar proceeds exceed the higher replacement value. (p.120, *emphasis added*)

Other similarities included:

- Both employed a physical capital maintenance concept. However as noted earlier in this section, although prima facie similar, there is a suggestion that Limperg's continuity principle and Schmidt's relative maintenance of value concept differed.

- On balance there appear few substantive differences between Schmidt's *replacement price* and Limperg's *replacement value*.

- Both attempted to place their theory of accounting in the wider context of a macro or social economics theory, suggesting that an "organic" view of the firm should be adopted. It could be inferred that this was the result of a common concern with the ongoing business problem of determining prices which would justify, economically, the continued utilization of an entity's resources. Managerial problems and the accounting data necessary for their resolution seemed to dominate their works.

- Both writers, although having recourse to the *current* economic ideas were not unquestioning users of those ideas. Witness Limperg's rejection of marginal utility theory and Schmidt's rejection of the quantity theory of money. In this respect, they were not simply followers but rather analytical thinkers.

- The examples used, particularly in the 1920's and 1930's articles suggest that the problems and resulting accounting solutions were in respect of single owner, or family owned concerns - in contrast to today's larger corporate vehicles. Examples often were crouched in terms of commodity dealers', often plantation owners' problems, leading to possible inferences *either* that their ideas were more applicable to simple organizational settings, *or* that a simplified example was devised by both to ensure clarity in expression.

- Both perceived inflation as having measurement implications. Support for this view is found in Muis (1980) and Schwantag [1951]. In a quote provided previously, Schwantag [1951, p.9, *emphasis added*], suggests "that Schmidt wants to analyse the substance of the production process of the firm from an economic point of view . . . (taking account of) the effects of inflation and falling productivity . . . it was obvious that the *measure* of economic figures formerly held to be fixed - the *money unit* - was *flexible* in reality and that this flexibility had to be taken into account when *measuring*". It was noted earlier, and is explained further in *chapter 6* that Schmidt's organic system was perceived as a form of stabilized accounting. Although recognising a measurement problem, Limperg's and Schmidt's respective responses, have however, led some to suggest that both failed to appreciate the differential effects of price changes and changes in the general level of prices (Zeff, 1976, and Tweedie and Whittington, 1984).

- Both Limperg and Schmidt were systematic, deductive thinkers whose premises were taken from their *casual* observations of business affairs. In this regard their methods of analysis, at least in Europe, were seminal (Schneider, 1981, p.137-39 and Burgert, 1972).

Although similarities exist *differences* are evident. These include:

- Unlike Schmidt's symmetrical treatment of increases and decreases in replacement prices, Limperg "did not admit to symmetry of capital accretion and impairment" (van Seventer, 1975, pp.74-6). Limperg's suggestion that any holding losses were to be charged to a special reserve account, *Wertberichtigungsconto* or *rekening voor prijsverschillen*, until the balance has been exhausted, with any residue then to be charged to the profit and loss account, begs the inference that his approach was more pragmatic, and certainly less systematic, than that of Schmidt.

- Whereas specific accounting adjustments for changes in the general level of prices were not part of either Schmidt's or Limperg's accounting mechanisms, Schmidt explicitly sought to neutralize the effects of any general purchasing power changes through the balancing of liquid assets and liabilities - his "identity of values principle".

- Although adopting similar methods of valuation Limperg qualified his approach, along the lines of what has subsequently been described as the *value to the owner* method of valuation. In Limperg's own words this appeared as:

> "The two theories [Limperg's replacement value theory and Schmidt's *Wiederbeschaffungswert* or reproduction value theory] have a different starting-point and only share a small amount of the theoretical argument. The theory I developed is based on the phenomenon that every good has a realization value and a replacement value and that the value of the good is determined by whichever is the lowest of the two, in business usually the replacement value." [Limperg, 1937, p.15]

- In respect of speculative assets financed with loan capital Schmidt was prepared to modify his income rule that holding gains did not constitute income. Schmidt [1926, p.390-391] is clear on this:

> From the viewpoint of the balance sheet one of the main issues is that of the *form of profit from speculation.* If a speculator, in order to buy real goods which he hopes will increase in value, takes a loan for which he has to pay interest, then his yield consists in *that price increase* which exceeds the *contractual* interest amount. In the case of a deliberate holding of the proceeds in the form of money from the sale of real goods the *profit of the speculator is the interest on the amount of cash at bank as well as the possible increase in money value.* In both cases after the settlement of the business and the distribution of the profit he has at his disposal the amount of money with which the speculation started. In the first case he can pay back his loan and the principle of maintenance of the firm is thereby observed. *But only the realized speculation profit is distributable.* In the context of buying real goods with borrowed money this means: it is only possible to distribute the increase in value of the real goods which exceeds the amount of the loan and the interest after the business has been settled by selling the real goods purchased for speculative purposes. Before that, the speculative profit is still tied up in the firm. Therefore final (profit) calculation can only take place after the speculation has been settled and, at the latest, it has to be done when the initially borrowed money is paid back. Also conceivable and quite common in practice is the form of speculation with borrowed money in which several of these transactions are *rolled over.* One buys real goods on credit, sells them and buys again. In this case the profit from speculation resulting from the increase in value of the real goods is tied up until after the last sale of goods, i.e. until after

> the final redemption of the speculative loan has been made. (*emphasis in original*)

Tweedie and Whittington (1984, pp.28-30) provide an extended discussion of this aspect of Schmidt's proposal, based on his 1930b article. It is clear that this was an antecedent of the so called gearing adjustment found in the 1977 U.K. Hyde Guidelines.

On the question of speculation, Burgert [1972, p.115], details Limperg's position. He notes that "the rule about the importance of price variations is now changed in such a way that only alterations in the value of the normal stock are credited or debited to the 'revaluation account'. Price changes on a surplus or shortage of stock give rise to profits or losses from speculation, which are entered directly into the income statement".

- Although both describe their theories as a form of *organic* accounting their concepts of organicism differ. Schmidt unequivocally viewed businesses and accounting for businesses as a part of the wider workings of the economy. The firm was a "cell" within the wider economic system. Limperg's variety of organic accounting appears more related to the organic structure of the particular entity, than to the economy as a whole. Again, if we draw upon Mey (1966) for clues as to Limperg's position, it appears that Schmidt's notion of an accounting system driven by a perceived need to maintain the *relative* capital of the entity on an economy-wide basis, is firmly rejected. To an extent Mey lampoons the *relative* notion. Whereas Limperg's theory "has its basis in the macro-economic view" (p.14) with a focus on maintaining the overall level of industrial production, it ". . . does not imply or prescribe . . . [relative maintenance of] the position of a firm within the industrial complex or society"; it is at the option of entrepreneurs to choose their specific positions. Entrepreneurs are free to vary their position, according to Mey; to argue otherwise he explains, would invite non-commercial action by fiscal authorities to shape the economy.

Some uneasiness with Mey's explanation is justified, for the element of industrial harmony at the macro level which he presents to be underpinning Limperg's ideas, distills into integrated action at the micro level, cooperation and joint action by individual firms are necessary, if economic harmony of the kind envisaged is to occur by design and not by chance.

Again, it is difficult satisfactorily to piece together exactly where Limperg stood on such matters. In particular, it is unclear whether the measure of confusion or contradiction which appears to emerge in virtually every description of his ideas are properly attributable to him or to those trying, with hindsight, to resurrect his thoughts so as to give them internal coherence. It could be that Limperg, working alone as he is presented to have done, had not refined his theory to that extent. Apparent inconsistencies may be more the product of the accounting *anthropologists* piecing together what they believe to be the pattern of Limperg's ideas, stretching them beyond the actual framework he had in place, than a failure properly attributable to him.

6. LIMPERG AND SCHMIDT - INFLUENCE, EVOLUTION AND ACTS OF FAITH

It appears that Limperg and (to a lesser extent) Schmidt are the most frequently alluded to *authorities* in the post World War II push by the Anglo-American professional accountancy bodies' drive for some variety of current-value or current-cost accounting mechanism. Some of that recourse to the authority of Limperg and Schmidt is explicable in terms of the attraction that the idea of an evolution of ideas has in obtaining support for proposals to depart from tradition.

In this case the firmly entrenched half-a-century tradition of historical cost accounting was to be unseated. And reference to accounting developments during the hyperinflation of 1920's Europe would appear to be of immense assistance in creating an impregnable basis for the current-cost case. Furthermore, although Sweeney's case for indexed accounting did not win support in any of the English speaking countries, it is understandable that the debt he expressed to major participants in the German *Betriebswirtschaftslehre*, especially Mahlberg, Schmalenbach and Schmidt provided an irresistible link with the 1920's inflation. If the more recent 1970's developments in Britain, the U.S., Australia, Canada, New Zealand can be linked with those 1920's events, it injects into the replacement case the attractive didactical tactic of giving the proposals an *evolutionary* flavour.

In some instances allusions to Limperg and Schmidt being forerunners to the proposals to account for inflation appear to have arisen from commentators' failures to distinguish between the variety of mechanisms promoted in both the *Bedrijfseconomie* movement and the *Betriebswirtschaftslehre*. Inflation accounting has been presented in much of the modern accounting literature as a generic brand of accounting. But, the subtle differences between the competing varieties of mechanisms, lie at the root of the prolonged debate in which they were participating (Whittington, 1983, and Whittington and Tweedie, 1984).

Not obvious in the pervading recourse to Limperg and Schmidt has been any awareness (or, at least the recognition) of Limperg's bitter criticism of Schmidt's ideas, Limperg's unequivocal declarations that Schmidt's ideas differed from his and thus were irreparably flawed (see *chapters 4 and 5*). Most important in this context is Limperg's assertion that Schmidt's ideas were not set in a general theory of the firm as part of a unified economic system. Yet, that is clearly claimed to be an underlying feature of more recent current-cost proposals.

Witness the Sandiland's suggestion that "CCA was evolutionary rather than revolutionary" (Report, 1976, para. 11). Virtually no objection to that assessment was evident. As noted in *chapter 2* others to support the evolutionary notion include

Whittington (1981), Mattessich (1982) and Bloom and Debessay (1984). Such suggestions invoke an air of *orderly refinement*, as opposed to what has been the disjointed opportunistic nature of successive CCA proposals. Modern versions of CCA might be regarded as the outcome of a long series of events and the consequential proffering of ideas over time. The postulation of a genetic link between modern CCA and the earlier (including *Betriebswirtschaftslehre* and *Bedrijfseconomie*) proposals is understandable. There appears to be a pattern in the emergence of those proposals - extensive levels of inflation followed by some *form* of replacement cost alternative. However, the pattern is not necessarily an *evolution* - an *orderly unrolling* of what was already there in embryonic form. Any flow-on of ideas, explicit or subliminal, from the 1920s in Europe to the 1970s and 1980s elsewhere is not discernible. We speculate that, in this context, *evolution* has been used as a synonym for *development*, as a synonym for occurrence. As such it suggests that every event in the course of history is evolution.

Name-dropping with respect to Limperg is even more explicable. For his husbanding of the Dutch *Bedrijfseconomie* movement through the 1920s and into the following decade is part of the folk-lore of western European business history. And most importantly, tradition has it that he developed the replacement price system used by Philips Lampfabrieken of Eindhoven, which survives (in one form or another) for all to observe today (see for example, Burgert, 1972 and Cattela, 1983).

Despite the various modifications it appears to have undergone over time, reference to "the Philips system designed by Limperg" is presented as a variety of living proof that replacement price accounting works.

Not so explicit in the references to Limperg's contribution are either evidence that those who indulge in history in that way have a clear understanding of exactly what Limperg's contribution to the Philips system really was, or how or whether it corresponds in detail with the current cost proposals promoted by, for example, the Sandilands committee in 1975. In fact, there is evidence that some aspects of the Philip's system (regarding the treatment of monetary assets) was in contrast to Limperg's ideas [Burgert, 1972, pp.122-123].

Reference has been made in the literature (Whittington, 1983) to the visit by members of the Sandilands Committee to the headquarters of the Nederlands Instituut van Registeraccountants in Amsterdam and therefore were influenced by the Dutch system and by implication Limpergian thought. But no specific aspects of Limperg's ideas are referred to as such in the Sandilands Report and no evidence is presented to the effect that there was any particular access to "Limperg's ideas" (in contrast with what others suppose to have been his ideas). Nor is it clear how anyone currently understands exactly what Limperg advocated. His failure to present his ideas in print in any comprehensive or cohesive fashion leaves a lot to be received as an act of faith. From the Limperg translations in *chapter 3* it is clearly the case that Limperg's valuation rule and Sandiland's value to the owner rule are similar in their effect. That is all, however.

The notion that the proposals of the 1970s were products of an evolutionary process has an immediate appeal. An evolution has been alluded to with respect to current value/cost proposals on a number of occasions.

(i) Pattern

Modern versions of CCA might be regarded the outcome of a long series of events, as proposals emerging in similar economic settings (Mumford, 1979), and as the outcome of similar threads of ideas weaving through thought over time. 1920's *Bedrijfseconomie* and *Betriebswirtschaft* theories emerged and prospered, gained coherence, during periods of inflation, only differing in intensity from those which spawned the replacement cost proposals of the 1950s and the full-blown Sandilands type CCA proposals of the 1970s. It is understandable that conscious and deliberate attempts have been made to forge a genetic link between modern CCA and those earlier proposals, especially those attributed to Limperg and the Dutch system. And, there can be little doubt that the awareness, however vague, of that background gave at least moral support to those developing current versions of CCA. In that sense there are connections, and there is a pattern.

But such a pattern is not necessarily an *evolution* of the kind alluded to in the Sandilands Report. Nor is it an evolution of the kind which bestows on modern CCA the inheritance of refined technical substance or the reward of intellectual persistence, or the privilege of *survival* by virtue of gradually having gained perfection. It is reasonable to infer that the (often throw-away) references to connections between the work of successive scholars grappling with the inflation accounting problem have been intended to create the impression of an integrated development; for example: the linking of Limperg with Bonbright (Peasnell, 1982), and the linking of Schmidt with Sweeney and with Bonbright, under a supposed pervading influence of Limperg (Whittington, 1980, 1981a and 1981b).

Distinguishing *evolution* from *revolution* has been a longstanding posture over the past two centuries by those wanting to drape a particular phenomenon with a mantle of an orderly unrolling of what implicitly existed. Unnatural occurrences, radical departures from what was developing in an orderly manner, have been contrasted as a specialized sense of *revolution* (Williams, 1981, p.122).

But, no such orderly pattern, nor violent overthrow of an orderly development, has characterized the promotion of modern CCA. And except by allusion and casual, almost careless, reference to the names of Limperg and (less often) to Schmidt, no specific drawing upon the explicit theories of either has occurred. Limperg's failure to publish his theories has been noted (for example: van Seventer, 1969; van Sloten, 1981 and Ashton, 1981). Outside the development of a replacement price system by the Philips Company of Eindhoven, it appears that no recourse could have been had to ideas reasonably attributable to Limperg prior to the edited version of *his papers* (in Dutch) as *Bedrijfseconomie* beginning in 1964 (Groeneveld *et al.*, Vol. I). Any flow-on of ideas, explicit or subliminal, is impossible to identify. Goudeket (1952), for example, makes no specific mention of which aspects of Limperg's theory of business economics the Philips system drew upon. Goudeket (1960) makes no mention of Limperg at all, nor do Gynther (1966), Vos (1970), Enthoven (1982) or (say) Cattela (1983). It ought also be noted that Limperg found imputation of an adjustment for price-level changes oppugnant. Accordingly, modification of Philips' accounting in 1982 to include adjustments of that variety and their presence in ED18, SSAP16, (indirectly) the Hyde proposal, in the proposal of the Richardson Report and the Report of the Ontario Committee, and (say) in Australia's SAP1, are at odds with what is said to be fundamental to Limpergian thought (van Seventer [1975, p.88] and Burgert [1972, p.122]). Over the same period virtually no specific link with Schmidt's work is evident in the literature. The same is true of the injection of Bonbright's notion of *value to the owner* into the debate.

This is not to deny similarity, even congruence in some instances, between the ideas and some particular aspects of the proposals of those authors. Witness the discussion in *chapter 5(i)*. Nor is it intended to deny the potential for a subliminal infiltration of ideas from the 1920's work of either Limperg or Schmidt, or both; and it does not exclude the possibility of Bonbright's work on the valuation of property having drifted, somehow, into the thoughts of those putting together CCA proposals.[1] But similarity is not necessarily the outcome of an evolution in its etymological sense. If, as appears the case, evolution is being used as a synonym for *development*, as a synonym for *occurrence*, then every event in the course of history is evolution. The import of using language to describe relationships in history is lost and we are much the poorer for it.

There may well be a pattern underlying the events from the 1920s in Europe to the 1950s, 1970s and 1980s elsewhere. But, if it does exist such a pattern is not what is generally accorded the distinction of being *an* evolution. There is no evidence of a

1 In an accounting *setting* this notion of a *drift* of ideas from one *context* to another was suggested by Clarke (1980).

deliberate, conscious, unrolling of what was already there in embryonic form. In fact, in many ways what Schmidt had in place by the early 1920s was far more refined and consistent, than CCA as it currently stands in most of the proposals. Nor can it be claimed that the emergence of CCA has been a revolution; not for the reasons that Sandilands implied, but because there has not been any radical, violent, departure from an evolving course of events. It might well be argued that in relation to the *Betriebswirtschaftslehre* of the 1920s modern CCA is more in the nature of a regression than an *evolution.*

It is difficult to imagine what purpose those allusions to an evolution were intended to serve other than to bestow upon the post World War II proposals the psychological benefits and the force that proceeds from having been subjected to the processes of a gradual refinement, an *evolution* over a period exceeding fifty years. But attempts to promote one mechanism in preference to another on evolutionary grounds is likely to backfire, for the historical-cost system might equally be taken to have survived and, accordingly, ought to be given preference as much as the agency theory literature suggests. That is exactly the opposite result those having recourse to Limperg have set out to achieve.

Curiously, appeals to the authority of Limperg and Schmidt do not appear to have admitted to the argument the possibility that their ideas may also have lent support to other mechanisms by which accounts might incorporate the effects on firms of price, and (or) price-level changes. Nor have they attempted to consider the likely consequences of extending what is known of Schmidt's and Limperg's reasoning beyond the points at which their work finished. Nor has there been any attempt to consider the social and political environment in which the *Betriebswirtschaft* and *Bedrijfseconomie* movements flourished, other than some of the financial impact of the inflation. Most importantly, the political climate in Germany has received virtually no attention. Consequently the impression has emerged in the Anglo-American accounting literature that the accounting mechanisms canvassed at the time to "account for inflation" were driven by a common desire to improve the serviceability of the data which resulted. A conflicting, or at least competing, thesis emerged in the economic history literature. It is reasonable to presume that where political considerations were as dominant as the economic historians suggest, Schmidt (and possibly Limperg), were not necessarily promoting solutions to the problems of accounting in a vacuum of financial reporting criteria. Speculation as to the possible impact of the political pressures of the day on the shape of their proposals is in order, for it produced conclusions no more problematical than those already in the traditional literature.

With only a vague reference by Sweeney (1936) to Limperg it seems that of the two, Schmidt's work had the greater impact. How great an impact, whether it was the dominant influence in the development of *Stabilized Accounting*, and whether Sweeney's end product contained strong traces of, *inter alia*, Schmidt's thesis ought to be enquired into. For evidence that the mechanism and underlying reasoning of Sweeney's *Stabilized Accounting* are traceable to Schmidt and or other members of the *Betriebswirtschaftslehre* strengthens the German evolutionary element up to that time. Though it does nothing for those who persistently point to a connection between the post World War II current value proposals and Limperg's *Bedrijfseconomie*.

(ii) *Betriebswirtschaftslehre* Participants in Context

Drawing upon the circumstantial evidence of Sweeney's casual reference to so many of the participants in the *Betriebswirtschaftslehre* makes it reasonable to speculate as to who had the greatest impact on Sweeney. Preliminary research by Clarke and Dean, (1986; 1989), Dean and Clarke, (1989) and Graves (1985 and 1987) suggests the German *Betriebswirtschaftslehre*, especially Schmidt, Mahlberg and Schmalenbach had a major influence on Sweeney's *Stabilized Accounting*. Sweeney himself (1964) drew particular attention to his recourse to the Germans - Mahlberg, Schmalenbach, Prion, Geldmacher, Strutz and Nimax, in addition to Schmidt; and to Leger, Valois and Faure from France. On balance it seems reasonable to accept that Mahlberg and Schmidt had positions of primacy in the scheme of things. But with the exception of Graves (1985, 1987 and 1989) and Clarke and Dean (1989), up to the recent past their respective roles have not been represented adequately in the literature. In contrast it now is well documented that Sweeney has been misrepresented in the literature with regard to a presumed promotion of adjusting mechanisms of the current purchasing power (constant dollar) variety (Clarke 1976a, pp.265-67; Whittington, 1984, p.34) and Clarke and Dean 1989).

Curiously Sweeney was as much a victim of the desire to compromise to achieve *practicality* as were the participants in the *Betriebswirtschaftslehre*. Kester, Sweeney's mentor and PhD supervisor, emphasised the need to be *practical* on several occasions. And his exhortations appear to have taken an ultimate hold on Sweeney's judgement in the matter. But the result would have been much the same even if he had not listened to Kester, for the evidence is strongly supportive of a view that much of the outcome of the *Betriebswirtschaftslehre* was politically motivated - to that extent, bent on the practical rather than what was *a priori* supportable (*Introduction,* Graves, Dean and Clarke, 1989, pp. xi-xlii).

Examination of Sweeney's work *pre* and *post* 1928 has been informative in the development of this thesis (Clarke and Dean 1989). But, for a clear understanding of the contrast we wish to make it is necessary to consider the contrast of the dominant financial characteristics of the German 1920's inflation and, in particular, the underlying political and social pressures driving the events.

(iii) Management and Replacement Cost Dictum

Against a groundswell of interest and articles on the problem of the rising price-level Geldmacher (1920) was considered by Mahlberg (1923a, p.ix) to have touched the real issues most effectively. But as noted he was in crowded company, particularly in the engineering and industrial press. Notable contributions included those from Schmalenbach (1919), Prion (1919), Klein (1920), and Kast (1920) amongst others including Geldmacher. But it was Geldmacher's most penetrating perceptions of the accounting problems arising by virtue of the prolonged changes in the value of money (*Geldentwertung*) which aptly captured the essence of the situation. Most importantly, he drew attention to the " . . . growing profits" which were being reported, being " . . . mere tricks with figures"; and he pointed to the problems facing businessmen of maintaining the level of activity when " . . . the money they were getting their hands on (through sales was) . . . often far less than what they would have to invest in immediately replacing the goods sold" (1920, p.364).[2]

Two elements of present day thinking and the rhetoric it spawns appear to permeate Mahlberg's thinking. We might presume that to be indicative of the general perception of the situation: first, the automatic *creative* consequences of following the rules as they currently stood without any attempt to deceive, though that might be the ultimate consequence; and second, the unjustified jump by which a problem in budgeting (inventory replacement funding) is translated into an income measurement problem - for even without the inflation between 1918 and 1921, inventory replacement with the associated inventory price rises could still be budgeted for. Income measurement and budgeting were confused much as they have been in the 1970's and 1980's discussions on the price and the price-level problem, half a century later.[3]

Most important during the period were the variety of *solutions* which emerged from that literature and from the numerous books which emerged at much the same

---

2 This article and several others of that post World War I period are provided in translation in Dean, Clarke and Graves (1990).

3 Clarke (1978) suggested that CCA's development had more in common with regress than progress because of this confusion.

time, including for example Prion (1919 and 1921); Schmalenbach (1919 and 1921); Mahlberg (1921) and Schmidt (1921) (see Appendix II for greater details).

As noted in *chapter 2* between 1919 and 1921 three basic varieties of solution to incorporating the price and/or price-level changes in accounts were promoted: a base stock method (Schmalenbach, 1919), which was a crude form of attempting to maintain the physical component of capital; *Indexbuchführung*, (Mahlberg, 1921; Schmalenbach, 1921) by which the accounts (primarily the balance sheet) were restated *forwards* to be expressed in terms of the number of contemporary paper marks entailing an equal amount of the same general purchasing; and crude forms of *current value accounting* (primarily from Schmidt, 1921) by which the inventory and assets were restated in terms of something approaching their current replacement price.

Whereas those *solutions* coexisted as competing alternatives and whilst Mahlberg and Schmalenbach might appear to have fickle allegiances and possibly might each be accused of hedging their theoretical bets, the urgency of finding a solution was such an imperative as to welcome an undisciplined canvassing of *alternative solutions*. It was a period in which experiment was not only acceptable, it was an imperative! The subsequent Index Commission was specifically charged with the responsibility of analysing the diverse solutions, sorting out the obvious conflicts between them, with the objective of recommending a practical mechanism for implementation in the inflation-ridden German economy.

Pervading German concern was over the impact of price and price-level changes on "cost estimation" and on achieving an effective delineation of "proper and fictitious profits" for taxation purposes. To a lesser extent, but nonetheless a growing concern also was the production of comparable financial data in accounts. Recall that von Kast had suggested "one cannot add apples to oranges" (1920, p.1), whilst Schlesinger was concerned that the length of the unit of measure "is rubbery and expands and contracts daily" (1920, p.507 - see footnote 9, *chapter 2*). Perhaps these were forerunners of Sweeney's (1936) observation that the "truthfulness of accounting depends largely upon the truthfulness of the dollar - and the dollar is a liar!".

These issues were captured by Mahlberg (1920, p.183) in his explanation that, whilst state price controls forced price setting to be determined on an historical cost basis, conditions were conducive for pragmatic support of the use of a current value basis for pricing. In this setting it could be argued that data comparability was the highly desired by-product that would emerge from a matching of current costs of goods sold with the contemporary prices for which the goods were being sold. But it is difficult to determine which, maintenance of true profit levels and its associated tax relief or data comparability, was driving the increasing pressure for accounting change.

Nonetheless, Schmidt's campaign for a variety of current value accounting to be adopted was clearly a significant development. His *Die organische Bilanz im Rahmen der Wirtschaft* (1921), was a seminal contribution to the thought of the period.[4] Current values (replacement prices) for physical asset valuation clearly offered a potential base from which a programme for the charging of cost-of-goods-sold and depreciation in a contemporary financial dimension could be effected. In the context of Germany's dwindling productive capacity because of the inflation, the ravages of war and the constraining pricing laws, Schmidt's promotion of such a current value technique had clear appeal. From the standpoint of theoretical structure it is most interesting to note the manner in which Schmidt captured the commingling consequences of the effects of changes in the general level of prices, and the general purchasing power endowment of the entity and the effects of changes in the prices of the particular goods and services the entity faced in the market. In this way Schmidt clearly indicated his thorough understanding of the differential financial purchasing power effects of inflation (Clarke, 1976a; Mattessich, 1982; Tweedie and Whittington, 1984 and Graves, 1985).

Concern over data heterogeneity underscoring most developments of 1920's Germany period has been noted. Schmidt's current cost approach captured the detail of the issues, but the question of interfirm and intrafirm intertemporal comparison pervaded the climate.

In making a comment that the *ownership* of assets was a shareholder hedge against inflationary losses Mahlberg (1920, p.182) might be taken to have exhibited an imperfect understanding of the financial consequences of the inflation. He appears to imply that shareholders were thereby insulated against the differential effects of inflation by virtue of holding physical assets. This appears to be the only purpose for distinguishing *bondholders* as "mere creditors" with "assets in marks . . . (whose) value had melted away". Yet the pervading feature of the German inflation, even at that early stage, had been the differential impact. How, and to what extent, an individual gained or lost general purchasing power depended not so much upon whether the assets held were liquid or physical, but the extent to which their exchange price *for current marks* changed in line with the rate of inflation. Holding money assets, simply predetermined the outcome; made the consequential loss of general purchasing power an indisputable and predictable outcome. Holding *Sachwerte*, the physical assets, though generally more desirable, did not necessarily insulate owners

4 Mattessich (1982) was an early commentator on Schmidt's contribution. In Dean, Clarke, and Graves (1990) two chapters from *Die organische* are reproduced in translation.

against indirect general purchasing power losses, nor guarantee general purchasing power gains, nor even some kind of neutral hedge. The outcome was dependent upon the extent to which the inflated selling prices of the *Sachwerte* kept pace with, or had outstripped, the rate of inflation. Differential impacts were the expected outcomes. Holding *Sachwerte* merely introduced a chance of hedging effectively.

It is to be noted that Mahlberg's 1920 contribution to the debate was part of a flurry of articles and books addressing the problem of how to best have accounts incorporate the financial effects of inflation. Of particular note was Prion's (1919) *Die Finanzierung und Bilanz Wirtschaftlicher Betriebe unter dem Einfluß der Geldentwertung* in which he illustrated through the medium of his *merchant example* (p.11) the problem of matching current costs with current revenues under inflationary conditions. It reinforced Geldmacher's aforementioned (1920) observations. Sweeney (1927, p.184) was to enter the illustration in the Anglo-American literature by drawing upon Mahlberg's reproduction of it in his *Goldkreditverkehr und Goldbuchführung* (1923b).

Relatively moderate beginnings of the inflation up to 1922 were conducive to *exploratory* solutions as accounting theorists grappled with the vicissitudes of the time. Mahlberg's early proposals were unquestionably "first attempts" to find a serviceable mechanism. Time had run out by June of 1922 (Feldman, 1982; Kindelberger, 1984; Holtfrerich, 1986), after which the inflation gathered momentum. May 1921 had seen the delivery of the London Ultimatum setting out the Dawes Committee's final assessment of Germany's War Reparation liability. As unwelcome information for the financial markets the Ultimatum was the catalyst for the take-off of the hyperinflation. Its onset removed the convenience the accounting theorists had enjoyed of having time on their side whilst sifting through the inflation accounting mechanisms mooted to date. The Ultimatum thereby removed the privilege of experiment and exploration that had been enjoyed up to that time and introduced a period of recapitulation, summarisation, factors which were most conducive to the compromise which was to emerge.

Against this background Schmidt's current value proposals had been rather early and impotent for the winning of converts and supporters. In contrast, as outlined in *chapter 2* the various formats by which accounts might be indexed exhibited a variety of mechanisms within what was perceived to be an understandable and acceptable framework of common goals, in particular *data homogeneity* and the facilitation of data comparability which it promised.

(iv) *Indexbuchführung* and *Goldmarkbilanz*

Although Schmalenbach had promoted the idea that costs for pricing policies ought be calculated according to contemporary replacement prices ("Die Abschreibung" in *Zeitschrift für handelswissenschaftliche Forschung*, 1908/1909, he properly is identified as the "father of *Indexbuchführung*". For there is little dispute that Schmalenbach's 1921 article, "Geldwertausgleich in der bilanzmässigen Erfolgsrechnung" changed the focus from income comparability to a forwards adjusting mechanism emphasis of *Indexbuchführung* (see Clarke and Dean, 1989 and Graves, Dean & Clarke, 1989).

Whereas that appears as a change in emphasis, it did not represent a change in *policy*, for no policy had emerged up to the deliberations of the Index Commission. To the contrary, up to 1921 the varietal prescriptions coexisted without the respective protagonists being distressed by the existence of the competing proposals. The breadth of those proposals was captured by Mahlberg in the 1923 edition of his *Bilanztechnik und Bewertung bei schwankender Währung* (1923a, pp.206-246) and in Schmidt's *Bilanzwert, Bilanzgewinn und Bilanzumwertung* (1924, pp.80-121). Developments generally lacked cohesion, except to the extent that the movement towards a variety of indexed adjustments appears (in retrospect) to have had considerably greater momentum than Schmidt's organic current value schema. One unifying element, however, was a common recognition by the *Betriebswirtschaftslehre* theorists that business decisions required calculations producing homogeneous data.

Thus, whereas Mahlberg and Schmalenbach had actively promoted the *Indexbuchführung* technique, their advocacy has to be seen in the context of the time. And whereas Mahlberg's advocacy was strong and persistent, though exploratory, his cataloguing and annotation of the various indexing techniques are indicative of his perceptive appreciation of the state of flux in which *Indexbuchführung* was being illustrated and explained. Most important for the understanding of the historical significance of Mahlberg's work is his recognition of Schmalenbach's greater exposition of the technique; Schmalenbach " . . . inspired (his) second revision . . . recognised the *account* distortion arising from balance sheet corrections due to money value changes" (1923a, p.viii, *emphasis added*). In contrast with Schmalenbach who demonstrated his more single-minded disposition to the issues, Mahlberg appears to have been tracking through the possibilities in the hope of discovering a satisfactory technique; in the present day idiom, a method which perhaps could *enjoy a consensus* of the business community and the Government.

Perhaps Mahlberg's unsettled position on the matter is demonstrated aptly by his experimentation in 1921 by restating only the *Realwerte* (physical items, plant, machinery, merchandise and real property, for example) in the opening balance sheet, leaving the *Geldwerte* (monetary items) and capital structure items unchanged. But contrary to the price-level or price change indexation methods, movements in the price of gold (*Goldägio*) were the basis for the scaling of the historical cost data. With the restatement of the closing balance sheet being based on capitalised or programmed values (*etatsmässiger Wert*), profit emerged as the increase in paper mark wealth (Graves, 1985, pp.141-155 and Graves, 1987).

Stabilisation under Schmalenbach's 1921 forwards method was far more conventional than that 1921 experiment by Mahlberg; historical costs of both the physical and liquid items were scaled by Schmalenbach. And whereas he used a *forwards* adjustment method, restating in terms of year-end marks rather than those of 1914 as his subsequent 1922 model required, he canvassed a variety of retail and wholesale price indices and currency exchange rates for the purpose. He did not at that time have any commitment to a particular restatement device (Graves, 1987). Putting aside Mahlberg's more tentative and experimental approach to the problem of which indexing method to use, several fundamental theoretical differences between the varieties of *Indexbuchführung* filter through from a comparison of Schmalenbach and Mahlberg. Schmalenbach took part of the wealth change arising from the indexation of the opening balance sheet data for all items and the paper mark closing values to be part of the profit; in contrast, Mahlberg regarded that as only a *value adjustment* relating to the *value fluctuation in capital* (Graves, 1987).

Perhaps a source of those differences lies in Schmalenbach having been wedded, *ceteris paribus*, to historical cost. In both the 1921 and 1922 Schmalenbach articles the necessity for historical costs to be indexed to achieve *data homogeneity* was promoted. Graves suggestion (1985, pp.61-64) that Schmalenbach's approach reflected a response to the level of inflation, is borne out by his switch to a backwards indexing mechanism in the 1922 article. Graves' proposition is that it all was an extension by Schmalenbach of his *dynamic theory* of 1908. Income comparability was the driving motivation according to Graves " . . . a concern with achieving comparable periodic income figures (1985, p.58), and the indexation to effect price level adjustments " . . . seems to be put forward as a temporary measure"; a view which finds corroboration from Schoenfeld (1979, p.60).

Further differences between Schmalenbach and Mahlberg are indicative also of the general lack of consensus on the details of which indexation method to employ. Whereas Tweedie and Whittington (1984) allude to similarity Schmalenbach's preference was for historical cost stabilisation, whereas Mahlberg claimed to have preferred *programmed values* (1925 and 1927) as is demonstrated by his alternative mechanism of distinguishing between, and differential treatment accorded, the

Realwerte and the *Geldwerte*. These differences in detail invite the inference that whilst Sweeney was showing an affinity for the backwards indexation mechanism in his 1927 and 1928 articles, Mahlberg's 1922 *Goldmarkbilanz* proposal probably had the strongest influence, with respect to indexation mechanics. But, it would appear that it was Schmalenbach's emphasis on data homogeneity which had the greater influence on Sweeney's expositions post 1928 with regard to that objective. Nonetheless, Mahlberg's penchant for experimentation and for deviating from the straight indexation of historical costs quite reasonably were also strong influences on Sweeney following his initial excursions into indexation methods.

Analysis of the influences driving the switching to *Goldmarkbilanz* from *Indexbuchführung* gives an insight to the pervading state of flux in the *Betriebswirtschaftslehre* thinking as the hyperinflation took hold in 1922. In particular, the search for a *quick fix* emerges strongly as the driving factor. Much more so than any express desire to effect a long term, or to produce a definitive, general theory of accounting, or of external financial reporting in particular. The emphasis on cost estimation and pricing, income determination assessment of taxation and assessment of the quality of management through financial data up to 1922, tended to cloud the full financial impact of the inflation. Distinctions between *price* and *price-level* changes were clouded such as to obscure the essential *selective* financial effect of inflation by virtue of the differential movements in particular prices and the price level, per se. Zeff (1976, pp.23-24) identifies that obscuration as a major influence on subsequent failure in the accounting literature to distinguish between *general* price-level changes and *specific* price changes. That may well be true. But the most cursory examination of inflationary behaviour illustrates the differential impact of inflation as arising from the impact of variations in the changes in the prices of the particular goods and services as they are encountered by different entities.

(v) Stabilized Accounting - The Product of Compromise

An unassailable element in Sweeney's post 1928 development of his variety of stabilized accounting is the emphasis he placed on the need to have *homogeneous data*. In the context of the German experience upon which he drew, that emphasis was to be expected. His shift from the stabilization of historical cost was equally explicable in terms of the influence of the German events upon him and the general trend in the *Betriebswirtschaftslehre* thinking. Sweeney's allegiance to the trend (and the law) on indexation *as he read it* is indicated by his initial 1927 description of *Goldmarkbilanz* and his subsequent recourse in 1936 mainly to the *Indexbuchführung* mechanism. His preference for the stabilization of replacement prices, rather than staying with historical costs, possibly is indicative of his affinity with the valuation trends which were permeating the movement from the mid 1920s.

Reading Sweeney, however, does not give a very clear understanding of why the *forwards* method of indexing replaced the *backwards* method. From Sweeney one might gain the impression that it better conforms to his aim of removing the mathematical defects of conventional accounting and better achieved his homogeneity objective. It is far from clear that much difference ensues in the switch from the backwards to the forwards method insofar as it affects the production of homogeneous data.

Sweeney's motivation does not align with the forces which were driving the changes in Germany. *Goldmarkbilanz* had been the only practicable indexation solution during the hyperinflation, on almost the purely arithmetical and psychological grounds of coping with the size of the numbers it produced. The 1914 gold mark was a stable reference point; the data representative of a purchasing power dimension that everyone might reasonably be able to comprehend. And the size of the numbers emerging from the scaling had psychologically manageable proportions. In contrast, the data of *Indexbuchführung* lost out badly on each of those points during the hyperinflation following 1922. One inference is that changes in Germany were more politically than technically motivated (Clarke and Dean, 1989).

Once the hyperinflation had subsided in Germany the emphasis of the *Betriebswirtschaftslehre* theorists could more reasonably be directed toward a meshing of their general concern with the development of a *general theory* likely to give homogeneous data and the more specific objective of accurate income measurement. Whilst this may be interpreted as a *higher ideal* than the search for a quick fix that dominated the development of both *Indexbuchführung* and *Goldmarkbilanz*, one might speculate that the experience was an important ingredient in the cognitive process.

That provided a focal point which may not have emerged without the economic events of the time. Considered as such, an understanding of the circumstances of the experimentation with indexation methods and the politically driven outcome of the Index Commission are indicative of a contextual dimension which *positive theory* type examination may make to *normative theory construction*. An understanding of the "what" and the "how" emerge as important elements in the development of the framework in which the normative issues, such as Schmidt's advocacy of replacement price valuation, might be pursued.

We might argue then that Sweeney had plugged into the mainstream of the *Betriebswirtschaftslehre* movement with his expositions of indexed accounting in

1927 and 1928. And that his ultimate preference for a forwards indexation based upon replacement prices (or the current costs of reproduction) was entirely consistent within that framework of events, rather than being somewhat "inexplicable" as has been suggested (Tweedie and Whittington, 1984, p.34).

These circumstances may well raise a question as to whether Sweeney actually *preferred* replacement price stabilization (Clarke, 1976), or whether his avowed allegiance thereto was merely a manifestation of his conformity to the *Betriebswirtschaftslehre* trend. Sweeney's recourse to Schmidt is unequivocal. Likewise is Sweeney's increased interest in replacement price stabilization after Schmidt presented his *Valuation* paper to the 1929 International Accounting Congress (*The Accountant*, October 1929). It is arguable that Sweeney's communication with Schmidt also appears to have had a salient effect on the shape of the subsequent development of his stabilized accounting. Sweeney's reference (1935, footnote 15, p.199) to personal discussions with Schmidt " . . . on the subject (of stabilized accounting) on September 29, 1929" invites the inference that they may even have met.

Less speculative is the incidence of their corresponding (1931, pp.176-177); and 1936, pp.40-42). Citing Schmidt on numerous occasions over a nine year period (1927, p.188; 1930, pp.280-284; 1931, p.166, 176-177; 1933, p.190; 1935, p.109, and 1936, pp.40-42, 47 and 193) lends weight to a reasonable inference that from 1927 onwards Schmidt's views, and exposition of them had not only continuous, but possibly an increasing, appeal for Sweeney.

That is understandable, for the meshing of the current values and the overall financial effects on the prices of productive assets had been a consistent theme in the organic stream of the *Betriebswirtschaftslehre* literature from its inception. Its presence in Schmidt's *Die organische Bilanz* has already been noted and in the context of the diminishing effect of the inflation after 1923, it was inevitable that thoughts were turning to the development of a more *general theory* of accounting.

The intensity of the *appreciation debate* in the American literature during the latter part of the 1920s is indicative of that trend as evident in the works of Moss (1923), Rorem (1929) and others (see Clarke, 1982 for details). And whilst the catalyst for that episode in the American literature was more the flow-on from the public utility pricing debate (Clarke, 1982), it had nonetheless been the problems in that monopoly setting arising from price and price-level changes that had been its beginning too. In that sense the German literature emerging from the *Betriebswirtschaftslehre* movement and the U.S. appreciation debate were linked to a common problem.

(vi) *Betriebswirtschaftslehre* rather than the *Bedrijfseconomie* Movement

Notable in the literature, and in particular in Sweeney's references to it, is the absence of any explicit injection of identifiably Limpergian thinking. That of course, does not ensure that some of the thinking of the *Amsterdam* School did not enter the development of Sweeney's ideas. But clearly, if such influence occurred, it did not have anything approaching the lasting influence of the work of the *Betriebswirtschaftslehre* theorists. No other conclusion is reasonably based on the analysis of events post World War I in Germany (discussed above).

Another inevitable conclusion from this analysis of the events is that the contextual vagaries of the German hyperinflation and the pressures to discover a workable solution *seem* to have been lost on Sweeney. It has to be noted that he was pursuing the development of a general theory of accounting to remove those inherent defects of *mathematical incorrectness, irrelevance, and incompleteness* which he complained undermined the serviceability of conventional accounting (1936, pp.3-23). He seems to have been unaware of the extremity of the social and political factors (described, *inter alia*, in Holtfrerich, 1986) which were shaping the development of the German solutions during the early 1920s and which played such an important part in the Index Commission's choice of *Goldmarkbilanz* and the Reich's recourse to the *Rentenmark*.

There is no doubt that the events of those times had a fundamental influence on the basic development of Sweeney's stabilized accounting. In particular the need to "match current costs with current values" had been raised long before the onset of the hyperinflation. Seicht has identified that trend as the European theorists drew from the ideas of Fisher. Concern to achieve data homogeneity, likewise, underscored the developments in post World War I Germany as the inflation gathered momentum. But the pervading methodological characteristic was the pragmatism driving the development of those accounting solutions. First were the forwards *Indexbuchführung* adjustments (Mahlberg, 1921; and Schmalenbach, 1921), then the switch to *Goldmarkbilanz* (Mahlberg, 1922; and Schmalenbach, 1922), and in the background was Schmidt's 1921 developed current value proposal and other partially developed proposals (e.g. Geldmacher 1920, Prion 1921) and the notion of a *physical capital* that this entailed (for details and reproduction in translation of some of these proposals see Dean, Clarke and Graves, 1990).

It could be inferred that Sweeney's *reading* of the German developments was *out of context*. German *compromise* and *acquiesence* could have been mistaken by him for refinements in thinking. An alternative proposition is that it fitted in with Kester's and Schmalenbach's reliance on a "practical" solution. Notable in the literature, and in particular in Sweeney's references to it is the absence of any explicit injection of anything identified as *Limpergian thought*. That, of course, doesn't ensure that Limperg's ideas did not enter his reasoning. But it is reasonable to infer that Sweeney did not regard any such infiltration of great significance.

Only one reasonable inference can be drawn with respect to Sweeney's stabilized accounting and the Anglo-American recourse to it in the post World War II development and promotion of varieties of mechanisms by which to have accounts incorporate the financial effects of price and price-level changes: they have their strongest roots in the 1920's *Betriebswirtschaftslehre*, and not in Limperg's *Bedrijfseconomie*.

7. CONCLUSION

Often "why study history?" is asked. Such a question is always inappropriate for every study of events is, "pro facto", a study of history. Only the deliberate style of analysis undertaken and the particular insights sought differentiate history as a *discipline*, per se. It is reasonable to expect that when inflation recurs, probably early in the 1990s there will be calls for some form of CCA again, and the accounting profession will be faced once more with the task of evaluating that system of accounting. An understanding of the contextual frameworks in which its underlying ideas emerged lessens the possibility of CCA being attributed unwarranted authority and refinement.

There is unquestionable diversity in the interpretation of Schmidt's and Limperg's ideas. Possibly this is due to the penchant for recourse to description by those referring to Schmidt and Limperg, rather than undertaking the task of translating the respective works and placing their themes in historical context. Schmidt's and Limperg's treatment in the English language accounting literature illustrates the need for recourse to primary sources in searching for the development of ideas. This monograph is the product, partly, of recourse to primary sources. However, recourse to secondary sources, such as Schwantag's biography of Schmidt and Burgert's analysis of Limperg's works has supplemented, helped fill the gaps in, and added a temporal dimension to, the translations of parts of the respective works of Schmidt and Limperg. A better use might thereby be made of references to those authors in the contemporary literature. In the case of Schmidt, exposure to often vague descriptions of his work, or at least, to parts of it, is considerably more extensive than might be inferred by the variable coverage of Schmidt's work in the literature. The attached translations of both authors' works and appendixes below are a source for further exploration into the *Betriebswirtschaft* and *Bedrijfseconomie* theories in general, and that of Schmidt's and Limperg's theories in particular.

With translations of primary sources, this fresh look at the background of modern CCA prescriptions imparts a sense of order into the literature, by (i) bringing forth new evidence, suggestive that as early as 1923 the essence of Schmidt's works had been published in Dutch. Recognition of the existence and the substance of the 1923 article adds support for MacDonald's claim that it was Schmidt's work, and not Limperg's, that might be regarded as the true seed of the development of the theory of current value accounting; (ii) highlighting the extent to which the features of modern current cost accounting systems (and their underlying theories) had been developed by the mid 1920s; and (iii) dispelling some myths related to the works of Schmidt and Limperg, in particular casting doubt on the suggestion that modern CCA proposals were the product of an evolutionary development. This study suggests that modified forms of CCA - the *value to the owner* variant or the *Hyde-type* containing gearing adjustments - are not the result of evolutionary developments. Rather, these tinkerings appeared in some parts of the original versions of either Limperg or Schmidt, respectively. The recent reemergence of such adjustments can be explained as attempts to placate special pleas (from various interest groups). The pleas have arisen because, in its pure physical capital maintenance form, CCA provides only a partial solution to the problems of how to account (simultaneously) for changing prices and changes in the general level of prices. Hopefully this analysis of the works of Schmidt and Limperg, should limit the possibility of unearned historical significance disturbing the course of subsequent inflation accounting debates.

APPENDICES

Appendix I

Summary Features of Major French and German Inflation Accounting Proposals 1921 - 26.

GERMANY				FRANCE			
SYSTEM TYPE	**DATE**	**AUTHOR**	**FEATURES**	**SYSTEM TYPE**	**DATE**	**AUTHOR**	**FEATURES**
[A] FORWARDS ADJUSTING STABILIZED				**[A] FORWARDS ADJUSTING STABILIZED**			
(i) Historic Cost figures indexed in equivalent paper marks at end of the period	1921	W. Mahlberg[1]	This was one of the earliest forms of indexation - only *Real* items were rescaled.	(i) Paper franc restatement of Balance Sheet items in terms of a Gold Standard Country, e.g. USA.	1926	P. Bayart[2]	This balance sheet adjustment was widely employed in France - all accounts except fixed assets and capital are divided by the international co-efficient of exchange rates between France a some gold standard country.
(ii) as per (i)	1921	E. Schmalenbach[3]	This was regarded as the first *complete* indexation method. Both *Real* and *Monetary* items were rescaled.				
[B] BACKWARDS ADJUSTING STABILIZED				**[B] BACKWARDS ADJUSTING STABILIZED**			
Goldmarkbilanz Historic cost figures were again rescaled.	1922	W. Mahlberg[4] E. Schmalenbach[5]	*Goldmarkbilanz* - which consisted of a backwards rescaling of balance sheet balances to pre war (1914) equality.	"Retrograde Method"	1926	Raffegau & Lacout[6]	Gold money correction - similar to Mahlberg's *Goldmarkbilanz*.
[C] CURRENT VALUE ACCOUNTING Organic Accounting	1921	F. Schmidt[7]	Relying on the paper mark unit of measure, balance sheet (*Real*) items were stated in terms of current costs.	**[C] MULTIPLE COLUMN REPORTING** "Four Columns - two gold/ two paper francs - all indvidual accounts are adjusted.	1924 1925	Delavelle[8] Faure[9]	- Rescaled monthly balances. - Daily rescaling, involving: (i) use of gold francs as unit of measure (ii) restatement by international co-efficient of dollar exchange (iii) Additional closing entries.

GERMANY				FRANCE			
SYSTEM TYPE	DATE	AUTHOR	FEATURES	SYSTEM TYPE	DATE	AUTHOR	FEATURES
[D] MULTIPLE COLUMN REPORTING			Both paper mark and Gold marks were provided.	[D] PAPER FRANC ACCOUNTING (i) "Progressive Method"	1926	Leger[10]	Three adjustments: (i) Depreciation based on the gold equivalent of fixed assets (ii) COGS based on replacement cost. (iii) A form of Working Capital Adjustment.
				(ii) "Heterogeneous Method"	1926	Fain[11]	- A combination of gold franc and the paper franc methods.
[E] RESTATEMENTS USING OTHER CURRENCIES AS MEASURING UNIT	1923	Berliner[12] Blume[13] Sträter[14]					

NOTES: Based on Max J. Wasserman, "Accounting Practice in France During the Period of Monetary Inflation (1919-1927)", *The Accounting Review*, March 1931, pp.1-32.

1 W. Mahlberg, *Bilanztechnik und Bewertung bei schwankender Währung*, Leipzig Gloeckner, 1921 1st Edition.
2 P. Bayart, *Les effets de l'inflation le bilan au point de vue l'inflation: fiscal*, Paris, Sirey 1926.
3 E. Schmalenbach, *Geldwertausgleich in der Bilanzmässigen Erfolgsrechnung*, Leipzig Gloeckner, 1921.
4 W. Mahlberg, *Bilanztechnik und Bewertung bei schwankender Währung*, Leipzig Gloeckner, 1922 2nd Edition.
5 E. Schmalenbach, *Goldmarkbilanz*, Berlin Springer 1922.
6 P. C. Raffegau & A. Lacout, *Etablissement des bilans en francs - or*, Paris, Payot, 1926.
7 F. Schmidt, *Die organische Bilanz im Rahmen der Wirtschaft*, G. A. Gloeckner, Leipzig, 1921.
8 E. Delavelle, *La Comptabilité en francs - or*, Paris, Nouvelle Libraire Nationale, 1924.
9 G. Faure, *Bilans et Comptes en Francs - or*, Paris, Nouvelle Libraire Nationale, 1924.
10 F. Leger, *Le redressement des bilans en francs-papier*, Paris, Editions Experta, 1926.
11 G. Fain, *Comment se défendre contre l'inflation*, Paris, Editions Experta, 1926.
12 S. Berliner, *Organisation und Betrieb des Importgeschäfts in China*, Hansche Buchhandlung, Hannover, 1920.
13 B. Blume, *Die Valutarische Goldmarkbuchführung*, Verlag für Wirtschaft und Verkehr, Stuttgart, 1923.
14 L. Sträter, *Papiermark und Sachwertbuchhaltung*, G. A. Gloeckner, Leipzig, 1923.

APPENDIX "II"

BIBLIOGRAPHY OF GERMAN PUBLICATIONS ON ACCOUNTING AND (HYPER)INFLATION

TABLE II.1
ARTICLES 1908-30 (CHRONOLOGICAL ORDER)

Notes:

ZfB = *Zeitschrift für Betriebswirtschaft* (F. Schmidt, founder and editor, 1924-50.

ZfhF = *Zeitschrift für handelswissenschaftliche Forschung* (Eugen Schmalenbach, founder and editor, 1906-33; from 1933 edited by Ernst Walb; since 1964 called *Zeitschrift für betriebswirtschaftliche Forschung*

ZfHwuHp = *Zeitschrift für Handelswissenschaft und Handelspraxis*

Author	Title and Source	Translation
Eugen Schmalenbach	"Die Abschreibung", *ZfhF*, 1908-9, pp.81-9	"Depreciation"
Eugen Schmalenbach	"Über den Zweck der Bilanz", *Zfhf*, 1910, pp.379-88	"The Purpose of Accounting (or Balance Sheets"
Erwin Geldmacher	"Bilanzmässige Buchhaltung: ein kritischer Beitrag zur Methodik und zur Theorie der doppelten Buchführung", *Handelsschullehrer Zeitung*, No. 37, 1914, pp.393-6, 401-5, 417f., 425-9	"Balance Sheet Bookkeeping: A Critical Contribution to the Method and Theory of Double Entry Bookkeeping"
Eugen Schmalenbach	"Theorie der Erfolgsbilanz", *Zfhf*, 1915-16, pp.379-82	"Theory of Profit Accounting"
Robert Stern	"Substanzwert" in *Buchhaltungslexikon*, Verlag Leopold Weiss, Bd 1, 1917, pp.12-15, Wien	"Substantive Values"
Robert Stern	"Abschreibung" in *Buchhaltungslexikon*, Vol. 1, Verlag Leopold Weiss, Wien, 1917, pp.54-86	"Depreciation"
Eugen Schmalenbach	"Grundlagen dynamischer Bilanzlehre", *ZfhF*, 1919, pp.1-60, 65-101	"Basics of Dynamic Accounting"
Willi Prion	"Abschreibungen und Geldentwertung", *Plutus*, 15 September 1920, pp.285-8	"Depreciation and Changing Money Values"
Gustav von Kast	"Falsche Bilanzierungsmethoden seit der Valutäntwertung", *Berliner Tageblatt*, 16 September 1920	"False Balance Sheet Methods Since Currency- Depreciation"
Willi Prion	"Ersatzanschaffungen und Neuanlagen", *Plutus*, 27 September 1920	"Replacement Acquisitions and New Plant"

TABLE II.1 - Continued
ARTICLES 1908-30 (CHRONOLOGICAL ORDER)

Author	Title and Source	Translation
Erwin Geldmacher	"Bilanzsorgen" *Industrie- und Handelszeitung*, 1920, pp.364, 378, 385, 392, 398, 406	"Balance Sheet Worries"
Walter Rathenau	"Produktionspolitik" *Vossische Zeitung*, 15 September 1920	"Production Policy"
Walter Rathenau	"Über die Veröffentlichungen von Prion und Rathenau", *Frankfurter Zeitung*, 24 September 1920	"On the Publications of Prion and Rathenau"
Gustav von Kast	"Falsche Industriekalkulation", *Industrie- und Handelszeitung*, October 1920	"False Business Cost Estimation"
Theodor Schulz	"Falsche Industriekalkulation", *Industrie- und Handelszeitung*, October 1920	"False Business Cost Estimation"
Georg von Schlesinger	"Abschreibung oder Ersatz?" *Werkstatt-Technik*, 1 October 1920, pp.505-6	"Depreciation or Replacement?"
Richard Buxbaum	"Ersatzanschaffungen und Neuanlagen unter dem Einfluß der Geldentwertung', *Plutus*, 27 October 1920, pp.334-7	"Replacement Costs and New Plant under the Influence of Inflation"
Richard Buxbaum	"Abschreibung, Erneuerung und Geldwert", *Die Bank*, No. 13, November 1920, pp.686-96	"Depreciation, Renewal and Money Values"
Richard Buxbaum	"Der Einfluß der Geldentwertung auf die Kalkulation", *Industrie- und Handelszeitung*, December 1920	"The Influence of Changing Money Values on Cost Estimation"
Ludwig Klein	"Einfluß der sinkenden Kaufkraft des Geldes auf Kalkulation, Bilanz und Steuer", *ZfHuHp*, 1920	"The Influence of Changes in the Purchasing Power of Money on Cost Calculation, Accounting and Tax"
Fritz Haussmann	"Steuerfreiheit für Erneuerungsfonds", *Bank-Archiv*, 1920, p.115	"Tax Exemption for Renewal Funds"
Julius Flechtheim	"Steuerfreiheit für Erneuerungsfonds", *Bank-Archiv*, 1920, p.154	"Tax Exemption for Renewal Funds"
Walter Mahlberg	"Wirtschaftsrelativität", *ZfHwuHp*, 1920-1, pp.133-6, 182-6, 195-7	"Economic Relativity"
Felix Pinner	"Abschreibung und Erneuerung", *Berliner Tageblatt*, 19-20 February 1921	"Depreciation and Renewal"
George Strutz	"Zur Frage der Steuerfrei Wert-berichtigungskonten", *Frankfurter Zeitung*, 10 March 1921	"On the Problem of Tax-Free Valuation Reserve Accounts"
H. Huebner	"Nachkriegsbilanzen", *ZfHwuHp*, 4 July 1921, pp.8ff.	"Post War Accounting (Balance Sheets)"
Eugen Schmalenbach	"Der Geldwertausgleich in der bilanzmässigen Erfolgsrechnung", *ZfhF*, Vol. 15, 1921, pp.401-17	"Compensating for Money Changes in Balance Sheets Appropriate for Income Accounting"

TABLE II.1 - Continued
ARTICLES 1908-30 (CHRONOLOGICAL ORDER)

Author	Title and Source	Translation
Gustav Nimax	"Quantitative Kalkulation und technische Buchführung", *ZfHwuHp*, 5 August 1922, pp.98n.	"Quantitative Cost Estimation and Technical Bookkeeping"
Fritz Schmidt	"Gewinn und Scheingewinn der Unternehmung", *Zeitschrift für Aktienwesen*, Vol. 32, 1922, pp.50-56	"Proper and Fictitious Business Profits"
Fritz Schmidt	"Bilanzberichtigung durch Indexziffern (Goldmarkbilanz)", *Zeitschrift für Aktienwesen*, Vol. 32, 1922, pp.484-9	"Correcting Balance Sheets Using Index Numbers"
Friedrich Lehmannn	"Der Einfluß der Geldwertveränderungen auf das Betriebsleben", *ZfHwuHp*, 8 November, 1922, pp.73 ff.	"The Influence of Changing Money Values on Business"
Fritz Schmidt	"Geldentwertung und Bilanz" in F. Schmidt, G. Strutz and R. Fischer (eds), *Geldentwertung und Unternehmung*, Berlin, 1922, pp.1-39	"Currency Depreciation and Accounting"
Georg Strutz	"Geldentwertung und Steuerrecht", in F. Schmidt, G. Strutz and R. Fischer (eds), *Geldentwertung und Unternehmung*, Berlin, 1922, pp.40ff.	"Currency Depreciation and Taxation Law"
Alfons Marichal	"Die Indexziffern", *ZfhF*, 1923, pp.70-80, & 172-225	"Index Numbers"
Fritz Schmidt	"Die Umwertung der Bilanzen auf Neuwährung", *Zeitschrift für Gesellschaftswesen*, 33, 1923, pp.381-7	"Balance Sheet Reevaluation due to the New Currency,
Ernst Walb	"Zur Theorie der Erfolgsrechnung", *ZfhF*, 1923, pp.416-43	"About the Theory of Profit Accounting"
Fritz Schmidt	"Scheingewinn, Kalkulation und Bilanz", *Mitteilgn des dt. Hauptverb der Industrie*, 1923, pp.383-87, 869-74, 905-11	"Fictitious Profits, Cost Estimation and Balance Sheets"
Editorial	"Wertbeständige Anlage der Dividendenbeträge", *Frankfurter Zeitung*, 22 December 1923	"Stable Investment of Dividends"
Ew. Brenken	"Indexbuchführung, Abstimmung gemischter Bilanzen und Gewinn und Verlustrechnung bei schwankender Währung", *ZfHwuHp*, 8 November 1923	"Index bookkeeping: Harmonization of the Balance Sheet and the Profit and Loss Account in Times of an Unstable Currency"
Fritz Schmidt	"Die neuen Goldmarkbilanzen und Goldmark Buchführung", *ZfB*, 1924, pp.2-34	"The New Goldmark Balance Sheets and Gold-Mark Bookkeeping"
Alfred Isaac	"Anschaffungswertbilanz und Tageswertbilanz", *ZfB*, 1924, pp.246-65	"Historic Cost and Current Value Accounting"

TABLE II.1 - Continued
ARTICLES 1908-30 (CHRONOLOGICAL ORDER)

Author	Title and Source	Translation
Josef Hellauer	"Kalkulation nach den Wiederbeschaffungs - oder nach den tatsächlichen Gestehungskosten", *ZfHwuHp*, 2 May 1924, p.40 ff.	"Cost Estimation with Replacement Costs - or Actual Product Costs"
Herman Grossmann	"Die ausschliesslich wertangleichende oder statische Abschreibung", *ZfB*, 1924, pp.75-82	"Exclusive (Explicit) Value Adjusting or Static Depreciation"
Ernst Walb	"Tageswert oder Anschaffungswert in der Bilanz", *ZfhF*, 1924, pp.228-40	"Current Values or Purchase (Historic) Values in Balance Sheets"
Editorial	"Die Generalversammlung der Deutschen Bank", *Berliner Tageblatt*, 28 June 1924	"The General Meeting of the Deutsche Bank"
Fritz Schmidt	"Unternehmungswert und Kapitalbemessung in der Goldmarkbilanz", *ZfB*, 1924, pp.209-20	"Enterprise Values and Capitalization in Goldmark Balance Sheets"
Herman Grossmann	"Die Abschreibung in ihrer Beziehung zu den betriebswirtschaftlich wichtigsten Werttypen", *ZfB*, 1925, pp.20-27	"Depreciation and its Relation to the Most Important Value Types of Business Administration"
Fritz Schmidt	"Kalkulation und Beschäftigungsgrad", *ZfB*, 1925, pp.378-82	"Cost Estimation and the Degree of Activity Levels"
Willi Prion	"Grundsätzliches zur Frage des Kreditwuchers", *ZfB*, 1925, pp.1 15-27, & 209-219	"The Fundamental Issues about Profiteering from Credit"
Eugen Schigut	"Das österreichische Goldbilanz Problem", *ZfB*, 1925, pp.149-56	"The Austrian Gold Accounting Problem"
Ernst Walb	"Zur Frage des Bilanzbegriffes", *ZfB*, 1925, pp.27-37	"Questioning Balance Sheet Understanding"
Anton Haar	"Die Geldwertveränderungen und ihr Einfluß auf die transitorischen Posten und Antizipationen", *ZfB*, 1925, pp.353-66, 414-33	"The Change in the Value of Money and its Influence on the Existing and Projected Position"
Willi Prion	"Auslands-Kredite und Inflation", *Bank - Archiv: Zeitschrift für Bank - und Börsenwesen*, 1 December 1925, pp.69-74	"Foreign Credit and Inflation"
Fritz Schmidt	"Die Anpassung der Betriebe auf die Wirtschaftslage", *ZfB*, 1926, pp.85-108	"The Adaptation of Business to the Economic Situation"
Fritz Schmidt	"Gewinn und Bilanzwert", *Het Internationaal Accountantscongres*, 1926, pp.378 - 436	"Profit and Balance Sheet Value"

TABLE II.1 - Continued
ARTICLES 1908-30 (CHRONOLOGICAL ORDER)

Author	Title and Source	Translation
Fritz Schmidt	"Gewinn und Bilanzwert", *ZfB*, 1926, pp.813-25, 906-20	"Profit and Balance Sheet Value"
Fritz Schmidt	"Die um ersparte Zinsen steigende Abschreibung", *ZfB*, 1927, pp.816-39	"Increasing Interest in Depreciation"
Franz Angelberger	"Das Problem des Kalkulationswerts vom Standpunkt der ökonomischen Theorie" *ZfhF*, 1927, pp.166-77, 227-37, 241-62	"The Problem of Estimating Cost from an Economic Theory Perspective"
Alfred Scholz	"Scheingewinne und Scheinverluste bei stabiler Währung", *ZfB*, 1927, pp.771-9	"Fictitious (paper) Profits and Fictitious Losses with a Stable Currency"
Fritz Schmidt	"Die Industriekonjunktur - ein Rechenfehler!", *ZfB*, 1927, pp.1-29, 87-114, 185-99	"Business Cycles in Industry - an Accounting Miscalculation!"
Fritz Schmidt	"Indexziffern", *Handwörterbuch der Betriebswirtschaftslehre*, 1927, pp.274-82; 191"; Vol. 2, pp.352-60	"Index Numbers"
Eugen Schmalenbach	"Zur Reform der Aktienbilanz", *Zfhf*, 1927, pp.49-58	"About the Reform of the Joint Stock Company Accounting"
O. Schwinger	"Ausbau der organischen Bilanz", *ZfB*, 1927, pp.282-97	"Elaborating on Organic Accounting"
Fritz Schmidt	"Ist Wertänderung am ruhenden Vermögen Gewinn oder Verlust?", *ZfB*, 1928, pp.1-19	"Do Holding Gains or Losses Generate Profit or Loss?"
Ewald Auferman	"Die Scheingewinne in französischen Steuerbilanzen", *ZfB*, 1928, pp.591 -9	"Fictitious Profits in French Balance Sheets for Taxation,
Fritz Schmidt	"Die verkrüppelte Erfolgsrechnung", *ZfB*, 1928, pp.81-99	"The Distorted Income Accounting"
H. Hausner	"Zum Problem der richtigen Erfolgsermittlung", *ZfHwuHp*, 1928, pp.57-62, 88-94, 108-116	"About the Problem of Determining the Correct Profit"
Fritz Schmidt	"Bilanz und Steuer", *ZfB*, 1928, pp.561-75, 641-59	"Balance Sheets and Taxation"
Fritz Schmidt	"Preispolitik", *ZfB*, 1928, pp.641-66, 731-54.	"Price Politics"
E. Mueller	"Zum jetzigen Stand der Goldbilanz frage in Europa", *Schweizerische Juristenzeitung*, 15 June 1929, p.369	"The Current Status of Gold Balance Sheets in Europe"
Fritz Schmidt	"Theorie und Praxis der Preis- und Lohsenkung", *ZfB*, 1930, pp.699-702.	"The Theory and Practice of Reduced Prices and Wages"

TABLE II.2

BOOKS 1910-28 (CHRONOLOGICAL ORDER)	
Author	**Title and Source**
Pawel Ciompa	*Grundriss einer Ökonometrie und die auf der Nationalökonomie aufgebaute natuürliche Theorie der Buchhaltung - Ein auf Grund neuer ökonometrischer Gleichungen erbrachter Beweis, dass alle heutigen Bilanzen falsch dargesellt werden*, C. E. Pöschel, Lemberg, 1910
Ilmar Kovero	*Die Bewertung der Vermögensgegenstände in den Jahresbilanzen der privaten Unternehmungen mit besonderer Berücksichtigung der nicht realisierten Verluste und Gewinne*, Berlin, 1912; Helsinki, 1911
Emil Fäs	*Die Berücksichtigung der Wertverminderung des stehenden Kapitals in den Jahresbilanzen der Erwerbswirtschaften*, H. Laupp, Tübingen, 1913
Erwin Geldmacher	*Bilanzmässige Buchführung*, Die Handelsschullehrer Zeitung, Berlin, 1914
Irving Fisher	*Die Kaufkraft des Geldes*, Berlin, 1916
Eugen Schmalenbach	*Dynamische Bilanzen*, Westdeutscher Verlag, Köln, 1919
Richard Passow	*Inflation und Geldentwertung*, Berlin 1919
Willi Prion	*Inflation und Geldwertung: Finanzielle Massnahmen zum Abbau der Preise Gutachten erstattet dem Reichsfinanzsministerium*, Julius Springer, Berlin, 1919
	Die Finanzierungen und Bilanz wirtschaftlicher Betriebe: unter dem Einfluß der Geldentwertung, 1921, Verlag von Julius Springer, Berlin, 1921
Manfred Berliner	*Die Bewertung des Vermögens für die Bilanz. Ein Ratgeber für praktische Kaufleute, Juristen Steuerbeamte*, Hahn, Hannover, 1920
Eugen Schigut	*Die Frage der Bewertung in der Bilanz*, Waldheim Eberle Verlag, Wien 1920
Walter le Coutre	*Bilanzen, Anschauungsstoffe aus dem Gebiete der kaufmännischen Wirtschaft*, G.A. Gloeckner, Leipzig, 1921

TABLE II.2 Continued

BOOKS 1910-28 (CHRONOLOGICAL ORDER)

Author	Title and Source
Hermann Grossmann	*Abschreibung und Steuer unter besonderer Berücksichtigung der neuen Abschreibungsfragen*, Spaeth und Linde, Berlin, 1921
Helmut Heberle	*Geldwertänderung und Bilanz*, Verlag Muth, Stuttgart, 1921
Emil Hofmann	*Indexziffern im Inland und im Ausland*, G. Braun, Karlsruhe, 1921
Rudolf Löwenstein	*Kalkulationsgewinn und bilanzmässige Erfolgsrechnung in ihren gegenseitigen Beziehungen*, Leipzig, 1922
Walter Mahlberg	"Bilanztechnik und Bewertung bei schwankender Währung", *Betriebs- und Finanzwirtschaft(BuFF)*, 1921, Monograph No.10, G.A. Gloeckner, Leipzig 1921; 2nd edn, 1922; 3rd edn, 1923
Fritz Napthali	*Wertschwankungen und Bilanz*, Buchverlag Frankfurter Zeitung, Frankfurt, 1921
Heinrich Sommerfeld	*Die Wertansätze in der Inventor*, Sammlung Grossmann, Bucherei für Bilanz und Steuer Industriewertung, Spaeth und Linde, Berlin, 1921
Willi Prion	*Die Finanzierung und Bilanz wirtschaftlicher Betriebe unter dem Einfluß der Geldentwertung*, Julius Springer, Berlin, 1921
Eugen Schmalenbach	*Geldwertausgleich in der bilanzmässigen Erfolgsrechnung*, G.A. Gloeckner, Leipzig, 1921
Fritz Schmidt	"Die organische Bilanz im Rahmen der Wirtschaft", *BuFF*, Monograph No.14, G.A. Gloeckner, Leipzig, 1921 (2nd edn, 1922)
Ernest Schmikl	*Bilanzen und Geldentwertung*, Selbstverlag, Wien, 1921
Eugen Schigut	*Abschreibungen und Erneuerungsfonds*, Peter Verlag, Wien, 1921
Ernst Walb	*Das Problem der Scheingewinne*, Walter Momber, Freiburg im Breisgau, 1921
Alois Zeiler, Adolf Mayer & Rudolf Wassermann	*Die Geldentwertung als Kredit-, Kalkulations- und Besteuerungsproblem*, Schweitzer Verlag, München, 1921

TABLE II.2 Continued

BOOKS 1910-28 (CHRONOLOGICAL ORDER)

Author	Title and Source
Rudolf Wasserman	*Die steuerfreien Erneuerungsrücklagen der Abschreibungen wegen Überteuerung*, Schweitzer Verlag, München, 1921
Richard Buxbaum	*Die Anlagewerte in der Bilanz bei schwankender Währung*, Frankfurter Societäts-Druckerei, Frankfurt, 1922
Doderlein	*Die Erfassung der Sachwerte industrieller Unternehmungen und ihre Abschreibung*, Karlsruhe Tageblatt 1922, Nr 326, 329 & 330 (inzwishen als Brochüre erschienen)
Irving Fisher	*Purchasing Power of Money*, Macmillan, New York, 1911, (Berlin 1922)
Wilhelm Kalveram	*Die kaufmännische Rechnungsführung unter dem Einfluß der Geldentwertung*, Spaeth und Linde, Berlin, 1922
Walter Mahlberg	*Die Notwendigkeit der Goldmarkverrechnung im Verkehr*, G. A. Gloeckner, Leipzig, 1922
Josef Nertinger	*Goldmark-Buchführung und Goldmark-Bilanzen, ihre Durchführung und Aufstellung*, 2nd rev. edn, Muth, Stuttgart, 1922
Willi Prion	*Die Finanzpolitik der Unternehmung (im Zeichen der Scheingewinne). Zwei Vorträge über Scheingewinne*, 2nd edn, Gustav Fischer, Jena, 1922
Johann F. Schaer	*Buchhaltung und Bilanz auf wirtschaftlicher, rechtlicher und mathematischer Grundlage*, 5th edn, Berlin, 1922
Schaefer	*Klassische Valuta-Stabilisierungen und ihre Lehren für die Markstabilisierung*, 3rd edn, Verlag C. Boysen, Hamburg 1922
Eugen Schmalenbach	*Zwei Vorträge über Scheingewinne*, 2nd edn, Julius Springer, Jena, 1922
Eugen Schmalenbach	*Die steuerliche Behandlung der Scheingewinne Zwei Vorträge über Scheingewinne*, Gustav Fischer, Jena, 1922, pp.1-75

TABLE II.2 Continued

BOOKS 1910-28 (CHRONOLOGICAL ORDER)

Author	**Title and Source**
Eugen Schmalenbach	*Goldmarkbilanzen*, Verlag Julius Springer, Berlin 1922,
Walter Sterz	*Die Ausscheidung der Scheingewinne*, ABC - Verlag, Leipzig 1922
Leo Sträter	*Papiermark und Sachwertbuchführung*, G.A. Gloeckner, Leipzig 1922
Wilhelm Thiele	*Marktpreis und Übergewinn*, Spaeth und Linde, Berlin 1923
Andreas Voigt	*Der Einfluß des veränderlichen Geldwertes auf die wirtschaftliche Rechnungsführung*, Mitteilungen der Gesellschaft für wirtschaftliche Ausbildung, Frankfurt am Main 1922
Otto Warneyer	*Geldentwertung und Vertragserfüllung*, Spaeth und Linde, Berlin, 1922
Theodor Althoff	*Goldmarkrechnung im Einzelhandel*, Frankfurt am Main, 1923
Gerhard Blume	*Die valutarische Goldmarkbuchführung*, Verlag für Wirtschaft und Verkehr, Stuttgart, 1923
Richard Fischer	*Goldmarkbuchführung - Goldmarkbilanz*, Spaeth und Linde, Berlin, 1923
Wilhelm Gerloff	*Steuerwirtschaft und Steuerrecht im Zeichen der Geldentwertung*, 2nd edn, Spaeth und Linde, Berlin, 1923
Erwin Geldmacher	*Wirtschaftsunruhe und Bilanz 1. Teil: Grundlagen und Technik der bilanzmässigen Erfolgsrechnung*, Springer, Berlin, 1923
Geiler	*Geldentwertung als Gesetzgebungsproblem*, J. Bensheimer, Mannheim, 1923
Harburger	*Gleitende Währung*, Verlag Dunker und Humblodt, München, 1923
Heymann	*Die Sachlebensversicherung und ihren Einfluß auf des Wirtschaftsleben*, Vertag Hartung, Hamburg, 1923
Kurt Hellriegel	*Der Scheingewinn bei Warenumsätzen*, Spaeth und Linde, Berlin, 1923

TABLE II.2 Continued

BOOKS 1910-28 (CHRONOLOGICAL ORDER)	
Author	**Title and Source**
Walter Mahlberg	"Goldkreditverkehr und Goldmarkbuchführung", *Betriebswirtschaftliche Zeitfragen*, herausgegeben von der Gesellschaft für wirtschaftliche, Monograph No.4 Julius Springer, Berlin, 1923
Oskar Mügel	*Geldentwertung und Gesetzgebung*, Spaeth und Linde, Berlin, 1923
	Die Goldmark als Rechnungswert, Vahlen, Berlin 1923
Wilhelm Osbahr & Heinrich Nicklisch	*Die Bilanz vom Standpunkt der Unternehmung*, (3rd edn 1923), Haude & Spenerische Buchhandlung, Berlin-Leipzig, 1913
Fritz Schmidt	*Der Wiederbeschaffungspreis des Umsatztages in Kalkulation und Volkswirtschaft*, Spaeth und Linde, Berlin, 1923
Heinrich Sommerfeld	*Die Goldmarkbuchhaltung, Goldwährung, Geldentwertung und Assignate*, Sächsische Industrie, 1923 Nr 22 Ihre Grundlagen und Technik, 2nd edn, Spaeth und Linde, Berlin, 1923
Leo Sträter	*Papiermark und Sachwertbuchhaltung*, Leipzig, 1923
Wilhelm Thiele	*Wiederbeschaffungspreis und Preiswucher*, Spaeth und Linde, Berlin, 1923
Reinhold Wolff	*Die Goldwertrechnung als gesetzgeberische Massnahmegegen die Wirkungen des Währungsverfalls im Privatrecht*, Georg Stilke, Berlin, 1923
Richard Fischer	*Goldmarkbuchführung - Goldmarkbilanz*, 2nd rev. edn, Berlin, 1924
Friedrich Klausing	*Die Goldmarkbilanz*, Verlagsgesellschaft, Berlin 1924
Wilhelm Kalveram	*Praxis der Goldmarkbilanzierung*, Spaeth und Linde, Berlin 1924 (Goldmarkbilanzierung und Kapital-umstellung), 2nd edn, 1925
Gustav Wellensten & Walter Loewenfeld	*Das österreichische Goldbilanzgesetz*, Wien, 1925
Ludwig Quassowski & Walter Susat	*Durchführungsverordnungen*, 2nd edn, J. Bensheimer Verlag, Mannheim-Leipzig-Berlin, 1923

TABLE II.2 Continued

BOOKS 1910-28 (CHRONOLOGICAL ORDER)

Author	Title and Source
Richard Rosendorff	*Goldbilanzierungsgesetz Systematische Darstellung der Verordnung über Goldbilanzen*, 2nd rev. edn, Spaeth und Linde, Berlin, 1924
Fritz Schmidt	*Bilanzwert, Bilanzgewinn und Bilanzumwertung*, Spaeth und Linde, Leipzig, 1924
Fritz Schmidt	*Scheingewinn, Kalkulation und Bilanz*, Teplitz-Schonau, 1924
Heinrich Sommerfeld	*Die Goldmarkbuchhaltung, ihre Grundlagen und Technik*, Berlin, 1924
Hermann Grossmann	*Abschreibung und Steuer*, Spaeth und Linde, Berlin, 1925
Hermann Grossmann	*Die Abschreibung vom Standpunkt der Unternehmung, inbesondere ihre Bedeutung als Kostenfaktor*, Spaeth und Linde, Berlin, 1925
Walter Mahlberg	*Die Tageswerte in der Bilanz*, G.A. Gloeckner, Leipzig, 1925
Arthur Nussbaum	*Das Geld in Theorie und Praxis des deutschen und ausländischen Rechts*, J.C.B. Möhr, Tübingen, 1925
Richard Malteur	*Die Zwischenbilanz als Mittel der Kontrolle und Betriebsleitung*, Spaeth und Linde, Berlin, 1925
Richard Rosendorff	*Das österreichische Goldbilanzgesetz*, Wien, 1925
& Emil Hofmansthal	
Karl Sewering	*Die Einheitsbilanz Die Überbrueckung des Gegensatzes zwischen statischer und dynamischer Bilanzlehre*, G.A. Gloeckner, Leipzig, 1925
Heinz Auer	*Die Praxis der Bewertung in der Goldmarkbilanz*, Robert Noske, Leipzig, 1926
Walter le Coutre	*Die Praxis der Bilanzkritik, Vols 1 & 2*, Spaeth und Linde, Berlin, 1926
Karl Hax	*Der Gewinnbegriff in der Betriebswirtschaftslehre*, G.A. Gloeckner, Leipzig, 1926
Max Gurtler	*Schweizerische Bilanz unter dem Einfluß von Konjunktur und Scheingewinn*, BuFF, Monograph No.20, G.A. Gloeckner, Berlin, 1927

TABLE II.2 Continued

BOOKS 1910-28 (CHRONOLOGICAL ORDER)

Author	Title and Source
Gottfried Haberler	*Der Sinn der Indexzahlen*, J.C.B. Möhr, Tübingen, 1927
Max Lion	*Wahre Bilanzen: Ein Beitrag zur Vereinheitlichung von Handelsbilanz und Steuerbilanz*, Carl Heymann, Berlin, 1927
Walter Mahlberg	*Konjunkturbeeinflußung durch Kalkulations- und Kreditpolitik*, G.A. Gloeckner, Leipzig, 1927
Heinz Mohr	*Bilanz und immaterielle Werte*, Spaeth und Linde, Berlin, 1927
Fritz Schmidt	*Die Industriekonjunktur-ein Rechenfehler!*, Berlin und Wien, 1927
Ernst Wagemann	*Konjunkturlehre*, Reimar Hobbing, Hamburg, 1928
Ludwig von Mises	*Geldwertstabilisierung und Konjunktur-politik*, Julius Springer Jena, 1928
Fritz Schmidt	*Kalkulation und Preispolitik*, G.A. Gloeckner, Berlin, 1929
Fritz Schmidt	*Die organische Tageswertbilanz*, G.A. Gloeckner, Leipzig, 1929
Ernst Wagemann	*Einführung in die Konjunkturlehre*, Quelle und Meyer, Leipzig, 1929.

TABLE II.3

MISCELLANEOUS PUBLICATIONS 1924-52	
Author	**Title and Source**
Unpublished Dissertations	
Richard Padberg	*Der Wiederbeschaffungspreis in Theorie, Praxis und Recht*, Frankfurt, 6 November 1924
Irmgard Palm	*Der Gewinnbegriff in der modernen Betriebswirtschafts -wissenschaft auf Grundlage der Theorien von Schmalenbach, Mahlberg und Schmidt*, Frankfurt, 10 July 1925
Heinrich Lieboner	*Wertgleichheit und Konjunktur nach Vorkriegsbilanzen*, Frankfurt am Main, 22 July 1926
Johannes Anger	*Die Bewertung des Betriebsvermögens nach dem Einkommens steuergestz vom 10 August 1925*, Leipzig, 1926
Anger	*Bilanz und Konjunktur*, Frankfurt, 1927
Kramer	*Konjunktur und Bilanz in der deutschen Schaumweinindustrie*, Frankfurt, 1928
Biographical Data	
Alfred Isaac	"Fritz Schmidt, Forscher und Persönlichkeit", *Zeitschrift für handelswissenschaftliche Forschung*, 1950, pp.93-6
Karl Schwantag	"Fritz Schmidts wissenschaftliches Werk", *Zeitschrift für Betriebswirtschaft, (ZfB)*, January 1951, pp.1-14
Reinhold Sellien	"Professor Schmidt und Prof. Kalveram zum Gedächtnis - Aus meinen persönlichen Erinnerungen", *ZfB*, January 1952, pp.121-4
Alfred Isaac	"Theorie der Betriebswirtschaft und allgemeine Wirtschaftstheorie", *ZfB*, January 1952, pp.125-34
F. Henzel	"Gegenswartsprobleme im Lichte der organischen Bilanzlehre", *ZfB*, January 1952, pp. 135-42.

APPENDIX III

COMPARATIVE ANANLYSIS OF DIE ORGANISCHE TRAGESWERTBILANZ (EDITIONS 1,2,3)

SECTION NO	SECTION HEADING	1929 Page Ref.	SECTION NO	SECTION HEADING	1921 Page Ref.	SECTION NO	SECTION HEADING	1922 Page Ref.	Articles pertaining to Section, written after 1st Edition	Comments re developments, if any, from the 1st Edition
I	Die Grundlagen der Marktwirtschaft	1-29	I	As per 1929	1-34	I	As per 1921	1-37		Pages 1-44 of this Section in 1929, contain only very minor alterations to the corresponding sections of the 1st & 2nd editions.
II	Die Grundsatze der organischen Tageswertbilanz	30-89	II	Die organische Bilanz	35-53		Die organische Bialnz	38-54		
A	Die Unternehmung in Marktwirtschaft	30-53	A	As per 1929	35-53	A	As per 1921	38-54		Virtually verbatim from 1st to 3rd editions.
B	Gewinn und Bilanzwert	54-81							"Gewinn und Bilanzwert" an article by the same title, orginally written for 2nd International Congress, 1926.	Subsection 'B' of Section II contains new material on "Profit and Balance Sheet. Values". It is virtually verbatim from material written for the 1926 Conference in Amsterdam. Subsequently it appeared in *ZfB* 1926, pp.813-825 & 906-920. It has been claimed by [Macdonald (1977)] that this article significantly influenced Philip's accounting systems. The ideas in this article were a spin off of earlier books by Schmidt (1923) and (1924).
C	Bilanzmethoden der Praxis	82-84	B	Die bisherige Gewinnermittlung und Vermögensrechung in der Unternehmung		B	As per 1921	57-61 54-57		Virtually verbatim from 1st to 3rd editions.
D	Die organische Bilanzauffassung	84-89	C	As per 1929	59-62	C	As per 1921	62-65		Virtually verbatim from 1st to 3rd edition.

COMPARATIVE ANALYSIS OF DIE ORGANISCHE TAGESWERTBILANZ (EDITIONS 1,2,3)

NO	SECTION HEADING	1929 Page Ref.	NO	SECTION HEADING	1921 Page Ref.	NO	SECTION HEADING	1922 Page Ref.	Articles pertaining to Section, written after 1st Edition	Comments re developments, if any, from the 1st Edition
III	Die organische Vermögensrechnung	90-138	D	Die Vermögens-rechnumg	63-99	D	As per 1921	66-107		Pages 90-138 are similar to to the 1st & 2nd editions. One subsection, "Die Vermögensrechnung die Anlagwerte", was substantially reduced (from 12-6 pages) while the sub-section on Depreciation was progressively increased from 6 pp. in 1921 (16 pp. in 1922) to 54 (pp.176-229) in 1929. A new section, "Immaterielle Werte in Der Bilanz", appeared in the 1929 edition.
IV	Die organische Erfolgsrechnung	139-272	E	As per 1929	100-119	E	As per 1921	108-164	"Die um ersparte Zinsen steigende Abschreibung" *ZfB*, 1927 pp.816-839. "Die verkruppelte Erfolgsrechnung", ZfB, 1928 pp.81-99.	Schmidt's section on "organic [dynamic] profit accounting" was substantially enlarged following the 1st Edition. This reflected the trend in German accounting thought, moving towards the dynamic from the static balance sheet approach - as well as Schmidt's particular emphasis on *profit* and *maintenance of productive capacity*. Regarding the latter, the article "Increasing Interest on Depreciation", is reproduced verbatim, reflecting depreciation's importance. Discussion on this matter increased from 7 pages (80-87) in 1921; 16 (pp. 77-92) to over 54 (pp. 176-229) in 1929. The need for German post War recon-struction is evident. Subsection F,G,H, are new, as are the lengthy subsections on "profit", J (theory) and K (practice).

COMPARATIVE ANALYSIS OF DIE ORGANISCHE TAGESWERTBILANZ (EDITIONS 1,2,3)

SECTION NO	SECTION HEADING	1929 Page Ref.	SECTION NO	SECTION HEADING	1921 Page Ref.	SECTION NO	SECTION HEADING	1922 Page Ref.	Articles pertaining to Section, written after 1st Edition	Comments re developments, if any, from the 1st Edition
V	Einzelfragen	273-396	E	Das Ganze der organ-nische Betriebs-rechnung	120-133	E	Das Ganze der organ-ischen Betriebs-rechnung	165-181		
A	Korrektur in Bilanz und Erfolgsrechnung	273-276	a		121-125			167-170		
B	Bilanzkontinuitat	277-281								Sections B-E contain
C	Totalgewinn und Periodgewinn	282-284								material not covered
D	Die Einheitsbilanz als Vereinigung von Erfolgsbilanz	285-289								by the 1st and 2nd
E	Die Einheit von Kalkulation und Erfolgsrechnung	289-292								Editions.
F	Erfolgsrechnung nach der Index-methode	292-300							"Gewinn und Schein-gewinn der Unternehmung" *Zeit. für Aktienwesen*, 1922, pp. 50-56. "Bilanzberichtigung durch Indexziffern (Goldmarkbilanz), *Zeitschrift für Aktienwesen*, 32, 1 pp. 484-492.	This section is verbatim from the 1922 Edition (pp. 147-164), and discusses the advantages and disadvantages of indexed accounting proposals. There were numerous advocates of such adjustments (see *Appendix II*) following the inflation that accompanied the end of the Great War. Authors such as Passow, Prion, Schmalenbach, Heberle, Mahlberg, Walb, Strater, Geldmacher were to name a few. In 1922 Schmidt wrote two articles on the topic and these formed the basis of the new section (pp. 147-164) of the 2nd Edition.

COMPARATIVE ANALYSIS OF DIE ORGANISCHE TAGESWERTBILANZ (EDITIONS 1,2,3)

SECTION NO	SECTION HEADING	1929 Page Ref.	SECTION NO	SECTION HEADING	1921 Page Ref.	SECTION NO	SECTION HEADING	1922 Page Ref.	Articles pertaining to Section, written after 1st Edition	Comments re developments, if any, from the 1st Edition
G	Die Technik der organischen Technik Wertberichtigung	301-304								Sections G & H are additional to the 1st and 2nd Editions.
H	Ist Wertänderung am ruhenden Vermögen Gewinn?	305-324							Article of the same title, *ZfB*, 1928 pp. 1-19.	The seemingly dominant issues of the 1920's [in the USA and Europe], Depreciation and Appreciation are discussed.
I									A mystery section.	It does not appear in the text.
J	Bilanz und Konjunktur	325-352							"Die Industriekonjunktur - ein Rechenfehler!" *ZfB*, 1927 pp 1-27, 87-114, 165-199.	
K	Bilanz und Recht	353-356	d	Organik und Recht	126-127	d	Organik und Recht	171-172		
L	Tageswertrechnung und Preisregelung	357-358	f	Organik und Preiseregelung	130-31	f	Organik und Preiseregelung	178		
M	Finanzierung und Tageswertbilanz	358-361	g	Finanzierung und organische Bilanz	131-133	g	Finanzierung und organische Bilanz	179-181		Sections K,L,M,N,O remain virtually unchanged throughtout the 3 Editions.
N	Bilanz und Steuer	362-394	e	Organische Betriebsrechnung und Steuer	128-129	e	Organische Betriebs-rechnung und Steuer	172-177		
O	Die organische Betriebsauffassung	395-396	a	Die organische Betriebsauffassung	120-121	a	Die organische Betriebsauffassung	165-166		

REFERENCES

References

Accounting Standards Committee (1977), *Inflation Accounting - An Interim Recommendation (The Hyde Guidelines)*, ICAEW, (November)

Ashton, R.K. (1981), *The Use and Extent of Replacement Value in the Netherlands*, (ICAEW, London).

Beusch, P. (1928), *Währungszerfall und Währungsstabilisierung* (Berlin: privately published).

Bloom, R., & A. Debessay (1984), *Inflation Accounting: Reporting of General and Specific Price Changes*, (New York: Praeger).

Bresciani-Turroni, C. (1937), *The Economics of Inflation* (London: Allen & Unwin).

Buckmaster, D. (1981), "Review of H.W. Sweeney, *Stabilized Accounting*", 1978 Arno Reprint, *Accounting Historians Journal*, (Spring), pp.126-127.

Burgert, R. [1972], "Reservations About Replacement Value Accounting in the Netherlands", *Abacus*, (December), pp.111-126.

Carey, H.C. (1837), *Principles of Political Economy: The Laws of the Production and Distribution of Wealth*, Vol. I, 1837; reprint Augustus M. Kelley, 1965.

Campbell, J. (1984), *Grammatical Man*, (Middlesex: Penguin).

Cattela, R.S. (1983), "An Introduction into Current Value Accounting and its Application within Philips, N.V.", *Current Value Accounting: Its Aspects and Impacts*, Ed. Enthoven, A.J.H. (Center for International Accounting Development), Dallas.

Chambers, R.J. (1966), *Accounting, Evaluation and Economic Behavior* (New Jersey: Prentice-Hall).

Clarke, F.L. (1976a), "A Closer Look at Sweeney's Stabilised Accounting Proposals", *Accounting and Business Research* (Autumn), pp.264-275.

__________(1976b), "CCA/CPP: A Technical Impossibility", *Accountant's Magazine*, (October), pp.394-397.

__________(1978), "CCA: Progress or Regress", pp.70-80 in G.W. Dean & M.C. Wells *Current Cost Accounting: Identifying the Issues*, University of Sydney, 1978, 2nd ed.

__________(1980), "Accidents of History", *Abacus*, (December), pp.79-99.

__________(1982), *The Tangled Web of Price Variation Accounting* (New York: Garland).

Clarke, F.L. & G.W. Dean (1986), "Schmidt's Betriebswirtschaft Theory", *Abacus*, (September), pp.65-102.

__________(1988), "Limperg and Schmidt: Pattern, Chaos and Order", *Proceedings, Fifth World Congress of Accounting Historians* (University of Sydney: Accounting and Finance Foundation).

__________(1989), "Conjectures on the Influence of the 1920's *Betriebswirtschaftslehre* on Henry Sweeney's *Stabilized Accounting", Accounting and Business Research* (Autumn), pp.291-304.

Clark, J.M., "Valuation for the Balance Sheet and Profits", pp.369-377, *Proceedings, Het Internationaal Accountantscongress*, (J. Muuses, Purmerend, 1926; republished by Arno Press, New York 1980).

Coenenberg, A. and K. Macharzina (1976), "Accounting for Price Changes: An Analysis of Current Developments in Germany", *Journal of Business Finance and Accounting*, (Spring) pp. 53-68.

Dean, G.W. & F.L. Clarke (1989), "A Note: Graves, Sweeney and *Goldmarkbilanz* - Whither Sweeney and Schmidt's *Tageswertbilanz*?", *The Accounting Historians Journal*, (June), Vol. 16 No. 1, pp.101-109.

Dean, G.W., Clarke, F.L. & O.F. Graves (1990), *Replacement Costs and Accounting Reform in Post World War I Germany*, (New York: Garland Publishing Inc.).

Edwards, E.O. & P.W. Bell (1961), *The Theory and Measurement of Business Income*, (Berkeley: University of California Press).

Enthoven, A.J.H. (1983), *Current Value Accounting: Its Aspects and Impacts*, (Center for International Accounting Development, Dallas).

Fisher, I. (1911), *The Purchasing Power of Money* (London: Macmillan). German edition, *Die Kaufkraft des Geldes* (Berlin: Julius Springer, 1916).

__________(1920), *The Stabilisation of the Dollar* (London: Macmillan).

__________(1925), *The Money Illusion* (London: Allen & Unwin).

Geldmacher, E. (1920), "Bilanzsorgen", *Industrie- und Handelszeitung*, (October), pp.364, 378, 392, 398 & 406.

Graves, O.F. (1985), *Accounting for Inflation: German Theory of the 1920s; Schmidt, Mahlberg, Current Value Accounting* (Unpublished PhD thesis, Alabama).

__________(1987), "Accounting for Inflation: Henry Sweeney and the German Gold-Mark Model", *Accounting Historians Journal*, (Spring), pp.33-55.

__________(1989), "Walter Mahlberg's Valuation Theory: An Anomaly in the Development of Inflation Accounting", *Abacus*, (March), pp.7-25.

__________(1990), "Economic Orientation and Choice of Accounting Models: An Inquiry into the Relationship between Fritz Schmidt's Replacement Cost Model and Henry Sweeney's Stabilized Accounting", Working Paper.

Goudeket, A. (1952), "Fluctuating Price Levels in Relation to Accounts", *Proceedings of the Sixth International Congress of Accountants*, (London: Gee & Co.).

__________(1960), "An Application of Replacement Value Accounting", *Journal of Accountancy*, (July), pp.37-47.

Groeneveld, G.I., *et al.* (1964), *Bedrijfseconomie: verzameld werk van Prof. Dr. Th. Limperg, Jr.*, (A.E. Klewer, Deventer; Vol. 1, 1964; II, 1968; III-VII, 1965).

Guttmann, W. & Meehan, P. (1975), *The Great Inflation* (London: Saxon House).

Gynther, R.S. (1966), *Accounting for Price Level Changes: Theory and Procedures* (Sydney: Pergamon Press).

Hans, J. (1925), "Amendments of Accountancy Laws on the Continent", *The Accountant*, (31 October), pp.675-676.

__________(1926), "Accountancy Law Reform in Central Europe", *The Accountant*, (7 August), pp.201-202.

Hendriksen, E.S. (1965), *Accounting Theory* (Illinois: Irwin; 1st ed).

__________(1982), *Accounting Theory* (Illinois: Irwin; 3rd ed).

Holtfrerich, C.L. (1986), *The German Inflation: 1914-1923* (Berlin: de Gruyter).

__________(1985), "German and Other European Countries in the 1920s", pp.123-140 in J. Williamson (ed.), *Inflation and Indexation: Argentina, Brazil and Israel* (Cambridge, Mass. Institute for International Economics).

__________(1983), "Political Factors of the German Inflation", pp.401-416 in N. Schmukler and E. Marcus (eds), *Inflation Through the Ages: Economic, Social, Psychological and Historical Aspects* (New York: Columbia University Press).

Hügli, F.(1894), *Die konstante Buchhaltung* (Bern).

Isaac, A. (1950), "Fritz Schmidt, Forscher und Persönlichkeit", *Zeitschrift für handelswissenschaftliche Forschung*, New Series, Vol. 2, 1950.

Kalveram, W. (1923), *Die kaunfmännische Rechnungsführung unter dem Einfluss der Geldentwertung* (Berlin: Spaeth und Linde).

von Kast, G. (1920a), "Falsche Bilanzierungsmethoden seit der Valutaentwertung", *Berliner Tageblatt*, (September).

__________(1920b), "Falsche Industriekalkulation", *Industrie- und Handelszeitung*, 16 October, p.1.

Kempin, W. (1910), *Entwicklung der Bilanzlehre und der Abschlusstechnik* (Köln: privately published).

Kindelberger, C.P. (1982), *A Financial History of Western Europe* (London: Allen & Unwin).

__________(1984), "A Structural View of the German Inflation", pp.10-33 in G.D. Feldman *et al.*, *The Experience of Inflation. International and Comparative Studies* (Berlin: de Gruyter).

Klein, L. (1920), "Einfluß der sinkenden Kaufkraft des Geldes auf Kalkulation, Bilanz und Steuer", *Zeitschrift für Handelswissenschaft und Handelspraxis*.

Limperg, T (1926), "The Accountant's Certificate in Connection with the Accountant's Responsibilities", pp.85-104, *Proceedings, Het Internationaal Accountantscongress*, (J. Muuses, Purmerend, 1926; republished by Arno Press, New York 1980).

__________[1937], "De gevolgen van de depreciatie van de gulden voor de berekening van waarde en winst in het bedrijf", *Maanblad voor Accountancy en Bedrijfshuishoudkunde*, (January), pp.14-31.

Littleton, A.C. (1936), "Review of Stabilized Accounting", *Accounting Review*, (September), pp.296-299.

Littleton, A.C. & Zimmerman, V.K. (1962), *Accounting Theory: Continuity and Change* (New Jersey: Prentice Hall).

MacDonald, E.B. (1977), "Postscript", in W. Baxter & S. Davidson (eds), *Studies in Accounting* (ICAEW, London).

Mahlberg, W. (1920-21), "Wirtschaftsrelativitaet", *Zeitschrift für Handelswissenschaft und Handelspraxis*, pp.133-136, 182-186 & 195-197.

__________(1921), *Bilanztechnik und Bewertung bei schwankender Währung* (Leipzig: G.A. Gloeckner, 1921; 2nd ed. 1922; 3rd ed. 1923a).

__________(1923b), *Goldkreditverkehr und Goldmarkbuchführung* (Berlin: Julius Springer).

__________(1925), *Die Tageswerte in der Bilanz* (Leipzig: G.A. Gloeckner).

__________(1927), *Konjunkturbeeinflußung durch Kalkulations- und Kreditpolitik* (Leipzig: G.A. Gloeckner).

Mattessich, R. (1980), "An Evolutionary Survey and Comparison of Current Cost and General Purchasing Power Hypotheses and Their Applications", International Accounting Historians Conference (London: European Accounting Association).

__________(1982), "On the Evolution of Inflation Accounting", *Economia Aziendale*, (Vol. 1, No. 3, 1982), pp.349-381.

__________(1984), "Fritz Schmidt (1882-1950) and His Pioneering Work of Current Value Accounting in Comparison to Edwards and Bell's Theory", *Proceedings of Fourth International Congress of Accounting Historians*, (Editrice, Pisa).

Mey, A. (1966), "Theodore Limperg and his Theory of Costs and Values", *Abacus*, (September), pp.3-23.

von Mises, L. (1919), *Nation, Staat und Wirtschaft* (Berlin: Spaeth und Linde).

Moss, A.G. (1923), "Treatment of Appreciation of Fixed Assets in the Accounts and Balance Sheet and for Income Tax Purposes", *Journal of Accountancy*, (September).

Muis, J.W. (1980), "Wie was Limperg? Outcast Who Blazed the CCA Trail", *Accountancy*, (October), pp.69-70.

Mumford, M. (1979), "The End of a Familiar Inflation Accounting Cycle", *Accounting and Business Research*, (Spring), pp.98-104.

Nicklisch, H. (1912), *Allgemeine kaufmännische Betriebslehre als Privatswirtschaftslehre des Handels und der Industrie*, Stuttgart.

Paton, W.A. (1920), "Depreciation, Appreciation and Productive Capacity", *The Journal of Accountancy*, July 1920, pp.1-11.

Osbhar, W. (1912), *Die Bilanz vom Standpunkt der Unternehmung* (Berlin-Leipzig: G.A. Gloeckner, 1912 1st ed.; 1923, 3rd ed.).

Peasnell, K.V. (1982), "Technological Change and Other Aspects of the Definition of Replacement Cost for Managerial Purposes", unpublished paper.

Prion, W. (1919), *Inflation und Geldentwertung* (Berlin: Julius Springer).

__________(1920), "Ersatzanschaffungen und Neuanlagen", *Plutus*, (27 September).

__________(1921), *Die Finanzierung und Bilanz wirtschaftlicher Betriebe unter dem Einfluss der Geldentwertung* (Berlin: Julius Springer).

Ricardo, D. (1953), *On The Principles of Political Economy and Taxation* (Cambridge: Cambridge University Press); originally Vol. I published in 1817.

Rorem, C.R. (1929), "Replacement Cost in Accounting Valuation", *The Accounting Review*, (September 1929).

Sandilands Committee (1975), *Inflation Accounting: Report of the Inflation Accounting Committee* (Cmnd, 6225, HMSO, London, September).

Schaer, J.R. (1890), *Versuch einer wissenschaftlichen Behandlung der Buchhaltung* (Basel).

Schlesinger, G. (1920), "Abschreibung oder Ersatz", *Werkstattstechnik*, 1 October, pp.506-7.

Schmalenbach, E. (1908), "Die Abschreibung", *Zeitschrift für handelswissenschaftliche Forschung*, pp.81-89.

__________(1919), "Grundlagen dynamischer Bilanzlehre", *Zeitschrift für handelswissenschaftliche Forschung*, (Vol. 13) pp.1-6- & 65-101.

__________(1921), "Geldwertausgleich in der bilanzmässigen Erfolgsrechnung", *Zeitschrift für handelswissenschaftliche Forschung*, (October), pp.401-417.

Schmidt, F. (1921), *Die organische Bilanz in Rahmen der Wirtschaft* (Leipzig: G.A. Gloeckner 1921; 2nd ed., *Die organische Tageswertbilanz*, (1922; 3rd ed., 1929a).

__________(1923), *Der Wiederbeschaffungspreis des Umsatztages in Kalkulation und Volkswirtschaft* (Berlin: Spaeth und Linde).

__________[1923], "De winst van de onderneming", *De naamlooze vennootschap roermond*, (15 February and 15 March), pp.301-4 & 332-4.

__________(1924), *Bilanzwert, Bilanzgewinn und Bilanzumwertung* (Berlin: Spaeth und Linde).

__________(1926), "Profit and Balance Sheet Value", pp.378-436, *Proceedings, Het Internationaal Accountantscongres* (J. Muuses, Purmerend, 1926; republished by Arno Press, New York, 1980).

__________(1927), "Die Industrienkonjunktur - Ein Rechenfehler!", *Zeitschrift für Betriebswirtschaft*, (Vol. 4) pp.1-29, 87-114 & 165-199.

__________(1927), "Indexziffern" (Index Numbers), pp.273-82, H. Nicklisch *Handwörterbuch der Betriebswirtschaft*, (Stuttgart: C.A. Poeschel), pp.273-282.

__________(1928), "Ist Wertänderung am ruhenden Vermögen Gewinn oder Verlust?" (Do Holding Gains or Losses Represent Profit or Loss?), *Zeitschrift für Betriebswirtschaft*, 1928, pp.1-19.

__________(1929b), "The Valuation of Fixed Assets in Financial Statements", *The Accountant*, (16 November), pp.616-629.

__________(1930a), "The Basis of Depreciation Charges", *The Harvard Business Review*, (April), pp.257-64.

__________(1930b), "The Importance of Replacement Value", *The Accounting Review*, (September), pp.235-42.

__________(1931), "Is Appreciation Profit?", *The Accounting Review*, (September), pp.289-93.

Schneider, von D. (1973), "Renaissance der Bilanztheorie", *Zeitschrift für betriebswirtschaftliche Forschung*, pp.29-58.

__________(1981), *Geschichte betriebswirtschaftlicher Theorie* (R.Oldenbourg, München/Wien).

Schoenfeld, H.M. (1979), "Inflation Accounting - Development of Theory and Practice in Continental Europe", *Quarterly Review of Economics and Business*, (Spring), pp.57-73.

Schranz, A. (1930), "Modern German Accountancy", *The Accounting Review*, (June), pp.165-67.

van der Schroeff, H.J. (1959), "Limperg's Theorie van de Vervangingswaarde", *Maanblad voor Accountancy*, (December), pp.557-561.

Schwantag, K. [1951], "F. Schmidts wissenschaftliches Werk", *Zeitschrift für Betriebswirtschaft*, (January), pp.1-9.

Seicht, G. (1970), *Die kapitaltheoretische Bilanz und die Entwicklung der Bilanztheorie* (Berlin: Duncker and Humblot).

__________(1982), *Bilanztheorien* (Vienna: Physica).

Sewering, K. (1925), *Die Einheitsbilanz. Die Überbrückung des Gegensatzes zwischen statischer und dynamischer Bilanzlehre* (Berlin: G.A. Gloeckner).

Sweeney, H.W. (1927), "Effects of Inflation on German Accounting", *Journal of Accountancy*, (March), pp.178-191.

__________(1928), "German Inflation Accounting", *Journal of Accountancy*, (February), pp.104-116.

__________(1930), "The Maintenance of Capital", *Accounting Review*, (December), pp.277-287.

__________(1931), "Stabilized Depreciation", *Accounting Review*, (September), pp.165-178.

__________(1933a), "Capital", *Accounting Review*, (September), pp.185-199.

__________(1933b), "Income", *Accounting Review*, (December), pp.323-335.

__________(1935), "The Technique of Stabilized Accounting", *The Accounting Review*, (June), pp.185-205.

__________(1936), *Stabilized Accounting*, (New York: Harper and Brothers, 1936; reproduced by Arno Press, 1980).

__________(1964), *Stabilized Accounting* (reprint New York: Holt, Rinehardt and Winston).

van Seventer, A. (1969), "The Continuity Postulate in the Dutch Theory of Business Income", *The Internationl Journal of Accounting, Education and Research*, (Spring), pp.1-9.

__________(1975), "Replacement Value Theory in Modern Dutch Accounting", *The International Journal of Accounting Education and Research*, (Fall), pp.67-93.

van Sloten (1981), P.J., *The Dutch Contribution to Replacement Value Accounting: Theory and Practice*, (Lancaster: International Centre for Research in Accounting University of Lancaster).

Stolper, Gustav (1967), *The German Econmomy 1870 to the Present*, translation Toni Stolper, (New York: Harcourt Brace & World). Excerpts reprinted in *The German Inflation 1923*, edited by Fritz K. Ringer, *Problems in European History: A Documentary Collection*, (New York: Oxford University Press, 1969).

Tweedie, D., & Whittington, G. (1984), *The Debate on Inflation Accounting* (Cambridge: Cambridge University Press).

Voigtländer, Dr (1952)., "Bibliographie: Das wissenschaftliche Werk von F. Schmidt", *Zeitschrift für Betriebswirtschaft*, pp.182-185.

Vos, J. (1970), "Replacement Value Accounting", *Abacus*, (December), pp.132-143.

Whittington, G. (1980), "Pioneers of Income Measurement and Price-Level Accounting: A Review Article", *Accounting and Business Research*, (Spring), pp.232-240.

__________(1981a), "The British Contribution to Income Theory", pp.1-29 in *Essays in British Accounting Research*, Eds. Bromwich, M., and A.G. Hopwood, (London: Pitman).

__________(1981b), "Inflation Accounting - What Next?", pp.60-84 in *British Accounting Standards: the First Ten Years*, Eds. Leach, Sir Ronald and E. (London: Stamp Woodhead-Faulkner).

_________(1983), *Introduction to the Debate on Inflation Accounting* (Cambridge: Cambridge University Press).

Williams, R. (1981), *Keywords: A Vocabulary of Culture and Society* (Flamingo, London).

Zeff, S.A. (1976), *Asset Appreciation, Business Income and Price-Level Accounting, 1918-1935* (New York: Arno Press).

For Product Safety Concerns and Information please contact our EU
representative GPSR@taylorandfrancis.com
Taylor & Francis Verlag GmbH, Kaufingerstraße 24, 80331 München, Germany

www.ingramcontent.com/pod-product-compliance
Ingram Content Group UK Ltd.
Pitfield, Milton Keynes, MK11 3LW, UK
UKHW022215190926
475702UK00003B/366
* 9 7 8 0 3 6 7 5 0 8 6 4 7 *